Sept - 02/04

Dear William,

Well, we've met in binary
only, but here's hoping this
book will fill you in.

Thank you for your
purchase, and I look
forward to your valued
opinion.

Allan Wills was born on a snowy day in Montreal, Canada, in January, 1977 to adventurous European immigrants. He holds a college degree in Police Sciences and a university Bachelor of Commerce, though most of what he does now is self-taught. Allan often seconded to other parts of the world, usually solo, with only his backpack and journal, to have adventures. He still isn't sure what's next, but as long as it doesn't involve a tie, collared shirt and a window with blinds, he remains optimistic.

Allan Wills

BEST LAID PLAN

Best Laid Plan
© Allan Wills 2004
Cover: Hjordis Petersen Wills
All photography and maps, unless
otherwise specified, are © Allan Wills.
Editing: Marc Lalonde, Andrea Belcham

Printed in Canada by AGMV Marquis
Published by Allan Wills, 153 Spring Garden rd,
Dollard-des-Ormeaux,
Quebec, Canada H9B 2N5
allan@wills-world.com   www.wills-world.com
Dépôt legal: National Library of Canada
et la Bibliothèque nationale du Québec

Library and Archives Canada Cataloguing in Publication
Includes bibliographical references.
ISBN 0-9736090-0-1 (pbk.)

1. Wills, Allan—Journeys—Australia. 2. Australia—Description
and travel. I. Lalond, Marc II. Belcham, Andrea III. Title.

DU105.2.W44 2004   994'.07   C2004-904765-5

Best Laid Plan

Foreword

Allan Wills and I became friends for much the same reason I think you and he are about to become friends: because he made me laugh like crazy. Allan has an interesting way of looking at things and after a while I think you'll start to see the same thing. He has a great sense of the absurd and a great sense of what will make an interesting story. In the coming pages, you will read stories of joy, pain, apprehension, loss and political intrigue.

Australia is a land of many paradoxes; how did a country made up primarily of convicted criminals a mere two hundred years ago churn out such unfailingly nice people? How is a country so lush yet so barren all at the same time? Why is the Sydney Opera House so grand? What's the deal with gumboots?

Actually, gumboots are just what Aussies call rubber boots. I don't know the answers to the rest of the questions, though. I'm sure Allan does. Come with him as he encounters drunk Russians, sketchy stock-scam artists, modelling-industry shysters and the strange inhabitants of the desolate outback. To paraphrase the Grateful Dead, it was definitely a long, strange trip, and that's exactly what travel in a strange country, and the stories that follow it, should be.

Marc Lalonde

Dedicated to my late grandmother – Anna Birmingham
Wills – and my unofficial godfather, George Pappadatos.
Both of them ended their journeys just as mine
was getting underway.
They never got to hold this book.

Also to my parents and brother, for encouragement
and for allowing dishes to pile up when
a writer's mind goes absent.

Prologue – The First Oz-Aliens

TRYING TO PICTURE your destination before you get there – that is to say, the stage and its the cast of characters – is a fatal flaw that all of us share in varying magnitudes. It is a tricky Catch-22, because you can either have your expectations excitedly exceeded, matched, or, conversely, you can be spectacularly wrong and wallow in descending levels of comparative disappointment.

Then again, you can have your dreams come true in a way you never thought possible and in circumstances that had previously seemed bleak.

It was, at the outset, the perfect time to travel to Australia. I was young and unattached, final exams were done, I had no debt and, unlike many people I knew, I never received one of those nefarious phone calls about morning sickness and pharmacy liquids turning a sweaty, life-altering tinge. Yes, it was the perfect time to go far away. Or so I thought.

I didn't do as much research as I should have. As it turned out, the only other trip that was plotted to the same location with even more unfailing ignorance happened long ago and under draconian conditions. Nevertheless, when you don't have much money and the world isn't giving you too much hope, you are only left to bargain and barter with creativity. Sometimes indecision, in hindsight, is the key to flexibility.

The saga that unfolded had all the elements of tragic comedy; language barriers, shock reality checks and psychotically damaging employment prospects that drove me to humiliating public nudity among bubbly blonds. But then somewhere in all that a dream dared hatch and the dreamers dared chase it.

The dream began under a shadow of uncompromising hopelessness, progressed through a fellowship of the financially challenged, flowered into $60,000 worth of sponsorship (including wheels) and ended with me taking a branch of the Australian government to court.

During this epic journey memories from a more distant past were unlocked that put much of current life into perspective – stories of sex, drugs, alcohol, humour and woe, of government conspiracy, profound loss and beginning anew.

* * *

My first actual thoughts of travelling to the abnormally outlying country bubbled up about six years previous to my first footfall in Sydney. I was dating someone at the time and we had planned to go Down Under together after completing our studies. However, with time she and I became distant, rather like the target country we had dreamed of.

I knew it was a warm place, and I had read somewhere that, because Australia was still part of the Queen of England's little commonwealth pink bits on the map, it would be fairly easy to get a visa to go there. Beyond that, I knew that Arnold Schwarzenegger came from somewhere similar-sounding and something about kangaroos ...

I came spiralling out of university at a time when most of my friends were content to undertake the banal quest of becoming their parents as fast as possible. I swam upstream against my demographic equivalents by not rushing off to buy a suit, print résumés or hit the snooze button of life, hiding in school by immediately enrolling for a master's degree.

I ran the other way as fast as I could.

I needed to get away, you understand – far away. To a place to romp and stomp. Just for a bit. Just to clear my head.

Travelling *always* helped. Change of scene, change of people to reflect off of, stripping one's mental state down to its nuts and bolts and adding some new experience.

Plus another northern winter was coming.

All things considered, Australia seemed like a good place to go. It was almost impossibly far away and I didn't know anything about it, but that never stopped me before. Inadvertently, however, I would be introduced to Australia in a drip-dosage sort of way, starting with a needle prick on my own native continent.

On his whim, my brother, Simon, and I headed for a year-long sabbatical in Whistler, British Columbia, to work and play in North America's number-one ski resort. Australians are a ubiquitous piece of the ski resorts in the western US and Canada, roaming around carefree and jovial, asking me "How I was going" (by car, thanks) instead of "How I was doing." They didn't "think" but "reckoned," they spilled out "no worries," offered that most things were "no drama," called people "mites," laughed for unknown reasons at the Roots clothing line, and I had to employ "Sorry, what?" fairly often in conversation with them. One of the biggest holidays in Whistler is January 26, Australia Day.

Without Australia, I concluded, North American ski resorts would be deprived of the bulk of their eager ski lift operators and joyous snowboard instructors, of people who worship snow in a pious fashion and willingly take all forms of menial employment – and overpopulated living arrangements – to be near it. They are to ski resorts what Greeks are to restaurants, what mortar is to brick.

"I'm a Jafa, mite," said one of my many new Aussie friends when I began working at a well-to-do hotel.

"What's that?" I asked.

"Mite, this is Whistla, whea you bin? J-A-F-A: Jus' anotha fuckin' Aussie."

"Oh. Say, I'm thinking of going to Australia, what's your country like?"

He cast an aimless yet pensive glance into the air, collected his thoughts, and replied, "Mite, you eva notice that Jafas and Canucks get on real well on the backpacker travel circuit?"

"True," I said, and he continued.

"You eva notice that we both lauff at the same jokes o' don't get fazed about drivin' fa dayz o' weeks to get to anotha tewn? Owa dollas ah wuff the same. We neva worry about being welcome ova-seas, take the piss out of owa-selves and tell seppos we live with pola beahs and 'roos as pets and they believe it?"

I pursed my lips and conceded most of what I could make out in his long string of observations.

"That's because 'stralia is like just like Canadia, but heaps wa-ma and a bit small-ah."

Aside from most Jafas' inabilities to properly enunciate words containing the letter *r* (or for that matter properly pronounce the demagogical condition *eczema*) the reasoning seemed sound enough in theory. Canada and Australia did have similarities, and one magazine article I came across spouted that Australia was "Canada With an Accent." Most of all, foreigners can never correctly guess either obscure federal capital city within three tries.

And for those counting, there is the case of outlandishness: both nations utilize only a fraction of their mostly useless landmasses and respectively have the statistical spread of 2.2 and 2.6 people per square kilometre. To put this in context, consider that only Mongolia (1.3 people per square kilometre) beats that and the US (about the same size as Australia if you take out Alaska) rings in with 25.8, China with 113.7 and Hong Kong (a measly 1,098 square km) with 5,435. So the two were related. Distant commonwealth cousins, you could say. Element of the familiar.

Another Jafa vehemently held that Australia was a carbon copy of the United States, and claimed that Canada and Australia were as different as deserts and ice caps. A book I read compared Australia's lifestyle to that of Mediterranean Europe, while another author claimed "Australia is not Europe, it is not Asia and it is not California. It is another way in the world." What is more, when Aussies flush their toilets, the water swirls concentrically in the wrong direction.

I think that if the world were to be viewed in the terms of artistic paintings, then Australia would be the result of a paint brush dabbed in all regions of planetary paint, producing a colour you have to see and breathe to believe, then stroked across a vast, austere and still largely misunderstood canvas. The end piece is a lot of everything, a lot of nothing, in some ways colourful, though in others dogmatic, with primal, mysterious and creative undertones.

So that's where I wanted to go, even though I had some rough notions and huge misgivings about how things worked Down Under.

Meanwhile, lots of sequels and circumstantial patterns were playing out in the wider world. The *Star Wars*, *Harry Potter*, *Terminator*, *Lord of The Rings* and *Matrix* franchises all pumped out their trilogies while George Bush II waged War On Iraq II, which I dubbed The Search for Something, and the Australian government decided was a good idea to join ... but I'm getting ahead of myself.

When our year was up, my brother Simon and I left Whistler and road-tripped our way around the United States for two months. Shortly after arriving home, I gleefully acquired a one-year visa and purchased a one-way plane ticket to Sydney with a month-long addendum through Whistler, Hawaii and Fiji. As my design was to stay away a year, I shipped off two crates of important stuff with plenty of lead time.

But these were no ordinary times to be going anywhere carefree. For one thing, my parents entered the thrifty world of semi-retirement as people right, left and centre were being axed from once life-long and steady corporate careers. My grandmother in England was ill. Just three days before I was slated to visit New York City for the first time in my life, two planes crashed into the World Trade Centre, the media went into a frenzy and everyone was horrified to go anywhere. Talk about bad timing.

What residual personal savings remained from the four-digit price of my plane ticket was allotted to health insurance and a provisional stash for eating and seeking work and accommodation once I got there. I had purchased and plotted pre-9/11, but post-9/11 there would be no refunds, and even less assurances.

In the end, after being encouraged by my parents, I would travel to the antipodes of the earth, to a land I knew hardly anything about. I would arrive with no idea of what to do and at a time when the world had seemingly just gone upside down.

In the journey to come, I would first became what I wanted to avoid at all costs, and then through inspiration and relative poverty, would be guided invisibly to a different fate rooted deep in the past. It was something that I would both do and yet that I would never have imagined.

What You Need to Know!

Throughout this book, I use the non-denominational dating system of CE (Current Era) and BCE (Before Current Era), which refers, respectively, to what others might know as BC ("before Christ") and AD (*Anno Domini*, "in the year of the Lord").

I have altered some people's names, and I have equally changed some company names. The rule of thumb is this: any organization of good repute has their name right; any company of dubious distinction has been renamed.

All monetary figures, unless otherwise noted, are in Australian dollars.

You also need to know this word: pom (prisoner of Her Majesty), or pommy (a person from the United Kingdom).

Let the adventure begin ...

PART I
GOLDEN HANDCUFFS

I was the convict,
Sent to hell
To make in the desert
The living well

I split the rock;
I felled the tree
The nation was
Because of me

– Mary Gilmore, writing of the first white Australian settlers.

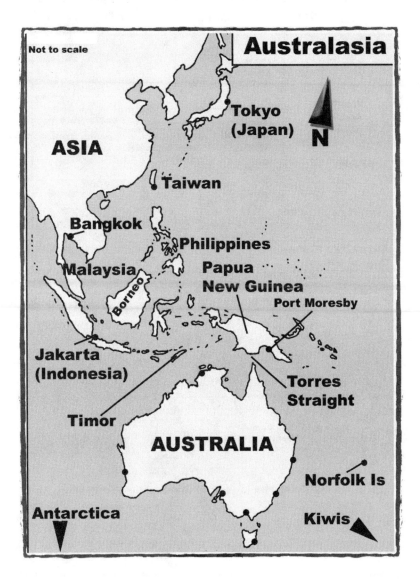

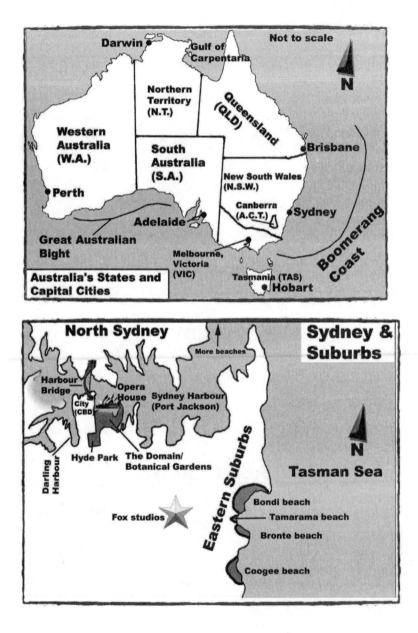

1 – Tired Steps

TO SAY THAT I knew a lot about Sydney or Australia when I first arrived is to say that Michael Jackson isn't much of an oddity. I knew sweet nothing. Well, I had seen *Crocodile Dundee*, but I have an inherent distrust of Hollywood portraying anything with any astute accuracy. Many Australians lament, with palpable sincerity, that Steve Irwin the croc hunter and his amphibious wrastlin', twang-infested ways have upstaged the previous mainstream cultural representative who jovially informed New York muggers, "That's not a knife." Add to this Fosters beer, and all that embodies Australia outside its borders trickles from unlikely representatives that are all too readily lapped up.

I, too, was an ignoramus, though I did act on the premise that unfiltered accuracy is best obtained in just taking it all in for oneself. How anyone can rationalize the option of a two-week, whistle-stop package to Australia is beyond me. No matter where you are in the world, Australia is always *really* far away.

My voracious reader of a father had given me *In a Sunburnt Country* (a.k.a. *Down Under*) penned by travel writer Bill Bryson. I polished it off on bus, boat, plane and rickshaw over a month as I progressed through the South Pacific. By his account, Australia was a land after my own heart – wild, to a large degree unexplored and promising adventure with obliging people of very dry and self-depreciating senses of humour. My other memory of that book (which I regrettably traded away, but immediately re-purchased) was the lengthy dedication of pages to venomous creatures that Bryson believed might kill him in a painful and unmerciful manner.

However, I do like second opinions, so over time after my arrival I would ferret out a collection of other books about mysterious Australia – ultimately because I would end up in the poor house, and reading is a free and time-consuming activity.

I was amazed when I realized that Australia has an official disparity of 10,000 square kilometres! One book indicates its area at 7,682,300 square kilometres, another at 7,692,030 and there are other counts. If Massachusetts or an area one-third larger than Connecticut went unaccounted for, you can be sure panic and government committees would result, but not in Australia.

Then again, Australia does cover six percent of the Earth's land surface and is equivalent to two Europes. It is 3,152 percent larger than its former colonial ruler, Great Britain, though with only one-third the population, so no worries, I suppose. To boot, much of the Australian landmass still awaits charting, as about four-fifths of it is so barren that only Antarctica can best it.

To cross from east to west entails a journey of 4,000 kilometres, and north to south is not too far off at 3,680 kilometres. Comparatively, the same distance would get you from Los Angeles to Pittsburgh in the US, and in Europe from the coast of Portugal to central Poland. The distance is akin, incidentally, to crossing diagonally from the coast of Chile to that of Brazil.

Speaking of coasts, there are an estimated 7,000 beaches in Australia, most of them deserted (and I would surmise uncounted), and a good number of them are claimed to be the best in the world. It surprised me further that some historians claimed Australia was the Earth's most recent discovery in terms of mapping (though others say it isn't *really*).

Australia is – to say the very least – still very much an enigma.

I must stray here for a second to let you in on something. You see, language can sometimes be limiting. For lack of a better term to describe many Australian situations that would arise, I coined my own. "Backorward" or "Forbackward" are two words meaning exactly the same thing: being forward or advanced in some ways, though not without being backward or behind in other areas. It's sort of like yin- yang, or the theory of compensating factors, but in a context that somehow makes sense only Down Under. Perhaps an illustration or two are in order.

The biggest irony is that Australia began as a place to sweep convicts under the rug, and in just under two centuries, it miraculously blew the whole theory of genetic criminal inheritance out of the water in the most spectacular and necessarily creative way.

Australia was federated in 1901 and immediately accorded women the right to vote ... but Australian citizenship didn't exist until after World War II and it didn't get its own flag until 1954 nor its own dollar till 1967, at precisely the same late stage that it recognized Aboriginal people as residents and extended to them the right to vote. Oh, and despite being a recent immigrant success story, the dubious "White Only Policy" (legislation that Australia allow only immigrants of white, north European descent) officially finished in 1972.

And there is trivial backorwardness: Australians produce and bottle world-class beer and wine ... but they use the yeast runoff from the brewing process to make something punishingly edible that they are obliged to enrapture with bright yellow and red labelling so no one mistakes it for tar or engine lube. What I'm referring to, of course, is Vegemite, and it tastes like a mutant salt blob; if you spread an amount of it on your toast equal to what you might when using butter, your nasal hairs will be incinerated by internal bushfire. Notwithstanding, advertisers will lead you to believe that it helps Aussies grow.

Australians have also built the world's longest fence (5,531 kilometres) and abolished pennies from circulation and pioneered aviation ... but they didn't get FM radio until 1974, and television until the late 1950s. You get the idea. Backorward. Forackward.

I now return you to your regularly scheduled reading.

While I was in Fiji, my grandmother in England succumbed to cancer and passed away. There is nothing worse than being so far away and being incapable – due to distance and more so to finances – to see an ill relative for the last time.

During the moments and correspondence I had shared with my Nan, she had absolutely encouraged me to pursue journalism, writing or some similar form of a career. I had never taken her advice seriously, but as it turns out she would get her wish posthumously, much by chance, but also largely due to the spirit of my new home.

I would fly into Sydney deliriously tired. Previously, I had been sick for three days on the binge on Beachcomber, a Fijian party island. I ate something that didn't agree with me and otherwise had travelled for two weeks with a hippie backpacker from Philadelphia, a distasteful combination. He was always looking for pot and his definitive moment was when he had tongue-wrestled a very inebriated Fijian woman only to slide his hand below and discover that "she" shared his plumbing. My last memory of him was when we parted ways in the Auckland International Airport, with exchanges of "See you in Australia." Ultimately, his budget transformed into more weed and I never laid eyes on him again. "Just say no," was the last thing I had told him. He didn't find it funny.

On my connecting flight the screens showed scenes of Sydney, and who was I to argue that this city boasted the world's most beautiful harbour, 40 beaches within city limits and an average of 340 days of sunshine a year.

In 1998, during a crippling ice storm in my native Montreal, my brother Simon met a lawyer from Sydney at the local YMCA, which at the time served as a refuge for people without electricity. In keeping correspondence over the years, the lawyer became a good friend of our family and even flew back to ski with us in marathons. He was my sole contact in Sydney and had been generous in allowing me to scrawl his name in the recipient box on the crates I dispatched weeks previous.

It was for him that I currently scanned as I cleared customs at the Sydney International Terminal, but I couldn't find him. I then sought to change some currency for the purpose of calling his cell phone.

I would learn an Aussie lesson right there at the exchange booth: colours in Australia are a lot more intense than anywhere else in the world. Back through the concave slot came a pile of bright prime-coloured notes. What is astonishing aside from a heavy saturation of dye is the feel. Aussie notes are rumoured to be waterproof and hard to tear (a great show of foresight for a nation that lives mostly near water), and indeed touching the bills is like picking up paper that had somehow been part of a laminating process gone half-wrong. Even if you crumple the notes, they reform immediately into their original shapes.

The woman behind the glass wasn't celebrating my trivialities with me, and didn't smile back, looking rather bored, her eyelids heavier than mine. "It's the little things in life," I thought to myself as I shuffled off with my fist full of rainbow Aussie dough, knowing that no evil water or malignant shark could tear away their value.

I didn't gamble that other things might.

I had gained a phone booth by the time I realized that Australians didn't seem to have quarters and muttered a disparaging comment to myself about outlaying 40 cents for a local call. I managed to enter the correct string of numbers to glean a ringing tone, but as soon as my friend answered three beeps danced over my "Hello?" A 25-second chat ensued before the line mysteriously got severed. I quickly fired another 40 cents into the slot, heard more strange beeps and this time got only 20 seconds. I repeated the performance and we managed briskly to arrange a location before the booth, to my surprise, played its hungry role again. There must be something wrong here surely, I thought, but I was too tired to bother informing whoever Telstra was that they had a defective unit.

I jumped into my lawyer friend's car, eyes heavy with fatigue, and he decided to zing me around the eastern suburbs of Sydney to show me their splendour.

"By the way," he said as we drove into the night, "I never received the stuff you shipped out a month ago."

As he negotiated the twisting and dark streets, he chattered away about houses, friends, restaurants and occurrences that happened in places like Double Bay, Rose Bay, Bronte and other suburb names that meant absolutely sweet bump-kiss to me, having only arrived in Sydney for the first time in my life, being startled by the colour and texture of the money, still rather at odds to justify the $1.20 charge on 60 seconds of local phone talk time and sour that my boxes of necessities had not yet arrived despite being sent out seven weeks prior.

His generous tour culminated at a place called Bondi where he drove me past a string of cafés and extolled how beautiful the beach was. I could roughly discern the white flecks of some waves and the outline of sand, but I couldn't really see much in the cover of darkness, and I just wanted to sleep at that point. How rude I must have seemed to my host, but I couldn't help it.

My friend then took me up the road to the residence he had arranged for me and I was greeted by Tehila, an energetic and lovable landlady who was a friend of his family. She jubilantly escorted me up to an eighth floor apartment boasting three bedrooms and six students and flattened out the futon in the living room. My lawyer friend told me that he had arranged a three-week billet for me with Tehila (including meals) until I got my bearings in Sydney and sorted myself out. I was so tired that I thanked Tehila and my friend, tossed my backpack on the side and dozed off.

I was finally here and all I could do was sleep. That night, I had nightmares about vicious telephones eating brightly painted money, spitting out a weird series of tri-beeps, and shipping crates disappearing into a mysterious dark beach called Bondi.

2 – The Overt But Intolerant Spy

A man should drink in moderation, be sensible or silent. None will find fault with your manners though you retire in good time.

    – Hávamál, *The Sayings of The Vikings*

THE ICON OF Australia, the bright and powerful sun, pierced into my eyes. My first rays of daylight on my first day in the antipodes! Everything was so new and full of promise, though, unknown to me at that point, I would only get to see one more sunrise before having to leave.

I jumped off the futon and absorbed my foremost visions of Sydney and Australia. The balcony looked out over a sprawling thicket of roofs and I took in the welcome sight of a glimmering gold sandy beach in the distance and, beyond that, an ocean of incomparable azure blue. I was speechless, and just as well, because some of the inhabitants of the apartment were stirring and well wondering who the heck I was.

From the semi-ajar door of one room, I caught sight of a cautious stack of Chinese eyes peering out at me; when I said hello, the door closed quickly and I heard rapid and frightened intonations. Not long after, a soppy Frenchman, a dough-eyed Brazilian and two Shrek-like Russian brothers emerged. This trend would be one that would plague me in Bondi for quite some time – I wouldn't actually meet any authentic Australians for quite awhile.

Well, I didn't see much of the Chinese guys after the initial door slam. They seemed content to treat casual passings as moments of discomfort with lots of smiles and nodding accompanied by a nippy sprint to the safety of their iron-curtained room. The Russians, the Frenchman and the Brazilian, on the other hand, were quick to welcome me in various forms of broken and accented English. As we chatted, I drew quizzical looks and after a little conference among themselves they managed to string together enough words to ask why I was studying English in Australia.

Before I could choose simple words for an answer, the Russians (16 and 18 years old) cracked open the freezer and ejected massive Smirnoff and Absolut bottles and a pile of shot glasses. It was seven in the morning, and they wanted to welcome me to the home. The French guy ran for the shower and the Brazilian started strumming a guitar.

I was flattered – as much as one can be – but with the taste of Fiji's Beachcomber bile still in my throat, I told them that I would probably be keener that evening, "Shall we have breakfast instead, boys?"

"In Russia, this is breakfast," they said in a very I-vill-kill-you-Mr.-Bond sort of tone. Nevertheless, we agreed that later would be better.

Tehila ran accommodations for students learning English in Australia. In the communal dining area, I cast my lot with the groups of worldly students and found myself repeatedly explaining – to all of them in turn – in a very pronounced and illustrative manner that I was actually there for reasons other than linguistics, that Tehila was a friend of a friend.

After lots of nods and smiles and breakfast, I batted off to the post office and – because I had just come from such dialogues – I conducted myself in a monosyllabic fashion using BIG and overly distinct gesticulations. As amused as they must have been, the smiles of the postal attendants did little to encourage me when I was informed that my two crates of clothing and other essentials had not seen Australian shores. As it turns out, they wouldn't for some time yet.

That evening, back at the apartment, the Russians made Absolut sure I sat at the table with them. They poured me a shot of vodka, then stared at me with strange Mongolian-like eyes, saying, "Ve drink now. Velcome." The Chinese guys buckled down behind their door, the sight of the Russians and vodka seemingly stirring some painful memories. The Frenchman was apparently out surfing and the Brazilian slipped into his room to "study." It was just me and them, and I felt like they wanted to know secrets.

Despite my yardstick male height and physical mass, I have to be the world's most lightweight drinker ... ever. There are theories circulating that I was born without a liver. "Two-Pot Screamer," "Two-Can Sam," "Cadbury Kid," "Lush" – the list of appellatives used to portray my massive inability to consume alcohol in correlation to my gait, or even normal human standards, goes on ad infinitum. It is a double-agent point of great mockery, and yet incredible jealousy.

I am not the type who becomes someone else when I drink – in fact, I don't change personality at all. Rather, the effects are physiological.

After one beer or half a glass of wine, my face and ears go flush, I slur my speech and my coordination declares war on my motor skills. Two beers (or the equivalent), and I'd rather not stand, for my fear of gravity and large objects becomes quite acute. Things move too fast for me to absorb, and I usually sit and smile politely to avoid any misunderstanding that might provoke a determined fist to adopt a speed too fast to dodge. Three equivalent units and I try to remember if I have written my blood type and address somewhere where authorities might be able to locate it in time.

I am often belittled by hardcore drinkers in a realm where a lofty footing on the ladder of manhood can be achieved only by those who can quaff obscene amounts of grog. My rebuttal, when the chorus of mocking voices finds a lull and the word "sissy" is repeated for the last time, is simply to state that my level of intoxication is often equal to theirs, though I outlay coins instead of bills of double and triple digit denominations. Who's the man now?

In any case, I will take you back to the conclusion of my first full day in Australia, where I was sitting with the stern boys and several glasses of a clear liquid that burns one's throat. Their idea of drinking was faster is better, and the vodka was going down at an alarming rate. I confessed to them my limits, and managed to negotiate that I would take one glass to their three, but even at that velocity I soon found my vision leaving trails.

Despite many limitations of English vocabulary on their part, the Russians seemed well versed in phrases associated with weaponry, female anatomy and torture. They had an affinity for the word "balls," and employed it surprisingly well and relatively often in sentences that conveyed themes of courage, cowardice and, in my case, a lack of ability to drink vodka.

The rest of the evening was placed in a file that was buried in the back of my very messy brain. At one point, my field of vision resembled the effect you get when you play with the V-hold on an old Hitachi TV set. I managed to find a path to my futon, some metres from my chair, and though it tried to move on me in a *Labyrinth*-like fashion, I pounced on it. The Russians exchanged looks and muttered something about "just getting started," but my ability to process external audio at that point would have required a decoder ring, an anti-delay mechanism and, moreover, a lot less alcohol in my system.

I lay on my futon with images of laughing Russians, swirling vodka bottles and a shot glass that enjoyed very little use from my numb fingers. A voice seemed to be saying to me, "Velcome to Ostraliuh, Mr. Bond. Things for you are about to get vorse. *Mu-ha-ha*."

3 – Here Be Dragons

Get your facts first, and then you can distort them as much as you please...Facts are stubborn, but statistics are more pliable.

– Mark Twain

STATISTICS, BOTH THE word and the framework of arriving at numbers that apparently paint pictures, came to be very jumbled in my imagination, a bizarre mix of alcohol and false follicles, starting when I was in college.

Bob had been a nut of a college teacher. He wore sandals to class in winter, was short and round, and he pulled his collection of a few abnormally long strands of hair from the left side of his head, over a glaring and exposed scalp, to the right side in a way that resembled grass in the wind over a savannah. He readily accepted beer from students, and his antics included (but were not limited to) throwing chalk, jumping on tables and chairs and (most famously) mimicking the sounds of an orgasm when he erased the blackboard. Bob was something one looked forward to when the title of his class weighed in as "Analytical Statistics and Applications in the Justice System."

Bob was in it for the fun, not the glory. During quizzes and exams, he would float between the aisles to respond to questions, or, truthfully, tell you the answer. Those too thick not to pick up on his hints would actually find Bob doing the work for them on their sheets. In fact, Bob was so good at doing the work that we really didn't learn much, not even the meaning of the Greek symbols one is supposed to use in formulating the numbers.

Furthermore, he concluded his semesters by taking our finals and his red pen down to the pub with the class in tow to buy rounds for him. We called him Professor Beer. By the time he reached my paper his eyes resembled glazed doughnuts, someone was running for another pitcher and we had lost track of n (n = number of pitchers in a set ... It was pretty hilarious then as I recall). Being as my paper was near the bottom of the pile, my final grade – scrawled slurry but lovingly on the top page – was 92 percent.

When I took stats in university, I got dealt an astrophysicist. This professor had a strange accent, an incomparable last name, and he spoke in a pompous tone. Immediately noticeable upon his person were the copious bandages on his fingertips – evidence that perhaps his evenings centred around beakers and bubbling tubes. He wore a strange and shiny raven-black toupée of lengthy hair parted differently each class. It forever seemed as though it would slip off but never did. In his clothing ensembles, he favoured tweed in tragic permutations.

He announced that this was to be his first time teaching "business statistics," and that he otherwise worked for NASA and taught in the engineering faculty. Thus, his levels of mathematical comprehension extended to nebulae and quasars, quantum theory and star spectrums and astronomy and its subtexts, while us first-year students were discovering that alpha, delta and mu had applications outside of fraternities and quite possibly in the business section of the newspaper.

Professor Wig's method of placing complex formulas on projectors that resembled someone spilling a can of Greek alphabet soup over a pile of lines, square root symbols and exponent ns, not to mention super- and sub-scripts to no end, did little for my overall comprehension. The class and I would stare shit-scared at tangled information on the screen while attempting some form of rough re-production in our own calligraphy. He would yank away the acetates spouting, "Well, that was obvious, self-evident rather, as you can see ..." We all became quite fascinated with his wig, though, strangely because it wasn't complicated.

I opted – under threat of repeating the year – to take the course by correspondence. I soon came to realize that, like politicians and media, I could make numbers back me and make others look bad. I had learned the "behind-the-scenes" workings, and could understand footnotes in magazines and newspapers, as well as impress girls by explaining complicated terms like "linear regression."

All of this to say that to me, all statistics are just "beers and wigs."

You are by now no doubt wondering what any of this has to do with the people who call theirs the "lucky country?" Well, everything and nothing, really, because history would show that the continent of Australia was the most hit-and-miss (or put more aptly, hit-and-leave) place on Earth, and all of it happened by sheer chance (or you could call it luck), in circumstances similar to what you have just read.

The person who first dreamed of Australia was bored and mentally meandering in a world of mu, sigma and delta letters, and his imagina- tion eventually gave a name to the big globule of sand with 60 million kangaroos. Claudius Ptolemy, considered by some to be the father of Renaissance geography, was very likely poking about his home in circa

200 BCE in Greece, considering what combination of diadems and sandals to wear to his next toga party, when he came up with the theory that in order for planet Earth not to topple off its axis, it needed a mass of land in the southern hemisphere to counterbalance the continents of the northern hemisphere. At the time, symmetry of the Earth demanded as much. He further dreamt that such a place was the source of the Nile and – after getting wind of the explorations of Alexander the Great in India (327 to 325 BCE) – a continent infested with all forms of freaks and sinners.

During his life, much of the known world around Europe, Africa and the Asian subcontinent was at least loosely charted, and in subsequent geographical charts Ptolemy represented his imagined counterweight continent as a massive sketched chunk of land that covered the entire South Pole. I have no doubt that as he drew things he made the sounds of orgasm and probably babbled, "Well, that was obvious, self-evident rather, as you can see …" before naming his dream *Terra Australis Incognito* (Latin for "Unknown Southern Land"). He would never find out that this mysterious upside down statistical 'beer and wigs' marvel land was not only sound, but also a lot smaller than imagined.

For many centuries after his death and well into the Current Era, other Europeans had an inkling that such a continent existed. In England, during medieval times, all territory that was unexplored and foreign was marked on maps with a single phrase: "Here be dragons." It was, at the time, the stamp that beyond the known lay danger and evil.

But dragons didn't scare everyone and thus all the early explorers were guilty of either completely missing the mass or finding it (by pure chance) and leaving without wasting good ink, feather and scroll to plot it. Before it became a British prison, Australia avoided detection for longer than any criminal mastermind – to all but a select few humans who had mysteriously arrived in a time beyond even the first thoughts of fire breathing lizards.

Putting aside for the moment discussion of the Aboriginal Australians (the real first people), still there is no consensus as to who "discovered" Australia. It would be logical for Asian cultures to take the title, but logic never played out. China knew about Timor, that much seems certain, as they searched avidly for sea cucumbers to smoke (you read correctly, smoke).

There are rumours about a Chinese map of Australia drawn circa 1426, but it has never tangibly been seen. For their part, Indonesian fishermen were making regular fishing drops to the Gulf of Carpentaria long before 1700 CE, and there are sketchy suggestions of intermingling between them and the Aboriginals. Nevertheless, supposed fishing sites cannot accurately be dated.

There was much, it seemed, that prevented the Indo-Asian societies from dipping Down Under. Aside from limitations in ship building (causing them to become coast-huggers), they also had superstitions about the end of earth in the south, spawned from ideologies about the shape of the world. It wasn't dragons that scared them, but evil spirits.

Ultimately competition, a considerable fund of lore and the joy of spreading Christianity would spur on the far more intrepid yet distant European sailors. They had pioneered two routes to Indian spice, one eastward via South Africa and the other westward from South America. Nevertheless, sea swells, winds and lack of layover land forced them ignorantly northward beyond the evasive Australia.

One theory holds that Marco Polo may have chanced upon it in his 1295 nautical meanderings, though opponents claim Mr. Polo only gained Cambodia and Singapore.

There is note about the 1503 voyage of French explorer Paulmier de Gonneville, who claimed to have found the Great Southern Lands, but it is largely conjectured that he was babbling under the influence of wine about South America.

Things get a little less grainy when gold-hungry and pen-loving Spanish expeditions came within a whisker. By 1595, Spanish captains had settled much of South America and the Philippines and sailed regularly between ports in Mexico, Peru and Manila, some with vague references in their diaries of the Inca legend of the "Great Gold in the West Lands."

Nevertheless, the Spanish had a spectacular succession of failures. One captain utterly missed Australia (by a hair) and reached the Solomon Islands, where he named a few dots of land. Another – who in a letter to the Pope described the Great Southern Land "[containing] millions of innocent heathen souls, ripe for salvation" – managed to gain Vanuatu in 1605 and immediately thought that a second Jerusalem would be born. In his Christian giddiness, he baptized a nearby stream The Jordan, but God was not on his side, for his crew grew mutinous and just as he was all but in Australia, his rudder made a forced wake back to Peru.

One Luis Vaez de Torres was left behind to continue on a south-west trajectory but, for reasons still unknown, when he was all but there, Torres capriciously decided to abandon the hunt and steer back north where he hit Papua New Guinea and named a sliver of water after himself. He died not knowing how close he had come, and his minor accomplishment in naming the Torres Straight lives on in modern Australia as a method used by the Immigration Department to discern Aboriginal-Torres Straight islanders from European descendants. Hardly cause for a celebration.

Enter the Dutch: the first official European sighting of Australia was made by William Jansz. In 1606, he was poking about New Guinea and anchored in the Gulf of Carpentaria, and his was possibly the first contact between Europeans and Aboriginals. Nevertheless, after one of Jansz's crew was speared by said natives, he nefariously logged that "there was no good to be done there," named the spot Keerweer ("Turn Back"), high-tailed it and forgot all about the place.

Several other Dutch vessels destined for the Dutch colony Batavia (present-day Jakarta, Indonesia) would miscalculate wind and wreck at locations along the inhospitable west and north coasts of Australia.

The Dutch East India Company (who dubbed the region New Holland) grew curious and sponsored missions to find (1) gold, (2) spices and (3) more people to convert to the Calvinist Jehovah Christian camp. They didn't find (1) or (2), but they did (3), and one captain wrote, "To our chagrin, [we found] a land of exceedingly black barbarian savages."

It might shock you to know that the Dutch, not the British, were the first to use the place as a prison – albeit on a on a very small scale. Most Australians know little of the singular case of the obscure Wouter Looes and Jan Pelgrom. Looes and Pelgrom were crew members on the vessel *Batavia*, which ran aground in Western Australia in 1629. Captain Pelsaert sailed off for help, pledging to all that he would return with provisions.

While awaiting Pelsaert's rescue, crew member Cornelisz would be seized with the bizarre intention to become the world's greatest pirate. His plan was to forcefully appropriate the *Batavia* and her silver chests and then hit the open seas to pillage and plunder his days away, possibly with a hook for a hand and a patch for an eye, though of the former and latter I cannot be certain. Looes and Pelgrom fell in with Cornelisz and with other supporters they raped the women brought along on the ship and murdered 125 stranded victims. A small contingent of rebels managed to flee and survive on an island and would later capture the mad Cornelisz just when, true to his word, Captain Pelsaert returned to collect everyone.

Pelsaert arrived in the throes of a very real game of *Survivor*. He helped overcome the mutineers, then tried, mutilated and hung Cornelisz and all his disciples, except Looes and Pelgrom. He decided to leave them marooned in the lifeless area and they were never heard from again. Some rumours have it that the two intermarried with Aboriginal tribes, but more likely they perished trying to sail north to Batavia. Regardless, they are considered the first European convicts in Australia, a full 150 years before the establishment of the first British penal colony.

By 1642, one Abel Tasman took up the unenviable charge of further detailing the forlorn region. True to form, he sailed right under Australia, not knowing it was there, and tumbled upon the island of Tasmania, which he named Van Diemen's Land. The financiers of this expedition of the Company were not happy. Noted one bottom-line–minded shareholder, "[Tasman] met with naked, beach-roving wretches, destitute of rice, excessively poor and of a very malignant nature." Hardly a report that inspires notions of a healthy return on investment.

Of course, if Tasman had pressed just a little bit further in his explorations, he would no doubt have discovered the resource-rich regions of present-day Victoria and NSW. Instead, his sponsorship dried up and he was ordered to stop bothering with the region, even when he found a piece of the north coast of the mainland.

To all of this exploratory misery the English and French only added echoes. Englishman Dampier went ashore on the west coast and saw nothing aside from the natives, of whom he would malignly write, "The inhabitants ... are the miserablest people in the World ... setting aside their humane shape they differ but little from Brutes." Frenchman D'Estrecasteaux wrote, "The most fertile imagination could find nothing to say about it."

And no one was the wiser for nearly a hundred years more.

Now take a small reflective intermission and consider Australia's reputation to date. To the Greeks, it was a dream and a means to balance the world. To the Indo-Asians, it was not far from a place to toke a sea cucumber and increase paranoia about the mythical end of the world just below established shoreline. To the Spaniards (who actually went looking), it represented mutiny, arbitrary decisions to change course and, ultimately, no gold. Then, for those lanky Dutchmen who accidentally washed up, it was a place to either get speared or have daft brain haemorrhages that induced delusions of pirate grandeur. As for the British and French ... well, precious little was added there. And all the while, to the Aboriginals it was home long before most of us can conceive. Until another catalytic blunder in 1770, this was *Terra Australis*.

By skimming over a few book titles, you can get an idea of what happened next. Consider Geoffrey Blainey's *A Land Half Won*, *Tyranny of Distance* and *Our Side of the Country*. Suggestive? For an understanding of prisons, I was told that my "must-read" list should include Robert Hughes' *The Fatal Shore* – a dense compendium of well-crafted workmanship. But next to the other recommendation, it was a pamphlet.

I had noted references to Manning Clark (described in one book flap as "controversial*") and was taken aback at the library when I spied his six teeming volumes, each averaging 360 pages of tight print. In stacking them they almost attained my knee. I found his aggregate *History of Australia* (567 pages), which contained a photo of him in the sleeve. He didn't look happy. Either he had suffered from having written too much, or had perhaps put too much Vegemite on his toast just before the photographer arrived. I grabbed his *A Short History of Australia* (with its 257 pages and large illustrations) and put the mean-looking photo of whitie back on the shelf.

Nowadays nine-tenths of the Australian population live within 20 kilometres of the ocean, occupying a south-easterly arc from Brisbane in Queensland to Melbourne in Victoria (about 5 percent of Australia's landmass), known aptly as the Boomerang Coast. All of Australia's major cities (you can count them on two hands and still have enough change to pick your nose) are built near water.

One of the first things you learn as a foreigner in Sydney is that "there's Sydney and then there's Australia." Regardless, no one can take away the beauty of the nation's most bustling metropolis. Sydney is just stunning, and I would be blessed with the opportunity to view it from the air on three day lit occasions. It's such a striking location that on every flight, the pilots would take immense free license and pride in pointing out beaches and landmarks.

Can't blame them, really. The Tasman Sea shimmers with irresistible colour, the shoreline comes in two major flavours – golden beach or sand-stone cliff – and the Sydney harbour is known to be (depending on who you ask or what you read) either "the" or "one of the" most

---

* His views on Australian Aboriginal prehistory are still passionately debated presently, but, to be fair, he isn't the only one.

beautiful harbours in the world.

As the eye scrolls inland, the layout of the sprawling suburbs present a blend of green vegetation and roofs favouring red brick tones, stretching to infinity among streets that wind about like a child's hand at play with a crayon.

One source puts Sydney's sprawl at 1,800 square kilometres, while another pegged it at 12,000 (including Gosford and Penrith). However, with mountains to the west, and desert beyond that, ocean to the east and national parks both north and south, everything naturally seems to point you toward Sydney.

And now we come back to the present, for I would awake after my first Sydney night with the Russians to a personal tale of eviction.

4 – Slip, Slap and Slop

"SORRY, YOU HAVE to move," said Tehila. As it turned out, she wasn't allowed to house people who weren't studying English. The Russians were sad to see me go, but I did go back several times to visit, as Tehila was nice enough to say that I was welcome for dinner whenever I liked. I took her up shortly after when I hit dire straits.

In what seemed like minutes, Tehila had kindly driven me to the doorstep of an agency called Aussie Homestay where – after they had separated me from a colourful $220 "finder's fee" – I was picked up by a woman offering billet in Bronte, a beach suburb next to Bondi.

My new landlady was reserved but nice, and she made it clear that there were to be no parties or sleepovers, and that I was to clean as I went. As I had no friends at that point, I had little choice, anyhow. But a bonus! A pair of colourful and aptly named Rainbow Laurakeate birds – patched with the world's brightest-feathered colour spectrum – would visit our windows regularly to sing songs and accept remuneration in the form of a few bread crumbs.

The eastern suburbs of Sydney are nothing short of gorgeous, and my new coastal lifestyle was simply unbeatable. The ocean is magnificent and along the coast is a well-trodden path that wraps around striking cliffs and beaches, from Coogee Beach in the south (and further I am told) to Bondi Beach and beyond. Within that relay are Bronte Beach and the quaint Tamarama (a.k.a. Galmo-rama) Beach. They say that if you don't sweat, you don't belong in Sydney, and with the neck-twisting amount of gorgeous bodies flowing past me glistening in the sun, I believed it.

As if to convince those of lesser physical conditioning that there's no time like the present to act on New Year's Resolutions, there is no shortage of chin-up bars, sit-up boards and other communal points at which to work out and stretch in the splendorous surroundings. Bondi and Bronte have cordoned-off pool areas where you can swim non-chlorinated laps as the water brims in from the sea. Dotting the grassy areas of the beaches are public hot plates on brick structures conveniently located next to picnic booths of unique (and unquestionably for some, romantic) design. This was a real slice of Australia, a place of sun and fun, surfing, swimming and "footie," of blankets and beers and marinated chicken.

I was in heaven, though a heaven that was about to disappear under weight of fiscal reality.

Reviewing my early diaries, I realize now that some of my first impressions of the buildings of the eastern suburbs, and of Sydney in general, were that they looked and felt very English. Take away the constant sunshine, the gorgeous beaches and the white smiles on many, and (aesthetically speaking) you could be in Any Hamlet, UK. The streets are narrow; often just lanes, and they conjoin at roundabouts. The cars seem abnormally compact, by North American standards, and the homes, though slightly varied, by and large are made of crimson bricks, with burgundy roofs of curved tiles, and are packed tautly together; they're usually only a few floors high, with postage stamp-sized lawns behind little gates that are double the stature of the surrounding low brick wall.

The inner city and suburbs are a mixture of Victorian-style homes (with elaborate lace ironwork and balconies) and California/Spanish bungalows. Further west of Sydney, things become a little more American: there are massive shopping malls and multi-storey parking lots, and many homes are "federation homes" with an additional lawn in front. It is amazing how muddled Sydney is in its buildings – one can see a grand old Victorian estate next to a bland and linear edifice, but there you go. Sydney's influences can be traced and architecturally eyeballed from the ocean inland.

One hugely British mark is Sydney's fragmentation, which resembles London's, comprising between 728 and 844 suburbs (depending on where you draw the line) – the complete opposite of the North American mega-cities with their amalgamated administrations. So blurred are their borders that in many cases two street directories will list a certain street as being in different suburbs, though always in the same general region.

Then there are constant reminders of royalty – the main streets in Sydney are Elizabeth, Victoria, George, Kent and York, and most suburbs have at least one of these. The artery that leads from Bondi Junction to the City is Oxford Street, which snakes through the suburbs of Paddington and Darlinghurst (not far from King's Cross*) and ends at Hyde Park, which also has a St. James train station.

---

* The "Cross" sprang up to cater to the vices of American soldiers in port during Vietnam. Today it is still the red light district where you can find lots of youth hostels, fine dining and derelicts, but also burgers and fries and titties and thighs.

Each borough has its own flavour, of course. Bondi (further divided into north and south Bondi, suburbs that are each less than a kilometre in size) is quite different in feel from Bronte. Paddington – a whole other world of artists and iron-wrought balconies – is just down the road a few kilometres. Initially I found it a bit frustrating to find my way around, but soon I liked the idea. Sydney's haphazard style forced upon people the necessity to get to know the place rather intimately. Conceivably, this spawned the obligation for Aussies to be friendlier at the risk of getting hopelessly lost.

An area of Sydney known as The Rocks is a little piece of yester-year Britain: cobblestone streets, old fashioned arches, steps leading to the wooden doors of old brick buildings. One might expect to see a hurried Englishman in a trench coat whistle past on his way to see Sherlock Holmes on Baker Street, as horse and buggy clop by.

The shops and commercial zones enjoy much of the same economy of space, with buildings squashed together, sometimes separated by a thin alleyway, but most often without. Rectangular signs hang down from jutting roof awnings and some shops one has to enter by striding up a trilogy of steps. But then that was the plan all along for the founding colonials: the far-flung continent was never really intended to be a place other than the Britannia of the South Pacific.

In what is today Barwon Park (just outside of Melbourne), one Thomas Austin, a keen English hunter, holds the distinction of having unleashed furry English sexual hell on Australia. In 1859, he brought from the homeland six pairs of rabbits and some pheasants, foxes and quail, and released them along the shore of the Barwon River so he could shoot them for fun. Jolly good then.

He failed uncompromisingly to consider the warm environment, a lack of natural predators and, above all, his own bad aim, and soon they multiplied thousands of times faster than Austin could pick them off. Within a few years, Australia was plagued with an environmental disaster. One source fixed the amount of damage done to crops and indigenous nature by rabbits as being well over the $1 billion per annum mark.

Then another genius dabbling in the science of opposites thought foxes would do the trick, and a second plague was born. It would take another century for Australians to use the poison myxomatosis, which has an almost perfect rabbit kill-rate. Nevertheless, the furry buggers have developed immunities and presently scientists can't agree if it is 100 or 400 million rabbits bouncing about the place.

Among other animals that made the trip were horses, donkeys, buffalo, sheep, camels, cows, goats, dogs and one of the most deadly predators of smaller indigenous wildlife, the domestic cat.

And – like a mother-in-law who reorganizes the natural state of your home starting with the kitchen – European immigrants also brought over seeds for melons, pumpkins and cabbage, along with oak trees, willows, jacarandas, hedges, bushes and all kinds of other flora. Although it might be said that some introduced species looked good and even flourished in Australia, the sad consequence was that numerous others, such as the noxious weed Patersons, have wrought untold damage on what was once very isolated and unique Australian nature.

Before all of this happened, Australia was teeming with riches: it had so many forms of new and untamed life, strange animals, fish and plants. By all early accounts, one might have expected to come to Australia in the early days of white settlement and climb a fat bean stalk to find a giant snoring away in the clouds. Alas, with time Australian nature was ripped up to make the place more homely. The horticultural statistics of destruction and extinction are stunning (estimates between thousands and tens of thousands), though there is in reality no way to know how accurate they are. Hundreds of thousands of native Australian birds and other animals were trapped for export, three-quarters of them dying before they got to their far-off destination, and it took legislators until as late as 1960 to ban such activity.

The possibly happy upshot is that, to this day, much Australian nature awaits cataloguing and naming, so it is hard to tell which species might still exist or how many million more could have possibly come and gone without ever seeing the business end of a scientific microscope and slide label.

Of course, one can't help but wonder how all of this destruction even came about. I leafed through Hughes' *The Fatal Shore*, Clark's *A Short History of Australia* and Donald Horne's *The Lucky Country*, among some other sources, to get an answer.

Hughes declares that Australia's convict past is "a stain ... a moral blot soaked into [its] fabric," and thus a source of "national amnesia" that most national history textbooks care not to cover. As a sixth or tenth generation Australian, it wouldn't be easy to think that one's recent ancestors might be a punting amateur of the five-finger discount method and his concubine a Southwark prostitute. Regardless, it was ignorance of the past that convinced Hughes to sift through the dense layers of Australia's felonious records and scribble it all into his substantial tome.

Truthfully, it is one of the most fascinating and sordid success stories in recent human history – the ugly duckling country of the world that blossomed into the grand swan.

So we'll back up a sec to before the time when the forests fell.

The story begins, unbeknownst to its protagonist, in 1768. James Cook (later known as Captain Cook, even though he wasn't a captain) of the British vessel *Endeavour* undertook a mission completely removed from charting the unknown. Quite simply, he didn't go looking for Australia, for he had his eyes on a higher prize – the skies.

In those days, calculating longitude at sea was still an inaccurate gamble and in most cases European ships were off by margins of 2,000 miles – just one of many reasons why so many ships of the epoch missed Australia or couldn't find their way back if they tried.

Cook's orders were to sail to Tahiti by June 3, 1769, in time to witness Venus crossing the sun's face. Using nautical instruments of the day, his team was to record the celestial movement in order to add a variable to the formula of using stars to calculate longitude.

Just as he was about to leave, Cook's superiors casually instructed him that "if he had the time" could he just make a stop in New Holland and either dismiss or acknowledge it? If you have time? Cheers, mate.

Riding shotgun was botanist and naturalist Joseph Banks, who was fascinated by the nature of far-flung tropical places. While in Tahiti, Banks took exorbitant amounts of samples, including a live Tahitian native man whom he wanted to introduce to British society as the Noble Savage.

Once their astral mission wrapped up, the *Endeavour* set out to New Zealand and then – since they had a bit of time – decided to sail west to the Cape of Good Hope in Africa, solely because the winds favoured the direction and Cook considered it might be a good idea to have a quick pit stop in New Holland and potentially bonus their already grand scientific booty of South Pacifica.

Wouldn't you know, Cook (who had Abel Tasman's old charts, which made New Zealand and Tasmania look like one big island) then did what no one else to date had managed to pull off: he sailed north to the elusive shoreline of the Boomerang Coast.

He laid anchor in 1770 at what became known as Botany Bay. Banks, for his part, was still reeling with excitement from the wondrous lushness of Tahiti and New Zealand, and compared the Australian landscape to "the back of a lean cow." He and the others spied smoke in the hills and concluded that the land was already inhabited by natives.

Then, after tracing the coast northbound all the way to the Gulf of Carpentaria, thrusting a pole with the Union Jack into the ground and naming – for reasons to this day mysterious – the whole east coast of Australia, from the top peninsula down to Van Diemen's Land, New South Wales for King George III, Cook and his crew buggered off. Aside from being delayed seven weeks by running the *Endeavour* aground on the Great Barrier Reef, Cook b-lined it for England to show and tell of all their wonderful findings, including the Tahitian Noble Savage. All of these outshone the newly claimed territory, which was not bothered further for almost two full decades.

As late as 1770, when America was in its adolescence and close to independence, the Great Southern Land still remained a huge disappointment. How, then, do you get a country of such nice people from criminal stock?

Return with Cook to 18th-century London. It was a bustling and dank city with a thin crust of nobles sitting atop a heavy mass of illiterate and impoverished peasants. The west end was rich and the east end was swarming with poor people who barely had room to bury their dead – which contributed significantly to the already putrid air. Children started working at age six in industrial sweat shops without regulation, equipment or social security.

At the time, English farmers had a surplus of corn, and some wise entrepreneurs mass-produced the most affordable solace a poor person could want in such a sombre world: gin. "Drunk for a penny, dead drunk for two-pence," was the saying, and by 1743 east-enders killed their pain by downing over eight million gallons of gin a year – a gateway to dereliction and a good reason to establish one gin shop for every 120 east-enders by 1751. In other words, Gin-Bucks.

Into the mix poured industrialization and a soaring birth rate. Between 1750 and 1770, the population of London doubled, whereas it had been stable beforehand. The more refined echelons of England's citizenry were gripped as statisticians churned out "beer and wigs" numbers that a swarming criminal class was rising. One in eight men lived off of "crime," it was said, though the definition was so overly general as to include scavengers and murderers in the same sample.

But London was not equipped with crime-fighting tools; the metropolitan police wasn't established until 1829, and even then, their beginnings were ragtag. They generally avoided criminals or were bribed with gin. Fingerprinting and registries were even further off. Bounty hunters worsened matters, for they encouraged crime for paycheques.

England was the laughingstock of Europe: other nations had stamped out their problems with militia, torture and executions. The English Common Law instead dealt rights that more often let those few who were stupid enough to get caught walk free on technical points of white-wigged, ivory tower theory. The solution, it was thought, lay in deterrence. More than 160 offences that today would earn one a light fine were quilled into the books carrying reprimand of death. One could swing for murder or "impersonating a gypsy," poaching a rabbit, scratching a fence and, yes, even abducting an heiress (because she was "property incarnate" and abduction was therefore theft of a family's "accumulated goods and rights.") Judges – bound by law and against their own better conscience – ordered boys who stole candy strung up with men who snatched someone's niece for ransom.

Soon after, ships on the disease-infested Thames came to be prisons, and murderers bunked with crafty accountants, women with rapists and children with paedophiles. The alternative of "transportation beyond the seas" came to be a brainchild and criminals were forked off to the colonies of America as cheap labour.

All well and good until 1775, when the Americans rebelled; by 1783, Britain had to recognize the United States as an independent nation. The US would go on to steal and transport black slaves from Africa instead of paying for the English castaway classes because "a new Republic must not be polluted with the Crown's offal." So, in a large way, Australia would have America to thank for its peaceful creation. It was then suggested that felons be swept deep under the respectable British rug to the recently claimed NSW.

Consider with me for a moment what it must have been like to live in the skin of a British peasant in the 1700s – illiterate, under the heavy hand of Christianity, getting all your information through hearsay, myth and church, ignorant of all geography, your life spent on a parcel of land and never travelling outside a 10-mile radius. Now imagine being done for a ridiculous crime, dragged trembling before a grim and high-minded judge and then being clapped in irons and dispatched unceremoniously away from everything and everyone familiar to the ass-end of the Earth.

* * *

I began to feverishly scour around for a job.

The 11 ships of the First Fleet contained just over 1,000 people, of which about three-quarters were convicted men and women. It left Portsmouth in 1787 and sailed 40,704 kilometres in 252 days waywardly via Brazil and South Africa before arriving in Botany Bay, NSW, 18 years after Cook and Banks had scrawled their preliminary notes and never returned*. The First Fleet captain and first governor of NSW, one Arthur Phillip, a semi-retired navy man, had no idea what he was in for. In a manner eerily similar to my own voyage to Australia, there had been no reconnaissance.

Consider the line-up of first Australians: one woman (age 70) was busted red-handed with cheese; another guy for nicking two hens (one in a state of being alive). Another female had had her sentence of death commuted to transport for appropriating butter, flour and raisins, and her companion on the voyage was a gentleman who had destroyed a bed of cucumbers. The oldest convict was an 82-year-old woman under penalty of perjury, and sadly she became Australia's first recorded suicide when she hung herself from a tree in Sydney. Among the younger convicts was an 11-year-old boy who palmed a pair of stockings and 10 yards of ribbon, a kid who had made off with a book and some tobacco and the youngest of the bunch, a nine-year-old child who filched some clothes and a pistol. Then there was a guy on board for grabbing barber's equipment from his boss. One male offender had tried to take a lady's handkerchief, which she later testified "put her into fear" and the hankie-hijacker had spent half a decade on death row before finding himself in the hulled presence of the above company, destination: NSW.

In this band of the ill-chosen, only one was a gardener and one a fishermen, and there were but a handful of bricklayers and carpenters. Most had none of the necessary experience required to settle a new land. Only one-third of the total could work, while the rest were reliant because they were either too old or just unskilled slum-dwellers. Hughes describes the scenario as "a motley crew, this Noah's Ark of small-time criminality, and for all the trades represented aboard, it was absurdly ill-chosen for the task for colonizing New South Wales."

Besides being ill-prepared, they were sent out over-packed and under-provisioned and arrived in the opposite season to what Cook and Banks

---

* They had returned in that time to chart Antarctica, thinking it might be the fabled Great South Land, but due to ice, they just turned away and didn't bother to further chart the Australian shore.

had seen. The new governor Phillip found swamps, low-lying scrub and scant supplies of fresh water – not at all what Banks had written about. But he would be momentarily distracted from his dire plight by one of the strangest coincidences in nautical history.

Two French vessels under command of the Comte de La Perouse were spotted poking about. The Frenchman had gotten wind of the new colony and put just that in his sails to pop down and check out the new set-up at Botany Bay. He ended up staying for six weeks. The chance of such a meeting was next to impossible, and governor Phillip extended every courtesy to La Perouse – which was essentially nothing because that's exactly what they had.

Meanwhile, a better location was scouted 25 kilometres north at Port Jackson, and Phillip opted to swap spots; as he wrote, it was "the finest natural harbour in the world, in which a thousand sail of the line may ride in the most perfect security."

Some of the convicts escaped and ran back to Botany Bay to beg of La Perouse to take them back to Europe. Instead *le français* flogged them and turned them on their heels back to Port Jackson, though none of the fraught convicts ever knew how lucky they were. It was discovered, some 40 years on, that his tandem vessels were driven aground by a cyclone and sunk with all aboard in the New Hebrides, Solomon Islands.

Today all that remains of the this remarkable French-English crossing is that Sydney has a suburb named La Perouse just south of the central city. One can grab the 371 Sydney Transpo bus from Circular Quay (where Phillip first stepped ashore) to get there. I had learned that much while reading aboard public transit and plodding around Sydney searching for a job, so far without success, and completely unaware of the snare I was about to step into.

5 – Fledgling Ignorance

PORT JACKSON WAS almost renamed Albion, but instead it became Sydney Cove (in honour of Lord Sydney, the British Home Secretary); eventually, the Cove was dropped. Australia Day celebrates the day the convicts had an arrival party along Port Jackson. But the inaugural party was very short-lived.

The first fledgling years of the convict settlement were spent in the perpetual pangs of starvation. Their meat was home to maggots, the plough would not come for another 15 years and their livestock wandered off. I don't supposed it helped that they couldn't catch any of the local game for food or clothes, or figure out which plants were edible. All the plants were complete enigmas to them, especially the ubiquitous eucalypt tree (of which one Marine wrote 'beggared belief'), and the kangaroos, wallabies, lizards, massive spiders and eccentric birds weren't like anything they could have imagined.

Soon thereafter, governor Phillip cut everyone's already meagre supply of rations. The Marines' uniforms turned to ribbons and they went barefoot, gave up any pomp and circumstance and just cried to go back to England as things plunged headlong for all into outright famine. They weren't sure if another ship would come, and when it did, it just brought more unskilled convicts and a dreadfully unwelcome story about their supply ship sinking off Africa's coast. Governor Phillip was raising huge objections in his correspondence with the Lords of England on the topic of trying to grow a self-sustaining colony with no tools and even less talent. Britain just didn't care.

Rum would become both a major problem and a currency – somewhat like the gin scenario in London. The Marines became the NSW Rum Corps, who drank to forget. The conditions were squalid, their tents were often blowing away and in one case, women begging for some more rum were chased and raped by male convicts and Marines alike. "As the couples rutted between the rocks, guts burning with grog ... the first bush party in Australia had begun with 'some swearing, others quarrelling, others singing,'" noted Hughes. Men outnumbered women six-to-one and Phillip sent more nagging emails to England, which back then took the better part of a year to go one way, if they ever got there at all.

Into the 1800s, things started to look up, thanks to burgeoning pastoral farms and a very budding mastery of the local fauna. In

Parramatta (24 kilometres inland west of Sydney) and along the Hawkesbury River to the north, semi-successful farms were springing up. When Phillip retired, the NSW Rum Corps became unofficially the ruling elite with convicts as cheap labour*. England was otherwise tied up in the Napoleonic Wars and thought little of their fledgling penal colony in the grips of alcoholism.

What happened next was most unexpected.

I often looked up from the history books to the paradise of present-day Sydney and completely revelled in being able to ingest such a fascinating chain of toiled events, while staring at hot bodies walking along the sandstone cliffs or frolicking on the beach. But I soon realized that I, too, would face some dilemmas eerily similar to those I had just read about. If I didn't find a job soon, I would starve and have no home, and what's more, despite my shipment of clothing that was still late, I would not be getting any other assistance from anyone overseas. It was up to me to make it or break it now, completely removed as I was from my sphere of familiarity.

You see, living on the Sydney coast did not come at rock-bottom prices. My savings account had not known the meaning of "deposit" in six months. I immediately purchased my very first pre-paid mobile phone, got a tax file number and took other necessary steps toward finding gainful livelihood. I was to discover, however, that this was probably the worst time and season to find employment in.

To start with, I didn't know anyone in Sydney aside from the lawyer, and, as anyone knows, the best jobs aren't advertised. Secondly, 9/11 had rippled out to Australia, causing economic anxiety, and thirdly, the 2000 Olympics had left town just a tickle over one year previous. It seemed like I had arrived when Sydney was economically at low tide, and I was fishing in a dry riverbed of classifieds. In fact, since the Olympics – a period in which jobs had outnumbered people – the city had, as Sydney-siders were telling me, deeply exhaled, in economic terms.

Ads in the *Sydney Morning Herald*, as well as online recruiting agencies, came under my acute gaze. What seemed to occupy more space

---

* Although the convicts lamented that "… the Crown used them as slaves until they were judged fit to become peasants" (Hughes), they were theoretically far from slavery. The "government men" enjoyed rights; they could work off their debt and earn pardon or a ticket of leave, they could bring their superiors before court for ill-treatment and their offspring were born free, and of course none of the above were enjoyed by the Negro slaves in America.

in the newspaper, however, were articles forecasting grim (yet always hopeful) economic outlooks, citing that even top Australians – CEOs and CFOs, among other professionals – were finding it next to impossible to return to Australia in similar positions to those they held overseas.

I revamped my résumé hundreds of times and fired it into thousands of advertised positions from accounting to temp work, to almost anything that was above bricklayer and sandwich hand. I was trying at all costs to avoid waiting tables, the hospitality industry or physical labour, but things weren't looking good. Over the span of an initial few weeks, I was forever receiving replies, written and emailed, that ran in a rather templated fashion: "Thank you for your interest in X. X strives to be an employer of high standards ... We are so great to work for ... Opportunity for advancement ... Thank you for your consideration ... HOWEVER, at this time you have been unsuccessful ... Will keep you on file should any position matching your qualifications arise ..." I swear, only the company name changed.

Wasn't that just like the replies Governor Phillip had received from England when he wanted help in NSW?

After his retirement, Governor Phillip was replaced by one Governor Bligh. However, the NSW Rum Corps became so powerful with their land and rum in 1808 that they seized power of the colony and ran it as their own military junta for two years! The deposed Bligh fled to Tasmania and churned out furious letters to England to have the mutineers court-martialled and himself reinstated. Things were out of control, and so the English powers sent down a bull-headed Scotsman named Lachlan Macquarie in 1810.

Now, sending a Scot to a region flooded with rum may not seem like the best idea, but amazingly it worked. As Macquarie sailed for NSW, the two chief mutineers who had ousted Bligh sailed to England on their own to face the courts. Bligh then returned to Sydney only to be told by the incumbent Macquarie that he was an idiot and to bugger off. Further embarrassment followed when Bligh arrived back in England expecting, at the very least, that the coup organizers would be swinging by their necks. They instead got slaps on the wrist and one headed back to NSW to a life of prosperity. Bumbling Bligh was quickly forgotten.

Governor Lachlan Macquarie, on the other hand, cleaned house. He was high-minded, with credentials of service all over the world. He strongly believed that the British way of life and Protestantism were the keystones of civilization. He wanted the upper classes to conduct themselves better and the lower classes to stay sober.

In that vein, he reinstated deposed officers from the Rum Rebellion and put competent people in office. He closed bars early, made rum too expensive to purchase in stupefying quantities, ushered people into church, expanded farmlands, encouraged inland exploration and was forever on hand to meet and greet all new incoming convicts. To the shock of the ruling classes, he told all convicts that by adherence to Protestantism and his rules, they could become emancipated and be involved in the building of a grand new colony.

Governor Macquarie also took one look at his Sydney and immediately requested that England send down trained architects, which they didn't, only maintaining the practice of dispatching more unskilled English rabble. Proud despite the refusal, Macquarie opened an architecture book his wife had brought and started revamping Sydney from a shanty town to a gorgeous Gregorian city financed by profits from the sale of rum. Beginning in 1816 and over the next six years, buildings flew up by convict hands.

New South Wales was losing its quality as a criminal deterrent and was fast becoming more of a wealthy new plantation, with wool and grain churned out at rock-bottom costs.

Notwithstanding, transportation of convicts to NSW didn't end until 1840 and to Tasmania until 1853, and the extremely hot state of Western Australian got a dump of Irish Fenians as late as 1868. In all, it is calculated that some 160,000 British convicts had been cast off to NSW over a span of 40 transportation years (a number still under debate) and by 1831 the first government-assisted immigration programs had begun to induce non-convict Britons to freely settle NSW.

Meanwhile, Macquarie's head inflated to proportions larger than life and he was known to say that his word came before God's. Toward his last days in office in 1821, Macquarie grew alienated and kept pressing inland explorers to name everything they found after him. His major concern, it seemed, was not the good of Britannia but his own legacy. Soon after retirement he passed away in grief and anguish, never knowing that later he would become known as the "Father of Australia."

Today in Sydney and Australia, almost everything is named for him; rivers, towns, streets, banks, universities, fields, plains, harbours, towns and even a dictionary. Not bad.

In only a handful of decades between the 18th and 19th centuries, Australia was fast turning its situation around and the current-day states of Tasmania, Victoria, South Australia, Queensland and Western Australia all struck off to become colonies sovereign of New South Wales. The oddest thing was that the six separate colonies all looked to Britain for cues instead of to each other. Each new colony formed its own identity as polar from the other, as Portugal would be from Poland. As forackward as it may sound, most things – including the cost of shipping – were cheaper to import all the way from the UK than going to the colony next door and paying very high import tariffs.

Each colony had its own separate militia (as there was no clause for shared continental defence) and sovereign postage stamps and divergent railways (gauges varied by up to half a metre!) to prevent the other colonies from attracting cross-border traffic. Anyone wanting to traverse the precincts would have to debark with luggage, swap trains and pay duty on anything they had purchased.

Over time, bickering and rivalries were smoothed out and there was talk to federate the separate entities (including New Zealand) for the common good. But Australians were keeping one eye on the Civil War in America, which to this day arguably makes the US a nation of fragmented mentalities and 50 conflicting criminal codes.

Despite the difficulties in convincing everyone*, the idea of independent federation came about with notions of equality for all. Australia was finally becoming a paradise and an example to the world, which, considering its origins, makes it the modern-day success story I'm telling you about.

Now we come back to my one month mark in NSW. Still no job.

Because my shipment of wardrobe had not yet arrived, I was trolling around Sydney from one employment agency to another wearing the same lime-green collared shirt and beige slacks, though I did fork out some bucks for black business shoes. I didn't have a briefcase, either, so I always pulled on my bright red backpack. I began to wonder if over lunch these agency people got together to say things like, "Did a guy with a funny accent in his green shirt, beige pants and red bag come in to see you about work? You, too? No way! What's up with him, mate?"

Prospects were looking grim. I had very little in the way of a safety net and I dipped into the money and plastic credit that I had thought would be my last meagre rations.

---

* New Zealand opted out of Australian federation at the last moment, but they are smarter than most give them credit for. Before leaving the negotiation table they managed to walk away with the right to live and work in Australia without visas, and the right to collect social security at Australia's expense.

I didn't want to do as everyone else does when travelling in Australia – going up the over-trodden east coast to Cairns in northern Queensland, picking fruit, sheering sheep or waxing surfboards for a menial existence by the beach. I felt over that, having been a backpacker in other far-off places of the world and ready for something a little less arbitrary. I endeavoured to get a long-term job with a steady income and save up and think about my next move in a world that was changing faster every day.

Sydney was, in effect, the proverbial golden handcuffs, for though it was such a gorgeous place, you paid through the nose to live even moderately. It has this latent power to squash any efforts toward saving money for all within its boundaries. The trend of well-educated people out of work, though, was a global one. Not that it was comforting in any way, but I didn't seem to be the only casualty.

Then another bombshell. The lady I was currently living with asked me if the Aussie Homestay Agency had informed me that my lovely room in Bronte was only available until the middle of the following month. No, they didn't, actually, so now I had to find a new place to live in a fortnight and there was not even a doomed French captain to run to for alternatives.

6 – Praying Man-tis

MY JOB HUNTING was turning out to be a nightmare, so in desperation I signed up for some quick and easy construction work, only to be told I had to buy steel-toed boots and some other assorted gear, which I couldn't afford. I was about ready to sign up to become a sandwich hand when I came across a posting placed by "Samami Modelling," which advertised in bold letters "No experience necessary." In my work-seeking delirium, I entertained the notion that perhaps they might require someone who knew how to take good photos.

I moseyed into a recruiting session. The waiting room was full of people of all shapes and sizes who – ranked in order of when they arrived – would saunter through a door for varying periods of time and emerge either beaming a smile or wearing a frown.

"Excuse me," I said to the magazine, I mean *receptionist*, "I am not here for modelling but photography; am I in the right place?"

"Yes doll," she replied without absenting her eyes from *Cosmos Sex Tips and Make-Over Miracles*, "Speak to Fredo when you go in. Don't forget to fill in the application," she continued, as if a recorded message, and handed me a transparent pink clipboard.

Soon enough, my turn to float through the mysterious door came and I entered Fredo's office, the walls of which were plastered with modelling magazine clippings. Fredo was in his mid- to late-50s, Mediterranean in appearance, wearing a brown blazer and large sunglasses with brown gradient lenses and his black hair slicked back. His desk was smothered in paperwork and magazines, and with swift steps and little eye contact I found myself briskly shaking his hand, then seated as he said in a strong European accent, "Smile for me, please."

I obliged – albeit begrudgingly and somewhat taken aback by such a request – and exposed my pearly whites.

"OK, we will continue," he said, while blindly slipping my application into a pile I am guessing was for some form of a second stage. Mere seconds after the word "continue" fell from his mouth, he launched into a speech designed to favour an exclusively one-way dialogue.

"... And this guy here," he went on showing me yet another photo, "was a traveller from England, like you, and walked into Samami Modelling, like you, and is now on catwalks in Milan and Paris and in Brazil making millions."

"But I –" I tried to interject.

"And this here," he continued as if I were mute, "is a letter from Christina, a German traveller, like you, who writes to thank Samami Modelling for her successful career, here read it," and he passed me the handwritten letter with portions highlighted.

"Actually, you see –" I tried again.

"Now you have done what very few people have, you have passed the first stage of Samami Modelling. We can make you a star. Do you want to make money?" Without missing a beat, he said, "Good, because you can be big with Samami. First you need a photo portfolio, then we will send you to our specialized training sessions, then ..." and as he went on, it became clear that the sign-up fee (his word: "investment") to become an instant millionaire was somewhere in the village of $600.

"But you need to pay as soon as possible to guarantee your spot. We need the money right away: competition is fierce," he said in a tone that suggested few people refused such an easy rise to the top of the modelling world.

Finally! I would have my chance!

To speak, that was.

"Fredo, I am not here to model. I was wondering what the odds are of becoming an in-house photographer with Samami?" I queried.

This must have thrown him off, for I got the impression that usually his big speeches were followed by eager listeners scrambling to pay him. The subject I broached was something out of the ordinary.

"I see. You can be big, you know. You have a special look ... Millions!" he tried again.

"Wonderful and thanks, but I don't have $600, so maybe I could do a few shoots as a photographer and then think about crossing over?" I offered. I suppose all salesmen who have just done a pitch hate the words "I'll think about it," and immediately he got grumpy.

"Speak to Carlo," he said as he ushered me out of the office with swift steps and little eye contact, telling the *Cosmo* lady to send in another victim. Carlo wasn't there so I was told to call back later.

A few weeks would elapse when one day my phone rang.

"This is Therese from Samami Modelling, is this Allan Williams?"

"Wills," I replied. In the background I could hear papers being shuffled.

"Dah-ling! We have been wondering about you! We want you to sign up, mate, because this is a once in a lifetime opportunity! Only one spot left for next month's Samami training session! Can you make a deposit to guarantee your spot, doll?"

"I asked to be a photographer, not a model. Is Carlo still there?"

"Who, dah-ling?"

"How about Fredo? He told me to call Carlo."

"Fredo has ... been reassigned. But he left your high-profile application with us, *and* with his personal recommendation before he went ... to Europe ... yes, back to Europe for a big show. So, how about it? Lots of other people who want that spot!"

"Thanks, but no thanks, Therese. Good luck."

Oddly enough, she had called me just when I had walked out of another agency, "Melly's Modelling," in Paddington. I had gone into the place with parallel notions, and a receptionist behind a funkadelic desk wearing two large picture frames around her eyes flashed me the industry smile and said that Melly would soon see me. The waiting room was smothered by magazines of hard-looking models.

Instead of Melly I was introduced to "Mike." Mike was a tall and well-built man who strode out with flowing grace and his chin held high. His voice was deep, but not powerful, and he lisped many of his words. When we shook hands, I was startled by the frailty of his grip; it was like grasping a dead fish.

We sat together on a couch that looked to have been dipped in neon residue. Mike crossed his legs and his arms on top of them, and looked at me in a peacockish manner.

"I will say this right now, mate: OK, we have too many boys on the books, OK," and he emphasized his words with eyelids fluttering and a hand that, though grounded elbow to knee, made a limp bow at the wrist as if someone had choked it.

"But perhaps you had place for an in-house photographer?" I ventured.

It seemed that I had spoken too many words, for I noticed that Mike's attention was riveted elsewhere. He was wearing the same expression one sees on cats before they pounce on something from a hidden vantage point. His gaze led to a square office, one side visible through massive glass panes, and within was a pack of bubbly girls dressed in all kinds of unmentionables, in tizzies of laughter over a pen that had a large pink feather on it.

Mike pounced.

"Girls! OK, girls!" he crowed with both hands flailing in the air, "OK, is this, OK, is there a party in my office?! Leave my pen alone, get out!" And he shuffled the sheepish ladies out of his workspace while they giggled evermore. He cast a vacant glance back at me on the neon couch without approaching.

"Sorry mate, OK, too many boys on the books, OK. Come again in three months," he said with a furrowed brow.

"But —"

"Three months. Bye."

Luckily, I would be employed elsewhere. In the vein of the world's opposites, my role would be one exactly like Fredo's, Therese's and Mike's.

I was destined to become a preying bullshitter.

7 – Hunting in All the Wrong Settlements

IT IS IN retrospect that I realize I had it all wrong from the outset: I hadn't properly weighed my situation. There it was staring me in the face in black and white on every job application, and I didn't get it for the longest time: name, age, sex, address, and "Tick one of the following: (A) Australian resident; (B) Traveller/backpacker."

I don't know why I didn't get it sooner, but maybe I had some misguided conceptions at the time. There is no (C) Not sure yet, but willing to work hard and see how things pan out. There is no (D) Not interested in backpacking at this point, so why don't you let me work for you and see how we go? There is no (E) None of the above. I had half the urge to write a note, but someone had thought of it before and the lines that bracketed the tandem choices left no room for essays of the most leeway-seeking nature.

Then everything happened at once. My mobile rang one fine day while I was simultaneously rifling through hundreds of "We'll keep you on file" emails from agencies, looking for shared accommodation and avoiding my online bank balance. My credit card was a pile of goo in my empty wallet. The woman on the other end invited me in for an interview, so on the following day, I donned my patented standard green-collared shirt and beige pants (then my wardrobe arrived a week later), borrowed a leather satchel from my lawyer friend to replace my backpack and travelled to Martin Place, Australia's response to Wall Street, also known as the Central Business District (CBD).

Martin Place is imposing. It is at heart a sloping and wide concrete walkway dotted with fountains and crossing the major arteries of Sydney's downtown core. The area is shadowed heavily by commanding business buildings and it constantly receives the hurried and clopping footsteps of flocks of people scuttling around in corporate attire. It is the land of briefcases and ties, where the majority of folks are engaged in heated conversation on mobile phones, looking important, firing back take-away as they speed off to their next meeting.

I was dazzled as I exited the Transpo station, though I found the building where my interview was to be easily enough and ascended it in an elevator with a few nervous-looking people. (I found out later on that Martin Place was where many corporate human-drone scenes for the movie *The Matrix* were filmed. How appropriate!)

Then there I was, sitting on the leather couch in the foyer of a company called "Many Excuses" (ME), named after the founder. The receptionist was chirpy, but I somehow got that *save-yourself-while-you-still-can* feeling from her, one that would prophetically prove founded.

"What we do here at ME is exciting," said a vertical guy in a suit.

Some of the nervous elevator people were in the conference room with me and presently we all also knew each others' names, courtesy of pre-printed appellative badges. "We are the best in the world," announced our host in a rehearsed manner that seemed a little too upbeat.

In the background somewhere a bell rang out and applause exploded. I had passed two interviews and was in group training to become something I wasn't even sure of yet, but they kept using the words "limitless earnings" in sentences containing "you *can*," spoken in crescendos of glowing enthusiasm. The ad in the paper had included the words "No experience necessary."

"You have just entered the world of high-powered executive sales!" said someone else perpendicular to the ground in a suit. "What you earn totally depends on you, and commissions are high. Some of our staff make six-figure incomes. We here at ME will teach you to be mavericks."

But the corporate welcome video took the cake. Mr. ME, in his mid-30s, spoke from the head office in London all polished in a suit and sitting in a velvet chair extolling the ME vision. In his younger days in his native England, Mr. ME had sold scalped tickets to events from the trunk of his car when inspiration (more likely dumb luck) struck him. Manicured images flashed on the screen as he told his story in voice-over. Mr. ME formed his company with a stellar sales team who organized high-end business events, summits and conferences in pristine locations all over the world for high-powered executive types. He expanded and took over similar companies and now he was a millionaire enjoying the good life. And we could be, too, if we followed their inspirational sales training program.

Our top regional boss, some youngish high-energy British guy, would grace us with his presence every now and then to deliver vigorous pep talks about sales, closing deals on the phone and other generally emotive, yet ultimately hollow, topics, before disappearing for long lengths of time. The movie *Boiler Room* was championed as the prime example of what we were trying to achieve in the office.

(Briefly; *Boiler Room** is a film about American junk bond traders who established illegal phone set ups and place high energy tele-sales calls to people to induce them with a powerful pitch to purchase stocks that didn't actually exist, before the cops could shut them down).

ME wanted a working environment wherein we wore suits not because we would ever be seen, but in order to retain a professional and high-end atmosphere in front of each other. In short, ME wanted us to get people we didn't know to stay on the phone in order to suck them into outlaying money for the ME product. And it was all legal, with offices existing all over the world.

Much like any fast-food chain with a managerial operations formula that dictates how to lay out their production line, the ME training manual assumed that by the second, or at worst the third phone call, you were to have a deal coming in. On the human side, we had coaches that basically taught us how to be smooth liars on the phone, so that we were telling people that we were closing out the registration for a stellar event the following week and that there were two places left, when in actuality there were two more months to go and hundreds of vacant seats.

The whole place was a sales pressure cooker, bells ringing, fast-talking sales people on the phone doling out smooth and energetic pitches, morning rallies to pump us up and make us want to get on a phone for nine hours a day. We were expected to research our list of call-up leads outside of working hours in magazines and newspapers and on the internet, in order to maximize phone time.

I was given a small desk and a well-used phone, and was told to share with five other execs a computer terminal prone to crashes and constant reboots that operated at a speed that made unionised snails look quick. I never entirely believed anything my ME superiors said, but a job was a job, and income was income, and now six unemployed weeks after my arrival, I could not be choosy.

Outside of ME, I was otherwise engaged paper-wise in house hunting, as the Bronte apartment would soon cease to be an option. I set up numerous interview sessions, favouring locations in the eastern suburbs. This, you understand, was for reasons of familiarity, as well that I felt ill of having travelled so far not to be able to live near the splendours of the ocean and beach.

The parade of potential shared accommodations that followed was a disaster, mimicking the early sea-explorers of Australia in the hit-and-

---

* Starring Vin Diesel!

miss department. I attribute this, retrospectively, to the ads that contained words like "broad-minded" and "seeking open-minded flatmates" ... but everyone learns at their own pace, I suppose.

The first conference was with a lady who owned a decent house, but the walls and carpet were so grey, and the interior so dimly lit, that I felt sure a skeleton might be chained up somewhere, or that I would one day slit my wrists in the throes of a melancholy and delusional belief that the walls should be painted red as I scream as if I were in a Van Gogh painting.

Down the road, I walked into a "colourful" abode replete with uncounted barefoot and hairy-legged hippies (two of them pregnant and seemingly in no rush to establish paternity), who stipulated that a condition of residence would be that I cook two days a week for everyone. I took a gander at the available room, which contained a dingy mattress strewn on the floor below a wall decorated with some form of artwork created by a chemically induced hand. The rest of the interior layout and backyard looked like what occurs when police drain a riverbed for clues and dreg up all kinds of useless keepsakes. I thanked them for their time and walked out hurriedly past a truck with blocks in its wheel hubs and two furry legs protruding from beneath. I looked back to see a small child occupying the door frame and wearing a "could-you-be-my-daddy?" face.

The next flat was absolutely stunning and located not far from Bondi Beach. It was well lit, had hardwood floors, laundry facilities and everything one could want. The interviewer was alone and described the two other absent live-ins as "a couple who were musicians." I inquired innocently what *he* did for a living, to which he replied, "This and that." During the conversation, his cell phone would erupt frequently and brisk conversations would ensue, usually containing the words "How much do you need? No worries." He conceded that he himself had only moved in three days previous after meeting the girl of his dreams at a "mental" rave.

My final interview of the day took place with three Australian women in a four-bedroom apartment but a hop, skip, and a jump from Bondi Beach. The apartment was massive in dimension – the kitchen had marbled counters and a gas stove, and the soon-to-be-vacated bedroom was everything I could want. The lease-holders were Sally – who worked for a well-to-do hotel chain and seemed to get promoted higher every week – and Tenille, who worked for a film distribution company. The

third roommate, Jen, worked an office travel/hospitality job. The ladies
were thus all nine-to-fivers like me, seeking a quiet, clean, reliable and
long-term flatmate. I brought wine to the interview, told the ladies about
my long-term plans for Sydney and then told them what every female
housemate wants to hear: when I use the bathroom, I am never in there
for more than four minutes.

That clinched it; I was in. Later the girls would admit (with some
more wine) that I was the first man ever to live in the apartment during
their three-year tenure. My competition had weighed in as a flock of
other females, a gay guy and some drop-dead gorgeous guy. So they
picked me, the happy medium, and I was over the moon to have found
such a place, though quite unsure of how to feel about how I came to be
chosen.

I outlaid the remaining sum of my credit to purchase a bed and other
bedroom furniture from the girl who was leaving, and happily got
established in my new surroundings.

But this, too, would eventually come undone.

8 – Assimilation

Ale has too often been praised by poets. The longer you drink, the less sense your mind makes of things.

– Hávamál, *The Sayings of The Vikings*

TO DISTRACT MYSELF from contemplating the slimmer qualities of my wallet, I found the nearby Waverly Library in Bondi Junction. It was time to learn more about my surroundings and the potential hazards of Australia.

Setting aside for the moment cute kangaroos and cuddly koalas (both of which have tempers and can grievously injure anyone if approached), there are other such cuties as the blue-ringed octopus, funnel-web spider, bluebottle jellyfish (so efficient it hasn't evolved in 600 million years), the box jellyfish, paralysis tick and stone fish – to name but a few – all of which can maim and kill with specialized and varied methods of torturous toxicity. Eighty to 85 percent of all that lives in Australia cannot be found anywhere else on the planet.

There are said to be over 50,000 types of insect, 350 species of butterfly, 7,600 varieties of moth, 18,000 forms of beetle and 900 types of ant who are preyed on by over 700 species of bird. And there actually might be thousands or millions more of all of the above that haven't been discovered, catalogued or assigned fancy Latin names.

Now wild creatures were nothing new to me. Indeed, the presence of bears, wolves and temperamental elk had been avidly explained to all employees who worked in Western Canada's, Jafa infested, ski resorts. I had often avoided all of them on my way to and from work and ultimately never ended up a statistic. Australia's critters, however, in the apt description of Bill Bryson, "seemed to have evolved as if they had misread the manual."

In 1906, only a third of the human population of Australia lived in cities. By 1921 it was 43 percent and by 1940, about half. Since then, and in spite of promises by the government to keep rural areas alive, industrialization induced flocking to the metropolitan sprawls and today only one in 11 Australians lives outside of urban belts (locally known as living "in the bush").

In a *Reader's Digest* book, I read a frightening tale. A 63-year-old Queenslander named "John" was walking home when he failed to notice a taipan snake (its venom is 50 times more powerful than a cobra's!) charging him with furious velocity. John's uncle had been killed by a taipan and he knew all too well that one bite meant a premature rush to the pearly gates. Nevertheless, he was not fleet-footed enough to avoid having his leg punctured seven times in rapid succession (the serpent is blessed with the ability of quick venom top-ups owing to a natural fang-mounted muscular refuelling program).

The narrative was written in agonizing detail, and luckily John managed to make it to hospital. The doctor couldn't be sure which snake had bitten him and was alarmingly undecided as to which anti-venom to use (the wrong one would accelerate pain and death). The good doctor decided to needle in a polyvalent – a mix of anti-venoms – and John doubled over in agony and screamed that his stomach felt as if it had been turned inside-out.

Miraculously, he managed to pull through, only to be delivered the news that he still might bleed to death on his hospital bed. The venom's ingredients prevent the coagulating of blood, and thus survivors become unwitting haemophiliacs. Blood was dripping from the puncture wounds as well as from his gums and pooling in his mouth. Over 15 hours, John slowly bled, but with more anti-venom he survived the ordeal. And that's just one story.

There are an estimated 140 different species of snake in Australia, of which 100 are venomous, and 11 of these comprise the entire list of *world's* most deadly. It would be an exaggeration to say that attacks happen often (if at all) in cities, but I will make the salient underscore that even travel guidebooks make a mute point about meandering in fields and parks with long pants and thick boots. They also advise looking before you sit, as snakes do seek warm spots under urban household objects.

One story I was told was of a man bitten on his hand by a full-grown diamondback rattlesnake. Apparently the lengthy incisors punctured clear through the meat and bone of his hand to emerge on the opposite side. What saved him was just that – the deathly venom sprayed harmlessly out the other side. Had the dripping daggers of the serpent been millimetres shorter – as would have been the case with a younger snake – the toxin would have travelled along the man's blood way arteries instead of hitting a bitumen highway.

However, it seemed what was more immediately threatening to Sydney residents were spiders and sharks.

Atrax Robustus, or funnel-web spider (because it knocks up a funnel-shaped web in a burrow), lives within a 160 kilometre radius of Sydney and usually turns up in backyards during the summer or before a heavy rain. The male is five times more toxic than the larger and scarier-looking female, who has a thorax the size of a golf ball and can lazily cover the top of a mug with her legs.

The local newspapers were certainly rife with their exploits. Between 2001 and 2002 alone, I read a score of articles about young and elderly alike being attacked while playing or gardening. There was one woman whose backyard was infested when a colony was disrupted owing to a neighbour installing a new pool.

One of the more outstanding stories was that of a Sydney engineer who trained to work with a funnel-web in his shoe. He was halfway through a meeting when he suddenly felt a sting. He survived (barely) because it had exhausted its death juice on the shoe leather. After the ordeal, he religiously checked his shoes and made his local hardware shop owner rich by nailing screen doors over everything he could.

Most of these stories were worded unpromisingly with descriptions of people violently vomiting, with their skin going funny colours, or of them breathing in strangled whoops and thrashing madly about after being injected with a payload. The unruffled reality is that the venom is one of the most toxic of the 30,000 known species of spider in the world.

Amazingly, the antidote was only concocted in 1980. This discovery owes its lateness to the fact that funnel-web poison doesn't function anything like snake venom. It instead overloads electrical impulses to muscles, nerves, glands and vital organs, and researchers can still not explain why the venom doesn't affect any other creatures aside from bugs, monkeys and humans.

The breakthrough remedy came when a doctor needled certain antibodies from rabbits into mice and monkeys. Next he needed a human, and the wait was not long.

One night a 49-year-old man was rushed to hospital in critical condition after being bitten in the comfort of his own living room (these spiders believe strongly that the best defence is an aggressive offence, and with sets of fangs that grow to seven millimetres (effectively the size of some snake fangs) ... well, you get the picture). The first dose of the new serum didn't work, but another did, and by 1981, Sydney hospitals were stocking the refined cure.

An Aussie workmate told me about her horrific ordeal. She was awoken suddenly by a pinching sensation on her face. Half-consciously, she brushed something from her cheek and then raised the alarm, and her mother dashed in and lifted the mattress to find the culprit, a white tail spider. They rushed her to the hospital and luckily the arachnid was a baby with ill-developed fangs, so her life was out of harm's way. Even then, her complexion, sadly, would not be.

"Picture what a mummy looks like, and that's what was happening to my face. It was falling apart," she said, as I recoiled. With time and lots of cream, her face was restored to normal with no vestige of the dermatological damage. Had the spider been a tad larger, the dosage, even if minute, would have been fatal. Unlike the man who survived because the fangs were more mature, this time underdevelopment saved a life.

Of the 370 known species of shark in the world, Australia is home to 166, though only four types are man-eaters. If ever a shark alarm clangs at the beaches, most Australians tap their foot impatiently as if these watery messengers of death are wasting their aquatic leisure time. One article described a shark jumping into a Jafa's fishing boat, and instead of freaking out, his mates took photographs to show everyone at work.

Nevertheless, brazen-talking Aussies had to sing a very different tune before the 2000 Summer Olympics. Many publications with international readership (dated just before the commencement of the Games) had run numerous articles detailing the very real fears of some tri-athletes. "The Europeans are pretty worried about it [sharks]," commented a world champion. "They're used to swimming in freshwater lakes, where the most you'll find is an eel."

Many recalled an incident in 1963 when a woman had her leg torn clean off in three feet of water in the middle harbour. Her boyfriend had an unsuccessful tug-o-war with the shark, but ultimately she fatally bled out where many Olympic events were scheduled to be held. To boot, a recent spate of sightings and attacks, including two in two days on schoolboy rowers, as well as another fatal attack in 1996, were a tad hair-raising. Many Olympic Australians downplayed any danger, citing that for years events had been held without incident.

Even so, the organizers had to take steps to avoid, in the words of one journalist, "the ultimate public relations disaster ... victims' screams echoing through the homes of a billion-plus viewers around the world."

The solutions undertaken were fairly rudimentary. Officials warned swimmers in several languages to stick together and to not stray from the pack. They slid a few more inflatable boats with loud outboard motors out and upped patrols, some from the air. Indignant Australians tried to brush it all off, including one *Time* magazine writer who tried to joke that Australians dominated both men's and women's water events because they instinctively got out of the water faster.

The following sums up the local attitude. In one recent story, a 49-year-old woman was catapulted more than four metres from her rowboat by a shark and then got back in to continue rowing for more than 15 minutes. The following day, the members of her rowing club (in Leichhardt, near the city) put up a drawing of her and a shark and wrote, "Are You For Breakfast?" She laughed and told a reporter: "There were plenty of sharks, no worries."

But you see this was what worried me: between 1990 and 1999, the state of Florida logged 186 shark attacks, though only one was fatal. South Africa was second, with 65 attacks and eight fatalities, but Australia got gold, for even though there were only 53 attacks, nine were fatal!

And what's more, those who encounter (as one survivor put it) "being hit by a train of teeth" and live to tell the tale always do so with several less limbs and more trauma and physiotherapy than any place else. Never mind that sharks don't like the taste of humans; being impulsive, they (like any human who eats a pizza at four in the morning knows) realize after the fact that it wasn't such a good idea, despite first urges.

In the year I lived in Bondi, five people died from shark attacks, most near Perth and in South Australia, but the last fatal attack to occur in Bondi was 1937.

One expert concluded (brilliantly, I might add) that "attacks are basically an odds game based on how many hours you are in the water." That's like saying you stand to burn your finger worse the longer you leave it in the flame of a candle. And if you thought that was a groundbreaking revelation, another defensive shark scientist quilled, "More humans are killed by falling coconuts and hippopotamus each year than sharks and other animals combined." Considering that there are actually no hippos – aside from obese humans who shouldn't wear Speedos but do anyway – on or near Australian beaches (or for that matter coconut trees), you might as well tell Californians that more people lose toes to frostbite in Alaska than in a San Diego summer.

Having just moved in with my three new roommates in Bondi, my acquaintance with several transient souls of low-scale bulk would be an abrupt one. I observed a hairy spider the size of my palm inverted and static on the ceiling above my bed. He or she or it was one of many I would come to know coming and going as they pleased, always looking down on me from above my place of rest, and always the first thing I looked for when I would nervously stir from an uneasy snooze. If I were bitten and did survive, I don't think having the face of a rotting corpse would have helped my job situation or possible love life (then again, I might meet a nurse).

Upon opening my closet to hang my garments, a couple of cockroaches rivalling the size of plump walnuts made quick pace down the hallway causing me to jump and cling twitching and inverted on the ceiling.

So I settled on a soothing sunset stroll to calm my rankled nerves and stepped into the dodgems world of hop scotching around blatant gangs of bold cockroaches pottering jerkily all over the place (it is rumoured that they are even bigger in Queensland ... and, I surmise, used for public transport).

If chance ever permitted a moment to look upward, the sight of broad-winged bats flapping in stealth mode was never uncommon. Sadly, they were the only form of silent air-born critter, and if all these visual frights were not taxing enough to a newly landed foreigner with his head awash in horror stories, there were certainly lots of audio in store.

When the sun was just about ready to come up each day, I would be startled from a precarious slumber by what I thought was the noise of a child screaming in excruciating pain, possibly trapped under the wheel of a moving car. It was actually a crow, and he had competition. Dawn and dusk were full of strange sounds, a series of strident *hoo-ha-ha* laughs coming from something called a kookaburra – which isn't a chuckling chimp or a hyena in hysterics but a bird – as well as an ear-piercing screech from a rather hammered and ill-mannered fowl called a cockatoo (or "cockie"), and then once more the scream of a child under car wheels.

Picture yourself taking off your clothes and getting into that state of private vulnerability (possibly with a mirror), when suddenly you hear a chorus of laughter outside your window. Thoughts?

The Aboriginals believed that kookaburras were spirits who brought the sun up each day. The Europeans, on the other hand, quickly called the annoying bird the "laughing jackass" and the "bushman's clock."

Then I read in the newspaper that Australians were more at risk than anyone of being hurt by birds. "Our feathered friends are more aggressive than their overseas relatives, live longer, have bigger beaks and raise more offspring," ran the article. Magpies, apparently, are the most dangerous urban bird as they might dive-bomb people's heads to take eyeballs out. I suppose that explained why I saw some people in Sydney walking around with bike helmets and no bike.

My roommates took great pleasure to my clambering up to them in a rather flushed state, asking why so many things in the house seemed to be moving freely, and why I could hear so many chorales from amused tree creatures with Cadillac beaks and other ear-shattering noises. "This is Sydney and this is Australia," was all they could say, in a tone that basically implied that "they are residents too." Not that I had never seen large insects before, but that was in places like Central America, where you dwell no-frills in an adventurous thatched hut on the beach for 50 cents a night, not in metropolitan Sydney for several hundred dollars a month.

Be that as it may, I assimilated and learned to shake my shoes before I put them on, agitate my clothes and accept normality in fleeting movement under and on plates, cutlery, kitchen appliances, beneath soap bars in the shower and other locations of hide-able potential.

One night, in the frame of mind that I had it all under control, I got a great shock. After a few glasses of wine with my roommates, I ambled for my room and lay on my stomach trying to convince myself that my bed would eventually stop making concentric circles and the contents of my stomach could be anchored by repeating: "I'm *not* going to throw up." On the floor was a massive cockroach.

Slowly – in the manner of Hollywood action stars releasing a secret weapon while uttering the ultimate one liner – the back shell of the roach splayed open and a set of wings jack-knifed out. In a moment the oversized insect was hovering like a harrier jet, pausing momentarily (and perhaps I imagined this bit) to give me the finger before he, she or it glided out the window.

Cockroaches in Australia can fly.

So there I was, living with bugs that could survive nuclear blasts, irksome birds that gave unwanted concerts and, as I soon found out, lots of English and Irish people in the area yelling obscenities at each other between dusk and dawn, blissfully unaware that the bricks around them might house people already learning to sleep in new realities. The upshot was that I did live near the beach and the ocean, thus distraction was always close at hand.

However, as is Sydney's nature, Australia's most famous kilometre of sand came at a price.

9 – What's In a Name?

CARE TO KNOW how *Australia* got its name from the dreamy Greek who didn't stick around 1,800 years to lobby for its adoption? If you guessed by pure madness, or possibly in a heated moment owing to an unhealthy relationship with a furry animal, you would be correct.

As the 1800s began, one Mathew Flinders was making sure that Napoleon's sailors stayed clear of the bottom lip of Britain's prison land (they had even begun naming certain portions Terre Napoleon). In doing so, Flinders mapped Van Diemen's Land to prove that it was separate from the mainland and then set out to end Australia's duping duality, for it was both New Holland in the west and New South Wales in the east. He attained notoriety in circumnavigating the continent between 1801 and 1803 and found that it was in fact one landmass.

In 1805 Flinders scrawled that "the whole body of land should be designated under one general name ... *Terra Australis* or Australia ... having antiquity to recommend it, and no reference to either of its two claiming nations ..." He then penned a book in 1814 entitled *A Voyage to Terra Australis*, and three years afterward, Governor Macquarie began to use the name often in correspondence to England.

In one prominent letter Macquarie wrote, "Australia, which I hope will be the Name given to this country in the future ..." Well, it stuck, and *Terra* was dropped and *Australis* made into the English "Australia," and the colony's first independent newspaper, the *Wentworth's Australian*, was published in 1824. But Flinders did more than make a name stick.

On the *HMS Reliance*, somewhere between the Cape of Good Hope and Botany Bay, Trim was born. Trim was a cat, and Flinders formed a deep bond with him. After Flinders had championed the name for the new continent he made a miscalculation and shipwrecked on the French island of Mauritius. He was captured by locals and thrown into prison with his hairball companion for seven years. During his term, Flinders penned the biography of Trim before the poor object of his manuscript ended up as a major feature in a bubbling cauldron surrounded by hungry slaves. The feline's life story remained obscure until the monograph was discovered in England in 1971 and posthumously published two years later. The conclusion of Trim's bio read, "The best and most illustrious of his race, the most affectionate of friends, faithful of servants and best of creatures ... never will his like be seen again."

I wonder what Australia would have been named if Macquarie had read the whiskered biography first?

The early wandering coastal Aboriginals called where I presently lived "Boondi" (pronounced "bun-dhi"), which means either "water breaking on rocks" or "a place where spirits battled with nulla-nullas" (Aboriginal clubs), but no one is entirely certain (or seems to deeply care) which it is. By the 19th century, Bondi Beach was privately owned and trains brought people in. Backorwardly enough, and stemming from strict Christian principles, no one was allowed to swim in the ocean until the law was challenged in 1907 by a bold brine-loving protester at another beach.

The 1920s saw Bondi boom as sand dunes were carted out, buildings flung up and the beach packed daily. Swimsuits (both male and female) would cover almost the entire body and until 1940 parliament actually regulated the number of inches a swimsuit had to fall below the thigh. Rule-breakers were promptly escorted off. But rules were meant to be broken, and the daring bikini was commonplace by 1948.

Although surfing was introduced by a Hawaiian as far back as 1909, it didn't become mainstream for a decade and sharks became a large issue as they tended to eat and mangle people every summer. The worst of the finned bunch were tiger sharks, who grow to be 14 feet long (which is four feet longer than the boats lifeguards used to scare them off). People got really scared in 1929 when two shark related-fatalities occurred within a month of each other. By 1937, Bondi had installed shark nets, and since then, there have been no shark fatalities.

Oddly enough, the worst day in Bondi's life-saving history has nothing to do with sharks. On a Sunday in February of 1938, a sand bank collapsed in the knee-high water and an ocean rip took 250 frightened people helplessly out to sea. The Bondi lifeguards scrambled to save as many as possible and amazingly only six people drowned. The day is still remembered in Bondi as Black Sunday.

Then, during World War II, a Japanese submarine scared some very docile residents by lobbing shells into the area and putting holes in homes, though no one was injured or killed.

Nowadays, Bondi enjoys a convoluted reputation. It is in many ways the Whistler of the southern hemisphere, for it's packed with tourists and transient travellers and hardly any authentic Australians, black or white. Over time it came also to be known as "the largest city in New Zealand" before the Kiwis were turfed down to Coogee Beach because of rising property values not matched by increases in dole pay-outs. Then an invasion of English and Irish toting their highly valued currencies followed. Those who permanently inhabit the Bondi area are as come-as-you-are as can be: seasonally unemployed photographers, models, artists, actors/waiters and dancers, but also well-to-do doctors, lawyers and accountants. Bondi is, however, a rather expensive locality to live if you want a place to yourself.

As a result, a large cash-strapped Bondi subculture exists and one never really has to buy furniture or most other items if one can't afford them. Although most pin-up boards and lampposts are avalanched beneath "flatmate wanted/travellers welcome" signs and second-hand sale notices bearing contact details for anything from cars to surfboards, you need only to take a walk around on the weekend and scores of shelves, mattresses, dressers, hangers and whatever else you could possibly need would be curb-side. Amazingly, some of the stuff was in mint condition, and all told I got two shelf sets and a chest of drawers for the mere price of asking friends to help me carry it down the street. Bondi is an extremely recyclable place to live.

And, despite the constant reminders from Australians that Bondi is not the nicest beach by a long shot, I was nevertheless captured by my new home. Physically, everything leads to it. A hill slopes to the ocean and the lanes cull in like tugging horseshoe magnets to the sprawling u-bay stretch. Going uphill and away from the sand seemed like such a task that it felt better to just stay there, for it was a Pleasantville with everything preventing you from wanting to leave.

But Bondi also has its own way of doing things, as if it looked to the dreamy ocean instead of Sydney at its back for inspiration. For one thing, the local buses, though decaled with Sydney Transpo, ran as they pleased, like a rogue biker gang chapter. I felt sorry for the dedicated person who had laboriously prepared the bus schedules, printed them and proudly mounted them in the glass cases at most bus posts, for the transport never arrived when slated to. In fact, you're always waiting for long stretches when a bus would drive right past your stop because it was crammed full. And they never staggered themselves, for always clumps of buses would roll by and leave gaping intervals between their assemblies.

So bad was the wait that graffiti artists had reflected the general mood by writing "Every 30 minutes, or four in a row" over the timetable. Another had written, "Walk, you'll get there faster." I eventually got used to the "service," but found difficulty in explaining it to some German roommates I would later have who were learning English and how things operated in Bondi.

"Vy ist zee bus not here? Zee schedule says now! No bus!" lamented a German friend.

"Do you have an expression in German for 'exactly and approximately' or 'roughly and precisely?'" I ventured.

"Vat?" and words would be punched into a hand-held translator. Ultimately, the concept of public transport not arriving on schedule was lost as the precise German mind struggled with the Bondi bus enigma.

So the timetable was a poisonous affair; on the other hand, retribution for tardiness in the form of entertainment would punch out. Taking the bus back into Bondi from the city always felt like a field trip or a vacation. The late-night buses were forever full of travellers on the piss singing and chatting and throwing each other's flip-flops out the window. One noticeable driver named Michael, a pommy, did sit-down comedy routines as he drove from Bondi to the city and back. If Michael were in North America or Europe, he would surely be in an asylum, but in Sydney he was trusted enough to be a bus driver.

And with time I would internalise a lot of things that initially shocked me. Certainly they could not be all that bad. Like an overachieving snake bite that ultimately saves your life, things could always slice both ways.

And as you are about to find out, so they did for me.

10 – Get Your Dogma Off My Karma!

AFTER A FULL month in the sardine can of ME, in the soul-sapping diorama of Sydney's Central Business District, I got my very first official paycheque, which was an event because ME issued pay only once a month! The base salary (emphasis here on *base*) was so piddling that it made people on the dole look lavish.

The big money, they kept drilling into us, was in the commissions, so we were to generate those sales! Nonetheless, the initial payout in question was so thin that once taxes, rent and living expenses were factored out, there was enough of a remainder to purchase a bag of rice (or two, with appropriate coupon).

I was also further flabbergasted when I finally clued in that Australians seem to quote rent and public transport rates per week instead of per month. I always thought I was getting a good deal until I heard them say "per week," which coincidentally was equivalent to what I paid per month back home, so everything was three or four times more expensive*.

The goal posts at ME were doing an evasive shuffle. When I was first brought on board, it was under the pretence that I would cut my teeth on some small-time summits and then be slicing the fat off of six-figure deals in the department that originally recruited me. The ME system was fairly straightforward. Each executive was given a letter split and within other parameters was expected to research the top 500 companies in Australia, find out how to get their chief financial officers on the blower and convert them to the notion of outlaying obscene amounts of money for ME summits and conferences (which were "highly regarded in case you didn't know, where you can be amongst your peers, have one-on-one discussion sessions with companies of your choice and hear keynote speeches from experts in the field that will guarantee sales into the future!")

So that became me: "Executive Salesperson, Director of the CFO Summit." Pretty snazzy title for a glorified telesales jockey. It was regularly brought to my attention that if I performed well and could make certain deals in my low-end training fortnight, then sumptuous commission awaited, tapping at my door when I hopped into the high-end department I was destined to be in. Nevertheless, it was always

---

* Maybe it was just me, but other companies I would come to work for also paid out only once a month or whenever they pleased, while debts had to be paid immediately.

underlined that I would have to work hard for such outcomes, hence the long days in a high-pressure, results-driven environment, and on Saturdays I would come into the office to do research, assuming promotion was as promised.

We were equipped with double-jacked phones such that our supervisors could listen in on our calls and instruct us how to create pressure, slip past PAs, handle objections and make call-back appointments to generate sealed deals. If there was enough interest engendered initially by us sales-vultures-in-training, the next call would be placed by our experienced bosses (while we trainees listened in on the double jack) to net the baited with "Fax your payment in now! Only two spots left!"

My reality, day in, day out, Monday to Saturday. My backpack gathered dust, I shaved, gelled my hair, tied a tie, trudged out to the bus stop to witness packed buses pass me by and get stuck in city-bound traffic. Dreary faces on the train to Martin Place. A drone-like march outside past people trying to get a quick drag off their cigarettes and taint their breath with coffee before going into the coffin-shaped and slate-coloured buildings to their desks, phones and computers. I would watch the clock make retarded progress until lunch, when it would of course speed up, and then run out the rest of the day in the same dawdling pre-lunch rhythm.

The routine continued in a *Groundhog Day*–like fashion that invariably comes with office roles. Out of the original 10 executives hired, I was the only one left. It was like watching some twisted reality-based version of the book *10 Little Sales Execs, and Then There Were ...* Myself and one other guy from my batch and kept asking each other, "Have you seen so-and-so?" until one day he never came back ... and then there was me.

No one else really asked any questions. The ME regulars appeared accustomed to people coming and going. Office ergonomics made it so that my desk and I sat facing my boss, who was always eyeing me and asking me what deals I had made while she simultaneously accepted new applicants replying to a classified in the paper similar to the one I answered to get me here. I would hear her peppering her sentences to the hopeful with words like "promising career," "possibility for advancement," "limitless earnings" and "no experience necessary" in sentences containing "you can" spoken in crescendos of glowing enthusiasm.

The irony was not lost on me, despite my dire financial constraints; I was on the other side of the globe, living by beach and ocean in the height of summer in a city with 340 days of average sun, but I only ever saw the sun's rays through a veil of blinds. I was so stressed and pressured, and so underpaid, that by the end of the day I was too tired to do anything but lie down and hope I would be shifted to where I was supposed to be so I could at least aspire to save some money and move on.

What compacted this sense of hardship further was getting on that train and bus to Bondi at the end of the day only to witness the juxtaposition of smiling people in suits holding surfboards. They bore expressions of knowing full well that they would soon be back by the ocean where they would shed their shirt and tie and glide their troubles away on waves.

All I knew was that I could barely afford to eat.

There was one advantage, albeit slight, in the grand scheme of things, namely lunch hour. ME had its healthy helping of office gossips. I steered clear of this activity and instead spent my time wandering outside of the incestuous world between Elizabeth, George, King and Market Streets. Outside of an office, the city of Sydney is amazing.

Only a short stroll west and south of Martin Place and her thumping corporate buzz are the typical smattering of metropolitan food courts and bustling downtown shops and pedestrian places like Pitt Street Mall, streaming with people and buskers. Swaths of the city centre are unbearably noisy places, I have to concede. Above the din of buses and people finding reason to palm car horns, there are shops that have the odd manner of "spookaning." Spookaning is, in effect, the practice of advertising wares via the booming (and annoying) voice of an announcer, played off a CD and channelled through pedestrian-facing speakers.

You walk by these places with the same voice yelling out, "Toothpaste for $1, six belts for $12! Sensational savings! You'll never pay full price again!" And if that repetitive jive isn't enough to edge the attending store cashier toward the fringes of dementia, there are also people (wearing clothing that would not necessarily distinguish them from anyone else) standing around the aisles spookaning, "Look here! Books for $2. Pens for 50 cents. Deals! Look, sunnies for $5."

Here is the thing I absolutely love about Sydney: that solace is close at hand. A little legwork a few hundred metres east will leave all of that behind in a verdant interlinked corridor that starts with Hyde Park, leads through the Domain and wraps up at the Botanical Gardens, skirted by the world's most beautiful harbour and Sydney's two most prominent icons, the Harbour Bridge and the Sydney Opera House. And it's all absolutely free.

The Harbour Bridge looks like an oversized and complex coat hanger without a hook, and it is a somewhat convoluted success story. Construction started in 1923 from both sides of the harbour with the aim of melding the arches in the middle. The whole shebang took nine years to build, with the most worrying aspect being a forceful 100 kilometre-per-hour gale that threatened to tumble the then unlinked arches. Nevertheless, they survived, the project cost only $20 million and though that was a bargain, the debt was only completely settled by 1988. Furthermore, it is said to be held together by six million rivets, and it takes a decade to completely repaint. But that isn't the most interesting part: the bridge had to be opened twice in less than 10 minutes!

In 1932, before 750,000 proud Sydney-siders and dignitaries, NSW Premier Jack Lang was about to cut the ribbon when Captain de Groot flew up on horseback, drew a sword and beat the startled premier to the slice. The "captain" was a hardcore member of the New Guard, a right-wing revolutionist band who were dead-set against Lang's socialist ideas of shepherding NSW through the Depression of the 1930s by feeding the poor with rich people's money. De Groot managed to cry, "For the decent and loyal citizens of New South Wales," when his blade fell and he was promptly carted off by police. The ribbon was quickly retied and clipped again by the rightful Lang, who proclaimed the Harbour Bridge open (again), "On behalf of [all] the people of New South Wales."

Aside from that incident, the Harbour Bridge was a complete success on every level, quite the antithesis of its neighbour, the Sydney Opera House.

I'm not quite sure what to make of its shape. Maybe a bunch of smashed up teacups or a massive white Loch Ness serpent with crunched curves, entering the water? It has also been likened to "a fleet of sailing ships, a rugby-scrum of angels, drowning nuns, mating turtles, birds, waves, shells or aliens, and some Asian visitors see a pile of crashing Chinese rice bowls, which apparently shocks the spirit 'feng shui.*'" The Sydney Opera House was such a complete disaster that it is still often referred to as the Sydney Soap Opera House.

---

* This list from my friend Louise, whom you will learn more about later.

The location was originally a garage for trams, but Sydney-sidersstarted questing for culture. The NSW government held an international competition in 1956, and Danish architect Joern Utzon, inspired by pieces of an orange, won the bid with his unquestionably never-before-seen design of "soaring sails" (to mimic those of the harbour), which he estimated would cost no more than $7 million to construct. Three years later, construction began and immediately difficulties, disagreements, narrow-minded politics and massive cost overruns were of the order. In 1966, a disgusted Utzon turned his back on the project and left the other head architects holding the bag of problems, which included designing a "compromised" interior. All told, the final tab for the Opera House, completed obscenely late in 1973, thudded in at $102 million, or nearly 15 times the initial estimate!

The financially strapped government raised the surplus by selling lottery tickets, (very similar to what Macquarie had done in using rum profits to build Sydney) which Australians snapped up readily. Ironically, the first play to open at the new digs was *War and Peace*, and during a dress rehearsal a possum ran on stage and ruined the inaugural performance. To this day, Utzon has never returned to see his completed masterpiece, and apparently still consults around the world building interiors that are not entirely compromised.

That it is nearly always sunny is a blessing, and Hyde Park is large and leafy, with two stretches of concrete ground gliding between tall trees in a perpetual Marine-like sword salute overhead. Here is a place of picnics, reading, relaxing, reflecting and all the good things that can result from sun and a fine green park.

Directly opposite is the AMP Centre-Point Tower, which looks like a golden-tipped needle thrusting through a large fishnet stocking. Although it measures only 325 metres, it is the second tallest building in the southern hemisphere (the tower in Auckland, NZ, is 24 metres higher). The AMP Tower, however, does have the highest observation deck. So far.

The Domain is just around the bend, a large field with its boundaries skirted by mysterious gnarled trees that look like old bearded men sitting around for a chat. The trees in Australia are certainly odd looking, with massive boughs large enough that one could easily imagine building Swiss Family Robinson-like communities on them, or at the very least, having an afternoon nap with magical creatures on the branches. The Domain area was set aside by Governor Phillip in 1788 as a place for public recreation, and it lives on in that vein nowadays as the field that plays host to Sydney's many festivals and outdoor events, such as Carols by Candlelight at Christmas, the Short Film Trop-fest gathering and the Gay Games, to name but a few.

The Domain's other endearing feature is that it acts a land bridge into the arresting Sydney Royal Botanical Gardens, which was Australia's first ever vegetable plot. This area is full of life – bird-life, plant-life and people making out in the bushes. It has restaurants, cafés and benches that all share incomparable locations under stretching canopies of the region's natural bounty.

The tree branches are always enchanted, with varieties of noisy and colourful birds or inverted twitching bats cocooned in their own wings, getting ready for the night shift. One of the most odd-looking birds is the Australian pigeon. Its unblinking red eyes and strange intense hops make it appear as if it has been binging all its life on a steady intake of coffee, LSD and Red Bull. It has a gelled spike of hair on its head that sticks straight up, somewhat resembling the helmets of biker gangs.

But for entertainment value, my dollar goes to the cockatoo. It comes in several varieties, but for the most part they are white-plumed with a majestic yellow headdress that cranes up and down to reflect their fickle moods. When trees are full of them, it looks as though the branches are laden with snow – but cockatoos are actually not very peaceful.

Their flight patterns are evasive. They will, for no apparent reason, and in airspace that is breezeless and widely accommodating, suddenly change direction, drop, roll, crash into each other or just start screeching, throwing their heads back and forth in the air in a manner that does little to improve their jostling, wanton and illogical aerial trajectories. Whenever they land, it always looks like a first attempt: feet frighteningly spread, akin to a barrelling, out-of-control skier who has just hit a jump that wasn't planned for, yelling what can only be bird for "Incoming!" But they don't *sound* like birds. They don't softly tweet, they screech as if perpetually trying out to be the lead singer in a heavy metal rock band.

And they lack coordination even when stationary: cockatoos just haphazardly tumble out of trees for no other apparent reason then to crash into each other as if they have accomplished something phenomenal.

However, there may well be a good explanation for their behaviour. Would you believe the boomerang*? How, you ask? An industrious

---

* Boomerangs may not actually be Australian. Europeans note that some Aboriginal hunters (notably in Tasmania and WA) threw curved sticks that never came back while others used none at all. Spears were the chosen weapon. It is quite possible that it was a European invention, but I'm not getting into all that!

Aboriginal hunter could approach a waterhole with trees full of cockatoos and scare the pack into flight. He would then hurl his boomerang just above the plane of water, watch it arc upwards and take out a few scared birds in flight. If he missed, his weapon would return to him for another try.

The early Europeans watched all of this with wide eyes. Noted explorer Sir George Gray, "In vain, the terrified cockatoos strive to avoid it; it sweeps wildly and uncertainly through the air, and so eccentric are its motions that it requires but a slight stretch of the imagination to fancy it endowed with life." Boomerangs enjoyed many uses, from war to digging to tapping rhythms during musical ceremony. Nevertheless, for the cockatoo it meant a sore anus before death, so maybe evolution made them into paranoid freaks.

The Botanical Gardens have dozens of other noticeables in the pleasant acreage, culminating at Miss Macquarie's Chair, which offers a sweeping view and the most photographed vantage of the Opera House and Harbour Bridge in parallax. At dusk, the air becomes frenzied as the birds all start yelling from the branches and eddies of bats start whirling in warm-up before heading off on winged, Dracula-like missions to the city. Photographers are omnipresent with hammer-head flashes, taking full advantage of Sydney's golden sunsets to capture wedding couples forever in their gilded black tuxes and white flowing gowns.

This interlinked corridor of verdure, which covers a little less than half of Sydney's downtown region, was my only mental salvation when I stepped blinking into the sun from the anxiety-ridden offices of ME and was besieged by the impatient ebb and flow of the CBD. In essence, Hyde Park and area were my only real reminders that I was in an antipodean country full of mystique and animal surprises. I otherwise could have been anywhere, really, London or Toronto, New York or Hong Kong, toiling away in an office on a phone in the presence of habitual coffee-drinkers and smokers, treating time as something to waste in the clatter-buk rush to reach life's finish line.

However, like anywhere else in the world, there were annoyances in the park. Beggars would shuffle up and ask for alms and seagulls would cluster around if you had your lunch out, increasing exponentially the possibly of your being shit-bombed. Then there was the most annoying lost soul–scavengers of all: Jehovah's Witnesses, seeping through Hyde Park with one hand always ready to shake yours.

It really got me to thinking how they all get sucked into it, I mean what were their reasons? Were they paid, fed, guaranteed a place in heaven? Did someone give them a rousing speech everyday and did they have conversion quotas and a reward point system? (Convert five people and win a copy of the *New Testament*! 10 points gets you to bible camp! Yay!)

And with that in mind, I would leave Hyde Park and head back to offices of human compression at ME, catch a pep talk from some over-excited salesman to his flock and then pick up the phone and try to convert people I would never even have the dignity to shake hands with to the notion that they and their companies absolutely needed a ME conference or summit ... all in the hopes that I would make another small commission toward hitting the heavenly deals that would free me from financial fire and brimstone.

My honeymoon with Sydney was showing cracks.

11 – A Girl Possibly Named Sue-me

Australia could remind the world of what it could become if it doesn't blow itself up.

– Donald Horne

ONE DAY I sat down on a bench in an underground stretch of a shopping centre beneath Town Hall in the city centre. I had some time to kill before I was to meet a friend, so I plied a few books out of my bag and began to read in a hunched over-position while straddling a backless bench.

An Asian girl from the nearby sushi bar – spotting my uncomfortable position – accosted me and offered to escort me to a street level terrace, which she assured me had comfortable alternatives. She then helped me gather my books. I wasn't sure if she was expecting a tip or some patronage at her sushi bar (tipping is actually not part of Australian culture), but after a friendly chat she patted me on the back and disappeared.

There appears to be many unspoken clauses that come with the Australian passport: friendly nods, conversations with strangers, people on public transport rising to give elderly, pregnant or less-mobile passengers their surrendered seat, sociable waves or open apologies for things that aren't always their fault.

Of course, Australia has been an intrinsically egalitarian nation almost from day one. If we dip back to the famine days of first settlement, the evidence is there that hunger makes for a better co-operation. Even when that problem was overcome, Australians have always striven to pat each other on the back.

Much positively resulted from federation in 1901. Women got the right to vote as well as maternity benefits, free education up to secondary level was the right of all citizens, pensions for the elderly were doled out (and double those in Britain), there was a massive decline in the infant mortality rate and Australia developed civilian militias that were far more advanced than those of the USA, Canada and England.

All this to say that Australians have a lot to be friendly about. They have one of the world's oldest functioning democracies – a national campaign lasts barely longer than a month and costs significantly less than a single senate race in California. As late as 1984*, they swapped "God Save the Queen" for their own national anthem "Advance Australia Fair," which in its wording invites all to share the "golden soil and wealth for toil" in a "home girt by sea."

On spec, Australian children (who wear equalizing school uniforms) are taught to be "little battlers," but also to be "true-blue Aussies," which implies resourcefulness, self-reliance, sharing and giving everyone a fair go. And, as dirty as it may read, the male side of public toilet facilities in Australia are designed with socialism in mind: they are not built with individual urinals as in North America. Everyone pisses in the same, open trough. Evenly.

And it seemed that this Australian quality was destined to be enshrined. Prime Minister John Howard pushed to make "mateship" (what he called "something definitively Australian") a word in Australian constitutional preamble (name me another country that would debate something like that?), though he did receive opposition. Some Aboriginals looked at the word another way, as "mates" used to be white fellows sexually abusing their women or murdering them and sticking together to cover it up. Then there were some allusions made to Australia's loaded White Only Policy, for "mateship" seemed to be something for the British descendants.

Yet just how far will Australians go to manifest friendly and fair play? Pretty far actually.

When Australia federated there was fierce debate as to whether Sydney or Melbourne should serve as the capital seat. The question was of such a turbulent nature that for nearly three decades, Melbourne served as interim capital as Australians thumbed about looking for a compromise.

New South Wales offered to cordon off a patch of 2,538 square kilometres in the southwest – roughly halfway between Sydney and Melbourne – and call it the Australian Capital Territory, inspired by the US capital of Washington, District of Columbia. The British parliamentary system, however, was retained. The capital city was designed and planned by an American who sought to contour it around the plentiful bushland and have buildings blend into gardens. To this day, people still get hopelessly lost in it, and they call this place Canberra (an Aboriginal term meaning "meeting place").

In all the time I was in Australia, I never made it to Canberra, though I did come close once in a visit to Kosciusko** National Park in south-

---

* 83 years after federation! But then again, they only got their own dollar in 1967 and in 1992 it was made from polymer for security and durability! Forbackward anyone?

** Named after Polish patriot Tadeusz Kosciuszko, but somehow an Australian magically made the *z* disappear in the writing of the name on maps.

west NSW. Strangely enough, I was never made to feel guilty about not having gone. Ask any Australian about Canberra and a dark, scornful look comes over their face (much like you might see on a character in a horror movie warning people about a haunted house in which they eventually die horrible deaths), followed by a "Don't bother."

Even on paper, the place looks bad. Canberra lies 310 kilometres inland. It is devoid of beaches or a surfing culture and compared to all other Australian cities, it has the highest amount of fog (on average 46.6 days a year). The winters are apparently dreadfully cold and the summers are so scorching hot and without ample precipitation that bushfires are forever a concern. And get this: Canberra is so disdained that even Prime Minister Howard couldn't find it in his heart to extend his own hand in mateship, flatly refusing to live in the official prime minister's residence, and travelling only as business dictated from a home in Sydney, a five-hour commute. Canberra residents – who had already made the sacrifice – were no doubt aghast that their own highest-ranking political official snubbed a free home. However, when you consider that one-third of Canberra residents are public servants, can you really blame the guy?

It is odd to say in the least that in a nation already so remote, they've decided to bury their nation's business in a far-flung and isolated capital, but there you have it – they went the distance in the interests of friendly fairness.

It soon occurred to me that lurking alongside this friendly and outwardly obliging national conduct were some backorward, off-shoot dark behavioural bi-products – just as nasty Vegemite is derived from the runoff of golden ale.

One pattern of speech I despise no matter where I go in the world has also reared its ugly head Down Under, notably the use of the words "like," "you know" and "uhhh" as a 90 percent component of all spoken sentences. One day, I got in an elevator with two youngsters speedily yakking:

"Yeah, like, so he says, like, yeah, so I'm, like, uhh, then its, like, you know, what's your problem?"

"Yeah, mate, it's messed up, you know, like craziness. Anyways, whatever."

For a country so creative in its turns of phrase and rhyming slang, I found it discouraging to think that so many were growing exposed to and assimilating a new-speak vocabulary of Californian surfers. But I was more amused by it than abashed, and noticed another curio in the elevator that day.

A sign announced that the *maximum* penalty for "smoking" or "over-loading the elevator" was, respectively, $20. $20 was also the maximum fine for being caught pulling the emergency stop latch on Transpo trains. This is curious, you understand, because the consequence for putting one's feet on a Transpo seat was $200, and riding without an appropriate ticket was $100. Further to this, being a "tosser" (litterbug) invited a levy of $550 or loss of your Transpo pass if you were a student*!

I also found out (through a sanctioned roommate) that if – as a registered Australian voter – you don't show up to vote, or at least present a valid excuse, you'll be issued a fine! Then one evening on the news, I saw a taxi driver livid over a $5,000 (!) fine he was issued for dropping clients (at their behest) near their boarding gate at Sydney International Airport. The zone was a "no-stopping" one, and given that cabbies are constantly in and out, enforcement officers had been turning a blind eye for years until some supervisor commanded them to clamp down. Aside from the outrageous amount of the levy, cabbies legitimately also asked where else they're supposed to let people out? On the highway?

Now let's put all of this in perspective: if one day I awoke so inclined, I could load all my friends into an elevator, light up some cancer sticks to celebrate, then take the train and cause it to grind to a halt, no doubt causing a lot of trouble for a lot of people. Provided I would be reprimanded by the appropriate authorities in all the correct manners, I would be served three infraction notices to pay a cumulative *maximum* fine of $60, a figure significantly less than the singular and less-lethal alternative acts of riding without a voucher, instinctively seeking back relief by putting my shoes up or refusing to turn up and lend my backing to a candidate seeking political office.

And if I decided to skip accumulated fines and the country? I could head for the airport and insist on hopping out of a taxi near my gate in an area that would cause the driver and his family to go without dinner for many months.

Now we come to a shocking revelation: it is written that, compared to Americans, Australians are having the second highest amount of cosmetic and plastic surgery and, get this: "In the past 20 years, the rate of obesity in Australia has more than doubled ... now equal to Americans as the most overweight people in the world," read one article that screamed for government intervention. One of the main culprits was, apparently, too much TV. (One article's sidebar has an effective one-frame

---

* There was even this public announcement ad on TV where a kid had to pay full price for the train because he got busted being a tosser. His peers make fun of him.

cartoon with a TV newsreader saying, "To avoid obesity, turn off the television and go for a walk," to which a fat couch-bound Australian family tells the podgy child holding the remote, "Change the channel, mate.")

But this absolutely seized me: Australians (more notably New South Welsh-folk) were second only to Californians for litigation rates. Like, oh my God!

Can anyone say US justice makes great anecdotes and party ice breakers? A cool $(US)2.9million settlement for spilling hot takeaway coffee *while you drive* with it in your lap? A guy who sued an ex-girlfriend for an unwanted pregnancy (they had an oral agreement, you see) under a clause called "theft of sperm?" Criminals who break into American homes, injure themselves, and sue for building code violations? OJ Simpson? The "Good Samaritan" law?

I take it you see where I'm going with this. Some snippets from NSW case law:

A drunken teenager tries to break into a pub *and* a private residence and is given a therapeutic thrashing. He sues the property owner for an "excessive flogging and trauma" and receives damages to the tune of $50,000. The kicker: the court instructed the property owner to pay an *additional* $18,000 to the mother of the miscreant for "the pain and suffering [sic] endured while seeing her son in hospital." While exiting court, the nouveau riche "victim" stuck his tongue out at cameras, something the media took great liberties to slow down in replay while explaining the verdict. It was joked that this would be a precedent such that all mothers who give birth to a child in hospitals could sue for similar trauma.

Shortly after a man dove headlong into a shallow sandbar in a river, broke his neck causing paralysis and sued the local council for a pot of money because there was no sign. Meanwhile, an Aussie girlfriend of mine was sued for rubbing bumpers with another car, and her last memory of the event was the plaintiff saying "No worries."

Litigation was the new Australian epidemic. I found it sad to read stories about volunteer and fundraising events being kyboshed solely because of the cost of public liability insurance on venues had reached, as one writer put it, "epidemic proportions."

But the following story – which I saw on the evening news as a filler – was particularly striking to me. A man in the Snowy Mountains of southern NSW ran the only dog sleigh rides in all of Australia. He never once had an accident, or an injury, or any claim against him, but he was forced to close down his business because he couldn't afford public liability insurance *in case* someone might slip in the snow and sue him and the huskies.

Now if this all seems very negative, it isn't intended to be. I tell you sincerely that Australia is a wonderful and friendly place; nonetheless, I didn't expect NSW to be second only to sue-happy California. And it shouldn't really be any of my business anyhow, right? But if you, like me, fall in love with a "fair-go" place that went through hell to get there, then it would be disconcerting to think Australians may one day be afflicted with having to pee into individual public urinals while staring at advertisements promoting the services of lawyers who charge no fee unless you win, and provide a free neck brace to boot.

And, if things continue, what will come to be filed in the annals of Australian justice next? "Man breaks ankle while being helped by friendly clerk to better seating arrangement, sues her, court awards millions and a life-time supply of sushi. To prevent such re-occurrence, Supreme Court of Australia introduces Good-Intention Sushi Samaritan Exception Bill."

12 – Just Nod and Smile

"SO WHAT DO you do for a living?" I asked. I was sitting in Hyde Park contemplating my escape from ME when a friendly Aussie had randomly struck up a conversation with me about the weather.

"I'm a bludga, mate," he replied with a grin.

"Really? How long you been in that business?" I queried with genuine sincerity.

"All me life! Fair dinkum," he countered with a bigger smile, though there was something I certainly wasn't picking up on at that point.

"Did you go to TAFE [community/vocational college] to become a plumber?" I pressed further.

His smirk disappeared and he looked at me as if I needed medication; it was a look levied often at me in my quest to understand all that is Australian.

"I said I'm a *bludga*, not a bloody *plum-ah*, mate."

In our brief exchange of less than seven ephemeral sentences, I realized that I hadn't the remotest idea what he was on about. A bludger – as I came to find out in a subsequent round of follow-on "I'm serious" / "You are not"–type dialogue – is someone who is wilfully lazy, often (though not always) a mooch, allergic to working for remuneration and afflicted with an incurable affinity for the dole and the fine, cruising life it entails. So my new Aussie friend actually had no vocation, as it were, though he did have a term for what he did, which was nothing.

As far as the other part of his sentence, it took me roughly eight months and a brave question to realize that he, and many other Australians, were not saying what I initially thought they were saying – namely, "fair income" – but rather "fair dinkum," an Aussie-ism that means either "really?" or "honest/truthful."

I was now in the world of Aussie slang, a vernacular that floated in mixed fashion somewhere between vague ancestral London criminal flash talk, introduced Irish jargon stemming from bad potato crops, post–World War II American new-speak and absorbed Aboriginal expressions. I would therefore like to dedicate this chapter to clearing up a few language issues, before I tell you how things got steadily worse for me and then miraculously turned around.

* * *

The Australian accent alone takes a bit of getting used to. It is formidably the hardest accent for anyone who speaks English to mimic. Outsiders attempting the Australian accent most assuredly achieve something of a really bad and twisted British accent, stained with bits of South African (and in my attempts, Jamaican – don't know ask why, mon).

An article I read announced that Steve Irwin was the best-known Aussie in the world with a following of 500 million people and a decade as a US TV star before releasing his first movie. On his tail was Karl Champley, an award-winning Sydney builder who moved to the US to pursue the role of TV handyman superhero and cash in on his Australian accent – though not without subtitles. Turns out that most Australian films are exported with English subtitles.

The accent is fairly homogenous across the span of the land, undoubtedly a trait of the larger continents of the New World and completely opposite to tribal Europe and especially colonial founder England, which in its small bulk boasts hundreds of mottled regional twangs that change every few hundred metres.

Australians do tend to speak liberally and swear frequently, though oftentimes the tone of their inflection, which tends to rise as they speak, can leave you alarmingly undecided if they are making a statement or have just asked you a question. Nodding politely is often the best counter if unsure, though not always.

A rather industrious friend gave me his theory that there are generally three levels of Australian accent.

ELITE: sounding sort of like posh British, though definitely Australian; well-pronounced and clear, usually by people who went to private school.

GENERAL: as the term suggests, just an average form.

AUCKER: heavy Aussie slang, like yokel or uneducated English, mostly spoken by people from the country or small towns (or by people taking the piss out of people from the country or small towns).

That this friend went to such struggle formulating categories is a sincere sign that even Australians find their drawl and argot fascinating (or that he was extremely bored and reflectively drunk).

My category-loving friend did well, though, as I did meet people from locations like Cambeltown and Dapto (south of Sydney near Wollongong) whose grammatically challenged aucker accents were as inviting as the idea of standing in a small convention hall between a team of bagpipers tuning up and a sea of dentists testing new drills without silencers. They spoke as though they didn't need a mouth, just their nose, in a pitch that brought to memory those nasal American telephone switchboard operators of yesteryear: "Owen moe-em-ent, puleez." (In a few Lonely Planet guidebooks there is a section on Australian accents that advises, "To obtain a close approximation, pinch your nose when speaking.") But I formed a theory of my own that one day – a few generations from now – these south and west of Sydney people would evolve to have no mouth, just a nose to speak with. I'm still working out how they will eat, but something about adapting to inhale food springs to mind.

I fair dinkumly wondered how the Australian accent came about and roughly when. There was a reference in Manning Clark's work that around the same time Governor Macquarie requested that Australia be the name used for the new continent, he also noted the citizens were "developing a pronunciation of their own ... copying flash and giddy language of their convict parents." Historian Hughes, for his part, had scribbled that 30 years after first settlement, the accent was, lamentably, "not so English." Then it tail-spun.

Between 1838 and 1844, Meredith Charles (an Englishwoman) visited NSW and scrawled these aghast comments in her correspondences:

> A very large proportion of both male and female natives *snuffle* dreadfully; just the same nasal twang as many Americans have. In some cases English parents have come out with English-born children; these all speak clearly and well, and continue to do so, while those born after their parents arrive in the Colony have the detestable snuffle.

Many other similar letters raised concerns in England, and some members of high British society were fair dinkum concerned that the "twisted vowels" and "barbaric noises" that Australians made needed correcting; nevertheless, over time the accent stuck and morphed.

Several theories were put forward by Dr. Halliday Sutherland, who believed Australians spoke as they do because of "inflammation of the nose, a complaint from which most Australians seem to suffer." He further added that because of pollen and the native flowering plants, hay fever was more common and gave Aussie voices their nasal twang and also made many people slightly deaf, which he claimed might suggest why Australians also speak "louda." Other plausible theories: a desire not to sound like effeminate pommys, aggressive masculinity or just plain laziness. I'll sign off on accents with this riley tale.

English author Monica Dickens was promoting her latest release in Sydney in 1965. An Australian woman approached her and said "Emma Chisit," to which Dickens responded by taking the book and flourishing onto the flyleaf "To Emma Chisit" followed by her autograph. The Australian recipient looked surprised and kept repeating "Emma Chisit," which befuddled the author, until it was realized she was asking "How much is it?" Monica Dickens also learned a few other turns of phrase, such as "hembairg" (a woman's purse), "scettin lairder" (it is getting louder) and "egg nisher" (air conditioner).

Many Australians retain British spellings (extra *u*s and all that), but there is still continental divide. Many words are interchangeable in day-to-day speech, such as "rubbish" and "garbage," "sauce" and "ketchup" and standing in "queues" and "lines" at the "chemist" / "pharmacy." "Pants" in Australia, unlike in England, are outerwear and not underwear (though often called just "daks"). The "hoods" and "trucks" on cars are "bonnets" and "boots," however Aussies rarely say "lorry" but "truck," and "toilet" instead of "loo" or "WC." Although they eat "biscuits" and not "cookies" and pronounce the last letter of the alphabet as "zed" and not "zee," they also say "guys" and "dudes" and are confused when spelling plough/plow.

However, sometimes Australians just plain opt for themselves. The British walk on the "pavement," the Americans on a "sidewalk," but the Aussies tread on "footpaths." They don't treat their children to "sweets" or "candy," but to "lollies," and the most notably ambiguous word in this has to be "chips," which can mean both French fries and the kind you get in crunchy packages with shiny interiors ("crisps" in Britain). There is also the oft-employed but tread-on-eggshells word "bastard," which can be used casually, as in "Poor bastard lost his job," or "G'day, you ol' bastard." But in a fiery exchange it could mean that your father thought you were ugly and abandoned you.

Sometimes Aussie writers interchanged *s* and *z* in words like realize, recognize and organize, or put single and double *l*s in words like "travelling" or "revelling," often on the same page. Paradoxically, though they spell labour with a *u*, the political party in Parliament is Labor.

Let's take a typical day for yours truly. I walked into a pub of Aussie women watching sports and inquired politely which team they were rooting. Man, you could hear a pin drop, and I'm standing there with a "Whadd-I say?" look on my face. I of course meant it to mean which team were they cheering for, but then someone explained that in Australia it meant the act of copulation*.

---

* Which begs the question why there is a suburb near Sydney called Rooty Hill, and was it used for conjugal visits?

One girl told me she was "on schoolies." I mistook it to mean that she actually was "on" something, enjoying the effects of some new synthetic drug I had never heard of, (possibly related to 'mushies' or 'ees' or 'pillees') rather than the actual sense, that she was on school holidays (though there may be a underlying correlation there).

Walking up to the bar I asked for a lemonade expecting in return a glass containing the sweet mixture of water, lemon and sugar – you know, lemonade. Without looking, I took a deep swig and my eyes immediately went red and watery while my nose bubbled with a tickling sensation that I had to spit out rather quickly. The barman, looking rather concerned for me, asked me what was wrong.

"I ordered a lemonade!" I sputtered through my prickling nose.

"Yea," he replied, as if I was an idiot.

Lemonade in Australia is Sprite (or 7-Up), not what I used to sell as a child on my street for 25 cents on a hot summer's day. Sprite, like any other fizzy drink, is not a beverage you would endeavour to slam down the hatch quickly. Turns out they also call it lemonade, and, like the word chips, it had a double entendre, leaving me a perplexed man with watery eyes, bubbly clear liquid running out of my nose and a bunch of pissed-off girls who thought I'd just asked them to openly announce who they had slept with, while I assumed that one of them was on some form of novel delusional pill instead of enjoying a break from educational burdens.

Well, it didn't stop there. When we were about to leave the bar, I asked someone to pass me my fanny pack and solicited a chorus of giggles instead of my waist pouch. "What now?" I said; "Is it called a kangaroo-pouch, or schoolie-flap or poucheridoo, or something else I'm not getting?"

"I think you mean bum bag, mate," said a girl as she handed me my fanny pack. A "fanny" in Australia, you see, is something a lot more filthy. I tried to tell them about the time I slipped on ice and fell on my fanny, but it didn't go over because either it wasn't funny or they didn't have a vocabulary that explained the condition of slipping on ice and landing on one's vagina.

I learned a few more that day, such as "bogan" – not something from your nose, but someone who is badly dressed and often stupid. To "pay someone out" is not to give them back money you owe them, but make fun of them. "Having a squiz" isn't to eat a small octopus but "to have a look" at something (synonyms include "ganfer," "bo-peep," "geezer," or "sticky beak").

"Chuck" has several meanings. It can mean to "throw," "pitch" or "hurl." It can be "Charles" but also mean to "vomit." However, it can equally mean to turn or veer somewhere, for you can "chuck a right" or "chuck a left." Someone can equally "chuck a sicky," which is to play hooky from work or school.

Even in the world of drinking, there is a confusing vocabulary. A "hotel" can be a bar, pub or gaming establishment (and is usually all of these at once), but it can also be the Marriott or the Hilton. To "shout" someone is not to yell at them, but to treat them to a round of drinks or food. A "schooner" is not a not a light sea-going vessel, but a quantity of beer, often in a slender glass. A "stubbie" is not the result of amputation, but a squat bottle of beer (the opposite of a "long neck").

Taken together, you can see why I was overwhelmed with confusion when I went for a drink, wondering why people were offering to yell at me from boats, asking me if I wanted a stubbie (which could very well mean they would tear me apart in a bar brawl), but instead being a polite means of offering me a nice cold one.

But of all the talk, there is one injustice in dialect that caused me great excitement and then ground-breaking sadness. An Australian girlfriend of mine asked me one fine beachy day to accompany her on an errand to buy some new "thongs." I was ecstatic, but let me tell you, it doesn't get any worse than finding out she doesn't mean razor-thin bikini bottoms, but rather a pair of flip-flop, toe-wedging sandals.

Help is at hand. If you walk into any major bookshop in Sydney, you'll find a section for languages where you can grab *Learn Italian By Tape* or *Polish in 24 Easy Hours*. But there is also a heavy availability (in one shop, two shelves full) of material for the non-Australian on lingo and slang. I had read in *Reader's Digest* that in 1965 *Let Stalk Strine: Stewnce, Vistas, New Strines! Learn the Strine Language** was published, but I couldn't find it on the shelves presently (though I did spot notable help-books *Sydney for Gay and Lesbians*, *Sydney For Europeans* and *Sexualalia*).

The first dictionary dedicated to Australian English was published in 1812 and written by James Hardy Vaux, though most, if not all, of the words he listed then are no longer in use today. Vaux was an unlikely guy. He was a habitual criminal and the only person to be known to have been deported to Australia as a convict three consecutive times for stealing a handkerchief, holding hot jewellery and one other minor offence.

---

* If you missed that, it means "Let's Talk Australian: Students, Visitors, New Australians! Learn the Australian Language."

While in prison, he wrote *The Memories of James Hardy Vaux, Swindler and Pickpocket* as well as his dictionary of Australian terms.

And we can't ignore the Aboriginals, for much of their language has been appropriated. To name but a few: koala, kangaroo, wallaby, wombat, dingo, cockatoo and kookaburra, then you have billabong (water hole), coolinbah (a type of tree), didgeridoo (the slender Aboriginal instrument), boomerang and willy-willy (a sudden twisting gust of wind).

There is one undeniable and versatile word (other than the f-word) that enjoys frequent use in Australian dialect as noun, descriptive adjective, adverb and quantifier: "heaps." It can be used in any sentence, and often is, without fail. A movie can be heaps good, you can have heaps of friends, and someone, if they are nice, can get you heaps of work. Oddly enough, a shitty car isn't a "heap," but "heaps shit." If, conversely, you are in trouble, you are heaps dead. There is no end to where you can put heaps to replace words that would otherwise be synonyms describing both quality and quantity, as well as volume, emotion and heaps more.

And don't get me started on how Australians will immediately and without your consent assign you a new name when they meet you, usually with lots of *zs** But I noticed that one unisex name in particular that was fairly common back home was absolutely absent Down Under.

I never once met anyone named Randy.

I tried on several occasions to blend into mainstream Australian society, offering up my own Aussie slang. I dished out the novel and synonymous "chucking a crookie" and "on workies" and told someone that something was "heaps tops," only to be told that I didn't make a shred of sense!

"Well, at least I'm trying," I always say when Aussies laugh at my attempts to blend in.

"Yea, mate, bewdy, that you are! You're a rippa! No wuckas."

"I got most of that, but what's 'wuckers'? Animals?"

"Short for no wucking furries!"

Blank and curious stare.

"No fuckin' worries, mate."

---

* For example: "How ya going, Gazza (Gary), Shazza (Sharon/Sheryl), Jezza (Jeremy), Alzki (Allan or Alexander), Gret-zki (Gretel), Bazza (Barry), Kezza (Kerry), Tezza (Terry) or Kazza (Karen)?"

13 – New Upgrades

SHORTLY BEFORE 1860, a man by the name of Ben Hall was being hounded by police. They were curious about the company he kept and his whereabouts at the time of a large gold robbery. Up until this point in his young life, Hall had led a most quiet and respectable existence, mustering cattle and horses. Then hard times hit. He was scorned by his wife (who took his children and married someone else) and subsequently incarcerated, on a weak charge, for a sum of weeks.

As if this wasn't enough, upon his belated release, he found all his livestock (and thus his income for the year) dead from the attention and feed he was not able to provide them through prison walls. More or less by default, and lack of options, Hall fell in with one Johnny Gilbert and one O'Meally and decided to seek a legendary way of Australian life; bushranging.

(The term is misleading. Bushranging does not imply noble employment in looking after national parks, or for that matter a keen interest in preserving botany. A "bushranger" is Australian for brigand or bandit).

For three years the Ben Hall bushranger gang terrorized NSW with guns and fast horses, though they were noted to be nice to those they fleeced, and in some cases treated any hostages to drinks, food and merriment. Though sadly, murder of police (argued in some circles as self defence) came to make the Ben Hall gang dangerous even to nod "G'day" to.

Soon thereafter the gang members were brought down either by bullets or very convincing priests suggesting surrender. The details of Ben Hall's final stand are sketchy, but basically after a snitch betrayed Hall's final hiding location, he was surrounded by police and between 12 and 30 bullets (depending on which book you read) found their way into his body. His last words were: "I am wounded, shoot me dead!"

This was one of the flashier stories. Famous bushrangers were Australia's Robin Hoods, earning the respect of the peasantry by "cocking a snook" at starchy and frustrated English authorities. Nonetheless, the first bushrangers, by all accounts, were uncompromisingly pathetic.

Most were convicts who simply walked into the bush to avoid work. The majority either quickly perished or wandered back "so squalid and lean the very crows would have declined their carcasses," wrote one David Collins in his diary. Rumours flew in their geographically challenged circles that inland and north was a sure road to China, freedom, opium, tea, subservient Asian women and a sublime career of importation to England. Those delusional enough to make the effort instead met with the tyranny of baking-hot distance, armies of toxic critters or the business end of spears.

When towns popped up, things improved and acts of petty thievery blossomed. There is no accurate count of how many bushrangers there were (possibly hundreds) and though many were feared, many more received little attention.

What heightened most bushrangers to legend were their alter-egos, the bumbling levels of the judiciary. Easy to spot, they would be the ones 10 steps behind. With a bureaucracy that would make communism seem slickly efficient, and under the delusional belief that geographically inept front line constables (wearing bright red and dragoon style uniforms) were apt to pursue wilderness savvy criminals with significantly superior weapons and horses, bushrangers forever had a long head start. What's more, the newspapers of the day were happy to print bushranger exploits ... next to lengthy columns about police incompetence.

Then one day a man named E.H. Hargraves returned to Sydney from California and – with his own complete geological and geographical ignorance – surmised that the California-like NSW must also contain bullion. Despite laughs, he marched confidently into Bathurst (300 kilometres inland from Sydney) panned some earth and extracted gold. Soon everyone was pinning it into the hills, pans in tow. A digger culture flourished, complete with quack field doctors who charged outrageous rates and used their instruments to cut tobacco or spread butter as well as operate. For their part, bushrangers (most notably the Ben Hall gang) had a new form of income.

I had opened my first account with a major Australian bank – something called an "Ezy" account. I walked proudly into my branch a week later to make my first deposit.

"Next, please!" beckoned a voice behind a plastic shield.

I sauntered up and placed my bank card and cheque onto the counter with a flourish, and soon afterward found it being slid back to me.

"Sorry, sir, you can't deposit that here," the clerk said in a manner that suggested I was wasting her time immeasurably. "You can only make Ezy deposits at the supermarket. Have a nice day. Next, please!" she said, with all the spark of a wet firecracker.

I looked harder at the clerk and realized I was staring at someone who wore the expression of those whose dietary regime required their lunch to consist of a lemon wedge and some salt.

So, here was a fact completely new to me: you could open an account at a bank branch, then never have anything to do with them again. Shortly thereafter, I found myself in the peculiar position of pestering someone pushing a cart full of peaches at the superstore. He pointed a curved finger over some pears and I saw the Ezy desk jammed in between ripe Italian vine tomatoes and a wall of packaged nuts. I can honestly say that I have never banked in such a fruity milieu before, but the best was yet to come.

I soon discovered that I could also deposit cheques at ATMs, but regardless where I deposited, a painful discovery surfaced; Australian banks just love to hold your funds for no apparent reason. In a moment that I assume must precede most cases of cardiac arrest, I brought these little discoveries to the attention of a tele-bank service rep who had cleverly barricaded himself behind several irrelevant touchtone options. He seemed little interested in my plight, and answered condescendingly, "It takes five to seven business days, mate, not including weekends, to clear all deposits."

"What?" I sputtered with disbelief, "Don't you clear cheques instantly or have night audit?"

Surely there was some mistake! Even when I lived in the third-world nations of Central America in the mid-1990s with only three hours of banking in sunlight hours, several lines of people, typewriters, endless stamps and siestas, I still got my money the same calendar day. This was ridiculous! I was smelling bushranger-hood!

Then they really rub the salt in. I received bank statements riddled with line after line of fees. There was something called an "excess fee" (and I hadn't even used a machine yet), an "under-$1,000 bank balance fee" and they were hitting me with $5 a month just to have an account with them!

"I am wounded! Shoot me dead!" I stammered. The interest was something of a fractional rebate, a puny dent in a monstrous debit machine. What would be next? A fee if your name is longer than eight characters and overloads the computers? A fee for every number in your PIN?

Then one fine day, I went and misplaced my bank card only to discover it takes 10 days (not including weekends) to get a new one ... by mail! Had they never heard of temporary cards? When I put forward what I considered to be the stock standard solution for first world nations, the bank receptionist shot me a look one ancient Greek must have shot the other when he boldly proposed the world was probably not flat, but round.

"Sorry! Ten business days. Thank you for banking with us. Is there any further assistance I can provide for you today?" she would say in a voice all too trained.

"Yes, send a food basket to ... Yes, loan me $100 for five to seven days, not including weekends ...Yes, alert the UN." All things I wanted to say, but I would have better luck throwing pebbles at a brick wall. The Australian banking industry certainly held the gold standard in bad help.

Then a scandal! My bank disclosed that they were paying a retiring chief exec (in his 40s!) a $33-million goodbye package. And so the bank went into public damage control over the incident and the big cheeses had to explain why they didn't disclose to shareholders (and another 1,000 grumpy bank employees who were about to lose their jobs) the pre-boiled retirement egg. The spin doctors sidelined the issue into regions of volatile markets and downturns in the economy and a cry was raised for new laws; meanwhile, record profits were posted and some other bigwigs had fled to other parts of the world on their bonuses.

Hmmm ... People being swindled, alleviated of their savings and the government (according to citizens and media) too inept to do much about it ...

In 1878, officer Fitzpatrick approached the residence of the Kellys who, one generation previous, had been Irish convicts sent to Victoria. The policeman was looking to have a stern word with a Kelly teenager named Ned. Ned was something of a mild juvenile delinquent. His favourite pastime was collecting rewards on missing horses that he helped to go missing in the first place. Two versions of the Fitzpatrick encounter are told.

In officer Fitzpatrick's version the Kelly clan (including the mother, daughter and friends) rushed him when he politely knocked on their door. In the ensuing struggle he is shot in the wrist by his own gun and then tied up at the dinner table and threatened with murder. Under oath he would not tell, the policeman claimed he secured his own release and fled for help.

The Kellys, on the other hand, tell of Fitzpatrick showing up at their home without a warrant, fully bent on arresting Ned and, in the process, making overt passes on one of the Kelly sisters. Ned and brother Dan, as any upstanding Irishmen would, tell him to lay off and a very sexually frustrated Fitzpatrick clumsily draws his service pistol and ineptly discharges it into his own wrist before skulking away fully embarrassed and in the frame of mind to mince facts to his superiors.

Whatever the case, these facts are certain: though a warrant did exist, Fitzpatrick went to the estate without a paper copy. When the police went back afterward, both Dan and Ned had fled and Mrs. Kelly, her daughter and two of the Kellys' friends were jailed for aiding and abetting. Most salient of all, no man who is lonely and without women in his life would welcome a wrist that doesn't work properly.

The tales of the Ned Kelly bushranger gang were born.

These fascinating narratives include lots of wilderness hide-outs, horse prowling, spirited armed robberies, and notably surprising four stalking policeman (with guns borrowed from farmers), shooting three of them in the testicles (thus letting the coppers bleed out to rather embarrassing ends) while one escaped and raised the alarm. Like the Ben Hall gang before them, Ned's troop were soon wanted murderers.

However, what Ned Kelly is most remembered for is putting what amounted to a cylindrical wrought-iron mailbox with a Cyclops-like eye-slit on his head, donning the door of a furnace for a chest-plate and coming out of a buttonhole position with his pistols speaking his mind to the band of police who had surrounded him (previously, he had tried to kill all of them by derailing their train over a ravine). Shots to the legs brought Ned down and into court. Turns out the bucket on his head hindered his vision and his armour (made of ploughshares) made him sluggish.

Despite arguments of self-defence, the 25-year-old was sentenced to death in 1880, and the judge unwittingly released him into an afterlife of martyred iconography. Mama Kelly (who was still a prisoner herself from the Fitzpatrick fiasco) was brought to see her son on his last night and said, "Mind you die like a Kelly, Ned!" Whether Ned's last words were "Such is life" or "Ah, well, I suppose it had to come to this" is still in refute.

To some, the Kelly gang were oppressed, to others, just savage for no good reason, though they got their money faster from Australian banks in those days than you can today with a plastic card, a PIN and a profound bucket of patience.

*　*　*

My roommate shot me the evil eye as I walked in one day, an official-looking envelope with the top open laying on the table beside her.

"Allan, can you explain why our phone bill is $270 for the month, mate?!?" she demanded.

With great disbelief (and subsequent financial loss) I learned that in Australia you are not only charged for the phone line service, but a rate per landline call AND rates based on length of call to mobiles, as well! Unbeknownst to me until the arrival of the bill, I had been making local calls under the assumption that they were free, like back home. Then, a moment of sudden clarity. I understood why the Telstra phone booth had beeped at me and hung up when I first arrived in the airport and called my lawyer friend. It meant you actually had to pay per second!

Now pause with me here for a second for a comparative reflection on the most puzzling of contradictions. You can buy a long distance calling card and enjoy international rates of four cents a minute (in case you missed that: *four cents* a minute), but on mobile phones you fritter at a rate of one cent per second. Thirty minutes on mobile, $18.80; the same length of call to Israel or Europe or North America on a card, $1.20 – anytime. This was the first time in my life I had seen international calling rates fall so far below domestic.

The newspapers were awash in complaint. One article detailed investigations by the telecommunications regulator on six mobile phone companies. Their survey concluded that 14 out of 83 operators were providing incorrect details about mobile phone fees and misrepresenting contract fees, and most failed to volunteer details of ongoing charges that could cost callers hundreds of dollars a year.

An alternative system of mobile communication and signals has arisen and it was remarkably similar to what famous bushrangers did; bush telegraphy. The bushrangers, you see, had scouts that could use quick signals to convey brisk information, warning or instruction.

Today, using mobiles, Australians call the technique text messaging, or SMS. SMS rsults in redced amts of spellin so tht ur msgs will weigh in undr 130 chractrs (incl spcs). Millions of scaled-down emotions and needs appear textually on Australian mobile handsets everyday. The standard message usually runs something like "call u l8r, r u hm?" which unzipped means, "Are you near a land line so I can call you from my land line or a phone booth and spend only 25 or 40 cents as opposed to millions?"

There was a new kind of bushranger in Australia in the second millennium, one that stole more aided by legal institution and laptop than pistol and mask. They didn't wear buckets on their heads or unhinged chest-plates, but nice suits – concrete-rangers running amok in Martin Place. They didn't buy you drinks or leave you money to get home with. Whether you liked it or not, if you wanted such services you had to be with one gang or another, and there were penalties involved if your friends weren't of the same feather.

So I griped to my Aussie friends. They listened patiently, staunchly agreed that something should be done, that the government should step in, and then they just as easily concluded that it takes all sorts to make the world.

So, aside from reading a lot, I also went to the beaches a lot, simply because I had been cleaned out of what little money I earned in that hellish ME job. Women were streaming past me, many of them tanned and topless. What was I supposed to do? Offer to shout them a drink in five to seven days, not including weekends? Send them my feelings in 130 text characters or less? I certainly couldn't have telephone deep-and-meaningfuls without racking up debit over debit, which, where I was from, didn't exist. And then ...

... I noticed how magnificent it all was. How blue. And the waves were so foamy and white and inviting. And the sky was blue and the sun almost always shone and two girls were putting sun cream on each other just in front of me. And there were public baths and 39 other gorgeous beaches in Sydney, all free – which I didn't have where I was from!

And Christmas was coming, which meant a week off from ME.

And in that moment I forgot all about the Australian banks and phone companies as I thought to myself, "Such is life."

14 – Out Of the Pan and Into the Fire

IT WOULD NOT be my first Christmas on a beach, not by a long shot. Nevertheless, when you have spent the majority of your Christmases surrounded by snowmen, twinkling lights, decorated conifers and reruns of claymation reindeers, your mind does invariably do a double take on the notion of strolling to a sunny beach in 35°C and calling it "summer" at the end of December. And there would be a surprise for me that year, a big one in fact.

The odd thing about Christmas in laid-back Australia is that is lacks spirit. Despite two massive fake and corny Christmas trees erected in Martin Place and Darling Harbour, Aussie Christmas just didn't feel right. The only holiday most Australians go full out on is something called Melbourne Cup Day – an excuse for men to dress in dapper suits and women to garb themselves in extravagant 1920s floppy hats and ballroom dresses, miss work and get pissed, all to watch thoroughbreds stream around a track and bet on them.

My roommates Sally, Tenille and Jen had all gone home to family, thus I had our massive Bondi apartment to myself. My kin were thousands of kilometres away and several deca-degrees colder, so I had to find surrogates.

My pseudo-family came in the form of a motley crew of travellers I had met, mostly in Fiji. There was Neil, an Englishman with all the wit in the world and a mouth to shoot it off with. There were two Scottish boys from Glasgow, soon joined by another, all of whom burred away; when alcohol was introduced, what little we could understand of them flittered away in descending levels of gibberish. Rounding the pack out were a couple of other English girls up to no good, a friend from Israel and a whole network of their friends, all of whom were touring South East Asia on lengthy sabbaticals.

On Christmas Eve, Fraser, one of the Scotsmen, decided to bare all. After lugging some beers down to the beach, the impulsive Glaswegian was soon naked and sprinting toward the ocean, a pearly rump glowing bright blue in the night against his otherwise tanned other bits. For all intents and purposes, his tan lines would make you think he was actually wearing white boxers, were it not for the dangling front piece suffocating in a ginger forest, and the crack at the back. His other two Scottish contemporaries were Derek and Gary, and together the three of them were forever up to no good at night and searches for each other at sun up. (One night, Derek drunkenly gave his credit card to a girl in order to prove that he would see her again. When his brain kicked in on Boxing Day, we lost him for two more days, but he did reappear with his plastic and – we hoped – a lesson learned).

There must have been about 16 networked travellers at my apartment Christmas Eve and Day, mostly from the northern hemisphere, and not one Australian. We all agreed it was bizarre that Australian TV and radio ran *Rudolph the Reindeer*, with its themes of snow and sleigh bells ringing, while the majority of Australians can't really conceive of snow or decorate accordingly. It was as daftly out of place as, say, running a sexpo booth at a convention for nuns. But we set about sprucing up my place in a northern fashion with tinsel and good cheer, crackers, gifts, laughs and lots of things to eat and drink, and everyone crashed on my floor.

On Christmas Day, we descended to Bondi Beach, the typical travellers' tradition, for certainly no Australians went. Before us, Irish, Scottish and Union Jack flags were planted everywhere in the sand, as if there would be a second coming of J.C. But the *Endeavour*, stewarded by James Cook, never did return that day to his lobster-red descendants, who had ubiquitously smothered the sands of Bondi. Why visiting British and Irish people in Australia don't readily understand how strong the sun is in the glaring face of peeling and bubbling evidence is anyone's guess, but there you have it. Throw white flesh from the British Isles into Australia, and voila, pommy flambé, and fookin' proud o' it!

Incidentally, British genetics are to blame for one of the largest misconceptions about the exorbitant skin cancer rates Down Under. It has always been a belief (even among 90 percent of Australian university students) that there is a gaping hole in the ozone that lets all the harmful UV rays into Australian skin. But according to scientists, the hole (which at its zenith in 2000 measured 30 million square kilometres, four times as large as Australia) is actually over Antarctica.

Although small decreases in ozone have been noted above Melbourne and Brisbane since the 1970s, no change at all has come in the north over Darwin or Cairns. A glance at Aboriginal skin, which has had thousands of years to adapt, shows that "it is not surprising that a migrating population essentially from Britain and Europe would be at risk to the sun related illness," as several studies conclude. The good news is that the hole is apparently shrinking: in January 2003, it was 27 million square kilometres, though it is thought that another 10 years will be needed for certainty. But back to the beach ...

On the horizon, an eerie cloud loomed a colour I had not seen before, though the rest of the heavens were blue and un-obscured. It was a perfect, sunny, hot summer's Christmas. As the day progressed, however, the cloud grew larger on our flank, cloaking the sun such that it became just a glowing red ball, perfectly round and safe to look directly at. The light it cast was ideal for photography, though of a hue unlike any I have ever seen. A smell of burned something began looming in the air as we splashed about in the ocean and expanded our entourage.

Meanwhile, the Scottish boys had discovered the nearby Bondi half-pipe, where skateboarders and rollerbladers caught air from inertia garnered through built-up momentum. Through their bleary eyes, the enterprise of skateboarding must have looked rather fun, safe and self-evident, but then doesn't anything after a few? It wasn't long before a crowd had assembled and were chanting, "C'mon! Do it! Do it fer Scotland!" as Fraser and Derek commandeered some skateboards from two kids who didn't understand what they were saying, but who were happy to see what they would do. They stood poised at the top of the half-pipe, skateboard deck like a pirate plank laid forth, their next step just to get on and ride like pros. We all stood by in alert anticipation ...

The shrill squeak and thudding that is a sound produced only by skin and bone screeching on wood is never pleasant, but with no blood drawn, the toddling, stubborn and indestructible Scots were happy to lick their bruises and limp away, having at least given it a go. "Wewl, at least ut isn't a cowld and snewwie out, laddy," Fraser offered Derek in consolation as they hobbled away and pulled another moon on the crowd.

Just when, with those words, they and their asses brought my mind back to snowfall and all things white, I instantly became aware that charred flakes were twisting down. The cloud bloom had grown, and I stared at the acrid skies with budding unease as it snowed black. In all of the Christmas jubilance, I had failed to listen to or read any current news. Then, when we all returned to my apartment and flicked on the tube, we learned that at the same time as the others and I were slinging back another eggnog, roughly 20,000 NSW fire-fighters weren't home with their friends or families; instead, they were engaged furiously in attempts to contain the 100 fires that had already blackened millions of acres of land on the fringes of Sydney.

The area outside of Australia's largest city was engulfed by a sulphurous curtain. Some 150 homes were burnt and later I would read that one man burned to death in a caravan while another died of a heart attack. A news brief estimated that thousands of koalas and their habitat were likely blistered and a satellite photo clearly showed smoke and flames were visible from space. The US sent over two water bombers to help out, but the hopes of the stretched and fatigued fire brigade was that rain would come and winds would die down. Anyone with asthma or breathing problems, especially the elderly, were advised to remain indoors and clamp down windows.

In the weeks following Christmas, I would continually emerge from my Bondi apartment and be systematically deprived of long-range vision because of the dense fog. On certain days, no one could see the Sydney Harbour Bridge or the Opera House unless they stood flush up against them, though oddly enough, locals just seemed to get on with things, while my parents and friends called and emailed me frantically after watching newscasts with Sydney in flames.

On my second Christmas in Australia, a group and I would be shuttled to Penrith (about a 45-minute drive west of Sydney) for a job. En route, we passed smouldering sections of highway and flashing police lights, and drove through smoke so impenetrable that visibility was almost nil. Once again, no one around me appeared overly apprehensive. At day's end, we jumped back into the shuttle only to be told we couldn't get back into Sydney because the roads were ablaze. To boot, many residents had lost electricity to their homes and certain areas were being evacuated. Instead of showing grave concern, most of the Aussies around me grunted expressions of anger at being "unnecessarily" delayed. One guy was overtly angry that he would miss drinks with a girl named "Sheila." After three hours, one highway was reopened and in driving back over black asphalt that blended into charred surroundings, we crossed a bridge near the city and I saw what amounted to walls of smoke in all directions on the horizon. All very apocalyptic-looking, but, again, strangely most Aussies remained calm.

That same Christmas, 505 homes in Canberra went up in smoke, four people died and 70 were admitted to hospital. 2,000 residents were evacuated from 12 suburbs. Some tried to fight the fire with their garden hoses, and one man commented, "The flames were licking at me car as I jumped into it." One media source dubbed it "Australia's worst natural disaster*" and reports came that a quarter of Canberra (population just over 315,000) was without electricity or a sewage plant, and two suburbs had no water. So much for a nice capital city in the bush.

---

* Note: I would come across that same title for several other Australian calamities in my research.

But this was all normal, you see. Early explorers such as Abel Tasman or William Bligh or James Cook all noted in their diaries that they observed Aborigines totting live fire-sticks and setting blazes on purpose – often favouring windy days when fires would spread more easily – and it unnerved them to no end. Were they burning their land so the new invaders couldn't have it? Maybe they were signalling each other? Or maybe they were crazy?

As the white explorers ventured further inland, they were subsequently stunned to see deliberately set infernos and vast tracks of smouldering ground. To the European mind, fire was destruction and it was no doubt befuddling (and criminal) that arson should be committed in broad daylight. To the Aboriginal, fire had been the unquestioned centre of their universe for tens of thousands of years and, after my ordeal on Bondi Beach, I wanted to know why.

It was, to say the least, baffling why anyone in their right mind would constantly tote around a lit fire-stick, even while walking casually or hunting, and many first settlers concluded in a "not-in-my-backyard" way that Aboriginals lacked the know-how or catalyst to spark a flare and thus – like current day Olympic torch ceremonies – they just contiguously shared the flame.

"Tobacco, iron tomahawks and tinderboxes ... were indeed the three boons which the Blacks received from the Whites in compensation for endless disadvantages," noted an early pasture-man near the Murray River. Early squatters in Victoria estimated that almost every part of New Holland had been, on average, swept over by fierce fire once every five years.

Scientists believe that between 110,000 and 120,000 years ago, the amount of burned matter – carbon – as well as samples of fire-resistant plant species (represented in fossilized pollens) rose sharply in Australian soils, confirming that fire had become much more common in nature. In short, this continent is designed to burn. Here be fiery dragons!

Historian Blainey noted that to Aboriginals, fire was technology far beyond what the internal combustion engine (invented in 1900) did for transport in Europe. Fire was used to cook, hold ceremonies, burn the dead, deter evil spirits, repel pesky insects, topple trees, chase snakes from camp, illuminate the night and provide warm in the winter.

White explorers were at a loss to explain how Aboriginals tracked both them and animals so efficiently, until they realized that they communicated with tendrils of smoke. They could mark migration trails, organize searches for food and call each other to help pick it up.

And Aboriginals had safety in mind. Everything was portable and perfectly abandonable. If things got out of control, it wouldn't be hard to walk away, and they had long ago caught on that fire fertilizes soil and encourages re-growth on a scale far beyond any contained European backyard bramble burn. It was Aboriginal recycling, and certainly no native, knowing Australia as they did, would build a home in one spot in such an incendiary environment like a white family would in Canberra or Sydney or fringe bush towns.

That would be crazy.

The problem today is that fuel does accumulate and a lightning strike or a tossed cigarette can ignite the stockpile, and if winds are right it goes on wantonly from there. All the old knowledge of where and when to preventatively back burn was extinguished and you can only imagine the present-day administrative dilemmas of telling some private property owners that they have to burn their yard, while someone else doesn't have to, to prevent a potential disaster that may or may not happen, anyhow.

Touché! The Australian eucalypt is by far the strongest example of a plant that learned to take advantage of the scenario, while many more perished by not adapting. Like any tree, the eucalypt faced the issue of not being able to drop seed pods farther than the stretch of its largest branches. When the galloping flames came along, they suddenly had an option to spread the passion more readily, so to speak. Seeds could go distances that would otherwise have taken six centuries to cover. The heat would burst the seed pod and the engendered wind would carry it to soil free of competitors and ready for germination.

In the book *Burning Bush: A Fire History of Australia*, Stephen Pyne writes, "Eucalyptuses have given the bush its indelible character. It is not only the Universal Australian, it is the ideal Australian – versatile, tough, sardonic, contrary, self-mocking, with a deceptive complexity amid the appearance of massive homogeneity; an occupier of disturbed environments; a fire creature."

Ninety-five percent of Australian forests are made up of eucalypt, and while one source says some 600 species of them exist, another claims to have lost count, and these bark-dangling trees* have co-evolved with

---

* They were wrongly called gum trees by Governor Phillip in 1788 and – despite being completely unrelated – the name has stuck.

the Aborigines over hundreds of thousands of years. It is also thought that animals have grown used to fire, thus some dismiss concerns for fringed animals as poppycock.

And you want to hear the forbackward thing about all this? Weeks after my big red blazing Australian surprise, Sydney was hit by torrential rains and some hospitals were forced to close as their beds bobbed in water. Strangely in concert with this, my pattern of life at the time was about due for some stripping changes.

15 – The Naked Struggle

NAKED. BUCK NAKED. That's what I was – bare, physically and mentally and financially. It amazes me how life can illustrate points ironically in one's existence, and that day was a fine example.

For one thing, I was actually pseudo-physically naked, standing in Martin Place, cold and afraid, with nine other stunning women in identical state. This wasn't a dream; there was no alcohol involved, it was not a streaking session with Fraser (the Bondi white-ass without a kilt). It was a lesson in life and a change in livelihood.

"Put him in the ice!" suggested the manager, and *whiz click* went the photographer's shutter and they poured cubes of frozen H_2O over me as the girls gathered around. I was so happy I had decided to wear my jockstrap that day.

Let's go back a week ...

"Look what I got today," spouted my ME boss as she paraded a new set of Mercedes keys around the office. She had just made a 20 percent cut of another $100,000 deal she closed the other day – a deal I was probably meant to close. Despite all the promises in the world, ME had moved the goalposts on me such that after seven weeks in office hell I was still nowhere near her department, where I had been promised I would be five weeks previous.

ME was some mutated form of a plot torn straight out of George Orwell's *1984*: everyone was constantly monitored, history changed and records were kept and conveniently updated. Here was a company that bugged your phone, scrutinized how long you spent on it, how many calls you made, to where, to whom, for how long and how many deals resulted. Somewhere there was a person (I suspect in a dark basement with a mask, back hunched over a synthesizer) producing "beer and wig" statistical reports every week to compare me with others.

In my first few weeks I set records for what I was assigned, unknowingly becoming an asset to the lower step. Then when I realised my identity and worth was being incremented in minutes per day and closed sales, I felt ill. Deeply ill.

All I would look forward to were water cooler runs and trips to the bathroom, and taken together I managed to have one be the catalyst for the other and generate more frequent getaways.

Aside from my sizzling Christmas week off on Bondi Beach with my travelling companions, I had enjoyed very little of life in that span of time. So crushed was I by it all that I had even resorted to faking calls in front of my boss just to pass the day. Surely this was going to show on the next round of reports. I would be discovered, and John Grisham could pen a novella about it. Devil and Angel fought on my shoulders ...

Angel: "We need out of the boiler room."

Devil: "But we also need money. A job is money."

Angel: "But we're in Australia to explore new avenues."

Devil (laughing derisively): "But there's terrorism. The global markets are unpredictable."

Life wasn't bright, it had been sucked out of me. I was living by the most famous beach in Australia and not enjoying it. I was *living in Australia* and not enjoying it. I had friends visiting from all over, but I had no money. I couldn't travel, I couldn't be free and wild. What were my options? I couldn't go home. I didn't want to just yet, you only get one Australian visa per lifetime, one chance, really. Would I end up on a tower with a rifle and scope and foam around my mouth spewing obscenities and fatal projectiles? (Mind you, how to buy bullets with no savings?) So before it came to that, I quit.

Angel won.

I went in one day, walked into Human Resources, told them a fat lie that I had to return home urgently, signed some papers and walked out. But it wouldn't end there. They wouldn't let me go. My mobile would constantly ring with blocked calls from various ME bosses, listening in on each others' headsets, asking me why I left, was I lying, what was the truth? It was as if I had left the mafia or something, perhaps the "Order of Telesales."

While walking around Sydney, I avoided Martin Place at lunch-time lest some of the ME minions spotted me. I kept a low profile on the trains and buses, sometimes seeing some of the ME staff, and suddenly finding reason to scratch my nose for a long time with my hand fanned to cover my face and my chin planted in my chest.

It was horrible.

Then I replied to an ad in the paper: "Fun-loving, energetic people needed for marketing and advertising work. No experience necessary!" I made my way to the offices of a promotional company called "DeVogue" Promotions. Its walls were lined with unframed and snap-quality pictures of hot cars, alcohol and beautiful women, some in bikinis and some more conservatively dressed. I sat through a group interview with lots of fine-looking ladies. I had just entered the bizarre world of promotions, something I knew nothing about, though something I hoped I could make some money doing. With DeVogue, and with time, however, I learned another well-employed Australian word: "dodgy," which eventually graduated into "heaps dodgy."

My phone rang and I jumped with paranoia. This time it was DeVogue. The chirpy voice said, "OK, like, I need you for a new shoe promotion. It will be you and, like, nine women, OK, can I book you on this one, mate?"

"For sure!" I wanted to answer, though to sound very important and not too eager I allowed a small increment of time to elapse. "Let me check my agenda," I replied, permitting a pregnant pause to feign calendar verification. "Yeah, I can be there," I said coolly, hiding my inward excitement. This was my first ever promotion.

Here's where the irony set in (and if I couldn't have a sense of humour about myself, all else considered at that time in my life, I may well have gone mad): the location of the promotion was Martin Place, in the shadow of the ME building, and as, if to rub more salt in, it would take place during lunch hours! And it only gets worse.

We were promoting a new shoe, and the theme was that it "cooled" the foot with some fancy built-in vents. The marketing company had us memorize some facts about the product, its obvious benefits and how much feet sweat, but as soon as I saw my beautiful co-workers, I started to perspire out all that information.

In order to theme the promotion aptly, the wonderful people who thought up the marketing strategy installed massive fans, ice sculptures and pools of frigid water, and dealt out globular alien-like silver water pistols to each of us. They also went the distance of dressing all of us in skin-tight spandex leotards – flesh-coloured, to give the appearance of nudity – aside, of course, from the very obvious foot apparel we were according vast prominence in our "cool" manifestations.

Once we stepped out of the van, I noticed that it was actually pretty cold out, cloudy and grey, and we were dressed for a day at the nudie beach. It was my first gig, but I had had the presence of mind to bring my karate jockey cup, which was pretty wise, if you think about it.

Put yourself in my shoes (no pun intended): crawl inside my skull and see if you can understand my feelings at the time. You are with a panoply of gorgeous gals, parading around in cold weather wearing something un-insulated and, by design, the colour of your birthday suit. You have just quit a hellish job, told them you are leaving the country so they never bother you again, signed up for promotions which you are not even sure is anything more than very casual, and are also poking your nose into some temping agencies in an earnest search for more work. And you want to impress the promotions people because it could mean more jobs. And there you are, in Martin Place, just around the time when everyone comes out for a corporate feeding frenzy.

Now let's change roles for a sec. Say you are (not that I would wish this upon my worst enemy) a boss from the ME firm who, one week ago, had yet another sales person quit, telling you that he has to leave the country. You harass him on his mobile for awhile longer, and scowl because another one got away without being brainwashed. Then you walk out on the hunt for some form of fast tucker, a bit of gossip and the like, and there, parading around in your environment clad in a flesh-toned one-piece is that very ex-salesman, firing a water pistol and wearing shoes with vents.

Or better yet, you might be a corporate recruiter from some hot-shot temping agency, having just interviewed someone who sat there composed in shirt and tie, with a loaded résumé, earnestly explaining that he is seeking some full-time work. You could swear you have a vague memory of seeing him previously wearing beige pants, a green-collared shirt and toting a red backpack, and then there he is, screaming around in "cool shoes" with very little between the outside environment and the curves of his body. Would you call him back for that second interview?

I had just been dunked in the ice, for the pleasure of the media, and emerged with the suit more transparent than before. This, you understand, just in case anyone missed the show and was in time to flick on the evening news.

When I say I felt naked – standing there in the observant gloom of the ME building, in a place I was trying my hardest to avoid – I mean I felt naked. Any second, any number of humiliating things could transpire: discovery, pointing fingers, suits surrounding me with their mouths agape or howling with laughter. This was the stuff of nightmares. This was the stuff of movies. This was where you woke up sweating and wondering if it had really happened. You, naked, the whole world laughing at you. Especially kookaburras.

STRANGELY ENOUGH, WITH all probability working against me, no one I knew actually walked by that day. This was the first day in a new lifestyle and ad lib means of employment. My bank account records were dogged evidence of just how little savings I had (both initially and even while working as much as possible) over the span of time I would end up spending in Australia.

One statement sparks the glaring recollection of a two-week period where I had only $0.01 in my account. Indeed, my income was correlated to my new work life, sporadic at best, and I never knew when the next cheque would come in, leading me to adopt a very short-term and haphazard approach to budgeting.

It is written that Australians pay some of the highest taxes in the world, and compound that with astronomical insurance rates, reproachable banks fees and expensive domestic phone system, you may have an inkling of what I was up against living in the siphoning city of Sydney. But I will never say that I didn't love my time there, despite the awesome (and I dare interject unexpected) rip of debit that washed over me. My circumstances proved in many ways to be a litmus test for friends and grand adventure. Not only that, but mixed with the heavy solvent of spirit that is native to Australia, things panned out for me in ways that were wonderful and that required little funds at all.

My roommates in Bondi were great. Tenille and Sally were rather busy girls, so I didn't see them all that much, though I did attend some of their soirées and nights out as an attaché. I ended up spending a lot of time with my third roomie, Jen. If not for Jen, my destiny would have played out radically different.

Jen was so lovable and would make a great doll or stuffed toy. She's not very tall, but more than compensates in other ways, namely in how loud she talks and how tough she can be physically. She also has a penchant for all that involved gossip and whispers, and found solace (and I daresay inspiration) in all incarnation of TV reality shows airing at the time: *Survivor*, *Big Brother*, *Temptation Island*, you name it. When I knew her, she loved trashy mags and celeb goss, and when that wasn't enough, she would find dramas in her own life, often coming into my room for chats and advice. It was like having a little sister, and whenever I came home I never knew what to expect (unless she was watching TV, and then I could only speak during ads).

Jen – possibly descended from members of the First Fleet – had a proclivity for rum and adored the rum and cola mix in Jim Bean cans. If I ever came home to find a trail of empty Jims (usually around payday or week's end), I could count on encounters with her alter ego, Jumpy Jen – same body, perceivably the same mind, but in hyperdrive.

She once heatedly seized a hand-wash soap dispenser from the kitchen sink-side from me because she perceived that I was using it wrong. With dirty hands upturned, I subsequently found myself in the peculiar position of negotiating its safe release through the keyhole of our bathroom door with the muffled sounds of Jumpy Jen muttering and opening and closing cupboards and drawers, looking for a cache.

Keeping up with the quickly derailing trains of Jumpy Jen's thoughts was a task made only more difficult if other people were around, for she simply sought to lock everyone down with choke holds. She even came into my room in the wee hours of the morning once and executed something called a "steamroller" over me, just for fun, to wake me up and chat about her theories on men and their bizarre calling habits. I loved living with her. She made me smile so much.

Up the road from where we lived, at a house that came to be revered in a legendary way by its civic number, 258, lived some of Jen's friends. Her main link in the scheme was Kim, but for the purposes of brevity it would be Kim's peripherals trickling through the 258 portal who would come to play a more prominent role in my destiny.

Kim would move back to Melbourne and unintentionally open the gate to a German invasion initiated by a Dutch/German girl named Joelle. Joelle obviously had Dutch in her, for she was tall and slender and was of the gentlest and most peaceful of dispositions. Soon came Yvonne, another German. Pour into the equation the endless parade of visiting transients that passed through a home designed for four and in strict definition, 258 was a train station with a charitable hostel attached. There was always a party or a BBQ or similar circumstances, and on one occasion we found somebody sleeping on a rancid couch in the side yard and, after giving him water to stir him and flicking a few cockroaches from his person, discovered that he didn't know how he got there but somehow just naturally gravitated to the place in an evening of intoxication. Nevertheless, the most notable staple of the original 258 foursome that made instant forays into my life were the duo of Matt and Aaron, seemingly the only white Australians living in Bondi.

Matt's most physical claim to fame is his spitting resemblance to Harry Potter, and he is certainly no less magical. His room, the largest in the house, was a veritable library of piled science fiction and fantasy novels, as well as being a profound collection on Australian history, animals and botany. If ever there existed a walking, talking encyclopaedia of knowledge about Australia, Matt was it. He also practiced a profession in league with his ability to natter on about relevant facts and names: he worked on the Sydney Harbour Bridge as a climb leader, guiding tourists over and along the 134 metre-above-sea-level climax point, while delivering the historical spiel with zeal.

Matt, as far as I (and others) were concerned, was a genius brimming with talent and promise, but like many geniuses, he was desultory and spasmodic. His brain ran much like a telegram. Stop. Let's do this. Stop. Bugger that, let's do that. Stop. To drive my message home, quite literally: it was observed by some of our friends on an outing that he drove cars exactly in the manner his mind operated, in energetic spurts of determined speed followed by coasting and sulking. In his spare time, he could be found at the pub (usually the famous Australian Hotel just down the road from the climb base), where long yarns, long nights and schooners never went amiss.

Aaron was another character altogether. Although he was younger than all of us, he certainly didn't look or act it, and no one could ever gauge his age correctly. He was a well-read person if ever there was one, and a great person to have a deep and meaningful conversation with if you liked tangled tangents that somehow related, but in a way that was never certain. His claim to fame was that he was likened to a cynical old man trapped in the body of a 22-year-old. He often complained about modern gadgetry and pontificated a return to simpler times, but that's what everyone loved about him. He had moved to the bustle of Sydney from the quiet upbringing of a country town, found a steady office job in exporting and ended up staying for four years.

Since 258 enjoyed such a healthy visitation, fleeting moments of cleanliness were a direct result. Certainly, it was not from lack of effort, especially on the part of Aaron and Joelle, but always chaos and mislaid items would quickly reassert dominance over the hard efforts at disciplined start-overs. Colonies of large cockroaches enjoyed free reign and little fear of persecution. To walk into 258's kitchen at night was to view a sea of dishes and a carpet of skittering black movement. It was something of an acquired taste, but the rent was always low for the boarders, the house was large and lively and Bondi Beach was nearby. For Jen and I, 258 was – in a manner of speaking – something like what

Tijuana is to underage Californian college kids looking to slum it but remain respectable when they got home.

As it turned out, the German 258 invasion was a reflection of the larger Bondi trend – lots of people from all over the world came to learn English in Sydney and Australia. I did see the Russian boys on a few occasions and other members of my initial Tehila days, and they were always wanting in correction of their English. It isn't really until you spend lots of time with those who don't speak your native tongue that you realize how formidable English is, especially to those recording the loose language over their own well-structured idioms.

I always found it difficult to reply to well-meaning questions about when to use "since" and when to use "for," and I often had to tell students to switch them (brief example: "I have been here since five years"). Then there is the case of when to write "then" and "than," or why "read" could be read as acts of the past and present, but spoken phonetically as "reed" and "red"; and then there's the ambiguous pronunciation of "either." I daresay that all of us intrinsic English speakers were at a loss to explain much of our own tongue, or explain why our language has a thesaurus so thick with synonyms (no other language has one). Like many English newbies, swear-words seemed more swiftly absorbed and frequently employed, especially when a lack of vocabulary arose.

It is a very fun and curious thing to see cultural differences spill over.

"Do you have any hand-shoes?" I was asked one day by a 258 German. She meant gloves.

"Can you help me? I am having a conflict," announced another.

"What conflict?" I replied, somewhat confused.

"Chocolate or marshmallows?" she asked, dead serious.

The linguistic entourage invariably took a toll on my English, as well, and I would soon come to over-employ "Ja, das ist cool" as a reply in the affirmative to everything.

One little undertaking of the 258 squad was dubbed "Project Yvonne" in which we tried to teach her sarcasm and "taking the piss." It ran something like the scenario presented by the android character Data from *Star Trek: The Next Generation*, where explaining a joke or inference heavily diluted its hilarity, especially to a brain programmed with a strict language. But Project Yvonne did succeed. One day I showed up at 258 and, quite to my surprise, she was so sarcastic that she took the piss out of me and I had no comeback. Then out of nowhere she made a disparaging comment to Aaron about taking a possum from behind and unaware, and his shovel-shaped jaw hit the ground. We had not only installed humour in Yvonne, but she, in turn, gave hope to all others with guttural tongues that laughter could be part of a spoken language. Later, just before Yvonne left, she confided in me that of all the Australians she had met and lived with, I was the most easily understood.

But soon a bigger project was to arise, one with a policy of our own, and it was a brainchild of Matt and I. It would, despite failure, help deliver me from turmoil.

17 – Just Do It

MATT'S PROWESS LAY in his encyclopaedic grasp of the elusive Australian bush, and mine in the organizational sector, so we co-launched the very loosely associated Do-It-Yourself (DIY) Tours. An application of method to madness, the policy was simple: all participants were close to broke, but we all wanted to see Sydney and NSW in interesting ways and sharpen our respective skills. That was the bar by which people could enter. We simply picked a destination, a day, packed lunches, split costs and ventured with whoever was interested in bush walks and adventures with Matt as MC and guide. It was joked that he was Harry Potter gone walkabout. I chronicled the adventure in written and photographic form then posted both on the internet as a means to perhaps one day helping Matt run his own business.

But that never happened. By design, DIY was supposed to be a bi-weekly event, but over about six months we managed six tours, each waning under an oppressive air.

The inaugural walk was to the Royal National Park south of Sydney, with 10 attendees (mostly friends of 258) and three vehicles to shuttle us all there and back. Matt was in fine form on his first day, gleaming with the zeal of Steve Irwin and dressed like him, as well. Our assembly pressed into the dense trails with solemn silence as, at the time, 80 percent of this pristine park had been scorched by raging bushfires. Although we walked upon charred soil and looked at trees resembling large burnt-out matches, a fresh coat of green was showing through. Matt extolled his facts and even lent his own flesh to discovery by letting a leech have a gorge on his finger.

The pièce de résistance was the view as we crested a hill and took in the vista of a vast and sweeping blue ocean glimmering below the cliffs. The sight was wonder-striking, and we came upon a small waterfall that offered a cordial resting place among caves and flanking rocks. In the distance tumbled a gallivanting waterfall into the torrid foam of the ocean hitting the rocks. We rounded the day out with a BBQ and a dip at the pristine Wattamolla Beach, and so ended our first adventure.

Through 258 and Matt and DIY, I met Melissa, a budding photographer, and we immediately became close friends and assistants to one another. Melissa would be one of the big hitters in my life in that she introduced me to the Australian Centre for Photography in Paddington. The ACP had all the facilities a photographer could wish for: fashion studio, dark room, exhibition space and digital scanning area. I volunteered at the ACP now and again and would earn hours redeemable for free use of the facilities. I met many like-minded individuals and subsequently exchanged my banked helper-time into printing and scanning my own work and taking paying models under the glaring studio lamps. But for the moment, we will return to DIY ...

The next few outings were just as successful, the weather forever blessing us, though the combination of trying to stir people on a Saturday morning and keeping Matt on track became an escalating challenge.

We would next assail the Jenolan and Lucas Caves in the Blue Mountains, which – despite being discovered in 1867 – still have not been completely explored. It brought DIY into the world of mind-boggling limestone stalactites and stalagmites, and through the impressive chain of subterranean chamberssome larger than cathedrals.

After some barbecued beer-marinated sausages (which pleased the Germans to no end), Matt guided our even dozen congress along a wondrous path that flanked a lime-coloured river and wound into bird-infested forests. From all tree branches bellowed majestic songs, and there was ground competition, too – large lizards would strike poses for us on rocks. In DIY tradition, we concluded the day back on the porch of 258 with some quiet beers.

But then alcohol would be one of the contributing factors of DIY's undoing.

A fortnight later, we returned to hike in the Blue Mountains, drawing DIY's zenith fellowship of 17 people! The Blue Mountains are so named because of the bluish glow that results from a low sun hitting the oil of the eucalyptus. They might also be so called for the blues they caused the first British settlers.

Not long after the first settlers arrived, explorers went looking for more pastures around Sydney and encountered foothills about 65 kilometres inland before finding the blind valleys, gorges with tumbling waterfalls and densely tangled forest of the Blue Mountains just beyond. For a quarter of a century, no one could penetrate 100 kilometres west of Sydney (even Aborigines, according to Robert Hughes). Only in 1813 was a pass discovered by explorers Blaxland, Wentworth and Lawson.

Governor Macquarie, ever the thirsty creator, rounded up 60 convicts he considered to be "well-behaved men, and entitled ... to some indulgence," and proposed that if they could sling a 126-mile path from Parramatta (western Sydney) to the other side of the mountains, they would earn conditional pardons. Whereas Macquarie assumed it would take three years to forge the path, the eager convicts took only six months, with losses totalling a few men who dashed off and died looking for the elusive path to China. The route, today covered by the Great Western Highway, was by no means flawless. Certain sections were so steep that many carts and oxen and their masters became saucer-eyed casualties of acute slopes and gravity.

The town of Bathurst, in the pastureland on the other side of the crags, was thrown up two years later, and by the 1860s, a railway service allowed wealthy Sydney-siders to construct getaway cottages and hotels in the hills. Although the Blue Mountains used to be fairly remote, Sydney's sprawling suburbs now smash right up against them.

On the morning of our hike, both the weather and the participants were dreary, owing to a big Friday night that had ended only hours before I rucked up to get everyone. We arrived at the must-see Three Sisters – a tri-headed rock formation – but what we met instead was a sheet of unforgiving fog that barely allowed a view beyond our own noses and gave most of us vertigo. The general feeling was one of fascination, however, for it is a strange sensation to be standing on the edge of a precipice far above a veiled valley – like a surreal floating dream sequence.

It was soon noticed that Matt was guiding us without placing much emphasis on time or direction. When he smiled and uttered, "Trust me," it was the beginning of the end. Although Matt took a stab at jocularity by saying that disorientation was part of the adventure, some didn't think it was all that wonderful that – tired, hungry and wet from a basin hike – we had to conclude our day by climbing 900 slippery built-in cliff steps in steep Z switchback profile. Aside from an incident where we actually lost Aaron (yes, we lost him!), and gained a City-Rail train guard who sang songs with us, some were enthused about future trips, though expressing very real concern over Matt's scattered ways. Some openly speculated about fatality.

Our next outing was a bold one, for it was to be an entire weekend in the Hunter Valley, a triangular-shaped swath of land in the wine region, a few hours drive northwest of Sydney. The valley is renowned for comprising over 70 vineyards, as well as producing three-quarters of New South Wales' electrical power supply.

Originally settled by pastoralists who managed a route around the Great Dividing Range and bumped the Aboriginals along, the first vineyards sprouted up in 1820, and a sample was sent to France and received favourably in 1835; however, it wouldn't be until after 1960 that the idea to mass-produce Australian "liquid gold" became popular. Since then, Australia has produced some of the best wine in the world, hands down.

With initial interest as high as 20 people, our numbers whittled down to a core half dozen when deposits were demanded. We realized that we were still one too many for Jen's little car, so Aaron, always the reliable one, offered to set off after work and take a three-hour, country-link train ride and meet us there. All but Matt were present, packed and ready at go-time, when Aaron was already on the rails.

Matt showed up late with the smell of the Australian Hotel on his breath and a grand fable of a life-altering conversation he had had with a stranger at the bar. After being further delayed by his "Trust me" shortcuts (which doubled us back into Sydney ... twice), we arrived greatly behind schedule in Pokolbin and found Aaron sitting nervously at the ill-lit and lonely Maitland country train station. Several suspicious youth were swarming around him, and they didn't seem pleased that he didn't have any cigarettes to dole out. Many of us were not impressed with Matt, least of all Aaron, who never even received an apology for the unnecessary tardiness and the train-yard tobacco threat.

Despite the dubious start, we had a great weekend in the hospices of a kindly elderly woman who ran a B&B. The following day, we took in the grand green land that stretched over rolling hills, dotted with ranches, shady tree groves, stables and horses, who lent some form of linear reference to the longitudinal vineyards and plantations.

We jumped on one of the winery buses, which took us to several regional and family wineries. The ranches and farms were splendid, often endowed with majestic and massive cellar casks and earthy décor. As was the custom, we tasted samples from each winery. Well, it wasn't long before my tolerance and unwillingness to give my sampled sip of wine back to any spit bucket played its role. There is a missing piece of my life somewhere in that valley ...

I do have a vague audio recollection of Aaron or one of the others saying, "No, he only had a few samples, sorry, mate," as I was lifted from a sprawling starfish position off of someone's lawn and crumpled into a bus seat with my face squished against the window pane and my mouth uncontrollably agape. A dip in the pool back at the B&B did me a world of good, I must confess.

We hiked the final day with Matt as nature guide and lots of kangaroos (some with joeys in their pouch) stared at our troop from shady tree groves.

But DIY was soon to crash and burn.

At ten to eight on the Saturday morning we were to hike through the Burning Palms Bushwalk south of Sydney near Wollongong, I rapped my knuckles upon the stained-glass portion of the door that shielded an unusually dark interior of 258. Ordinarily, one of the Germans or Aaron would at least be awake and having muesli. I entered the quiet household and verified three independent time sources to confirm that it was indeed the right time and day that we had arranged.

Aaron popped his head and naked shoulders out of his cryptic bedroom and sized up my silhouette down the hall, his eyelids fighting a harsh battle to keep light out and sleep in. He realized that he had set his alarm but hadn't turned it on. While he collected himself, I pressed on through the house to Matt's room and swung open his door, expecting to see him slipping on his standard hiking pants and Steve Irwin shirt with an exploratory glint in his eye.

He wasn't there! When I asked aloud where he could be, a shrouded voice from deeper within the house mumbled, "Probably still next door."

I rebuilt the previous evening's events in my mind. Party at the Irish girls' place next door ... Fridge full of beer ... Lots of people ... Music ... Chips ... Smoke ... Couches ... People talking ... and where there are all these elements, we always find ... MATT! I was soon rapping my knuckles on the neighbours' door. It took awhile, but he eventually stumbled out looking like he was being re-introduced to the world. After a shower and a kick in the ass, he was ready to head for the train station.

This time it would only be Aaron, Matt, myself and my British friend Neil, and three-quarters of the foursome were in Friday night recovery mode. We were each to have had more friends come along, but, alas, sleep had conquered them on this gorgeous day. En route we met a lone German hiker, and she joined our band.

The hike was a grand one that took us through a fascinating forest to the gorgeous coast and blue waters. We would pass a queer home built with a foundation of beer bottles before eventually coming out onto a beach and taking a dip, while trying not to let the strong rips take us out to sea. Matt then suggested that instead of returning back via the forest trail, we should hug the coast at the base of the cliffs. Daylight was waning, thus Aaron and I expressed real concern about darkness enveloping us and the wide berth in rural train service timetables.

Nonetheless, we all took up his suggestion and furthered our course along the rocky shoals, at intervals scrambling over jumbled configurations of boulders, betwixt the torrent ocean and in the shadow of impenetrably steep and overhanging cliffs. Matt did find some interesting marine life and birds to talk about, but Aaron and I were looking ahead and noticing that our path appeared all too temporary. The sun was preparing for bed and we were still presumably a fair distance from the train station. To boot, the alternatives paths for getting back up the cliffs were disappearing as quickly as the advancing tide, and the spires of water – like exploding geysers – indicated that the creamy waves would soon be licking at our feet. Then we got the prophetic words as Matt pointed down the pernicious coastline that somehow to his mind was a path: "Trust me."

As soon as the words tumbled from his mouth, the flags went up and Aaron and I (the significant meaning of Matt's admission being lost on the others) swiftly sought a way back up the cliffs as Matt stubbornly pressed on, leaving the German girl and Neil in a state of confused loyalty. The hike back was a gruelling uphill slog, though eventually, with ravenous hunger hampering our spirits, the trail spat us back out where we needed to be. We had missed our train by minutes and would have a two-hour wait, though we found an apple pie and ice cream shop and no doubt forked over what would amount to a quarter of their annual revenues as we hungrily consumed their wares.

People would admit to me that while they loved Matt's presentations, the obvious financial benefits and my organization of DIY, getting lost in the wilderness was not always something they wanted to do in Australia. As a result, our final outing occurred long after and also only had four attendees, half of whom were Matt and I.

The final trip as follows: I and two others went hiking with Matt in Ku-Ring-Gai-Chase National Park ... came to an intersection ... "Trust me" ... met deaf and dumb hiker, equally lost ... risked life by running through train tunnel in a staggered fashion.

And thus ended DIY, as Matt and I organized none further and friends faded back to Europe or travelled elsewhere. Months later, under a new banner you will eventually come to learn about, we launched one other DIY outing, returning to our original location, Royal National Park.

Sadly, Matt had spoken to a lawyer and found out that even if our tours were non-profit, organized but loosely associated, NSW law stipulated that Matt would have to take out a $10,000 insurance policy in case someone twisted an ankle on his outings. The fact that we spread information on my website and by word of mouth brought the legal world into it all.

To boot, the Royal National Park was heavily dry that day. There were no more waterfalls and the vegetation was brown. All rather symbolic, wouldn't you say? But one thing was for sure: despite all the lack of funds in my world at the time, I was never lacking in good friends and good times. There would forever be a positive spirit of innovation, the presence of mind to give anything the "good old Aussie go," to boost me.

Even if I had to run around naked for cash.

18 – Got Somewhere To Be?

MARY BRYANT, OF Cornwall, England, was pregnant and in need of a larger cloak so she stole one, wound up on a ship of the First Fleet for seven years of transportation and gave birth to Charlotte on the way. Once in Sydney, she married Cornish fisherman (at the time the *only* fisherman) William Bryant and bore him a son, but they and seven other Englishmen had grander DIY plans of their own.

They took to scheming ways of getting back to mother England. They managed to solicit some navigational equipment and a sea chart from the captain of a Dutch trading vessel, then picked a time when hardly any ships were around and stole out of Sydney Harbour in, of all things, Governor Phillip's cutter.

In hugging the coast, the dozen-minus-one crew ignorantly earned themselves the distinction of becoming the first Europeans to navigate the precarious waters of the Great Barrier Reef since James Cook had wrecked there 21 years earlier. They managed to withstand Aboriginal attacks and stave off hunger by making jerky out of sea turtles.

Sixty-nine days and 3,250 miles later, they washed up in the Dutch colony of Koepang, in Timor. The local governor was fed a story that their group had accidentally shipwrecked on his turf and wanted only to stay until the next vessel to England arrived, to which the governor agreed wholeheartedly. But then, for reasons unknown (possibly intoxication or an act of male bravado), William Bryant told the governor of Koepang the true story and the whole band was taken to the brig.

Shortly thereafter, the crew of the *Pandora*, who were searching for them, smacked into the coast at the same place, and thus the escapees and their pursuers were thrown into the unquestionably unique circumstance of staring at each other, each without transport. Somehow, Mary and her crew all made it to Batavia (Jakarta), but her husband William and their son died en route. From there, Mary, her sole-surviving child Charlotte and the other survivors travelled on to Africa and while at sea, another three men in her party perished. They then managed to board a vessel that was, coincidentally, carrying tired First Fleet Marines from Sydney back to England. Some of the officers knew her from the First Fleet voyage, and many others knew of her plight and were glad she had survived. Wrote the captain,

> I confess that that I never looked at these people without pity or astonishment. They
> had miscarried in a heroic struggle for liberty; after having combatted every hardship,
> and conquered every difficulty ... I could not but reflect with admiration, at the strange
> combination of circumstances which had again brought us together, to baffle human
> foresight, and confound human speculation.

Sadly, young Charlotte died at sea when they were all but home, and Mary and the survivors landed back in English prison as escaped felons. Mary was about to be dispatched back to Australia when someone took up her case, heralding her as "The Girl from Botany Bay," and she was released unconditionally and accorded an annuity from the British government. Her four surviving companions were also pardoned, and one returned to Sydney as a member of the New South Wales Corps while Mary settled back into Cornwall and obscurity, having lost two children and her husband to be "free" in England.

At about the same time as Mary undertook her odyssey, a group of 21 convicts (one female) in Sydney blundered into the bush headed for China and were swiftly recaptured. Three of them escaped again, with fatal results, believing that a white Utopia existed 300 kilometres southwest of Sydney. (Although not recorded, I'm sure their leader said, "Trust me").

Meanwhile, on Norfolk Island, a convict perished by taking a door off its hinges and trying to use it as a raft to paddle his way back to England. Other more industrious homesick "government men" went to (literally) great pains to hide nails and supplies in their assorted orifices, only to build escape vessels that all sank.

As the 1800s rang in, it was calculated that as many as 60 convicts at a time were making a break without compasses or bearings, only hand-drawn maps derived from imagination.

"Every person who came out with a design of remaining in this country were [sic] now most earnestly wishing to get away from it," wrote one lieutenant-governor.

Aside from the harsh conditions, being separated from family and the familiar at such distances was traumatic. News only arrived by letter onboard ships coming in monthly or yearly intervals. Once sentenced to transportation, a convict had little hope of return, and back in England it caused many victims of crime to petition on behalf of the accused to not punish him or her by separating them from all that was familiar.

* * *

"I'm not really supposed to be here, but," clucked another blond for the ump-teenth time. ("But what?" I ventured, but it was another peculiar Aussie-ism for some to place "but" at the end of a sentence, like a punctuation mark, but). "I model and act heaps, though I do promos once in awhile, but," she concluded (I think).

Working in the DeVogue promotional world brought me into contact with a sea of people from all walks of life, from struggling university students to "seasonally" unemployed models, to travellers looking for a quick buck and actors between gigs. Many of my co-workers claimed to be destined for Nyder, which is seemingly one of Australia's tip-top acting schools producing most, if not all, of the country's top theatrical talent.

There were the committed lifers, of course (as there are in any vocation), but promotional work to the majority was always a provisional means to an end, in much the same vein as the first convicts saw Australia as a hindrance to getting back to the motherland, instead of a chance to make good in preferable weather.

There were many beautiful promotional women (or as one radio reporter put it, "sexy sirens of merchandise") on the DeVogue roster who air-kissed and then spent their remunerated working hours complaining, squabbling, back-stabbing and bickering over who got what gigs and at what rates of hourly pay. They were bent on reminding themselves that they actually shouldn't have been promoting – that Sydney's Fox Studios (as a proxy for Hollywood) or some higher modelling agency would be calling any minute to magically whisk them away from this form of lowly casual existence.

Product sample in hand, I would be the patient ears listening to sob stories about how rich football players or race-car drivers treated them badly and cheated on them constantly. What struck me the most was how it escaped many of them to flee such treatment.

"Typical Sydney chicks, mate," said a male promotional co-worker one day. "Bloody strategic survivalists."

True premise or not, my situation as a promotional DeVogue male was a bit of an odd one, all the same. I worked with some stunning women, yet I seemed to be one of those not-rich guys who was neither a threat nor an attraction, just a friend.

Working for DeVogue was fun, but always stressful. The proprietors were a husband and wife team who were extremely short-sighted in their approach to business, often calling staff last minute for gigs and unpaid briefings that were many times cancelled just as quickly without compensation. DeVogue habitually took more than a month to issue a paycheque, and they did so without any payslips. What's more, staff (some smart enough to keep records) would have to subject them to a blitzkrieg of phone calls before anything even got to the issue stage. Furthermore, DeVogue was the only (I found out later) promotional company that not only paid lower than most, but dinged staff 5 percent of total pay for finding us work. Heaps dodgy, indeed.

The bulk of work was early morning stuff, six in the morning starts in train stations all over the city handing out leaflets, product samples, oat bars or instant soup tasters. Though essentially boring (and often times exhausting), I would come to encounter all forms of fascinating humanoid: homeless folks, lonely office people, Sydney Transpo officials (who, incidentally, demanded the most free samples) and a whole host of other individuals, some of whom appeared to me in their disposition to prove that some prescription drugs wouldn't go amiss.

I think my favourites were the six to eight in the morning corporate crowd train dumps. They all looked like trolling zombies, and if I crossed their programmed paths with a product, suddenly many of them would wear expressions similar to what my computer does when I run too many programs with too little memory. I guess they never budgeted to be interrupted in executing their established algorithms. I also kept an eye out not to cross any ME staff who thought I was out of the country.

"Do you have a problem with gay people?" I was asked by the DeVogue booker one day*.

"What? Of course not; why?" I replied indignantly.

She then sent me to Fox Studios near Paddington for Mardi Gras, the biggest gay street party in Sydney – so big that hotel rooms are booked out in anticipative advance. The major downtown arteries close for the energetic passing of flashy costumes, floats and masks – all creatively fashioned with a fastidious eye – as well as wacky hair styles, transvestites and drag queens in all their glory. Organizations come out in supportive abundance to secure their own floats with dancers and blaring music, bands, performers and so forth.

I had injected myself into the Fox Studio scene via the staff entrance, and was swarmed by a homogeneous Noah's ark crowd of Vikings, Roman gladiators, S&M slaves and their masters, dolls, bikers, police

---

* Sydney does, apparently, have the second largest gay population outside of San Francisco.

imitators, firemen, angels, devils and everything in between. My favourite was a Canadian Mountie in fishnet stockings that were strung up with a garter. I can't imagine how many whales may have met their end to create all the make-up. It was in this gay scene that I dished out samples of whiskey into the wee hours of the morning.

My partner that evening was a short and stocky Italian guy who looked horrified to be there, walking as he was with his back forever at the walls and asking me to stay near him – but not *too* near him. Upon finishing our shifts he bolted and I stuck around to dance and have fun with another female co-worker. She claimed never to have seen so many good-looking guys in her life, but that being said, she also said she had never felt safer as a woman in a male crowd. Once again, I didn't seem to be a straight threat to her, but the mood was cool and kept going until it rained and people scattered (I guess they didn't want their make-up to run).

And so ended the world's largest oompahpah gay party. I walked home amongst large street-sweepers culling pink materials, confetti, scattered wigs and discarded beer bottles. And there were some big men wobbling about in high heels, skulking home in hope of finesse and balance, looking like they would have sore ankles the next day.

Promotional work would also bring me into contact with Kiwi Simon, from whom I learned that the word "Kiwi" in Australia meant more than a furry green fruit – or a certain type of bird – and actually wasn't derogatory. When I first heard Australians calling other people "Kiwis," I assumed it was an insult (and sometimes it actually is meant to be). In general, though, it wasn't: a Kiwi is someone from New Zealand, a country with a team called the All Blacks, who perpetually steal Australia's thunder in Rugby*. But NZ is also a nation that is the butt of many Aussie jokes, usually on the subject of abusing social security nets.

"I'm a Kiwi, cuzzie-bru," said Kiwi Simon when I met him one day at Central Station for an early morning dole-out of oat bars. He was a lively guy who had no end of quick wit and self-mocking humour, one blessed with the ability to make anyone laugh with his quick-fire turns of phrases. If it weren't for working with Kiwi Simon once in awhile, I would have gone mad in a world of dubious DeVogue, whining women and tedious target demographics. Kiwi Simon also came to play a major role

---

* The NZ All Blacks put out a t-shirt claiming, "I support two teams, the All Blacks and any team that plays Australia."

in my life down the road, and brought a lot of good nature into my life in Australia. Kiwis seemed good at that – making light of hard situations.

Over time, we both noticed that aside from the issue of getting paid in a reasonable time frame, the quality of our DeVogue female counterparts tailspun. Once stunning (and reasonably intelligent) ladies dwindled into groups of raucous, gum-chewing and generally very unfit women wearing tight clothes they really shouldn't. Most turned out to be backpackers, and we realized that DeVogue wanted people who wouldn't be around in a month to pester them for cheques. There was a heavy circulation of complaints among the closely knit world of promotional girls, and many staff were escaping DeVogue and taking others with them to other potential promotional utopias.

Meanwhile, now roughly halfway through my visa, I had to think about where my life was going in all this and how I would ever escape.

19 – The First-Ever Australian Extras

ALONG WITH MY dribbles from DeVogue, and because of the large margins of space between paycheques, I also managed to sign up with two other agencies of better repute: Julia Ross (for office temping) and Pinnacle Hospitality (for waitering and bartending). Cumulatively, work still came in spurts and drips, but I needed more and so, because of my limiting work visa, I found "no experience necessary" in the classifieds and made a list of agencies promising exciting backdrop roles in film and television, and began doing the rounds.

The agencies I subsequently approached all had flighty bookers who addressed everyone as "dah-ling" and "number one." Most wanted hefty joiner fees up front and promised heaps of work on TV and film stages, with a hint and a practiced undertone that one day everyone might be a big movie star. Two of the agencies I revisited were boarded up the day after they asked me to return with photos and the sign-up fee.

"Crucial Casting" was a small operation based out of some obscure suburb with a very flamboyant booker. He was the nicest guy you could ever meet, though he was very full-on and flirty, so I just turned all of his advances into safe forms of jocularity. He liked me, so I ended up getting quite a bit of work through him.

Another agency, "Mock-Up HQ," was run from a Bondi Junction home with a full reception area – complete with headshots, articles and magazine clippings littering the walls. The mystery of it all was the woman who ran it, someone whom I never actually laid eyes on. Mock-Up HQ had a few agents in the foyer who floated around like empty-brained pixies yelling to the boss-lady, who was somewhere in the hidden depths of the house (I never could tell where). Her haggard voice would come rasping and coughing down in reply. She was always out of sight, but never out of earshot, something I found very strange and shadowy, as if she floated around but was never really *of* the room. I gathered that at one time she might have been a model or actor, but now sounded (and I am assume looked) much like any candidate from an anti-smoking advertisement, inhaling through a surgical hole in her neck.

Nevertheless, I let them give me their spiel on making everyone a star, paid them a fee and was cast as a "background artist" on a low-budget Australian soap called *Home and Away* ... though when asked by friends what show they should look out for me on, I perpetually answered *Neighbours* (another Aussie soap, filmed in distant Melbourne; to this day, I still can't tell the difference between them).

Extras come from all walks of life, including the spectrum of the freaks. This one particular 6oish extra always turned up to sets wearing the same unwashed pinstripe suit and air of vanity. He would crack open his brimming briefcase to reveal magazine clippings and amateur snaps of very whacked out–looking girls in the buff. He confidently allowed that he was a hot-shot female model scout for top mags, and then would circulate the washed-out polaroids (probably against the wishes of those in them), while promising any nearby cuties they could be earning millions. Needless to say, most were spooked by him, and I would often see him off-set sitting at outdoor terraces along Oxford Street in Paddington, forever in the pinstripe, briefcase by side, drinking a glass of water and no doubt waiting for the talent to flush over to him and his professional disposable camera.

But in the profession of extras, you need imagination. For all extras do on and off camera, one can never aspire to be more than a blob of unfocused or moving colour in the backdrop in the final cut. But then again, I was never one to expect anything above my station. I got paid to do nothing for long hours, was fed like a king and polished off much of my "to-read" list. In my readings and chats I began to learn about many subjects, including something hardly anyone seems to know much about, the Australian Aboriginal – the oldest continuous culture on Earth.

Aboriginals are in essence the first Australian extras – peripheral, always part of the background but never a major feature. When you are in Sydney, you don't actually see many of them, if any at all. There are no Aboriginal news anchors that I can name, or, for that matter, radio announcers or big-name actors*. There were a few notables in the sports arena, but not really anywhere else that I could clearly discern. In all honesty, the only Aboriginals I saw in Sydney were either derelict and begging in King's Cross, or playing didgeridoos and clacking cadences with sticks in the hopes that tourist change would spring out from behind Sony digi-cams. This needed looking into.

Aboriginals were not "Australian citizens" until 1960. Then they couldn't vote for another two years after that, and in 1966, they appealed to the human rights division of United Nations regarding their plight. As late as 1967, the Australian government decided to include them in national population census. Later still, in 1992, 'Reconciliation' began –

---

* There are actually some, but I just never saw them.

the result of several rulings that in principal established that Aboriginals had owned Australia before Europeans arrived.

Only recently has Australian Aboriginal culture and history seen a resurgence and a movement to preserve and cultivate it once more. Thus, as a fellow extra who was sometimes seen but never heard, I paid them a professional courtesy by employing my ample on-set time to brush up on who they are.

The time frame is unimaginable. Aboriginal Australians are thought to have been on the continent for anywhere between 20,000 and 60,000 years previous to European settlement, and quite possibly longer. No matter what you read, two conclusions can safely be drawn: one, that all estimates share the commonality of six digits and at least four zeros in their composition; and two, that despite such a chasm of disagreement among specialists, or regardless which number it is, Aboriginals have most certainly been around for yonks longer than dreaming Greeks or the blueprints for early Asian or European sea vessels. They are the most mysterious and, indeed recently, the most mistreated species of human on Earth; the indigenous enigma of the world.

What renders the Aboriginal historian's task most knotty is that, in the scope of humankind on Earth, Australia had always been isolated and never part of any other landmass, so how did the first migrants get there? Of the many books I read, *Triumph of the Nomads* (by historian Geoffrey Blainey) was an eye-opener.

In 1968, the ground-breaking Mungo discovery was made in southern NSW. Some burnt human remains were unearthed and taken away for analysis. The skeletal structure had at one time been a woman who was of "gracile build and small stature," and her phrenology matched the common-day human skull. Carbon dating offered that she was 23,000 years old, but in 1981, other remains were dug up nearby that were estimated to be 68,000 years old.

Discoveries in the Northern Territory put the bracket of first arrival even earlier, with a margin of error of 20,000 years before that. This made the human habitation of the Americas seem like the latest news, and Aboriginal ground-edged tools dated back 10,000 years before Europeans began thinking that dragging knuckles with jaws agape might be going out of style. But then scientists found something even stranger to put in their pipe and smoke.

At Kow Swamp – a few hundred kilometres from Lake Mungo – remains were found of an archaic humanoid race that had existed some

300,000 years previous in what is now Indonesia. The difference between these and other skulls were of such a towering disparity in the timeline of mankind's development that nowhere else on Earth were two such remote variations of human found in such proximity. Even more baffling, the Kow Swamp bones were dated back only 10,000 years, not 300,000. Thus, did two completely different sets of immigrants from significantly sundry eras come to Australia and exist separately? No one seems certain, and to deepen confusion they don't appear to be related to anyone around them. The main theory has it that primitive hunters came by sea-craft from the north – Timor or New Guinea or Indonesia. Whoever undertook the dangerous trip did so either blindly, at the risk of being carried out to sea, or with intrinsic knowledge of what might be there.

Most regions of the world, including the South Pacific, had societies that had learned to tend gardens and domesticate animals up to, if not over, nine- to 10,000 years ago, so what remains even more perplexing is why Australian Aboriginals didn't store food, set up permanent camps, create justice systems or have churches or a class system with slaves and nobles. They were happy with a simple way of life.

Stranger still, how did they fan out across Australia to procreate all the way south to Tasmania within a few thousand years? Naturalists have found that the Indonesian island of Bali, once part of mainland Asia, is the rough cut-off point for zoology: animals and plants in Australia and Bali, you see, are completely unrelated. In short, not even birds, with their aerial vision, flew the distance to procreate or drop seeds.

So what would motivate people 50,000-plus years ago with "no experience necessary" to embark upon such risky business? Suggestions include wars, volcanoes, overpopulation, changes in sea level, religious or tribal persecution and possibly banishment – in which case, Aboriginals would be the first exiles to Australia.

So that's roughly what is known about how Aboriginals got to Australia ... sort of ... in a nutshell.

When Captain Cook and company arrived, they expressed sheer dumbfoundedness about how little regarded they were. The botanist Banks, who came within a quarter-mile of a bunch of fishing Aboriginals, noted that they "scarce lifted their eyes from their employment." Aboriginals in the hills further north could be seen looking at the massive white sails, and seemed unconcerned that they might signal the end of their long-established way of life.

To Joseph Banks, his entourage, and even the Tahitian Noble Savage, black Australians were "rabble" and a "swinish multitude." Later, when Governor Phillip and members of the First Fleet walked ashore, native adults fled and completely abandoned their own children on the beach. When some blacks did re-approach, the Europeans observed that they were completely naked, doused liberally with funky-smelling fish oils and appeared to have invited soot from their fires to accumulate on their bodies. These features were only momentarily forgotten when Marines stared in wide-eyed wonder at an Aborigine who approached their bubbling cauldron and repeatedly (at the sound of his own tormented screams) plunged his hand in to retrieve a fish.

Here were two races of human completely alien to one another. Unlike other natives such as the Amerindians, New Zealand's Maoris or the Pacific Islanders, Australian Aboriginals seemed to throw no welcome ceremonies, hold no possessions worth swapping or have any handy skills to exploit. They were condemned as improvident and apathetic.

Following the establishment of the first colony, in which a few dozen first settlers were killed by spears, Aboriginals became the hunted. Only a year after the arrival of the First Fleet, black corpses were a regular sight. Persecution and slaughter followed, though many more would die from European diseases their immune systems could not combat, as well as from the onset of alcoholism. The notion of "educating the savages" arose, as it was assumed a change of faith would sort them out.

I cannot for a moment imagine what it must have been like: undisturbed for time unimaginable, Aboriginals are told by a strange race – with skin that burns easy, who can't find water in the desert and who actually have an aversion to holy fire – that they must give themselves to Jesus. And who was he? Someone born only 1780 years previous (or, at best estimate, roughly 0.03 percent of their estimated cultural span) who died for everyone ... including them.

Complications would arise when it was realized that Aboriginals were not a homogeneous group, which partially explains why they didn't band together and resist in the first place. As tribes were forced from their terrains, they met their neighbours for the first time ever. Thus, thousands of independent cultures were within kilometres of each other and never having block parties. Outside of 100 kilometres, anyone met would be speaking an unintelligible language. Whereas one tribe might say, "I am sitting on the ground," the next group over might express it as, "Another is standing in the sky." One early estimate placed the number of distinct dialects at 300, while others said it was in the thousands.

Governor Phillip, despite having been speared in the shoulder, sought peace between races and captured two north-shore Aboriginals named Yemmerrawanie and Bennelong, both of whom he wanted (some say forced) to act as goodwill ambassadors between the dogmatic cultures. The two inductees took walks with the governor, dined at his table, learned European manners and travelled to England for two years, where they met King George III. Oddly enough, no one actually went to the bother of recording any scrap of detail about the momentous journey. The visiting tribesman were, metaphorically speaking, not part of the script.

Yemmerrawanie would die of pulmonary problems and Bennelong returned to Sydney declaring he would do his best to bring peace between Aboriginals and the new Colonials. But Bennelong belonged nowhere; he was shunned by his own people as being white and seen by white people as being too black. He drifted into obscurity for the last 15 years of his life, became an alcoholic, and died in anonymity in 1813 at Kissing Point in northwest Sydney.

Aboriginals were ushered blindly into the destructive cycles of tribal wars. And no white man saw it more clearly than did William Buckley. He was an imposing figure, over six feet, six inches tall and tattooed head to toe. William escaped transportation in 1803 in Port Phillip Bay (today Melbourne). He roamed the bushes as a hermit, realizing he had no way of getting back to Sydney or the fledging colonies in Tasmania.

Unwittingly, but luckily, he snatched up a walking stick and bumped into two Koorie women, who mistook him for the outsized ghost of an ancestor. The stick he carried was actually a sacred spear from the grave of a revered tribal elder. For 32 years, William lived as an un-official, nomadic Aborigine. He witnessed many brutal intertribal murders and revenge killings, mutilated women and children and the disfigurement of other members of Aboriginal society as white society impinged on their culture.

One day in 1835, William crossed a band of white people and was unrecognisable to them. Gradually he regained his ability with what was once his mother tongue, and then he rejoined the white world, where he would tell stories of what he had witnessed. He was inducted to become an interpreter, though like Bennelong, neither culture really paid him any attention.

Some observers believed he may have exaggerated the intertribal death toll. Nonetheless, time would prove only to add to Aboriginal woes under new colonial rulership.

Warning: if any of you have an aversion to gory detail, skip the next section.

In 1838, near present-day Bingara, inland NSW, stockmen from the Myall Creek Station rounded up 28 local Aboriginal men, women and children and hacked them to death before making a half-assed attempt at burning their remains. Law officials never did anything, for it was not illegal to kill Aborigines. They weren't *really* people was the argument of the time.

Eventually, the sordid story reached the ears of Governor Gipps, who ordered the stockmen prosecuted. Many white Australians were furious that their own were being done for what wasn't a crime. One of the loudest voices of protest was that of well-educated Englishman and Myall Creek proprietor Henry Dangar, who had help set up the huge Australian Agriculture Company. He raised considerable funds to defend the murderous members and they were acquitted in the first trial in under 15 minutes. On appeal, however, seven out of 11 stockmen were hung for the Myall Creek Massacre. It was one of the first and last times when whites were punished for killing Aboriginals.

Sadly, this is only one of a few well-documented events (that is to say, one that saw the rigid documentation by court), and we may never know how many Aboriginals went under the gun and sword. Stories of killing Aboriginals for standing in the way of expanding farms were abundant, and such action was largely viewed at the time as a part of the "clearing" of new grazing lands.

But it sliced both ways. In one case, a white man was appalled when, in 1796, he found his Aboriginal maidservant in the bushes hacked to pieces: tribal punishment for serving the white man. Many farmers complained about being victims of livestock theft or having a fire-stick chucked into their dry grass, and in retribution they poisoned flour hand-outs that many churches and government bodies gave the Aboriginals in good faith.

It was a big mix of business and pleasure, and one settler summed up the sentiment in 1849 by saying, "Nothing can stay the dying away of the Aboriginal race, which Providence has only allowed to hold the land until replaced by a finer race."

In the interests of presenting both sides of the argument, Aboriginal Australians hadn't always been treated that badly. When Captain Cook first observed their ways, he countered earlier reports of disgusting brutes by writing,

> ... They may appear to some to be the most wretched people on Earth, but in reality they are far happier than we Europeans; being wholly unacquainted not only with the superfluous but the necessary conveniences so much sought after in Europe, they are happy in not knowing the use of them. They live in tranquillity which is not disturbed by the inequality of condition.

Aboriginals were sometimes treated better than crew and convicts under Governor Phillip. He forbade any revenge killings (even after he tried to conduct one of his own), and when some of the settlers were caught hunting for natives, they were flogged and thrown into irons for a year. In 1815, Governor Macquarie had insisted on pushing more Aboriginals toward the Christian bosom. A year later, in Tasmania, Tasmanian Governor Davey pinned up several pictographic posters around Hobart showing Aboriginals and white men getting equal justice (hung by the neck) if they murdered each other.

Many historians today compare their treatment to that of Amerindians, Asian Aboriginals or South American indigenous cultures, or any other that has been pushed on rudely and violently. That Australian Aboriginals still remain today is a show that early white Australians didn't go all the way in extermination as many other nations have done (except Tasmanian Aborigines: more on that later).

As in North America, Aboriginals are today enjoying a reprieve and a helping hand to bring their culture back from the brink, despite those who pessimistically claim that all the law has done is smooth their pillow before they completely die out.

It is impossible to say, however, what the Aboriginal populations were before, during and after the years of English settlement. Early estimates put the number of Aboriginals between 150,000 and 300,000, and another at one million. In 1901, the Bureau of Census and Statistics estimated the population of Aboriginals in the state of Victoria at 66,950, though when they went to count heads, they only managed to find 521, a mere 1 percent of the estimated total.

I noticed one day, while strolling around Bondi, that the word "sorry" was spray painted on the sidewalks. Because Prime Minister John Howard and his hard-liners had refused to officially say sorry for the past, outraged members of the public took to the streets themselves to express it in aerosol paint.

To this day, it is recorded that Aboriginals still live in deplorable conditions and don't share in the generally rich fabric of new Australian society. Their mortality rates are still high, they are more often jailed than non-Aboriginals and die more often in custody. All recent statistics reflect poorly on their condition.

To lighten the mood, I feel compelled to tell this story. When Captain Cook began to speak to the naked natives, they delighted in the white men's bright uniforms and their big feathered hats. It became apparent that the Aboriginals couldn't tell what sex the Europeans were and they "poked at the Marines' breeches," wrote one sailor.

Lieutenant King ordered one of his Marines to satisfy Aboriginal curiosity. The embarrassed sailor fumbled at his fly, and the first white cock was flashed on an Australian beach. "They made a great shout of admiration*," King wrote proudly, and soon after they were offering up their women as gifts.

As I was skimming through all of this fascinating material one day on a film set, the assistant director burst into the room to call lunch. I then shoved my books into the dark recess of my bag, talked to a fluffy girl about rumours that a TV police drama series was being cancelled next season and then muscled into line to grab a sandwich, and forgot all about the Aboriginals.

Because in Sydney they are not much in frame.

---

* Wouldn't he just write that!

20 – Swim Home? I'll Bet!

AMERICA AND HER allies were still hunting for Osama Bin Laden, despite Bush's claims that they were closing in on him. Somehow the interest of the president shifted to Iraq, and much of the world was asking what the connection was. Meanwhile, images of parched and cracked earth continued to highlight that Australia was in the midst of a very dour drought and farmers were suffering massive losses. I was otherwise oblivious, scraping by with erratic agency employment.

They might be household names to nearly 20 million people, but it was only with time that I came to know who Kerry Packard (media giant) and Rupert Murdoch (some rich guy) were, and acquire bits and bobs about the names of major sports teams, their captains and, once in awhile, a significant player. Australians are always quick to point out which Hollywood actors – such as Nicole Kidman, Naomi Watts, Russell Crowe, Mel Gibson, Guy Ritchie or Hugh Jackman – originally came from Australia (and a third of that list actually don't come from Australia, I found out later).

"And sorry, who is Kylie Minogue?" I had asked in the first month of my landing. She is, wouldn't you know, Australia's biggest female pop solo singer export, pre-packaged on an Aussie soap before heading off to the UK. Nevertheless, I had no clue who she was at the time, and it culturally offended many Australians.

Then one fine sunny day I was cast as an extra in a TV ad promoting a new chicken burger. The assistant directors had instructed all extras not to speak to the star, one Jimmy Barnes, a blue-collared rock hero. During the establishment of the first scene, I was placed next to the man himself, not having the faintest who he was. We exchanged some pleasantries and then I asked my new friend "James" what he did for a living, and with a tone of edged surprise, James replied, in a husky voice, "musician."

"Cool," I replied, "So which extras agency are you with?"

Not everyone, however, was as easy-going about my unawareness.

One evening, I assisted a friend in the marketing biz by gathering male participants (my friends) for a "speed dating" event, in which contestants rotated for quick five-minute chats with an end to, hopefully, discovering true love. The media was present to Sony it all up, and I ultimately wound up in several repeat performances owing to a shortage of males (I "fast-dated" 27 women in 135 minutes, and boy, was I tired). In the end, it turned out to be a set-up in the true sense of the word: the majority of the females were equally friends of the coordinator who, like me, were helping her fill spaces. They were thus already spoken for, married or undercover journalists. In waiting for the cameras to get set up, I launched into dialogue with a guy and girl who had just strode in.

"*Big Brother*," spouted the guy when I introduced myself, as if I were a coat check attendant. The girl ignored me.

"Really?" I said. "I think you might be in the wrong place. You can't bring a little tyke into the bar! You'll definitely lose the sponsorship if the agency gets wind!" I added with concern.

I must intercede here for the benefit of the context of this conversation. For one thing, no matter where I am in the world, I don't watch much TV.

Secondly – and slightly more relevant – I know little about reality TV, quite simply because I respect my brain, its potential, and stay leery of manifest hazards to both. Hence, I did not know that there not only existed human beings who devised the notion of sequestering other humans in a 24/7 TV psychological aquarium, but humans (lots of them) stupid enough to audition to be put there *and* (the kicker) a supportive, lurid audience, large enough to justify it all *and* vote them out one by one.

But most relevant of all, growing up where I did, I came to know the Big Brother Program as the noble cause of volunteering one's time (subject to a background check) every week with a child who didn't have someone to look up to.

Now, back to the paused discussion in the bar.

Suddenly they were both staring at me with expressions often employed when startled by pushy homeless people bawling mindless things from dark and steamy alleys. In the ensuing discussion, they explained to the crazy foreigner who they were and what the show was.

"Oh," I remarked sheepishly. Then I thought for a second, grew bold, and said, "So, what do you do now? On the outside? Do you support children in your communities who've had hard lives?"

I can't recall the exact answer – something between shock of ignorance and realising a heavy truth – but I gathered that they did appearances at small televised events before obscurity set back in.

I would learn more about the Australian Big Brother 'phenomenon', namely from my alter-ego roommate Jen/Jumpy Jen and other addicted members of society. The broadcast blitz marketed on almost every medium but there was also a service offered (at a cost) that would allow the production to text message your personal mobile handset with updates! Now this is bordering on ludicrous. I immediately pictured myself in an important situation (say about to romantically embrace a girl I met on 'Speed Dating' before her husband came home) only to be interrupted by a text message that might read 'B.B. FLASH: Johnny just took a shit...now heading for shower, apparently holding a toothbrush...more to come...'

Nevertheless, aside from an illustrative anecdote, I cannot admit to drawing any other benefit from the speed dating show that evening, and it just made me feel that I might be doomed to tromp this planet alone into eternity. I am joking, of course, but later that same week I did head to the Australian Centre for Photography to volunteer in mounting an exhibition – without a date.

A fascinating new display featuring large-format black and white prints depicting obscure outback sports was being erected. There were monochromes of camel races, rooster sprints, crab relays, snail contests and blurred lizards in various forms of austere bouts. Haggard outback humanoids were equally engaged in strange playoffs with an assortment of other objects you would never guess could serve as trinkets in gaming heats. All the images were well composed and loaded with iconic symbols of strange desert sports: fat swarthy men sat in chairs with cigars and wads of cash, columned betting boards covered in chalk and handy stopwatches under thumbs. Below, a quote read, "Australians will bet on anything that moves."

True, true. Aside from Greece, Australia is the only country that has attended every single Summer Olympics. To boot, Australians watched more of the 1996 Atlanta Olympics TV coverage than any other nation on Earth, which is considerable if you take into account that the telecasts aired in the dead of night for them.

When other national governments lay embargoes against ambivalent African democracies, Australia sends cricket teams. For many Australians, playing, watching and winning sports events gives life one of its principal meanings.

And it started way before many think. Take William King (known as the "Flying Pieman"), who I found in *The Reader's Digest Book of*

Australian Facts. He beat some astonishing records, or, rather, created some that none had previously thought of. Intermittently, he was reported to have walked backward for 800 metres in six minutes, beat the coach from Brisbane to Ipswich by one hour while carrying a 45 kilogram weight and then went on to pick up 100 cobs of corn (each a metre apart) in 53 seconds. Subsequently, he carried a 42 kilogram goat plus a 5.5 kilogram weight from a pub in Sydney to another in Parramatta and back again (a distance of about 46 kilometres) in six hours, 48 minutes. On December 26, 1847, King supposedly ran a mile in 3 minutes, 36.3 seconds – a feat yet to be equalled by any Olympian. Either this makes him one of the world's greatest athletes, or 19th-century timekeeping was not entirely reliable.

William King, son of a London Treasury official, had been dispatched to the colonies in 1828 at the age of 22 to spare his family embarrassment – though his life would end in 1874 at an asylum for old men.

Although most don't know it, Australians held the first-ever ski competitions. The fur hunters of Tasmania used to ski circa 1830. Then Norwegians (who else?) introduced skiing in certain New South Wales goldfields and then went about organizing the world's first ski races, all on crude homemade skis.

(I did get to ski in Australia, a strange sensation: can you picture a ski vacation on what they call the "Australian Alps?" I went to Thredbo ski hills, the highest point in Australia at 2,228 metres. Where I'm from, we call that a speed bump. However, where else in the world might you ski among eucalypt trees and then see a kangaroo in the base parking lot? Still, for what little you get in the way of skiing, the price to engage is astronomical, until you consider that there is no regional competition for thousands of kilometres and with necessity of flight. It goes a long way in explaining extended migration patterns to Whistler.)

All you have to do in Australia, it seems, is try. In the 2002 Winter Olympics in Salt Lake City, Utah, Australia won gold in speed skating, not because their skater was the fastest, but because everyone else fell over.

Oddly enough, I did attend many sports events live, though always without a clue about who was involved. In Australian eyes, this is equivalent to finding a rare and treasured document – despite never having searched for it – and then using it for a placemat. You see, the agency Pinnacle Hospitality called me sporadically to work in the capacity of a banquet server, which ushered me into venerable venues such as the SCG (Sydney Cricket Ground), Telstra Stadium or Homebush (where the 2000 Olympics were held).

The process of mustering hundreds of front-line hospitality staff at packed out stadium events seemed to forever be a case of the left and right hands never agreeing to see each other. To be fair, the Pinnacle managers were great, and so was the company, but because we were agency staff we were thrown into the conflicting, chaotic world of stadium management.

Communications devices only heightened the pandemonium. It was with mixed fascination and sheer fright that staff would watch supervisors scurry about with clipboards and squawking walkie-talkies, mobile phones that spent very little of their existence mute and rosters dripping in pen marks – yet they never quite managed the desired task of keeping each other abreast of changes. Mix into this the fickle world of dealing with perfectionist chefs (an experience not much unlike telling a drug lord with gunmen around him that he should consider another line of work), being assigned to partners who had lost their brains and who enjoyed smoke breaks during rushes (or who didn't speak English) as well as dealing with pushy guests, not to mention managers seeking to cut agency staff, and there you have a typical shift. But over and above all of that bedlam, I did manage to steal glances at cricket matches, rugby* and similar sports chaos in what is called Aussie Rules Football (AFL).

During one shift at the SCG, I came upon a paradox (a backorwardness if you will): the popularity of the game called cricket. At first glance, the game appears to be a docile yet maddening mélange of baseball and golf, injected with a large dose of barbiturates. It should not be classified as a sport, but rather as a branch of yoga.

I would, on occasion, flick on the TV for noise value while getting dressed and a game of cricket would be in progress. I would have a full day, return eons later with stubble and longer fingernails, only to turn on the TV while undressing and see the same game in progress, and even the next day! Something was fundamentally wrong here. How could Australians *endure* – let alone *enjoy* – something like this? I immediately thought that Australians who didn't turn up to vote in elections could commute their fines to attending cricket matches as an alternative punishment. Turns out, despite my perfect logic, that I was wrong. So I *tried* to figure out cricket.

I would often look up at the monitors in the stadium to see complex

---

* I am told there is League and Union, though don't ask me to tell the difference.

charts, tables and graphs with all sorts of nonsensical information. It looked vaguely familiar, something like stock market day trading – the practice of refreshing tables of information on screen for subtle changes in figures. But cricket enjoyed some higher-end technology, as well. There were even three-dimensional graphic recreations of the curve, trajectory, angle, speed and spin on the most recent bowl. It looked eerily like the computer-generated CSI diagrams used in the criminal justice system to graphically represent crime scenes for the benefit and clarification of jury and judge, who were trying to grasp just how a victim had been shot.

On top of all this, you have commentators talking like the tapes you buy to help you sleep. They reminisce about the good old days when they thrashed India and Bangalore in 1,000 BCE, leaving me to wonder if indeed that same game could still be going on somewhere today with no final score.

I once sat through a news-sports segment where a heated discussion ensued over footage of an English captain kicking a box in his locker room. The debate raged over whether or not, in a moment of anger, he should be allowed to.

I bring this story up only because this is the kind of announcement on Australian news telecasts that immediately precedes a "millions die in earthquake in another part of the world" story.

Then I got it one day while working the bar. For one thing, Aussies at cricket matches are always pissed.

Second, Australia takes dedicated interest in any sport they might thump the British at. They love mopping the floor with their former colonial masters, and the fact that they can do it in a sport the pommies invented is ever sweeter, like sleeping with the warden's daughter.

And lastly, the soap-opera scandals – just as anti-climatic as the game – help keep a fan base.

A player by the name of Shane Warne enjoyed the most coverage. Among many other indignities, he was caught taking two banned steroid substances, and told the press that the first dose was to get rid of a double chin and the other a cure for the flu issued to him by ... his mom.

His most noteworthy ignominy takes the cake: a 40-year-old woman from South Africa accused him of sending her dirty mobile text messages. Just to be abundantly clear: Warne was not accused of cheating on his wife with a younger and more attractive woman, but of sending dirty messages to an older one from far away, who had kids.

During an interview, one of Warne's team-mates called the woman a "dopey, dirty, hairy-backed Sheila." In a media retort, the woman stated that she would then come Down Under to *fight* the offending player (side-bar: she was an expert in Thai kick-boxing). Whether or not the physical altercation ever eventuated I never found out; meanwhile, on the same news-spot, a volcano eradicated a third-world village.

But who can blame Aussie cricketers? Their game didn't start out gloriously. During the latter part of the 1800s, the only team Australia sent to England was a novelty Aboriginal group that drew attention for throwing boomerangs and blowing rhythmically into didgeridoos during breaks. They were to England what the Washington Generals are to the Harlem Globetrotters.

Then in 1878, one Mr. Cornway of Melbourne and a Mr. Gregory of Sydney decided to send a "real" cricket team to England, and everyone around them had a good laugh. The Australian team had to raise their fares (50 pounds), but instead of supporting them, most people joked that they would have to swim home. When they arrived, the British completely ignored them, most of all journalists. Despite losing their first match, the Aussies still had enough gall to challenge a high-profile English team called the MCC, and somehow they "made fools of the greatest bats in the world." They returned home as underdog celebrities and from that day forward, Australians pretty much mopped the floor with the English – and never again worried about having to swim home.

There is, however, another explanation for cricket in Oz, one that also explains why AFL is played on a circular field. In 1856, Tom Wills (as far as I know, no relation of mine) took a good, long, hard look at his line-up of cricket players and was appalled at how out of shape they were. Wills and his cousin agreed that they had to come up some alternative that would at least help register their pulse. Rugby and soccer (and probably even tai chi) were too rough and strenuous, so they set about developing a refined version of a type of football played by miners on the goldfields, while also borrowing heavily from hurling and Gaelic football. The idea was to improve (or more likely create) skills and range of motion.

True to the nature of their own sport, the cricketers played this new game over a month and not one could claim victory or gain advantage, partially stemming from confusion over the rules. By 1866 a very basic list of 11 rules was drummed up. Wills' cousin, in particular, wanted to eliminate "scrimmage from which half a dozen men merge in a seminude state." He favoured, instead, good kicking, dexterity and strategy, so the ball could be kicked, caught ("marked"), carried (if regularly bounced) or punched to other players. A year later, an oval ball replaced the round one. With time, the new sport gained in popularity because AFL games have everything cricket doesn't – most of all, a score and a clear winner after 70 to 110 action-packed minutes.

Today, AFL has been recognized as one of the toughest sports to play, and it also has cult status in the states of Victoria and South Australia. Nevertheless, AFL sadly did not supersede drowsy cricket, which still has a hardy national following. Unless alcohol is banned, it looks bound to stay that way.

I guess I can live with that, but if ever it is announced that people can sign up and pay to receive cricket text updates on their mobiles, I'll opt for ignorance, thank you.

WHEN YOU'RE DRUNK, and alone, on a Sydney Transpo train, and you don't have a book, you do strange things. As a result of my spread out employment scenarios, I got to know the Transpo trains quite well.

Actually, on this particular day, I did have a book, and a beer in my veins. I turned my lurid attention to thumping through the paperback directory of Sydney's streets. It occurred to me that perhaps it might be a way to see what Sydney-siders valued the most, i.e. what they named their streets. My findings reflected quite a bit about Australians in general, and what they deem important.

"Railway" (91 listings, third place in a top 40) is by far one of the most prominent designations of thoroughfare, and why not? Australia has an absolute necessity for railroad transport. The Australian Indian-Pacific is the world's largest transcontinental train linking two oceans, three time zones and the 4,350 kilometres that separate Sydney and Perth. It was built as recently as 1970 and comes second only to Russia's Trans Siberian. In Europe, the same distance will take you from London to Istanbul. There is, in fact, a stretch of rail that spans 478 kilometres in an absolutely dead straight line, which very imaginative Australians named the Long Straight. Even more crazy is that in 1917, Australian workers managed to lay 1,600 kilometres of track in only five years across unforgiving desert.

"Station" ranks 12th, with 56 hits, tied with "Arthur" (both the first name of the first governor of NSW, Arthur Phillip, and the last name of Tasmanian governor, George Arthur) and "Campbell," the man who established wharfs and buildings to trade with India. (Campbell was also a tax collector and a founder of one of the colony's first savings bank in 1819. Must have been a hit with the ladies).

Australia's British ancestry plays heavy in the name game, with William (76), George (74), Elizabeth (72) and King (70) rounding out importance just under Railway's bronze position. Ironically, the bottom rungs of the Australian ladder of naming are Princess (11) and Queen (34), though there are no Prince Streets, other than a highway. These titles seem more often used to name highways, which means, figuratively, that British royalty played important roles in arterial life.

In late 1999, Australia had the chance to sever ties with the British monarchy and become its own republic. What was ambiguous was how things would work – something of a myriad of two political systems with a prime minister *and* a president. Prime Minister John Howard (whose first act in office was to hang a picture of the Queen) proposed a different voting structure, which seemed to have been a major factor in the undoing of the referendum, and the razor-close outcome only slightly favoured staying with Britain.

"Church" scores 69 hits. I found that like most progressive and plural immigrant nations, Australia – mostly in cosmopolitan Melbourne and Sydney – has a shrinking number of Christian adherents. While Christianity used to be the majority religion (early on tensions between Protestants and Catholics were very real), it is now so only nominally. As early as 1870, New South Wales dug religion out and made the public school system non-secular. Followers of the Islamic faith are an increasing part of the fabric, though Buddhism is apparently the fastest growing, and 13 percent of those polled in one recent survey claim to have no religion.

But the oddest street to earn a name is Druitt: it doesn't really factor into the list (there is only one main street in Sydney, and two more back lanes elsewhere) but perhaps it is a muffled listing, if only because the story is rather embarrassing.

After sailing from England in the 1800s, George Druitt was appointed chief engineer, artillery officer and inspector of public works in NSW. He built roads, churches and the enormous Government House stables, and a region west of Sydney was named Mount Druitt in his honour. But Druitt also stole a man's bride.

Starving Irishman Terrence Burns enlisted with the British Army and in 1817, his regiment was ordered to proceed to NSW. His one true love, Peggy Lynch, a very pretty girl from Cork, snuck onto his ship and was only discovered far out to sea. She was alone with 700 men. In the name of decency, the colonel ordered that Terrence and Peggy be married at sea, but as the ship was without a chaplain, the skipper performed the ceremony.

The captain of this ship was George Druitt, on his way to colonial wealth. He had heard that there were no pretty ladies in NSW and rather liked the look of Peggy in her wedding dress. During the voyage, he bent her ear such that when they reached Sydney, Peggy considered Private Burns a very bad deal. She took one look at Druitt's seven-room house and Burns' ragtag barracks, and made her choice. Burns stormed around Sydney with his sad tale, but no one listened, and seven years after he went back to Ireland alone.

Druitt, on the other hand, became one of the richest men in the colonies. Peggy bore him several children, and, as high society demanded, he married her, believing the ceremony at sea was illegal. As a Druitt, Peggy bore four more children. Back in Ireland, Burns met a widow and wanted to marry her. He, too, thought about the absurdity of marrying Peggy on a ship and the new Burns couple had four offspring of their own in poverty.

Meanwhile, back in NSW, the Druitt offspring inherited wealth and homes in Sydney when George and Peggy passed on, and apparently some awaited them in Ireland, as well. The Druitt daughters set off to meet their uncle in Ireland, though when they greeted him he shot them a look and sputtered that they were illegitimate children and that their father had been a party to flagrant bigamy. Unckie Druitt knew all about the marriage between their mother and Private Burns. It all wound up in court, but Uncle Druitt was favoured by a decision on the legality of the sea marriage. The girls fled silently back to Australia lest their uncle get ideas about bringing the case to them there.

And laughing all along as he read the papers was Terrence Burns. He wasn't worried about Peggy's kids not getting Irish property that his brood would soon prove their rights to because, before this case, he didn't have any property to bequeath.

So what conclusion can we draw from all these street names? Maybe nothing other than the fact that travelling in Australia is important; however, Australia's first people (the Aboriginals) are not very present in this census and not even close to competing against British Royalty, who play next to no role in present-day in Australia but rather a peripheral and recently forgotten one. The only top Aboriginal street name contenders were Kurrajong (18), Burragorang (15), Warringah and Wonga (13), none of which even made top 40.

But the most interesting thing about this little inebriated experiment I decided to conduct was not the result that in some bizarre way, certain segments of history could be pegged to the numerical value of street names, but that the second most important name in Sydney avenues – "Victoria" (103 listings) – was a fair distance behind something that is next to impossible to do in Sydney and on most people's minds daily:

"Park" (122).

But, oh, how my own path was about to change.

22 – The Regal Drama Series

WILL THEY SLEEP TOGETHER?

Will she find out?

Could it ruin everything? Career ... Their partnership?

What will happen next?

If we keep repeating what we just said, will you watch?

One day, while absolutely bored, I surfed through my choice of four uneventful channels of constant advertising*. I came upon an Australian police reality show called *NSW Patrol*, or something similar. Having watched the American shows *Cops, Highway Patrol, Best Chases* and all other incarnations, I thought I would be in for some action – you know, cop spots someone smoking a joint then helicopters, dogs, obscene amounts of back-up and drawn guns follow.

Instead, a youngish NSW patrolman pulls a man over for speeding, and finds out he's wanted. The check is taking awhile, so the suspect exits his car and walks to the lone patrolman, who makes no haste to draw his gun and command the man back into a secure position. The two have a chat while the seated and vulnerable cop informs the free-standing suspect that he's going to have to come in.

Without calling for back-up, or for that matter finding crack wrapped in duct tape in the tire hubs of the suspect vehicle, the patrolman lets the wanted man sit in the front seat with him unrestrained. A conversation about "footie" ensues. The segment closes with the policeman taking photos of the tattooed man and then getting locked in the room with him because he forgot his keys outside. All smiles when he calls for help on the radio.

As its goes to commercial, a trailer of the upcoming segment comes on.

Voice-over: "Coming up next: watch this officer issue a littering infraction to a tosser." (A tosser, you'll remember, is a litterbug).

Tosser: "I'm not paying that!"

Policeman: "Up to you, mate, I'm just giving you the ticket. If you don't pay it, you go to court."

Fade to commercial.

And that's about how pandemic Australian TV plots can get. Watching any Australian TV drama (or in my case, being an extra in almost all of

---

* Is it just me, or no matter where you go in the world does advertising seem to use more airtime than actual programming?

them) reminds you that Australia doesn't really have huge dramas, or for that matter a large audience ... or even something resembling a decent budget.

What is full-on, however, is the promotion. There's one guy who must be making a killing off of his voice, always plugging the latest episode of the latest Aussie drama in his deep, digitized, cut-and-paste speeches. The heavy voice-over begins another sentence before he even finishes the last one, and the visuals are cut to create synergetic intrigue.

VO: "Where will she go next? Who can she turn to? Can she trust Nick? You won't believe what happens next episode! Next Episode! NEXT EPISODE!"

New dramas with recycled actors come up to replace old ones, and in chimes Mr. VO with, "New Aussie/NEW AUSSIE/drama/DRAMA, you YOU won't WON'T beliEVE what they DO NEXT!"

At the bottom of the food chain are shows like *Home and Away* and *Neighbours*, which are to the brain what fast food is to the stomach: something that looks appetizing at first and that doesn't take long to make, but that ultimately makes you feel nauseous after consumption. Then you forget about the effects and, strangely, do it again, ad infinitum. They do have redeeming features, though, namely that both the above productions do very well overseas, though not locally*, and they both occasionally launch a pop star or two. I am almost certain that the writers make extra cash scribbling dialogues for WWE wrestlers.

That's the comforting thought in all of this. With all the real dramas and tragedies going on in the larger world, it's nice to know that there is a country going to the effort to produce regular low-grade drama that strives to create lacklustre plots, recycle material regularly for the benefit of the up-and-coming and that actually succeeds, even on a small (and admittedly nationally embarrassing) scale, in attracting some kind of audience. One can fake death (known in the industry, I have no doubt, as "job security") and come back in a blaze of dramatic glory if things don't pan out elsewhere.

Now here comes the forackward theory in practice once again. On the flip side, I have to admit that Australians who act in feature films and in theatre – both locally and abroad – are for the most part

---

* *Neighbours* was watched by over 20 million people in Britain in 1990, and 45 million all over the world, and it was sold to several countries including France, Belgium, Greece, Sweden and Bulgaria. It began in 1985 and ran 170 half-hour episodes before being dropped by its network and picked up by another. It was almost dropped again after an uninspiring seven months, then hit big elsewhere and remained.

phenomenal at what they do. Many Australian-made movies are creative, ingenious, dry and witty, and with the budgets they get they do exceptionally well. One of Australia's first nation-wide talent hunts (something of an early version of *Australian Idol*) came about very un-officially in what is known as the account of the Vice Regal Fizz.

The first governor general of Australia, Lord Hopetoun, tendered his resignation in 1902, but decided on a grand final act of kindness for the "unemployed and distressed people of Melbourne." He proclaimed that he was going to spread 100 pounds and 300 bottles of champagne among the destitute masses. When the local brewery got wind, they thought wise of gaining publicity by charitably donating six hogsheads of their brand of beer. Two independents then contributed five pounds each to the pile. The trouble lay in figuring out who qualified for the funds.

The task was given to a socialist-anarchist named Fleming, who had his own list, though he lost complete control as all of Melbourne came out and became actors. Convincingly, the population put on performances of being unmarried, broke and even sick. The thirsty actor-citizens specialized in contortion, putting on crippling deformities, paralyzed arms and buggered backs, and some even crawled to the distribution point. Fleming couldn't sort the sheep from the goats, and after police quelled the riots, he had to explain to the real poor people that he had given away their rightful dole-outs to people playing them.

Perhaps it is the lack of domestic drama that manifests itself in the creation of great Australian stage men and women. And there is a theatrical corollary in Australia's transmission history ...

VO: "But first/FIRST! ..."

My tenure at the gorgeous apartment in Bondi came to a head after five months, to the surprise of all of us – especially Sally and Tenille, who had been installed there for three years. Jumpy Jen decided to stage her own drama and gave abrupt notice of departure for her native Melbourne. At the same time, our landlord felt obliged to raise the rent by an increment that was seemingly small to the other girls, but quite substantial to someone in my meagre financial standing. But for this place, I was willing to shell out a bit more and suffer, at least until an irresistible offer came along*.

A German doctor I met through a 258 soirée suggested that I take his lavish apartment in the well-heeled suburb of Elizabeth Bay for two

---

* It wasn't a lead role in *Neighbours*. Just want to dispel that myth.

months, as he would be away on some remote surgery stint. He would allow me to pay next to nothing in rent, an opportunity rarely seen by anyone in Sydney. With a bank balance perpetually shying away from even two-digit levels and opportunity knocking, I gave my understanding roommates notice and accepted the doctor's offer. This would surely get me back on my feet. But it was not to be.

One week before I was about to move out, ein doctor called to announce that someone had offered to pay him full rent per week for his place – a figure that wasn't too far from equivalent to the GDPs of some small nations, and an amount I could not even begin to imagine matching, let alone earning. This was a real-life drama.

Into Jumpy Jen's void, enter another Drama Queen. Keshana (Shanni for short), an Aussie friend from Whistler, was the product of a great set of Canadian parents who moved to Australia in the 1970s and shuffled around the country for years before settling down on the beachy and pleasant central coast of NSW. Shanni had met my brother in the banquets department at the Whistler hotel we all worked at. I woke up one day in my queen-sized bed for an early-morning start and found her snoring next to me.

"Your brother said it was cool if I slept over," she said politely enough, stealing my warm covers as I got up to get dressed for work and warm up the car. I didn't even know her name, and she was crashing in my bed!

Shanni came to be the sister the Wills brothers never had. She was a ball of energy, seemingly always got her way and had many connections – and if she didn't, she would make some on the spot. She had originally planned to come to Australia with me via the South Pacific, though the word "plan," to Shanni, is a very loose term. Everyone knows someone like her – an individual so scatterbrained that in well-meaning bids to make everyone around them happy, they invariably overbook themselves, lose track of time and let everyone down in one fell swoop. But because people like her are so lovable and seemingly have endless good intentions, you can't help but forgive them and their speckled ways.

On a visit from Vancouver, Shanni knocked on my door in Bondi with suitcase rolling behind her, asking rhetorically, "Guess who's visiting? Can I stay?" as she walked in and got comfortable. I was happy to see her, inasmuch as she's my polar opposite and thus a companion who provides entertainment that never ceases. Shanni farewelled me a few days later and headed back out the door with a return ticket to Vancouver in her back pocket but, as was her nature, knocked on my door again the next morning announcing that she had opted – in what can only be termed a "Shanni decision" – to miss the plane. This, of course, meant that she expected to stay with me, but my roommates were strict on long-term visits and Shanni – against my wish to accommodate her – had fend for herself.

Well, fend she did, and despite the fact that she spent obscene amounts of money on her mobile phone to get all the latest goss from friends, not to mention coordinate, direct and star in her own series of self-created dramas, she ultimately ended up talking her way into sharing a fabulous apartment in the well-to-do Darling Harbour area of Sydney. And, like a well-timed omen, her roommate moved out at the very time when Jumpy Jen was steaming for Melbourne and the German offer fell through.

In what was initially a temporary deal between us, I chipped in some cash and stayed in her living room on a fold-out bed for a few weeks until I (and she) figured out where to live next. In the interim, I loaned all my furniture to the boarders at 258. Nevertheless, the Shanni arrangement ended up lasting nine drama-filled months.

VO: "And NOW ... "

Concerts and stage theatre peaked in Australia with urbanization in the 1930s. In 1928, some of the first talking pictures were shown in Melbourne and Sydney, and many critics sneered at the American accent as being "nauseating, nasal and inane." Nonetheless, Australians took to movies.

Meanwhile, though radio broadcasting was regular almost everywhere else in the world, the task of getting a good signal from England in Down Under was onerous from the outset. Nevertheless, Ernest Fisk was able to receive the first direct wireless message from England in his Sydney home in the 1930s, and soon thereafter local radio stations were established.

The Australian Broadcasting Corp was brought along by the government to transmit "adequate and comprehensive programs ... in the interests of the community." However – nauseating, nasal and inane or not – American musicals dominated the airwaves up until WWII, though Australians always got their news from Britain. Soon after, the gramophone hit Australia and, by 1939, people were regularly jitterbugging at all major city beaches.

In the mid-1930s, there was unprecedented interest in an England v. Australia cricket match. Two years previous, the same cricket match was almost a diplomatic incident, and by the time it hit the pages of Australian papers it was yesterday's news in England. So Aussies were excited about being able to listen to a live feed. In reality, though, the transmission technology was still somewhat unreliable across the chasm, so Australian radio announcers did the next best thing: they acted it out.

Cables from the cricket ground in England were sent to Australia in brief code, play by play and over by over. The transmissions were decoded, rushed to a broadcasting studio where the announcers read a fluent description of the match complete with noises and applause to simulate them being field-side in England. Their arsenal of background blare included tape recordings of ovation and tapping a pencil onto a specially threaded piece of wood to create the reverberation of the ball being batted.

Listeners were none the wiser, until one announcer was handed an ambiguous translation of code and called the wrong batsman out. An angry listener, who was partially awake and caught on, called the radio station to complain that the announcer had confused two batsmen of completely different height. Nevertheless, 163,000 new radio licenses were sold that year. Shortly after, radio dramas and programs and adventure series for kids began flooding the airwaves to the entertained ears of those who had a radio set. Although TV did eventually take over, radio programs and commercial dramas continued until 1971. *Blue Hills* (a show about country folk) ran for a record 5,795 episodes and 27 years.

In 1926, the first demonstrations of TV were ongoing in London, but it took another nine years for the first transmission using a cathode ray tube to hit Brisbane. Most households in the US had TVs by the end of WWII, and the first images they received of Australia were of Bondi Beach. But Australians had to wait until 1956 to get Channel Nine, which was based out of Sydney and transmitted to some 3,000 proud TV set owners and people crowding around shop windows. Colour would come much later.

The building Shanni and I lived in was a hotel/apartment complex known as the Goldsbrough Building, which at one time was a sheep-shearing warehouse, and presently was hot property near central Sydney. The apartment was long and narrow, had very high ceilings and gorgeous deep brown wooden floors, and was designed for one person to live in. Shanni had melted her plastic decorating the place in a very earthy and African theme.

Shanni, of course, had the only bedroom and, with the help of her amazing brother-in-law, we installed a ladder to a storage loft above the bathroom that I converted into living quarters with all the grandeur a Japanese company man would enjoy at the Toyota plant in Osaka. It barely had enough room to accommodate a mattress, a midget couldn't stand erect in it, every time someone in the building flushed a toilet I would hear it *whisssh* through any one of the many pipes near my head and if Shanni ran the dryer the heat coming from the silver duct would turn the area into a sauna. It was a storage closet, and currently my bedroom.

I installed a pole into a small enclave at the back and hung my clothes, and I built a very taut and crude shelf system, put in a reading light and stacked a few crates behind some valves to put things in. Because both Shanni and I were struggling financially and never agreed on how much I would pay, the rent fluctuated and I paid what I could, which some weeks was more than others. I couldn't much complain, for I had everything I needed: a trusting sibling relationship with Shanni and secure place to sleep. The bottom level of the building had a 24-hour concierge and full pool, sauna and gym facilities.

Central Sydney was a five-minute walk away, thus I saved a fortune on Transpo. From Thursday to Sunday, I shopped for my fruits and veggies at Paddy's, a warehouse-type location full of flea markets and a chorus of farmers spookaning, "Dolla! DOLLA! Fresh! FRESH!" With $20 I could walk out with enough food to last two weeks. As far as entertainment, there would never be a dull moment living with Shanni, the queen of all dramas.

On my first night, I lay naked in my cot under covers in an empty apartment, about to drift off to sleep, when I heard a key in the door and a tall man strode confidently into the abode. I was startled, but he was conversely calm and just nodded affably to me as if we knew each other. "G'day, mate," he said and he opened the door of Shanni's new fridge, extracted my milk and made himself a cup of tea, while simultaneously making small chat. All the while, I had no clue who he was or if I should have had a bat handy.

Turned out he was one of the Goldsbrough Building security guys and Shanni – friendly and innocently open soul that she always is – told him that he could use his security key to access her apartment and facilities whenever he wanted to have a break. His name was Rick, and he was a really cool guy, and minutes later I received a text message from Shanni announcing that people might be coming by while she was out. After that, I always had clothes close at hand.

VO: "So what/WHAT happens/HAPPENS NEXT?"

I am sad to report that one of the biggest tragedies in Australian history was about to unfold.

23 – Genetically Altered Asian Lesbians and the Gastronomic Fortune Cookie

DARLING HARBOUR, ADJACENT to China town and the city centre, used to be an area of shipyards, docklands, factories and warehouses until it was revamped in 1988 into huge tacky leisure centre that apparently hasn't had all the success that was hoped for. The mental change for me was immediate, from Coppertone tanning to concrete jungle. However, the beauty of Sydney is that a quick bus ride would easily put me back with my friends and beloved Bondi.

During my time living with Shanni, I avidly continued to pursue and improve my photographic endeavours, made simpler by virtue of the walking distance to my suppliers. A girl I had been in a TV commercial with contacted me and asked if I would mind tutoring a Chinese girlfriend of hers in the basics of photography, and I was more than happy to oblige.

I received a call from Candy, aptly named, for she was the sweetest girl one could meet. She was fresh in from Taiwan but didn't let her still-budding vocabulary get in the way of thanking me in continuous reverence for agreeing to help her. We arranged to meet for the first lesson at a spiralling fountain in Darling Harbour.

In the interim, as it was a sweltering hot day I took up camp in the shade to read a Paul Sheehan book called *Among the Barbarians*. In many sections, Sheehan describes the true sharing quality of most Australians. By 1914, a sense of adventure, youthful jubilance and patriotism for their nation (then 13 years old) was running high, despite the fact that two-thirds of wheat crops had been lost to drought and unemployment was towering.

After WWII, a "populate or perish" mentality seized Australians. In little more than a generation, the population increased two-thirds, as the gates of immigration swung open, though not to everyone. Sheehan states that since WWII, not even the Untied States had remade itself on all levels "so comprehensively, so equitably and with such unselfconscious ambition, as Australia ..."

Australians are nevertheless aware that just above their vast and empty country, the teeming masses of the Indo-Asian subcontinent hold a stifling one-third of the world's population. For comparative purposes, Australia has 0.25 percent of the world's population, and China alone weighs in with 20 percent. China grows by 16 million people per year, which is roughly equivalent to the total Australian population. To boot, Sydney is 17,036 kilometres from London, and 16,028 from New York, but only about 6,300 from Singapore and Manila. Australia is – geographically speaking – an Asian nation.

Worrisome also are regional economies of scale. Hong Kong and China, Australia's second largest trading partners, scrambled blindly for the bottom of a once-ballooning economic bubble in the 1997 Asian market crash. One of the many contributing factors was China's tightly controlled economy, which is seen by most other countries as being rife with deceitful business practices. Microsoft, for example, contends that 99 percent of their Windows operating systems on China's computer networks is pirated, and there are no shortage of other international companies who find that things are done cloak and dagger in the Dragon economy.

Amazingly, Australia weathered the regional bubble burst. Economists praised Australia's resiliency and adaptability, and its clean financial foundations. Then again, perhaps the Australian economy is so small and diversified that it didn't get pinched. Regardless, worry over trade with such dubious partners is not the only friction.

Sydney bested Beijing to host the 2000 Olympic Games. Chinese officials – who had poured untold sums of investment into facilities they felt certain would tip them the bid – had their sense of honour very deeply offended. It was noted that the Chinese view most non-Chinese cultures as inferior, but the sword slices both ways. Recall for a moment Australia's White Only Policy, which made room in the preamble of the first Australian constitution to state that the Asian race (and, it was inferred, others) was "inferior" and "vile."

But that was then, and this is now. Now the worry is that Asians are snapping up Australian property with rabbit like quickness. Newspapers are rife with stories, and one comedian turned the Queensland vacation blurb from "Ah, Queensland, beautiful one day, perfect the next," to a beaming Japanese business man spouting "Ah, Queensland, beautiful one day, Japanese the next!"

Then there were piles of articles on illegal Asian boat immigrants attempting to gain Australian shore under the cruel conditions of overloaded vessels and overbearing snakehead smugglers. Aussie officials would controversially turn back sinking vessels to prevent affording asylum due process on Australian soil. Those captured wound up in the Woomera Detention Centre, located in a barren desert in South Australia. The UN Human Rights Commission, already heavy on China's abuses, was making concerned overtures about the Australian government's handling of sanctuary seekers. Shortly after, I read an article by a *London Times* writer who blasted Australia for not taking more immigrants into her "endless bosom."

Therein lies the debate. How much land and how many people can "the lucky country" support? There's actually not that much usable space. A book I read entitled *The Future Eaters* holds a theory that the Australian continent can only support a stagnant human population of 12 million people. Fanciful premise or not, currently the real number is almost double.

And so, while I waited to meet a Chinese girl named Candy, I read my way into the politically incorrect quagmire.

Many ideals came from a man named Paul Keating. At the age of 25, he entered politics and then apparently morphed from a polite chap into a visionary, yet foul, mouthpiece of a prime minister. It was no doubt ironic that his riding was Bankstown, an area of Sydney heavily populated by immigrants, because once in Canberra he claimed "the best migrant is the infant Australian." In 1996, he was reduced by voters to a backbencher and he threw in the towel. His time in office is remembered fondly and distastefully, as he was prone to tantrums and calling people names like "boxhead," "pig" and "clown," and asserting some of his opponents had "criminal intellect."

There was (some say still is) much unrest. Many rural Australians feared, with evident sincerity, that urban politics were putting their concerns out to meadow. Invariably much blame fell on immigrants – notably Muslim and Asian communities – who inherently distrusted police and government and who were seen as eroding the open Australian way of life. Matters were not helped in 1994 when NSW MP John Newman was shot twice after campaigning rigorously against the burgeoning drug market in his riding of Cabramatta, which is largely populated with Vietnamese. The phobia of drug triads reached dizzying new heights.

Then, at the same time as Paul Keating was heading out, another mouthpiece was incumbent. A woman by the name of Pauline Hanson – whose previous feats include that of running a fish and chips shop in her native Queensland after birthing a child – delivered her inaugural speech in Parliament, smattered with phrases like "I believe we are being swamped by Asians." Immediately, the Liberal Party dumped her and she went on to become an Independent.

To be fair, that was the phrase the media grabbed hold of, and apparently her whole speech had a broader context, but I never actually got to read the transcript myself. Afterward, whatever she said seemed to open a political Pandora's box. Although her opponents initially thought her views would fade her out, in 1998, one million rural Australians backed her (23 percent support in Queensland and 8 percent nationwide) and Hanson formed the One Nation Party and became the face of a seething undertone of Australians who genuinely feared that immigrants would do them out of jobs and that Aboriginals needed less attention.

Hanson then penned *Pauline Hanson – The Truth*. On the cover, she was draped in an Australian flag, but between the covers she made allusions to Aboriginals as "cannibals" and apparently, there's also a parody about a future Asianized Australia run by a lesbian Asian who's partly genetically engineered. But the story gets even more twisted.

Both her party and her son were the objects of insults, projectiles and protests, and one expert noted that the campaign against her was a systematic assault on freedom of speech – all in the name of tolerance. All around her, bigger issues bubbled over to include undelivered promises of globalisation, the loss of socialism and the pursuit of capitalism.

Hanson recorded a paranoid videotape that opened with: "Fellow Australians, if you are seeing me now, it means I have been murdered ..." It all tanked after that. Whether it was because her pulpit practices were bad to begin with, or because the media made her a scapegoat for intolerance, I cannot say. The more opinions I read, the more confused I got, though I gathered that her existence was rather bushranger-like – she was a villain or a superhero: no shades of grey.

Hanson stepped down in 2002, declaring she had no regrets and pride in diluting political correctness. And something very Michael Jackson happened to her later, but Pauline Hanson's story will end here for the moment.

Asian takeover – by cyborg lesbians or otherwise – is very much myth. Has been for awhile. During the gold rush of the 1800s, the government of Victoria appointed a committee to stop Chinese influx to "... prevent the Gold fields of Australia from becoming the property of the Emperor of China and of the Mongolian and Tartar hoards of Asia." The measures included a levy per Chinese head against ship captains, as well as a quota on how many Chinese each ship could bring into the country. Many

Chinese workers got around this by porting in Adelaide and then patiently walking, single file, to the fields of Victoria.

In 1861, to the cries of "Roll Up," about a thousand white diggers grabbed bludgeons, hired a marching band, unfurled a standard and swaggered under both to bash the Chinese from their plots. Luckily, most of the hunted were quick enough to escape harm. The police quelled and arrested many white diggers, but the courts released them all without charge and the press openly supported that decision.

Most people don't consider what happened next.

Apparently some 40,000-plus Chinese men made the journey, and behind them were only 11 Chinese women! Certainly that would put a serious damper on schemes for exponential reproduction. And to quell even further consternation, consider that when the gold rush died down, nine-tenths of them went back to China (and took the girls with them).

Following WWII, the British-bulldog leash was happily exchanged but not fully removed. The government of the day aligned with America's belief that communism was evil and should be stopped in Korea and Vietnam; meanwhile, they had to keep an eye on regional investment (between 1939 and 1979 trade, especially in exports and cars, swung almost completely from the UK to Japan).

With the tumultuous 1960s came a massive identity crisis. Protests were held against the Vietnam War, and it was wondered if participation in such a conflict would be merited. Australia's biggest neighbours were communist regimes, but their new best friends were staunch capitalists a hell of long way away. Then one day in 1967, Prime Minister Holt disappeared, and many saw it as an omen that Australia was lost. In actuality, Holt had gone to take a dip by a beach in Victoria and was washed out to sea in a rip, never to be found again.

American films, music and pop culture continued to flood in. Writes Manning Clark – who titled his chapter covering 1969 to 1983 The Age of Ruins; "American pop culture, with its money values, its emphasis on sex and its presentation of material well-being and creature comforts as the greatest good in human life, were corrupting Australians, calling on them to worship false idols."

A big slap in the face came with the 1970s. In only three years, Prime Minister Whitlam spun everything on its head. He officially recognized the People's Republic of China as the sole legal government of China, he pulled Australian forces out of Vietnam and abolished compulsory military service. He then aimed to place Australia heavily into the socialist spectrum. He paid attention to Aboriginal land rights and wanted to atone for the past. He granted Papua New Guinea independence and went about seeking ways to cut ties from the British colonial past.

Many established orders were fearful of his reforms. The governor general stepped in and dissolved his government in 1975, which infuriated Australians because until then, a governor general had been a hangover from colonial times. The Queen of England was still their official ruler, even by proxy, and a man named Fraser was installed.

In an odd twist of fate, despite all their griping, two years later Australians quietly voted Fraser back in over Whitlam. They, in essence, went status quo. In six years, Fraser undid everything Whitlam had put in place, and kept a keen eye on immigrants, especially Asians.

Attitudes have changed considerably in the past decade. Whereas Italian, Greek and Eastern European communities were blamed for problems by British-descended Australians following their post-WWII influx, the shift in scape-goating recently arrived Muslim and Asian peoples is essentially a shift in paradigm. Lest we forget that before the 1900s, Aboriginals were blamed for many nuisances to good and respectable British society, and before them, an underclass of British were blamed for corrupting London society (and that's how Australia began).

But then one of the biggest tragedies in Australian history happened just after I moved in with Shanni.

On October 12, 2002, a few days before I was to meet Candy, things got very shaken up for the lucky country in a nearby Asian location long considered a premier tourist destination. Inside Paddy's Irish Pub and outside the flanking Sari Nightclub – frequented by Australians in the Kuta Beach strip on the island of Bali, Indonesia – two horrendous bombs went off. It was Australia's 9/11, as nearly half of some 200 instantly incinerated victims were Australian. A third bomb exploded about 45 seconds later near the US Consulate, without injuries.

Australians were mortified why anyone would attack their youth at an apex hour, when maximum human casualty was no doubt the sinister intention. Sickening stories poured out to an abhorred public: bodies without heads or limbs, people missing skin and screaming, survivors who would have to undergo extensive surgery and heroic accounts of people banding together to help. One journalist labelled the attacks a "wake-up call for Australia." The prime minister said, "Terrorism ... has happened to our own, on our doorstep." It was notably the first overt act of terrorism against Australians, despite rumours that Americans were the intended targets. Furthermore, with tensions already building between the US and eastern Islamic states, in part due to American foreign policy and calls for pre-emptive strikes, Australia was being painted as an allied lackey.

Evidence surfaced that Jemaah Islamiah – an Al-Qaeda branch in South-East Asia – was behind the assault. A 41-year-old Indonesian mechanic named Amrozi, as well as many others, were arrested in connection to the attack, and Amrozi smiled without remorse and chanted extreme Islamic slogans with his fist in the air. A day later, a tape attributed to Osama Bin Laden praised the Bali attack.

A feeling of regional vulnerability seemed to pervade the media, and the Bush and Howard Administrations took up closer mutual friendships. Australia was of course a strategic placement for US interests in the region, and the Australian government once again saw the benefits of defending their way of life against swarming enemies with a big and well-armed friend.

Without trying to sound too off-topic, I can't say that the Bali bombings helped my already dire position in Australia. Not yet – and not directly – anyway.

Candy had called me to advise that she was bringing a friend, and it turned out to be none other than her father. Ostensibly he didn't speak English, and I surmised that his presence was a show of protective caution for his precious daughter. Our triad headed to the apartment, where the table lay awash with camera gear and illustrative books.

As Candy and I took up position at the table, her father sank into a bean bag not far away, raising his arms into a diamond shape to support his head and keep his eye on me. I went into the fridge and procured a bowl of grapes and a drink for him, then sat down to figure out how to explain cameras to Candy. As I spoke, her father chewed loudly in the background and then released the loudest *BURP* I think I had ever heard. It was so raucous that I ceased speaking, but Candy didn't bat an eyelash and looked back at me, expecting me to continue whatever line of thought I had been on at the time.

The father continued to quaff and erupt with belches from the pit of his core, while Candy was oblivious to it all and fixated on what I was saying and on the photos in my books. I continued the lesson as her father lay down on the couch, only to seep a very vocal burst in irregular intervals and emit a series of lip-smacks until the lesson concluded and they both left.

I gave an account of the events to Shanni upon her return home and she burst into hysterics and swore that had she been present, she would have been unable to contain herself as I had done. But then it dawned on me that in certain Asian cultures, belching and eating in an overly noticeable fashion was the equivalent of thanking the host profusely! What Candy's father was doing, in his culture, was parallel to what everyone I know does at dinner soirées: burying their hosts in endless compliments. He just did so in another language – the universal idiom of gas.

After that, I taught Candy a few more times unmonitored; thus, I surmised that her father deemed me to be a non-threatening foreign entity. Then again, he did know where I lived if he ever needed to find me, and the paradigm of threat would probably shift onto some other guy in the future.

I sometimes wonder if all we need to achieve world peace is for everyone just to get together on a few occasions (even if we can't speak each other's languages), gorge ourselves on each other's food and then just pass gas in the same room. It might well be overlooked ancient wisdom, the universal understanding all macho men in power are looking for.

24 – Out of a Tub of Smelly Bull-dung Can Grow a Rose

"UHH ... LOUISE, AND ... um ... I'm 47 and I'm Irish," she said in a barely perceivable tone as she came into the room, slightly late. One of those had to be right: she had red hair and green eyes, and by deduction, she was a long way off middle age. She was definitely one of those low talkers, always speaking such that you had to strain to hear her. It could be a strategy, but one could never tell with her. She had something about her, and who knew our destinies would meet like this?

"Great! Cool ... Good one," chimed Angie, with wide eyes, windows to a programmed mind. "OK, who wants to go next?" she continued excitedly in the fashion of teacher addressing her kindergarten class. Louise took up the last seat at the opposite end of a populated table.

"My name is Allan," I offered, as others in attendance seemed unwilling to go next. "I am a photographer and I work for *Playboy*." Geez, that was a hard one.

For all intents and purposes this could have been an experiment in actively reducing the IQ of mature adults. Perhaps someone in a lab coat was observing us out of sight. Could our brains eventually be shrunk until they could be rolled out of our ears?

I'll fill you in.

My relationship with dodgy promotions agency DeVogue had come to be severed shortly before I met Angie and Louise that day. I had to resort to siege. I showed up at DeVogue with my records and threatened not to leave until I got my two-months-overdue paycheque. Previously, I had been subjected to a firewall of excuses, including that only one co-owner could sign cheques, but she was pregnant and when staff called her she told us to get them signed by her husband, and he sent us back to her.

So I barrelled in and threatened to squat. Well, the tactic worked, I got my cheque (which was, strangely enough, not far from the counter and readily signed, as if I wasn't – and wouldn't be – the first or last to employ such drastic measures). To phrase it in my best Australian, I couldn't be stuffed; they had made me spew heaps but* (?).

---

* "Can't be stuffed" is Australian for "won't bother" and "spewing" is not "vomiting" but "being angry." Review Chapter 12: Just Nod and Smile, for assistance.

The following day, I had called Kiwi Simon to tell him that I had quit and he brought my attention to a newspaper classified section advertising a major recruiting campaign for upcoming alcohol promotions. The ad promised lots of hours, exciting shifts, good wages and the all-important term all people like me who have sweated through a prestigious university education like to see, "No experience necessary."

This recruiting company was called "Krap Field Marketing" (KFM), and it was located in some fancy north suburb New Age box of glass that looked like an oversized fishbowl. A Lego-like logo on the roof announced the building as "Idea-Works." Mix this information with a glance at the lobby's directory plaque, and one could only deduce that this milieu was some manifestation of a marketing think-tank housing multiple like-minded agencies. In 20/20 hindsight, in a fashion similar to Australia looking away from Britain and more toward America, I had traded dodgy DeVogue for dodgy KFM, which existed on a whole other plane of wastefulness.

An Irish-Aussie girl named Louise had also replied to the ad and we were sitting with several others in a funkadelic meeting room complete with fluorescent bean bags, some rhythmic CD bumping away in the background, a jar of crayons, a plate of cookies, a long meeting table and the tell-tale signature of the marketing world – endless flip sheets on easels salivating for ideas in brio.

The crux was simple (and they are most abashedly so for front line staff in the KFM promotional world): a number of new funky alcoholic drinks in colourful bottles was about to be unleashed into an already saturated market. Angie was our trainer for the day, our bridge, as it were, to a better understanding of the campaign. I don't wish to demean Angie, for I know rather matter-of-factly that many things weren't her fault, but the whole show was flaky, shallow and misleading from the start. I had to remember that I was here for remuneration, not any other reason, not even career advancement or free cookies.

We had spent a painfully long portion of the allotted training time playing the types of name association games shirted in playschool. "OK, go around the table, say your name and tell us one thing that is true about you and one that is false," Angie had said with a bubbly smile, hence the Irish-47, *Playboy*-photographer responses elicited from Louise and I. We then dutifully scrawled our names on cardboard and bent them to stand up and be visible. But that was only the beginning.

We were handed environmentally unfriendly stacks of bound paper, entitled "training manuals," which contained excruciatingly overstated details about the promotion, the product, some well-meaning ivory tower theories and other useless and less practical shit.

"OK, now we are going to go through the manuals, so have your highlighters ready, because there will be a quiz at the end!" chirped Angie.

Angie devised that we should each read a portion aloud. Two things became blatantly apparent at that juncture, whether it was intended or not: first, that we were wasting huge swaths of time for little in the way of retentive education; and second, that many at the table had to sound out polysyllabic words slowly. I also noticed massive errors in grammar and spelling as we charged through the pages, and concluded that either someone had prepared the document only moments before the briefing, or that they did not recognize the significance of green and red zig-zag squiggles in their word processing software, and printed them anyway.

"I see that you're not highlighting, Allan," observed Angie, breaking me from some daydream.

"Yea ... uh ... me memorize better, no highlight," I forged half-consciously.

"Cool. No worries. Whatever works!" she said.

You would not believe what happened next.

"Everyone stand up. How we feeling?" she inquired, in one of those sickly overly positive I-went-to-a-seminar-and-am-self-actualized tones of voice. "Shake! Jump! Change seats! Grab a bickie, max out on the bean bags, chill, get comfortable," she went on.

"I am going to ask you questions and if they are true, move to this side of the room, and if they are false, this side," she indicated with such laboured gesticulation that only an actor (or possibly a wrestler) on a far away stage would be able to compete with it.

"Question one: the new drink, Do-Me-Drunk, comes in five exciting new colours ... True or false?"

We shuffled accordingly.

"Good! It *is* true! Question two: 30 millilitre sample of the exciting new beverage Get-Me-Sloshed contains 8 percent alcohol ... True or False?"

Again we moved accordingly.

"Good. That's great, you guys are doing so well! Question three: you can purchase the new brand I-Have-Issues in six-packs of 350 millilitre bottles ... True or false?"

The room seemed divided on this one and – though I am not medically trained – I assumed it was because our cranial wave paths had flatlined. "FALSE! They come in six-packs of 500 millilitre cans! It's in the manual," she pointed out.

Once again – at this point about eight months into my visa – I reconsidered why I ever came to Sydney.

For close to a week, we would sit through wasteful preparation sessions. All of us were confused about almost every aspect of the gig, from our hours to our locations to their system of assigning shifts by sending text messages to our mobiles. In fact, what started as an internet site to inform us of our rosters soon became a message board where irate staff posted rants. We went through several trainers other than Angie, all of whom I am certain qualified for the job by reading the back of a marketing textbook.

They gave energetic presentations, though when fielded with a relevant questions such as, say, "When are we starting?" would scrawl the query on a large piece of wall mounted paper known as "The Kelvinator," which was meant to be a repository of all questions they would seek answers to later.

Once the bedlam of training ended, KFM proved to be as coordinated as an intoxicated guy who thinks he can fight. We had been asked to list the areas we preferred to work in, but people were getting asked to work in places opposite to their choices. I placed a call in to the company to speak with someone specific only to be told they didn't work there anymore. In one case, Angie told me off the record how bad things were, even telling me she hired some blond girl with big breasts on sight alone. I later saw that girl at the immigration offices. Turns out she was Russian and not actually legal.

Then one day I called in and Angie was no longer there. The voices of the people calling me changed every few weeks, ever more lively and energetic; it was a place where staff had the equivalent shelf life of a Big Mac.

For all its wastefulness, something good did come out of KFM. Without quite realizing it at the time, three-quarters of the core team that would chase and eventuate their dreams in these troubled times were all working for the same dodgy company to make ends meet.

At break I sat down next to Louise and initiated a chat, mainly because others had gone to smoke outside or drag their knuckles to the bathroom, and because Louise had been the only one who answered the name game question quickly.

And she was good-looking, so what the hell.

"I'm a freelance journalist, and I do mostly pharmaceutical writing, but I would love to do more travel writing," she said in her soft voice. Well, things developed from there, and chats got a bit deeper. We were both ecstatic that we hadn't completely lost all of our active vocabularies, and I eventually invited her out for a drink to talk to her about a very loosely burgeoning idea Aaron and I had.

And meanwhile, in the Middle East, things were getting just as haywire.

25 – The Dawn of Professional Dreams

THERE CAME TO be swift transitions from one level to another in many areas of my life; though, in theme with my time Down Under, they were ill-timed.

My photography had reached new levels through shadowing and use of the Australian Centre for Photography. I was not by any means earning my bread and butter with my camera shutter, but I was catering to a small burgeoning and self-created market of promotional staff, musicians and would-be actors in need of affordable studio and scene photography.

The only clients I declined were a male and female who wanted artistic shots of the girl wearing a suit made out of leather, raw meat and dangling fish hooks. As I sat in interview with them in their King's Cross apartment to go over what they would have me photograph, the man, a very fragile-looking human being, was quietly forging something out of leather strips and studs, hung heavy with fish hooks. I don't know how he did it, but he glided his effeminate fingers through the linking process without snagging himself. The girl, who had a very dominating presence about her, did all the talking while the suit-maker lisped his opinion every now and then, and retracted it just as fast.

They never did call me back, and aside from them I had no other industrious clients wanting to swing from rafters fastened to flesh.

Slowly but steadily, money was trickling in, practice was mounting, my portfolio was fattening and my name was being passed around. I had procured an Australian Business Number, a surprisingly simple process consisting of logging onto the Australian Taxation Office web-site and essentially announcing via online submission that I wanted to start my own business and then, Voila!, I did. You don't even have to be a resident of the country to start up your own business; how incredible, I was now a sole trader! I had my own invoices, I kept my own books, I had my own cards; I was impressed with Australia and started taking a lot more interest in its economy, but at the wrong time.

There came a shake-up in the nature of my casual agencies, a transformation from bulk crap to refined and singular quality. I still received calls from the very excellent Julia Ross Agency and equally first-rate Pinnacle Hospitality Agency, though even with the two combined, work was sporadic at best. The flamboyant and flirty booker from Crucial

Casting called me to say he was leaving to dabble in the theatre world, some new girl was taking over and aside from one role as a member of a 300-strong crowd of extras on a *Matrix* film set, I never heard from them again.

I constantly put in appearances at Mock-Up HQ for work, but I only ever got two small roles and was owed pay in arrears on both. I never would see the persona of the coughing and haggard voice from above in the flesh, though I would forever be fed the same old stencilled excuses by the desk pixies.

"Big work coming, dah-ling!"

"Yes, but how about those cheques?"

"Big work coming, dah-ling!"

Then one day, I showed up to a locked front door hung with a "For Lease" sign. A cursory glance through the window revealed an empty interior – no desks, no walls with posters of hopeful stars, nothing. Gone. I checked repeatedly to make sure I was in the right place, and sure enough, I was. The voice and her pixies had done the grab-and-dash as sure as though the place had had wheels. I can honestly tell you that there is no more vile a feeling than being owed back wages for a stint on the painful set of *Home and Away*. It borders on the definition of cerebral punishment.

I would surely never go back to DeVogue, KFM was just a nightmare and I needed more steady employers. But I also quested for a little more professionalism. I mean, at that point I had been toiling in Australia for almost three-quarters of a year. Through meeting other people in the industry, I managed to make myself privy to an "unofficial list" of promotional and acting agencies that were reputed to be top-notch and certainly not prone to advertising "No experience necessary."

"Finally," I thought to myself, "networking, instead of desperados in the classifieds." I gathered up a small series of personal head-shots and placed a few phone calls that only yielded the discovery that many had their books full and weren't taking newcomers. I did, however, manage to land two golden interviews with two companies I would become very fortunate to work for.

The first was a Central Sydney–based company called Extras, by far the best background acting agency anyone could ask for. The core quadruplet that worked in the spacious office were cut and dry, promised no Hollywood roles and took no initiation fee without first garnering some work and offering deductions as an alternative. I would come to be cast in the backdrop of several commercials, Australian TV dramas and films at their behest. Extras would also inadvertently lead me to another person who would play a central role in my destiny.

The second agency was my saviour, as far as income and promotional sanity were concerned. Australian tennis legend John Newcombe had started his own sports and media company and named it after himself (as you do). Within the structure was Newks Group, the promotional wing that catered to the upper-end promotional markets, namely in major sporting events, though nominally with fingers in all nature of marketing activities. I drifted into the offices of Newks Group for my interview and was first taken aback by how clean and organized the office was. Photos on the walls were not of a salacious or degrading nature; they were framed and protected by glass, and the women within them were not sprawled over cars or prancing around in thin slips of cloth, holding alcoholic bevies.

As a male in the promotional world, I knew instinctively that the lion's portion of labour went to the ladies, but Newks never let me down and I owe all of that to the head booker – a woman with Duracells in her back, an experienced business brain and a name that was French for *beautiful* – Belle. Belle had the remarkable ability to think proactively, not frantically, as was the case with any of my former agencies. She asked if there was anything else I would like to know and I slipped her a few of my business cards and asked if she would recommend me to any of her girls in need of imaging, which she did!

From my first gig onward, I noticed an immediate and remarkable difference in the staff and their attitudes. I never heard any complaints against Newks or Belle (indeed, rather praise), nor stress about receiving due payment, or having a job cancelled, switched or inadvertently being left in the dark. All relevant information was emailed or discussed and distributed in paid briefings. Belle managed to cater to all angles of the operation, from client to staff, single-handedly and gracefully. I met some strikingly intelligent individuals (some former DeVogue) in my roster of Newks co-workers. I also worked for some refined clients such as Microsoft, Disney and Commonwealth Bank, and a long fancy list of other big names. I would work at concerts, with radio stations, at major events, openings, on beaches, at parties and so forth. And I got to drive posh four-by-four trucks detailed with heavy promotional graphics and loaded with gadgetry.

That being said, driving in Sydney takes a certain kind of courage, and not just because everyone's driving on the wrong side. It occurred to me one day, while I was multitasking a plate of cooked 99-cent spaghetti and the planning of my route to my next job with an open *Sydney Street Directory* before me, that the two could be twins. It was a strange process, comparing food to paper-bound diagrams, but you get my point: Sydney is quite simply a big jumble, a game of pick-up-sticks gone awry. There is hardly any rhyme or reason to its layout, and its street "system" is anything but.

For one thing – despite a complete lack of proof or piece of written legislation – I strongly suspect that there might be a secret law or unwritten rule that exists strictly forbidding turning right along most major arteries for a *minimum* of five suburbs. Whoever got the contract to mass-produce signs that say "No right turn" must have a private jet and visit Hugh Hefner on a regular basis. His prohibitive handiwork is everywhere.

Conversely, you would be hard pressed to see any streets or intersections named with physical signs. Much falls to guess work. There may well be another reason for it, possibly that street names in Sydney actually change every few hundred metres. What few designations exist are often obscured by overgrown foliage, anyhow, so you have to snap your head to realize you just passed your turnoff. Then you can't turn right for minimum of five suburbs, and the name changes again.

While initially I found it frustrating, I soon came to feel that it was rather charming. Driving in Sydney is like being on a scavenger hunt or going orienteering in the woods. What's more, if you're being paid by the hour until you get back and driving a flash car knowing full well that you have to return it before boarding a train or bus homebound and thump through your street guide to pass the time, it isn't such a stress to miss an exit.

After close to a year of the lowest denominator in promo and acting agencies, I was nominally stable in my living arrangements, and my new-found memberships with Extras and Newks rounded out a quartet of casual agencies whose combination allowed me flexibility in my time and a reasonable income. Now I had quality of agency, a worry-free quantity of gigs and a lot less associated stress, as well as running my own business.

But remember the rule: no yin without the yang. Despite all my struggle to finally achieve some harmony, my one-year Australian visa was not too far from expiring, and I wasn't necessarily in any frame of mind to leave the country just yet – quite the opposite. It seemed that my times of starvation were finally over, and Sydney and Australia were starting to look like good places to build!

26 – When Madness Sets In, the Mad Get Going

ULTIMATELY, AUSTRALIA'S CAN-DO attitude and ambitious spirit infected me, rather like a non-fatal spider bite, and despite my financial hardships, living in Sydney-the-city-that-always-siphons-money, I dared to dream. It is hard to go there and not be inspired in some way, despite some of the shortcomings I've outlined. Something would come to blossom for me, and others as well.

The fact that my work/travel permit was about to expire, despite the challenging slog to make contacts and establish myself in a place so far from home, were in fact minor compared to my overall concern: I had been in Australia for almost a year and I had only spent a handful of days outside of Sydney, and I hadn't even been outside of NSW or seen anything of the country!

Remember, there is Sydney and then there is Australia.

I felt no urgency to go home just yet. There was so much more I wanted to do and see, so many places I wanted to wander ... but I needed to remain legal, of course.

I consulted pro bono lawyers and immigration officials and my options boiled down to the following: get married, get sponsored or bring a six-digit amount of capital in to start up a major enterprise. Each presented its own problems, namely that I hadn't fallen head over heals for any Australian woman (and would never marry for a visa), nor did I wish to be under the exclusive thumb of one company; and regarding the final choice, I think I might have had six digi– ... uh ... dollars. It was strange for me to be speaking to immigration officials, because I was neither sure that I wanted to stay long term, nor for that matter immigrate. I just wanted a little more time, if such a thing was possible.

And there was something more, something that made me wonder ... Something that was bubbling in the corners of my imagination ... Something that was stirring in the back of creative minds. I didn't know it at the time, but it would overflow more than we could ever know.

I will have to take you back some eight months from the present narrative in order to weave into the story the thread that will lead to the next yarn. You see, something has been going on behind the scenes pretty much since you started reading this book. I haven't mentioned it until now, and please don't feel dismayed, because not even I knew how it was going to pan out.

We go back to the period when I lived in Bondi with Sally, Tenille and Jen and down the road from 258. At that time, I was temping through Julia Ross two days a week in the city for NSW Rail, building a database and organizing their library. Aaron worked in the city, as well, and together we would spend our unhappy mornings on the crowded Bondi bus to the city (if we managed to catch one with space), each knowing that a full day in the office awaited us. But then something struck – the bus drivers. They stopped working for a few days to protest ... um ... something ... and this meant that Aaron and I would either have to walk to the train station or find alternate means of getting to work.

So we did. The notion of morning rush hour trains teeming with drones seemed very unappealing, so we decided to walk to the city instead. The trajectory along Oxford Street to City Centre (about 12 kilometres) took an hour and 20 minutes to complete, which was exactly the same amount of time it took by bus, if we summed our periods in wait with the stretch in rush hour traffic. We would dangle our corporate wear from our backpacks, strut off and arrive at work in the opposite condition of many of our co-workers, who sought deliverance in coffee. People thought we were either crazy, cheap or in need of therapy. They were right!

Despite the resumption of bus services a week later, the walks continued. We had grown addicted to the fresh air, the exercise and the opportunity to discuss politics, professional wrestling and their commonalties. One recurring theme was the desire to jump the rails, escape the rat race and see the rest of the world, starting with Australia.

These ritualistic walks spawned some concepts about just what we might do to achieve some travel. US president Bush was just starting to trump up his case of weapons of mass destruction in Iraq, and many countries were curious about his line of reasoning. Mr. Bush, despite all his assurances, had not yet found Bin Laden in Afghanistan. To boot, there had been some SARS scares, and generally the world just seemed like a mad place altogether.

During my lunch breaks at the NSW Rail gig, I would chat with another temp, a creative Londoner on the same visa as I named Emma, and – in tandem with ideas generated while walking – a little mere of creativity began to pool between the three of us at the same time as I left Bondi to live with Shanni in Darling Harbour.

Even once I had wrapped up the gig at NSW Rail, Emma stayed in touch and we had a few meetings at my new digs to discuss this loose idea of seeing Australia in a creative fashion. Aaron – phenomenal at coming up with jingles – spawned the name "Mad Nomads," and also drummed up a two word-slogan that reflected our frames of mind: "Wonder? ... Wander ..."

With time, we found out that Emma had other ideas. She absolutely hated the name, said she could not work with it, and would offer up alternate concepts that were drawn from the realm of hardcore, in-your-face London marketing ploys (that was her background, as it turned out). Over the span of our arranged meetings, she would not show up due to all kinds of excuses ranging from hangovers, to "coming down from a rave," to seemingly endless emotional bang-ups with a series of men I could ne'er keep track of, even had I been provided with graphical aid. Despite some great initial energy and ideas, Emma chemically sputtered out of our lives, leaving only Aaron and I and a loose concept.

We pressed on, laying down colour schemes and notions for the Mad Nomads project, coming up with ideas, and, with the help of our friend Melissa, the photographer, we illustrated who we were with stills. The whole idea was put out there, emailed to friends and family all over the world. A flood of ideas and criticism came back and we slowly began to polish the look of an un-posted website. I held meetings with several other people to seek their involvement: an architect I had designed a website for, a furtive photographer who never returned calls, someone I met at a bus stop, a worker from the ACP who turned out to be unreliable and a girl I had worked some promos with. All seemed keen, all seemed primed, all fizzled out quickly.

Then I met Louise at KFM and she turned out to be just what the team needed: a freelance journalist, keen-eyed editor and a token all-rounder. She would bring a woman's touch to the project and come to be an immense creative force in the band, not to mention being a magnificent streamliner. But we still didn't have a definite direction, until I met ...

"Action!"

Craig and I exited the police vehicle, opened the back door, extracted our suspect and walked into the jail entrance. We did this repeatedly. Once again, Craig and I had been cast through Extras as NSW police officers on some TV cop drama that would be cancelled by the following season. I crossed paths with Craig on a fairly regular basis (read:

whenever a cop show needed extras), and over time I let him in on the Mad Nomads project. Craig became a regular contributor at our meetings and for months thereafter we honed our product.

Despite having heavy imaginations, we were all extremely light in our wallets. We had a concept, some material and ideas for a website, but very little moola. We all sought to see the country, especially the three Australian members of the Mad Nomads quartet who hadn't seen their own land, but we would need vehicles, and if we wanted to be proficient at updating the website with images and words regularly as we went, we would first need a web host and some other gadgets like film and/or digital cameras and some laptops. The website was functionally complete, though not yet posted in cyberspace, and after a series of brainstorms, Craig came up with the idea that would come to be the basis of our plan of attack – but he did so just at that moment my visa expired.

As it turned out, there was an option to stay, albeit an expensive one: ETA (Electronic Travel Authority, a branch of Australian Immigration) offered online visas for three-month business stints and they only took seconds to get on the internet, at the meagre fee of $20. The catch: you had to be *outside* of Australia to qualify for one. Seeing as how Australia is the only continent that is a country, and the only country that is an entire island, it meant a flight to somewhere else! It was a ridiculous situation to say the least, but it was my only choice, so I hastily purchased a return ticket to Auckland, New Zealand, a three-hour flight from Sydney, and set out the night my visa expired.

This option was nerve-wracking, to say nothing of being the major contributing factor in the formation of a thriving moth colony that was lapping up new tracts of property in my wallet. But something amazing happened just before I left, something that gave us all hope ...

Only moments before I boarded the plane to briefly leave Australia, Mad Nomads would get their very first official sponsor.

27 – Roller Coaster

MANY YEARS AGO, when I lived in Whistler with the roving Jafas, I decided to teach myself the art of web design. I created a very crude site consisting of text about some of my travels, and then found out that one needed a web host for it to be accessible online (something seemingly every child knows instinctively by kindergarten these days). I confess that I was very web-dazed-and-confused when it came to that sort of thing, so I went a-huntin'. Word of mouth brought my browser and I to a company called Blacksun, based in Saskatchewan, and I opted for their service and have never looked back since. Blacksun was a lucky hit, just what I needed in the myriad of online hosting companies – an honest corporation that didn't die in the crash of the dot-coms, and one that boasted great customer support for web virgins like me, answering all my silly questions and even taking care of things on my behalf.

Flash forward a few years to appreciate my frame of mind on that fateful day when I stood in Sydney International Airport contemplating the outlay of a considerable amount of already pinched funds simply for a slap-dash visit to the land of Hobbits, with the only benefit being to remain above-board in Australia (I would never actually get to see any of the gorgeous land that is New Zealand: it would be an in and out affair). Add to this the considerable outlay of eight months that Aaron, Louise, Craig and my laptop spent constructing and pursuing this Mad Nomads enterprise, as well as my intermittent jobs, and my worry about my immediate future was very real.

I had sent off a proposal to Blacksun and decided to ring them from a pay phone metres from the gate boarding passengers for the flight to Auckland ... Now consider how I felt when they offered the Mad Nomads one of their hosting plans for our site! They instantly became a beacon in the fog, and once again they were just what I needed.

Shortly after my return to Sydney, the Mad Nomads went live on the web. We constantly updated the site with our plans, sought lots of feedback and chiselled it into a well-presented visual. A girl by the name of Wendy – one of my friends from back home who had journeyed to Australia – came complete with web animation skills and funnelled her talents to the project, giving us a great, Flash-y introduction. Now this was more like it!

The site had all our bios and aspirations and our contact information and, acting on one of Craig's initial ideas, the Mad Nomads went out to explore and document Aboriginal Sydney. Our combined efforts garnered us a free ride on an authentic Aboriginal boat around the harbour and attendance at some festivals, so lots of words and images came to be posted over a span of months. Aaron, Louise and I became the contributing writers, though we multitasked as Louise edited for all of us and I became the photographer, while Aaron continued in his prowess of creating great slogans and concepts. Craig's ambitions in the plot rested more so in documentary film–making; he had actually made his own documentary about epilepsy not long before he met us, and presently wanted to make a Mad Nomads "docco."

Because I had worked in so many offices as a temp, our team offered some free advertising space on the site to two Australian charities, Smith Family, who gathered clothing and items for the poor, and the Australian Red Cross Blood Service. With the help of a programming-savvy German I worked with at the Sydney Car Show, our website was soon rigged with the capacity to accept online financial donations to assist our project.

It wasn't long before all kinds of people were coming forward to bring their grain of sand to the growing pile. Some highly placed individuals from a few of the companies I temped at lent us their time and aptitudes by attending our meetings and being necessarily ruthless in giving us crucial feedback on our presentations and processes. A Newks co-worker, as well as another friend in Canada, edited proposals that we drew up to solicit sponsorship from a list of potential companies. Louise made some calls and garnered free deodorant from L'Oréal, but better yet, she managed to receive a pile of free guidebooks for all states and regions of Australia from my favourite travel publisher, Lonely Planet!

Then Craig nailed down our concept – one that was timely and well-received. The Mad Nomads would embark on a national project entitled "In Search of Hindsight." At the time, Australia was experiencing her worst drought in 104 years*, the lucky but quiet nation had to come to terms with the formerly unknown threat of terrorism, and was poised to possibly participate in offensive action in Iraq. Australia, like the world at large, was facing economic, social, political and technological changes, and the future was not all too certain.

Our mission was this: to seek wisdom from the grandmothers of Australia – a very often ignored demographic – who have themselves been through tough times before. We endeavoured to travel Australia

---

* The worst drought in recorded Australia history was "the seven-year drought," from 1895 to 1902, which killed over half of all farm animals and did untold damage to agriculture.

in search of answers, ideas, notions and feedback. We would seek accommodation via our website, by doing radio interviews, by word of mouth and by putting our intentions into the hands of members of the Country Women's Association, among other like-minded community organizations and clubs. Our website would serve as a forum for all of this, and we would collect clothing for Smith Family along the way.

So, now we needed support and more sponsorship. Kiwi Simon was good enough to give me the password for his dial-up internet service. After sitting down and deciding what we required, I spent a spine-busting amount of time researching Australian companies and their marketing big cheeses. My old training from ME kicked in, only this time, the intent wasn't dodgy. The process took a few more months, but I compiled a database of 50 major companies in five categories, then our team geared proposals for each one, outlining our project and stipulating what they would receive if they sponsored us.

Then a strange omen appeared.

One of the companies we were going to approach was named Britz. I misspelled it all over our proposal as "Brizt," and on the day we were preparing our packages, the keen eye of Louise caught the glaring error and made me reprint it. That evening, we kissed the pile of manila envelopes that were our hopes, shoved them into the post box and bid them God speed.

A week later, my ETA visa expired and I had less money than before, which is to say negative numbers. Nevertheless, I procured a return ticket to Auckland and headed for the airport. My luck was about to get a whole lot worse.

While in line to board Air New Zealand, an announcement was made that they had over-booked the flight and were offering a substantial rebate to anyone willing to wait six hours until the next departing aircraft. I could live with that, I decided. Just five minutes before boarding, they told us volunteers to get on the original flight because in the end there was space, sorry for the inconvenience and no rebate! Off I dashed.

At a checkpoint, a security officer deemed the corkscrew tucked away in my backpack a dangerous weapon (I kept it there for my hospitality shifts), so I was forced to give it up. This was followed by me having to remove my shoes and belt and repeatedly shuffle through the scanner arch as if I was on a film set with a director who couldn't get a good take; finally, they let me go on, while above me the PA screamed my name and the warning, "LAST CALL TO BOARD." I handed over my passport at the ultimate checkpoint, only to be told that my visa had expired two days earlier and I would have to speak to an immigration official. "MR. WILLS, PLEASE GO TO THE GATE!" beseeched the PA as I speedily explained to an official that I was leaving the country precisely for that reason. She released me, and after a knee-to-chest sprint in the general direction of two frantically waving flight attendants, I boarded the aircraft flushed in the face, belt in my teeth, pants riding low, shoes in my hands and the stare of several impatient passengers upon me.

I fell into my seat next to a gentleman who offered a jocular "What, did they give you the ol' rubber glove up the arse, mate?" to which I didn't reply and just went to sleep, having lost an expensive corkscrew and my dignity in the process.

I arrived in Auckland and took the bus into the city, washing up at the door of the same hostel of my previous permit procurement session. In repeat fashion, I logged onto the internet for another shot at three legal months in the Commonwealth of Australia. I then went to get a room. But all of Auckland was sold out – the America's Cup boat race was underway.

With no other option at hand, I got back on the shuttle bus to the airport and sat bolt upright in chairs designed to thwart attempts at lying down, my head rolling in circles on a loose and lolling neck in conscious/unconscious bouts that stretched over a hugely uneventful, 10-hour overnight session at Auckland International.

Come to think of it, there were a few occasions to gather some insight into a country I had now visited twice and yet not seen. In one scenario, I entered into a brief exchange with a Kiwi who struck me as frightfully confused in the use of his vowels. I was asking him directions to the toilet and he kept telling me to take a "lift," but I could see no elevator where he pointed. Then I realized that he meant the opposite of right. "See ... Jist ufta the bun, aye bru," which I deciphered as being, "Turn after the garbage can, my brother."

Back in my chair, I watched reruns of the local news on a mounted television. A top New Zealand political story was afoot: an offended politician was making a national stink over the use of the word "bugger" in NZ parliament. The upset parliamentarian was spending time and effort in an attempt to eliminate the "inappropriate" term, and had "diddly-squat" pegged for banishment, as well, in the course of parliamentary debates. There were of course rebuttals to this, though you might agree that the tale is fascinating if only by virtue of its existence and the fact that such a high national office appeared to be in dire need of more hobbies. I vowed thenceforth never to make fin of an Australian bugga or accint agun.

Once back in Sydney, I discovered in my email account a few stencilled rejection letters, most from banks, regarding the Mad Nomads sponsorship. Déjà vu – I was reliving my first days of employment agency rejection letters.

To add to that, my roommate Shanni, in her classic last-minute-but-I-can't-help-but-love-you style, announced to me via mobile text message that she was going to move out of our Darling Harbour apartment in a week and thus I would be forced to relocate. In the end, for financial reasons and because my furniture was there, I moved back to Bondi Beach and into 258 with Aaron, Matt, two Germans and about one million gazillion relaxed cockroaches.

Matt, my former DIY co-conspirator, decided in a life-altering epiphany that the party atmosphere at 258 was bringing him down, so he threw a party, invited lots of people and moved out on a whim with two co-workers to begin life anew. Matt, however, was our saving grace, for he kept hold of the lease on 258 and allowed us to stay, making Aaron the chief operating officer by default. To Matt we will always tip the hat, for otherwise Aaron and I would have been homeless.

Soon 258 would become even more of a bustling metropolis, as we invited several people to move in, thereby reducing our rent by filling the house to double its capacity. In the end, it actually turned out that despite numbers, things had never been more harmonious in the congested annals of 258's history. The house came to be comprised of five Canadians, two new Germans (the other two left but not without arranging substitutes) and Aaron, seemingly the only white Aussie in Bondi, and all together we managed to give the place a reasonable upkeep.

Our Mad Nomads deadline grew closer and closer, and with it many potential Mad Nomads sponsors trickled in with tentative interest and a keen curiosity to see who else would come aboard. Some major car companies looked about to bite, but many managers declared that because of the looming Iraq conflict, they were slicing or freezing their sponsorship budgets. It was like watching fish in clear water come near the bait but never take a chomp.

Then it happened – keen-eyed Louise's omen.

I was standing in North Sydney, about to get on a bus to a Newks employee party, when my mobile rang with a Melbourne number. The voice on the other end of the line was the marketing manger from Britz Australia, a company in the business of renting motor homes and four-wheel-drive vehicles altered to be camper vans.

"Is your Mad Nomads project still going on?" he asked.

Out of all the interested vehicle companies, Britz had the most synergy with our concept, namely because they flaunted a magnificent fleet of varied vehicles modified to accommodate adventurers, not to mention having depots in all major cities across Australia. Their slogan was "No Boundaries" – need I say more?

Soon after Britz came onboard, the dance floor came to life! For the following two weeks, I slept very little indeed, suddenly seized with a million arrangements to make as well as flogging off all my hard-bought furniture to fatten up the petrol fund.

Then a company very dear to my heart came forward: Nikon. In all aspects of my photographic work I have sworn by them and their methods of creating the best gear in the industry and their foresight to make it all backward compatible so you don't always have to start over so much as upgrade. Upon meeting the top man one night at a soirée at the Australian Centre for Photography, Nikon/Maxwell loaned me a high-end digital SLR camera body, battery pack, memory cards, zoom lens, flash gun and sync cord – simply everything the Mad Nomads required for their still imagery needs, not to mention cross-compatible with my already built-up kit of professional Nikon film-based cameras and accessories.

A few days later, I popped into Platinum Imaging in Paddington, the only photo processing lab I used for my professional work. Through their generosity, I obtained 65 rolls of professional Fuji transparency film *and* development costs covered! I could – and did – mail the exposed rolls back to the Platinum lab from locations around the country to be picked up upon my return. Things were looking up!

Not long after, and to Craig's delight, Sony Australia loaned us a PD-150 broadcast-quality motion camera, and a small Sydney-based company called A Magnet Force (AMF Magnetics) created two magnetic tags scrawled with "Mad Nomads" and our web address so that as we changed vehicles we could keep advertising ourselves. Alongside this generous stream of corporate approbation, friends of mine would give their own assistance: an Englishman named Will who worked at Ted's Camera Store in central Sydney donated a few photographic bits and bobs to help out; my friend Nick, a multi-tasker whom I met through Newks promotions, donated some DV cassettes to go with our Sony-

Cam and interviewed our team for a weekend broadcast on his community radio show in Bondi Beach; and Craig's mate Broderick, a sole trader who ran his own computer business called Prodigi, came in with some minor equipment and an offer to take care of things when we were incommunicado in far-flung locations of Australia.

The ecstatic feeling evoked by all this sponsorship was felt by all of us: we were simply over the moon and prepared to hit the road with vehemence, having all of this gear, a great concept and only three months to tour as much of this large nation as we could get under us. Our dream of seeing Australia and furthering our own personal creative agendas was coming to blossom in a way we could never have imagined.

But there was a down side to all this. One major Australian company came forward with a home brand of laptop and then, just when the arrangement was all but sealed, the manager ceased all communication with me without explanation and I never got the goods. Both a credit card company and a major bank were enthusiastic, and then just dropped off the face of the earth without a trace or any replies to my emails and calls. Then our website was hit with a virus that placed garbled text everywhere. I had to debug the site page by page, line of code by line of code, and considering that it was thousands of pages and millions of lines of code, it took me almost a fortnight; at the end of it, my eyeballs were nearly hanging on my cheeks.

As well, the Australian Taxation Office was supposed to refund me a significant amount of money that would have been very handy for the trip, but they delayed payment, reassessed me wrongly and then ordered me to pay them a significant amount of money. I filed objections, but bureaucracy held my rightful funds until we hit the road and I could do nothing.

Then the Mad Nomads regrettably learned that Craig – after all his efforts to get producers on board to make a documentary – had his end fall through and would ultimately not join us on the trip for financial reasons. He stayed behind to try and give it a last go, but at the end of the day, worldly events would smother his fundraising endeavours.

Meanwhile, there was a far greater bar of sadness that would descend onto me personally. Across the world, back where I was reared, my godfather, George Pappadatos, lay extremely ill. George was by no means my godfather on paper, rather as a consequence of his presence in my life and more notably in his appearance. His origins were Greek and he actually resembled and acted in manners similar to that of the godfather from the Mafia movies. He had a weathered but handsome face under his thick-rimmed dark glasses, and a slicked-back silver mane graced his head. In gesticulation and character, he kept alive the vestiges of his Mediterranean background: he motioned his messages with ostentatious hand movements and spoke grandly, giving a clear indication that Greek society had coined the democratic system. He had hot blood and a short temper, but could always turn the charm on just as easily.

Since my young days, George had been there, alongside his son Paris, whom I came into acquaintance with at a primary school level in my life. My childhood memories were flooded with George. He taught my brother and I how to drive, we would see him most weekends, he often took us out for ice cream or skiing and we would always watch him launch the most acrid one-sided debates imaginable with the CNN channel. He had worldly intelligence and political theories, and a character like none other I have ever known. When he was 40 years old, he dropped everything to lead safaris in Africa for half a decade, crossing the continent 19 times. Indeed, his life had been a riley one, full of trials and tribulations and global movements. He had truly lived.

At the age of 70, George was still as strong as a bull and described by doctors as having "the heart and lungs of an Olympian." Indeed, he seemed invulnerable, as all men do in children's eyes; he was someone you expected to be around forever. I spoke to George on occasion from Australia when rational international time zones would meet, and he bid that he was proud of me and my endeavours and couldn't wait to see me again.

Then one day, after stubbing his toe and visiting a hospital, doctors would take a very standard blood test and raise eyebrows over the results. Something inexplicable was wrong with his blood and, medically speaking, it was a bold claim for all to hear that his life should have theoretically ended many moons ago. The mystery was singular, as no medical team could guess what ailment he had nor how this particular and fiery man had existed so strongly in body and mind and ignorance of his rare condition.

With great speed, George deteriorated and then passed away, thankfully in a peaceful manner. He was gone forever. At the exact moment when an exciting and hard-earned journey in my life was about to be undertaken, my godfather came to his end briskly and I never got to say goodbye.

It was a hard time.

PHOTOGRAPHY PART I

The Bronte baths

Bondi Beach

The eastern suburbs coastal walk

Sydney Opera House

Sydney Opera House and Harbour Bridge

The drones of Martin Place, CBD

Sydney Opera House and Harbour Bridge

Fire performers on the beach

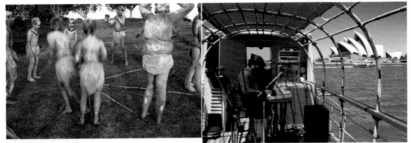

Aboriginal performers at a festival

Riding on an Aboriginal boat in the harbour

View of Darling Harbour and CBD from the Goldsbrough

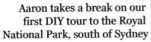

Aaron takes a break on our first DIY tour to the Royal National Park, south of Sydney

Hiking the woods of the
Blue Mountains, DIY tour

Something one doesn't expect:
skiing in the Snowy Mountains
of NSW

Exploring the Lucas Caves,
Jenolan, on a DIY tour

The Hunter Valley, NSW's wine
region, DIY tour

PHOTOGRAPHY PART II

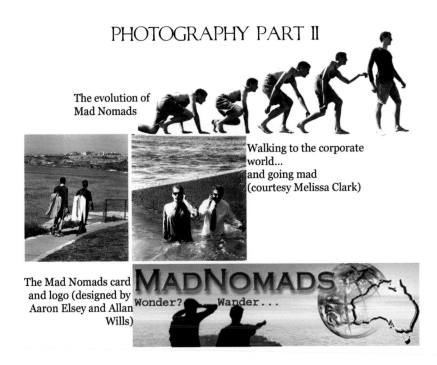

The evolution of
Mad Nomads

Walking to the corporate
world...
and going mad
(courtesy Melissa Clark)

The Mad Nomads card
and logo (designed by
Aaron Elsey and Allan
Wills)

MadNomads
Wonder? Wander...

Gold Sponsors

BLACKSUN

No Boundaries
Britz

Nikon

SONY.

CHAKRA ALLIANCE
PLATINUM IMAGING SERVICES

FUJIFILM

Silver Sponsors

MOTOROLA

amf
magnetics

prodigi

Special thanks:

lonely planet

Mad Nomads was proud to assist:

THE SMITH
FAMILY

Australian Red Cross
BLOOD SERVICE

Sharing life's best gift

The means by which we executed our journey ...

The Britz Nissan Patrol   The Britz Explorer motor home

The Britz Hi-Top   The Britz Elite and Hi-Top

The Britz Adventurer

The Britz Bushcamper

Aaron and Craig unload donations for
the Smith Family charity (Nikon D100)

(L to R): Louise Goldsbury, myself and
Aaron Elsey (Fuji Velvia)

A common site all over the nation;
bushfires and back-burning (Nikon D100)

The charm of small-town Australia
(Fuji Velvia)

The giant pelicans
of Nelson Bay, NSW
(Fuji Provia 100)

The Alma Doepel,
stolen from another
era (Nikon D100)

The Mad Nomads, Bulldog and his plane

View of Port Macquarie from the air
(Fuji Provia 100)

Being welcomed to the Toora
Lions Club, VIC

The CWA: helping communities and
Mad Nomads all over Australia
(Nikon D100)

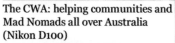

Rural VIC
(Fuji Velvia)

The alpacas, VIC (2nd photo
on Fuji Provia 100)

Sunset over the glens, VIC
(Fuji Velvia)

Wilson's Promenade, VIC (Nikon D100)

Drought in Tasmania

Freycinet NP and Hobart, TAS (Fuji Velvia)

The Tasmanian world of mailboxes and large trees (Nikon D100)

Wineglass Bay and Cradle Mountain, TAS (Fuji Provia 100)

Full moon and sunrise over the Twelve Apostles, VIC (Fuji Velvia)

Stopping along the Great Ocean Road,
VIC (Fuji Provia 100)

Heading into the outback, SA
(Fuji Provia 100)

Sunsets in the outback, SA (Fuji Provia 400)

Seeing faces in the stone at Wilpena
Pound, SA (Fuji Velvia)

The ridges of Wilpena Pound, SA
(Fuji Provia 100)

The Barossa Valley wine region, SA
(Fuji Velvia)

Underground churches, Coober Pedy, SA
(Fuji Provia 100)

Coober Pedy,
including
Hollywood
leftovers, SA
(Nikon D100)

Heading into the red centre,
and the sight of salt lakes, SA and NT
(Fuji Velvia)

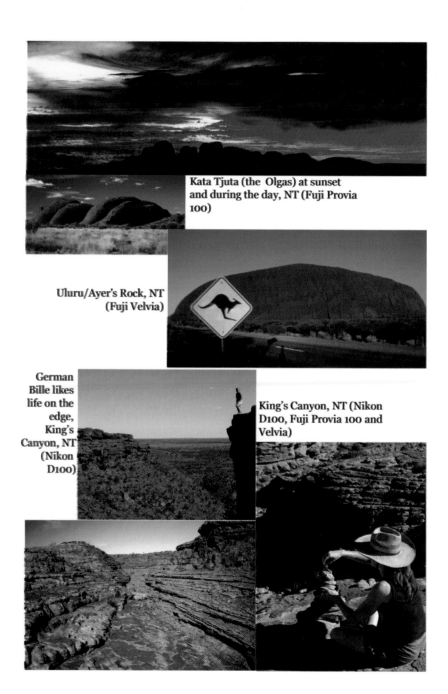

Kata Tjuta (the Olgas) at sunset and during the day, NT (Fuji Provia 100)

Uluru/Ayer's Rock, NT (Fuji Velvia)

German Bille likes life on the edge, King's Canyon, NT (Nikon D100)

King's Canyon, NT (Nikon D100, Fuji Provia 100 and Velvia)

The Devil's Marbles, NT (Fuji Velvia)

Stars over the desert, NT (Fuji Provia 400)

Louise opts for a swag, Alice Springs, NT (Nikon D100)

Rodeo, Katherine, NT (Nikon D100)

The termite mounds of the top end, NT

A billabong, Kakadu National Park, NT (Fuji Velvia)

Bille relaxes in a billabong in Kakadu and the
Mataranka Hot Springs, NT

Residents of Kakadu NP, NT (© Louise Goldsbury, Nikon D100)   (Fuji Provia 400)

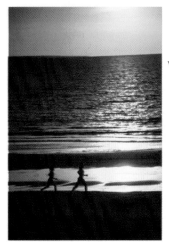

Louise relaxes in
waterfall, Litchfield
National Park, NT
(Fuji Provia 100)

Sunset in Darwin, NT
(Fuji Provia 400)

Buley Rock pools in Litchfield
National Park, NT (Fuji Provia 100)

The Mindle Markets and sunset in Darwin, NT (Nikon
D100 and Fuji Velvia)

PHOTOGRAPHY PART III

The ramshackle streets of Kuta

A popular pastime in Kuta: cockfighting

Final sunrise in Port Macquarie

My last visit to Bondi (photo
courtesy Melissa Clark)

PART II
THE MAD NOMADS
IN SEARCH OF
HINDSIGHT

Where are we going?
Where ever you want
First we see the small
Then we see the big world

– From Goethe's *Faust*

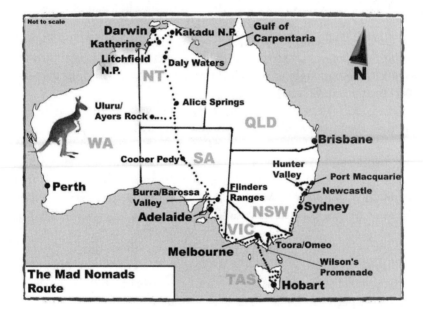

The Mad Nomads
Route

IT IS A near-impossible task not to *wonder*, above all things, how Australia *wandered* to where it is presently – I mean, before James Cook, before the Dutch and the Spaniards and even way before the original Aboriginals, whose descendants would eventually skewer some of them. Little is known about the pre-pre-history of Australia, but one thing seems certain: it has been around almost since the beginning of time, four billion years ago.

There are quite a few books on the subject, most written in pragmatic scientific lingo. Consider for a moment a human lifespan of 80 to 100 years. Most people possess the ability to think back a few years, especially if a summoned memory is vivid, but then again, in the day-to-day routine of life, many more can't remember what they had for breakfast. Now try to stretch your imagination back a number of years with nine zeros in its composition. Go on, try it.

One good read in particular did a very dandy thing for a layman like me: Reg Morrison, author, photographer and documentary filmmaker, wrote *Land Beyond Time: The Four Billion Year Journey of a Continent*, and peppered it full of his illuminating photographs. Technically speaking, Australia is one big fossil; much can be culled from it that might one day lead to numerous discoveries of how life first formed on Earth. Impeding these discoveries, however, are a few obvious factors, including size, the harshness of conditions and the fact that most people are not empirically qualified to recognize what they stumble upon, if they even stumble on anything to begin with. So the task of gaining perfect knowledge about Australia looks impossible, but many things can be deduced to offer a nutshell explanation.

Morrison attempts to reduce 4.6 billion years of Earth's life and creation – 90 percent of which Australia has been around for – into a graspable human diorama: a 24-hour day. So, the Earth begins at midnight and Australia begins at one o'clock, and the present day occurs 23 hours later.

The tale unfolds in the icy voids of space when our solar system was forming. Traces of zircon, the oldest known fragments of the Earth's crust tracing back 4.1 billion years (the Holy Grail of science) were discovered in Western Australia and presently collect dust in a university in Canberra. It would seem that Australia had once extended much further before a cataclysmic shearing came along. Portions possibly lay crumpled and suppressed beneath the mountain wilderness of eastern Tibet, nearly 8,000 kilometres away.

Some of the oldest forms of life, such as 600 million-year-old multi-cellular fossils – from which blood stock for most of the world's animals come from – had remained mostly preserved from alteration, until the Aborigines and Europeans arrived.

It is calculated that the Australian land mass drifts, on average, at the same speed at which a fingernail grows – between three and four centimetres a year. If you rewind at that velocity over three billion years, it results in a total journey of about 100,000 kilometres! Thus – guessing from tectonic postcards – Australia is thought to have visited both poles twice and grown from two crustal blocks into one of the world's major continental units. What a trip!

And, at the risk of debasing science but raising Australian pride, it is thought that sex first took place (*ahem*, scientifically speaking, the act of copulation between two of Earth's first beings) when Australia was young, mingling with the north pole and having a more than serious fling with Antarctica for about a billion years before separating and wandering off. (Antarctica still plays a modern role as the last preserved refuge for such inaugural bonking species). Fifty-three million years ago, the two separated and then Antarctica was bolted to the pole under a new ice age that would doom many of its life forms. Australia escaped with a stock of living cargo. It made its way toward the tropics, leaving the island of Tasmania as the last link and, in a big brother/small brother kind of way, a microcosm of its own, with nature not quite of either mass.

To put some names to this, it is said that all of Earth's present-day continents were at one time clustered together, about 225 million years ago, in one big super-continent called Pangaea. About 180 million years ago, it broke up to form two separate continents, and one of these was Gondwana (a name drawn from Sanskrit), which was comprised of the modern-day Australia, Antarctica, South America, India, Africa and New Zealand. "Clearly these two regions [Australia and Indo-China] were very close and probably contiguous," writes Morrison.

Between then and now, the continent drifted to where it is presently, and it's conjectured to be drifting back toward the Southeast Asian continent as the coasts also erode inland at a rate similar to that of the growth rate of finger nails. Where Australia will end up a long time from now, no one knows, but in some ways this explains why Australians travel so much. It seems to be in their DNA.

29 – Drifting Faster Than Fingernails Grow

FIFTEEN MONTHS HAD passed since my arrival in Sydney, and with joy bubbling in my veins, I acquired the Mad Nomads' first Britz, a throaty Nissan Patrol Turbo-Diesel four-by-four. Aaron, Louise and I had opted to take this vehicle because initially we would have places to stay.

It was with clear admiration that I pulled into the driveway of 258 in the Britz and we placed our AFM Mad Nomads magnets on its sides. The infamous Bondi address bulged with well-wishers and, thanks to Wendy (my recently arrived friend from back home) we had special guest Michael Jackson drop in for a performance! OK, not exactly, but no one was the wiser when we cut the lights and were treated to the divine and precise grooves of Wendy's friend Raddi, who executed a rhythmic routine rivalling that of the glory days of Jackson's past. As part of our Mad Nomads project, we placed out a bin and asked all comers to bring second-hand clothing and other items they didn't need, and soon it overflowed with donations. We concluded with a grand hug, and under a hail of several "See you soons," we got underway the following day, wondering whether we had tied up all our loose ends.

Our first stop was the Smith Family charity, and before the great beaming smile on the clerk's face, we commandeered a cart to transport a few boxes of the donations we had collected on their behalf. With that, we turned north and headed up the Pacific Highway, placing the bustling sights and noises of Sydney safely in our rear-view mirror.

It was the beginning of my second Australian winter as we coasted along the slippery dual carriageway under a sky of slate. I soon learned that the designation "highway" in Australia is rather like the word "hotel," for it could mean many things. There's no guarantee that the term implies pavement or anything over one lane in either direction. The Pacific Highway we were presently on could not have been much wider than the residential street I grew up on. Conversely, there were several upshots of absenteeism that served as blissful rewards: Australian major arteries are also satisfyingly free of the things that make thoroughfares in more populated nations impersonal: huge turnpikes, spaghetti junctions or layered bridges. For the most part, you cruise forever at street level, even in cities, so the feeling is not one of being segmented or walled off from society by concrete barriers, or of feeling minute among a sprawl of six or seven lanes in both directions.

The news was full of war and protest. In many cities across Australia, demonstrations against the federal government joining any coalition against Iraq were rife. In some cases, students cut class to protest and police otherwise had their hands full with pickets against the prime minister.

And, of course, Murphy's law: Just as the Mad Nomads were getting under way, fuel prices spiked.

Nevertheless, the weather and the clammy news served better to heighten than dampen our moods as we arrived on the doorstep of Aaron's mother's home: a comely estate of a warm, wooden interior and a green, lush exterior.

The next day, Aaron showed us around his native Port Macquarie (often referred to just as "Port"). The town was the quintessential representation of Australian coastal life. It was flanked by ocean and green hills, and between the limitless body of azure water and the land stretched strands of immaculate beach and cliff heads. It seemed that no kid was without a surf or boogie board. The harbour area was pristine with boats bobbing gently in the heaving dock areas.

It was be whilst ambling about that we noticed something out of the ordinary, namely the moored vessel *The Alma Doepel*. Its appearance was strange – a grand and curved wooden ship flaunting three spiralling masts and sails replete with cross bars and rope ladders, as well as all the trimmings: a large rudder wheel on the aft, small round windows, ropes and pulleys. Had I drank a beer, I wouldn't have had too much trouble imagining that some bizarre time-displacement vortex had wrongly spat it out near Port, and that pirates might soon spill over the decks with raised swords for pillage and plunder and the sheer pleasure of sealing their captives' fate with a plank walk. Cockatoos would no doubt find shoulders to land on, and their toothless and bearded sea-faring brigand friends only too easy to laugh. Of course, I hadn't had a beer ... yet ... but the *Alma Doepel*'s presence in a modern-day dock with Sea-Doos and up-to-the-minute yachts skimming around was surreal, to say the least.

We will return to subject of the strange vessel in just a bit. Meanwhile, an exciting and contemporary treasure chest awaited us a few paces away at Port's post office. Motorola had come aboard the Mad Nomads project as a silver sponsor and shipped us a hefty box. After we eagerly tore it open, we found inside two Motorola PTX-700 walkie-talkie handsets, batteries and chargers, and a pile of branded pens, mugs, hats and t-shirts. These radios were just what we needed to coordinate ourselves, our photo shoots and video endeavours, and we played with them as Aaron's hometown tour continued.

In 1818, John Oxley was very disappointed with what he had found. After helping to open up the Blue Mountains and the town of Bathurst, he – like others – was still under the impression that a great lake lay in the middle of the continent dividing it into two islands, New Holland and New South Wales. Oxley and his exploratory party, under another mandate from Governor Macquarie, set out to find more pastures inland. They travelled down the Lachlan River through swamps and marshes and arid lands and completely gave up looking for any inland sea. They instead came back through the Great Dividing Range and discovered the fecund Hastings Valley (some of the greatest grazing lands in the world, they say) before giving the name Port Macquarie to a coastal spot 407 kilometres north of Sydney.

Around the same time, a bunch of convicts had commandeered the ship *The Trial* to make a break for freedom and wrecked it near Port, only to be recaptured. The site was called Trial Bay and a prison was immediately erected. One of Governor Macquarie's last acts in office was to make Port Macquarie a penal settlement to which convicts who found life in Sydney a little too easy were sent. In WWI, Trial Bay's prison was used to contain German prisoners; today, it is a museum overlooking a splendorous cove.

This was not my first time in Port Macquarie, but it was my first time exploring it up close. I had been to the suburbs of South West Rocks, Kempsey and Bonny Hills and spent time with my gracious pseudo-family the Grants (Shanni's parents). They treated me like a son and hence I have an affection for the region, having passed holidays there far away from my immediate lineage.

The popularity of Port and its periphery has surged in recent years, with new suburbs and housing units being snapped up by young families and retirees alike who want out of an expensive and stressful Sydney existence. A small town it is no more, for its actual growth rate had been hugely underestimated by early real estate forecasts. Some of the life-long residents we spoke to revealed that Port Mac had indeed become a major swelling dot on the Australian map before their very eyes. One elderly woman spoke of a population of 9,000 in 1960. "Everyone knew everyone," she said. She was bested by her contemporary who boasted,

"It [the population] was only 3,000 when I got here in the late 1940s. Tarree was the main town*." Port Macquarie rang in, at the time of our visit, with a teeming 46,000 residents (add 20,000 more if you consider the surrounding area).

We ambled upon an intersection that was an ill-defined mix of pedestrian walkway and vehicle thoroughfare, with no roundabout or stop sign. Two cars almost brushed and a teenaged driver let loose a barrage of cursing and honking, all of which were layered on top of his already booming stereo, which we had heard long before he made way into sight. He managed to execute all of this while shaking his fist and talking on a cell phone. The other driver, who appeared to be a retired gentleman, looked quite frightened by the onslaught of decibels and didn't know what to do. Junior then gunned his engine impatiently, squealed his tires and sped off down the road with his cloud of din in tow. Some further reading and news would underscore that Port Macquarie was indeed burgeoning with the unwelcome trappings of major cities, including road rage and increased juvenile crime (juvenile criminals, by the way, are called "hoons" by Australians).

"When I was a kid, I could bike a few minutes from town and be in the complete sticks with no one around," said Aaron, himself somewhat saddened by the loud hoon we had just come by. "Now it's all homes for miles."

Animals were feeling the pinch as well, and Aaron took us to the very necessary Koala Hospital, set up by volunteers and donors, and he logged the tale for our website. The intensive care wing was made possible, in fact, by John Williamson. If the name means nothing to you don't worry – he's an Australian country music artist and quite possibly someone I had been in chicken burger commercial with without fully realising. He penned the song "Goodbye Blinky Bill" to raise awareness and funds for the hospital, and one wing bears his name.

The Koala Hospital rehabilitates 150 to 200 koalas a year, and can house up to 90 koalas at a time. The limited resources also stretch to cover lobbying for protection of existing habitat, as well as tree planting and corridor programmes. There are an estimated 2,000 to 8,000 koalas in the Australian wild, and though they're not officially classified as endangered, the population of Australian koalas has dropped by 90 percent in less than a decade thanks mainly to loss of habitat. The cute cuddlies we saw that day appeared well healed on the surface, though

---

* Our Lonely Planet guide opens its introduction of Tarree with, "It's hard to get excited about …"

they had apparently been admitted with injuries stemming from encounters with human contraptions, most notably cars and domestic cats. Our presence did very little to disturb their Yoda-like slumber in the tree tops.

Koalas are of course Australia's most recognized animal next to kangaroos, and they have their own collection of ubiquitous diamond-shaped yellow signs along roads that sling though wooded areas. Contrary to their name, they are not bears, and contrary to what most college kids will tell you, they don't get stoned on eucalypt leaves and tumble half-baked out of trees (that's the cockatoo). They are mammals, related to kangaroos and wombats, but they only *look* like cuddly bears with bloodshot Buddha eyes.

Aaron took us along a wooded path to Harry's Lookout, a cliff top location accessible only by two paths that offers a view over the ocean and the incomparable Shelly's Beach. Harry's Lookout earned its name in the most interesting of fashions, and Aaron told us the tale.

In the 1960s, a man named Harry and his wife won the lottery and immediately gave up all pursuit of remunerative income. They quested for a serene existence away from anything resembling a city and came to Port. Their commode of choice was a caravan, which they parked rather permanently on a grassy spot on the beach just below the lookout. With time, Harry would build a staircase and blaze two trails by his own means so all could enjoy access.

However, as is the nature of all small-town politicians with nothing to do, the council was quick to notice his rent-free situation. But the locals loved Harry and successfully blocked any administrative efforts to compel his disappearance. In time, he was deemed a local treasure, earning the title of "Mayor of Shelly Beach." The municipal ruling body even gave him funds for his lawnmower's petrol so that he could upkeep the area. He became a jovial fixture for dog-walkers and tourists alike, forever present at sunset with wine and obligingly enthusiastic for a chat or a photo.

Sadly, Harry passed on in the 1990s. Shortly after, the council removed his caravan, though they did pay homage by officially naming the spot and erecting wooden statues and picnic tables. The story is no less singular for the fact that he was a man who was rewarded for parking illegally for a very long time. At the very least, it was a demonstration of embracing the disarmingly hearty spirit of this "criminal" man. At the very most, it served to show that Harry picked a great time to check out:

just before the local population, ridiculous Australian court decisions and outrageous fines were all simultaneously on the rise.

Later that evening, we went to visit Aaron's father for dinner. Elsey Sr. (nicknamed Bulldog, but the cute kind) is a fabulous cook, and as we broke bread with him and his girlfriend, it fast became evident from whom Aaron had inherited his wisdom and broad but well-read theories.

At that very moment, eccentricity would invade the peaceful scene. Aaron's mobile rang, and the caller was looking for me. It seemed strange enough, but it got weirder and requires a brief historical backdrop.

A month previous, I was working for Newks during a Valentine's Day promotion at a North Sydney shopping centre. Once again, I was the only male, garbed as a Romeo, and my four rotating co-workers were stunning women clad in flowing red dresses. During the promotion, we were accosted by a woman who wanted to know more about us. She was very upbeat and fast talking, and announced that she had just launched her own promotional agency and would we consider working for her? We told her to call Newks if she wished to book us, though the conversation soon jumped to web design and photography, so I slipped her a card.

I did email her a few times to see about doing some final ad hoc design for her start-up just before the Mad Nomads tour launched, though I never heard from her again – that is, until Aaron's phone rang under the hospices of Bulldog's soirée. How she got Aaron's number was a mystery, but four million people or not, Sydney could be the smallest world at times. The caller never did explain the puzzle, and Aaron claimed he had never heard of her.

She had called to see if I could be an actor in a movie she was apparently getting produced by some big backers. The location was Byron Bay (a famous Australian surf spot in northern NSW) and the scenario a romantic one. The role she insisted I would be perfect for was that of a foreign sky-diving instructor living in an Australian surf town, and she went on to reveal other bits of the plot. The condition of her voice gave me cause to speculate that she was either drunk or heavily self-medicated. She spoke in an accelerated and jittery manner and often jumped topic in mid sentence. I was flattered, though, fanciful delusion on her part or not. I told her that I was otherwise engaged for the next three months, but she further pressed that Aaron had a sexy voice and she could most assuredly find a role for him in her blockbuster.

"I'll be in touch, dah-lings," she said, and a few days later I received a text message inviting me aboard some yacht in Sydney, though she knew

I was far away (or maybe she didn't remember). You can't always escape Sydney, it seems.

The following day, the strung-out phone call was dashed from my mind as we drove to an airfield. Among Bulldog's many talents was that of flight, and he took each of us up in turn in a little two-person Cessna that wasn't much larger than things I used to build as a kid out of Lego. After Louise helped to ease my cameras and I into the passenger seat with a crowbar, Bulldog checked his list of things to do (recorded on a scrap of paper) and executed a smooth take-off. Once way above the ground, I felt like I was in a cardboard box with a kite attached. The shell of the aircraft was so thin that there wasn't much separating me from the air rushing past.

Nevertheless, the skittish behaviour of the miniature plane was placed on the back burner of my mind as I took in the spectacular view of Port Macquarie. Suddenly, the town didn't look so big anymore. It appeared rather insignificant next to the endless coast, beaches stretching over a horizon that seemingly wrapped back around in the other direction. The foamy waves cascaded inland, lending a hint of rhythm and timelessness to the still and verdant tracts of forest and mountains that lead into a misty distance opposite.

The aerial view served to reinforce what I already knew, that blessed is this town for its surroundings. Could Bulldog have tunnelled back through the space-time continuum and bring Governor Macquarie up in the air, I doubt strongly "prison" would ever have been associated with Port.

Thus ended our initial few days, time spent with both physical flight and the strange phone call of a flighty nature. The theme of aviation wasn't over yet, and the next day the Mad Nomads would come into legendary company.

30 – Don't Let Sex Stop You From Getting High

Whether you think you can, or whether you think you can't – you're right.

– (Not sure who said that).

"I WOULDN'T WANT to be in your generation," quipped the woman across the table from us. It was coming up to the ungodly hour of seven in the morning, and it was only recently that we had been ripped from slumber and tumbled from warm beds. Once again, it was cold and rainy outside. Aaron and Louise waited patiently for their coffee and I, not being a coffee drinker, had to rely on my brain to kick in without the benefit of addictive bean-derived agents.

"Your generation has so much competition. We always had a path in life, a chosen career. Now you retrain every few years or months! You study one subject for 10 years, it becomes obsolete and you have to re-train. Crazy! So much pressure from an early age," she went on, while simultaneously chasing an elusive piece of cantaloupe around her plate. The bacon and eggs were coming.

We were seated at a table in a place full of members of Zonta – business women dedicated to bettering the community, of which Aaron's mother was a member. Thanks to mom, the Mad Nomads would hear a grand speech and have a fitting first interview subject for our three-month project: Nancy Bird Walton, a legendary woman who became a disciple of Sir Kingsford Smith, an aviation legend, and spent years flying around the country.

After a bit of club business, the Australian aviation marvel, 88 years young, strode to the podium and delivered an energetic oration about her life. Of course, at any event there's an agenda, and Nancy's dialogue did go overtime; however, the crowd was so absorbed with her enthusiastic stories of heroism, tales of sheer terror, near death and humorous twists that no one cared.

No one, that was, except one Zonta member (no doubt the one who had printed the agenda), and I saw her repeatedly looking nervously at her watch, multiple chins wobbling, then back to Nancy, then to the schedule. Later I would find out that Miss Many-Chins was a notorious clock-hen, the frittish member obsessed with protocol. In the presence of a hero who had come from a time of male domination and who, in 1933 at the age of 17, became the youngest Australian female to gain a pilot's license, it takes a special kind of control freak to jiggle her jowls by tapping her watch.

"There was a magnetic attraction between me and aeroplanes," Nancy told the Zonta crowd. At age 13, Nancy took a joy flight and greased the pilot an extra pound to do aerobatic tricks. That only served to heighten her fever, and she returned home "walking on air." Amazingly enough, her father didn't discourage her from pursuing her love or try to force her into a more "feminine" role for the epoch. With the help of good old dad, she bought her first plane, a Gipsy Moth, the very same plane, coincidentally, that she had had her first thriller ride. A year later, she obtained her commercial license and became the first female in the Commonwealth to fly aeroplanes.

All the fly boys were out and about breaking sky records, so Nancy did something very different indeed to stake her claim in history. She enlisted co-pilot Peg McGillop and together they became somewhat of a tamer *Thelma and Louise* by executing the First Ladies' Flying Tour around outback NSW. By virtue of Peggy's Catholic schooling and connections, they came to board under the roofs of many aristocratic Catholic families, and hence they always had places to "barnstorm." Down the road, the male pilots lodged at pubs.

"We would visit the families, tie the plane to the fence and be wined and dined in these great houses," remarked Nancy. "And all of that without a website," I couldn't help but think to myself. They would industriously subsidize their voyage by charging passengers for brief air tours. Later, Nancy was paid 10 pounds a week to file sky-written articles and advertise the new magazine *Women* (now *Woman's Day*). "I felt like a millionaire," she said. (Today, Woman's Day circulates glossy pages laden with Hollywood gossip and partner-compatibility quizzes that are the bane of all males).

Her second tour was a solo one, and she came under the employment of the Far West Children's Health Scheme. "They saw an opportunity in me," she said. "It was the first medical service provided to women and children in the outback. I was 19 years old and the bank gave me a 12,000-pound loan. I couldn't believe it." The position was that of an essential carrier and mobile baby clinic that flew nurses to and from remote towns. Before the famous Flying Doctors came along, Nancy and her new Leopard acted as an air ambulance when emergencies arose, serving further to give her the title of the first woman to commercially operate an aircraft in Australia.

But it wasn't all glitz and gold, magazines, saving babies and big bank loans. Isolation and lack of resources wore away on her. The subsidies evaporated and Nancy retired from flying, openly declaring to the press that there was "no future in the air for women as pilots."

However, not long after, Nancy was given came to be treated as John Travolta is today (he is a "good will ambassador" for Qantas). She would have an exciting year overseas at the behest of Dutch KLM airlines, who recognized her value and quickly made her a worldly "goodwill ambassador" who jet-setted with numerous dignitaries. In a better, faster metal plane, she soared across Burma, India, Singapore and Indonesia to England, with visits to Germany, Sweden, USSR and America.

When WWII began to brew, Nancy returned to Australia and married, though not without remaining passionately active in aviation. She became the commandante of the NSW branch of the Women's Auxiliary Australian Air Force (their acronym sounds just like a plane: *WAAAF!*). After the war, she took up political employment for several years by joining the Liberal Party, though her true calling was never too far away. In 1949, she formed the Australian Women Pilots Association and as a result, women became more prominent in flight throughout the 1950s, 1960s and 1970s. She was appointed an officer of the Order of the British Empire, and then in 1990, was awarded the Order of Australia for her "service to aviation, particularly the participation of women in aviation."

I of course found out all of the above information well after her speech thanks to Louise, who wrote an article on her.

Nancy concluded her amazing narrative in a manner that is very Australian: she humbly cast the spotlight away from herself and on to the feats of other pilots in the country. "The contribution of Australians has been enormous," she said. "Nobody outside Australia, and not many within, know that Australians pioneered every major ocean in the world in one way or another." It is such an Australian thing to do, to say that the country inspired the feats of the person, and I cannot more aptly describe how proud most are of this wonderful nation. But that hardly is surprising: so much goes on in this country that never makes news elsewhere, or isn't discovered or known altogether.

"Listening to Nancy makes me feel that my life has been nothing but inactivity," said a woman next to me as the applause roared. Clock-hen and her chins butter-balled her way up to the podium, wearing an expression of impatience, and most ignored her in the afterglow of the speech. Nancy signed copies of her aptly titled book, *My God! It's a Woman*, and was then interviewed by the ABC.

That same evening, we attended a dinner with the Zonta members and Nancy Walton. "So, you are the Mad Nomads travelling around Australia in Britz vehicles, are you?" she exclaimed upon shaking our hands and we were all dumbfounded. She was sharper than a tack! So amazing was her memory that in conversation she rattled off names, dates, situations and related facts without pause.

While Aaron continued chatting with Nancy, I spied a fresh plate of hors d'ouevres and magnetically coasted across the room. The quest for free food would prove noteworthy, as I came to shake hands and speak with another character who equally championed vessels. Although his methods of displacement also employed air, he was bound by water. He was Captain Adrian Button of *The Alma Doepel*, the wooden ship stolen from time that we spied on our first day in Port! He did have a beard, but thankfully he spoke modern English, didn't have a large and ill-mannered fowl on his shoulder and, ultimately, wasn't a pirate. (I had had a beer then, as I recall).

"I am now the master of this ship – it's in my care," he said as we simultaneously downed some feta cheese and quaffed a drink. "I am 65 years old and that makes me the youngest ever to hold the position," he continued. "There are barely any people left who are interested enough, or patient enough, to learn how to sail this ship. It isn't worth the time to any of the younger generation. Old vessels are quite complicated. I once tried to train a young bloke, but he was too gung-ho and didn't have the patience. Yep, there aren't many of us old timers left, you know." He then offered us all an invitation to visit him and *Alma* anytime we wanted.

The following morn, then, we strolled out to the dock and once again became transfixed with the mirage-like vision of the ancient ship and Captain Button in full uniform and with his grey beard, sailor hat and naval attire. It looked as if he might have a crewmember on board whose forearms might bulge if he inhaled a can of spinach. We were ushered onboard and allowed to amble about. I tried to make heads and tails of all the roping and masts, but succeeded only in confusing myself more. Before me stood technology that required vast knowledge and intuition and a crew to command. They didn't have a GPS or satellites, just the open sea and a sixth sense earned only over a lifetime.

The ship was named Alma for the builder's daughter, and launched in 1903. In Australian tradition, the ship had gone through many careers, from setting racing records, to the transport of raw goods, to WWII service in Papua New Guinea as a de-rigged troop carrier. In 2002, she came to occupy the post of Port Macquarie tourist attraction.

A crew of young cadets requested permission to come onboard, so the three of us left and stumbled back into the 21st century. With all of this air and water travel, it was somewhat disorienting to amble back into our road-constrained Britz. We put in a visit to the beach-front home of the Shanni's parents and then bid farewell and thanks to all and headed inland to the Hunter Valley ...

... Where we had some dancing girls and wine waiting for us.

31 – Reunion With Tea and Scones

TO THE CHAGRIN of the United Nations Security Council, President Bush was telling many opposing nations that he would be storming Iraq to depose Saddam Hussein. Last-minute stop tactics were not faring well.

As we coasted inland, we left the ocean behind and came to the celebrated dale-ridden Hunter Valley wine region. En route, Aaron shivered at the sight of the dark and lonely Maitland train station where he had spent those long and nerve-racking moments surrounded by dubious tobacco-seeking youth. But Aaron and my DIY history with the Hunter Valley thankfully didn't taint the present, and a strange turn of events involving dancing girls would lead to the narrative I am about to present. Once again, we go back in time several months ...

It was a case of six degrees of separation. Through the Australian Centre for Photography, I was sourced by the University of Sydney's Canadian/Australian Studies Department to chat about living in Australia and being a photographer. I was asked if I would be willing to go, all expenses paid, to Canberra and do a presentation. But it was not to be. The powers in that scorned capital had stipulated that they wanted an academic, or someone in that circle, and certainly I didn't qualify.

It ended up, however, that a trip to the Hunter Valley did result, at the behest of the Country Women's Association (CWA*), for at the same time, they were studying Canada and wanted a presenter. I invited Aaron, and the two us boarded for a weekend with Fay (regional cultural officer) and her husband, Tim, at their swank abode in Bolwarrah, near Maitland. The couple had recently retired and sold their B&B operation, though by their graces showed they still had the touch.

Tim and Fay fed Aaron and I like kings and gave us a little tour of the region. The following day, we were ushered into a community church where 130 CWA women were in attendance among a décor that paid homage to Canada. Some were dressed as Mounties, others as natives, posters of the major landmarks adorned the walls and there were more flags than I dare count. I was warmly received, gave a quick talk and was rewarded with two bottles of local wine. During the discourse, I

---

* The CWA was founded in Sydney in 1922 at same time as the Smith Family. It is largely a rural organization of women dedicated to bettering their communities. In 2003, for the first time ever, a man took over as its president.

announced that Aaron and I both desired to see Australia and at the conclusion, ladies were running up to us both and swelling our pockets with addresses and phone numbers of people to stay with.

To our delight, there was no shortage of the sandwich and fruit plates that only grandmas can make, and we ate heartily among the swarm. Many of them informed me that their children and grandchildren were off living in Alberta or Whistler or Vail or the state of Washington, and did I know them? Did I have news of them? Surely I knew Jacob: he's a liftie at the Creekside chairlift in Whistler? Good bloke, I was assured. How about Melanie? She teachers snowboarding to kids on Blackcomb? Sadly, I knew none of their travelling offspring, though they delighted in telling me all about them, as all good mothers and grandmothers do.

We eventually resumed our seats and the little stage lit up. Each chapter of the CWA from neighbouring areas played out skits, read poems, did stand-up routines, danced, lip-synced and sang. Although I'm not talking Hollywood special effects here (rather, tape players that didn't work, cardboard cut-outs that represented things and a lot of ingenuity in costumes), the show delivered. It was easy to forget that many of these ladies were grandmothers as they performed with the energy of kids who had eaten too much sugar. The finale was a tap-dancing extravaganza that was so spot on it looked as if they had trained for years! They even had judges and awards, including a trophy cup and some silver serving plates.

When the day concluded, Fay whisked Aaron and me back to her place in Tim's old Jaguar (which he had earlier proudly pointed out had the modern feature of automatic windows), but along the way, the car fizzled to a stop on a lonesome country road. Fay wasn't pleased initially about being left to drive Tim's Jag, so you can imagine how she felt when it died en route. While waiting for roadside assistance, we noticed bands of kangaroos bounding over the valleys around us as the setting sun cast the famous golden Australian glow. Once back at the ranch, we watched Fay prepare the dog house for Tim while we assembled our stuff for departure. (I am joking, of course: she made *him* get the belt ... Oops, there I go again!)

"Before I met Fay, I was in every dog fight in town," said Tim, wonderstruck that his Jag had failed. "Then I met Fay and settled down and we had three kids before we realized what was causing it."

Fast-forward and presently the two of us were there again – some seven months later – with a Britz vehicle and Louise, under the Mad Nomads standard. Fay had been very helpful by giving us CWA information in our nomadic search for accommodation, and once again we were treated to plump country beds and succulent meals at their comely estate.

We awayed to a CWA meeting at Muswellbrooke in search of leads and people to interview. Once again, I found myself standing before a crowd of women, a microphone in my hand and their attention on me. As I spoke about our project, the room came alive with chatter, points of order, ideas, contacts and stories. At lunch break, the patented CWA sandwiches, pastries and fruit came gliding out on trays and between delicious mouthfuls, the three of us jotted down names, addresses and ideas. It was a flood!

I will declare now that I love small towns and country life. Quite frankly, having lived in big cities for so long, I had forgotten that there are still places stuck in time. You see, I foolishly locked the keys in our Britz so I hung my head in sheepish shame and headed back to the CWA's hall to admit my grand stupidity to everyone. But on the way, I met an electrician who afforded me a small-town "G'day, how ya going?"

"Not good," I replied and after I admitted my grave blunder, he quickly advised that his mate ran the local NRMA (roadside assistance) and was simply around the next lane. I wandered not 50 metres to find a garage and a friendly bloke who was heading out for a distress call. He grabbed his sidekick, a young oil-covered teenager fiddling with an engine, and they managed to get into our truck and retrieve the keys.

Our team left the comforts and culinary feats of Tim and Fay to accept the invitation of another CWA member to stay on her farm not far from Nelson's Bay. As we headed through wine country, the ranches grew sparser and time turned back as we passed general stores that looked as though they'd been stolen from old Western movies. We felt like the Beverly Nomad-Billies as we coasted down a dirt road, passing fields where copious cars and tractors came to die, to arrive at a gorgeous two-storey home by a creek. Therein was CWA member Janet on the Cromarty family plot, located in a place called Bob's Farm (yes, that's actually the name of the area). As we coasted out that way, the news on the radio made it clear that War in Iraq II was starting to look inevitable.

On advice, we barrelled off to visit Nelson Bay, which was out of this world. The beaches were serene and I could not believe my eyes when I saw the coastal locals: pelicans on steroids! I know things are bigger in Australia, but this was ridiculous. They were almost three-quarters my stature and probably had wing spans greater than Bulldog's plane, not to mention strange eyes in yellow frames and beaks that were about half a metre long. In fact, they were so outlandish in bulk that Louise had a phobia of them – and she ain't scared of much. They were milling around some fishermen who were cleaning and de-gutting their catch. After watching the sun set on the beach, we headed back to the farm under the cover of darkness, only to be impeached in our journey by a driveway of idle and cud-chewing cows. They eventually ambled on and we made it home for a good old fashioned home-cooked meal.

The next day we were told that an expanse of sand dunes lay nearby, and because we were driving a four-by-four, we naturally thought, "When in Rome ..." The day before, I had sunk our tires on a beach, and thankfully we learned a very necessary couple of off-roading tid-bits from a friendly Aussie before getting underway again.

"Mate, ya didn't lock ya wheels or deflate the tires! No bloody wonda!" he stammered as he fixed the problem and delivered the Britz from the boggy sand. The properties of sand are unique, don't you know, and turned out to be more complicated than I thought.

Once we found the entrance to the dunes, Louise was first to try her hand. The sensation of dune-bashing is not unlike being in a hovercraft over sand. You just kind of glide and float. Soon progressive caution gave way to letting rip, and floating turned to bumping and bouncing and *yeeehaaasss*. Louise left the marked trails and blazed her own in virgin sand. Later, she would write this for the website: "We were so in control, in an out-of-control sort of way!"

The Patrol handled beautifully for Aaron, as well, and then it was my turn. I smote everyone's joy in one swift and stupid bungle. If you haven't noticed already, there are several themes in this book, one of which is my inability to make correct assumptions in Australia and another, the necessity for me to learn things the hard way. The assumption of which I write presently was another grand chalk-up on the long list. All of this buoyancy and glimmering sand made me instinctively feel as if I were driving on ice and snow. It looked the same to me: it glistened, it shimmied, it formed into wind-swept gullies and little eddies spun grains in the air. So I thought a little gliding handbrake turn would impress the crew, like I used to do back home in wintry parking lots.

I planted us halfway to China.

We sank gently right into a cushion of dune. Then I remembered, a little too late, why we used sand for traction in snow. Aaron and Louise were not impressed, not impressed by the sand up to the bumper nor, least of all, by the realization that we had no shovels save our arms.

Thankfully, we managed to make our way out, but I opted not to drive for awhile. We all thought that best.

Later that day, over tea and scones, we spoke to Ross Cromarty, a 94-year-old who told us stories of his time working on planes during World War II. We then thanked the Hendersons and headed to Wauchope (pronounced War-hope, though don't ask me why), a sleepy town that used to rely heavily on the timber industry.

As a result of the Bali bombings and in the months leading up to Australia joining the US coalition threatening to enter Iraq, images on TV of armour-clad men toting machine guns with skimming red laser beams in training to be "Australia's Elite Anti-terrorism Unit" were something more than a tad frightening.

Members of Parliament seemed oddly inexperienced as they debated and grappled with enacting new anti-terrorism laws that tried to prevent too much encroachment on civil liberties. The feds undertook an initiative that was coldly received by most citizens: they mailed out millions of brochures on the subject of terrorism to Australian homes. Many citizens saw this as an opportunity to protest and simply scrawled "Return to Sender" on the brochures, which effectively blocked up the mail system (yet did no justice for landfills).

The *Sun Herald* published an article entitled "Easy-Going Aussie Under Threat." It was quip, stating, "60 percent of those surveyed believed Australia's classic, relaxed way of life has been changed forever." A large part of the conclusion was based on the Bali bombings, which it called "a moment of lost innocence for Australia."

But getting that terrorism brochure in the post was a welcome change for Nora, who during World War II lived in Townsville, 1,367 kilometres north of Brisbane in Queensland. In those days, she and others would send their children to school with a government-recommended homemade kit consisting of a large sheet of brown paper, a few turfs of cotton wool and a clothes peg. Sound a bit different? It certainly struck us as such.

Nora, 87 years old, spoke to us from her home and remarked that the kit was there in case of a Japanese air raid. "Every day before school, I had to make sure my kids had a big sheet of brown paper, which was for putting over themselves if they had to crouch down and blend into the ground, a wooden clothes peg to bite down on if a bomb was dropped, and cotton wool for putting in their ears. It was very frightening for them." Nora had three little ones to worry about when, in July of 1942, the dread became reality and Townsville was targeted*.

"It was 12 o'clock at night when the siren went," said Nora. "My family and I were sleeping. I know it was silly, but the first thing I did was turn the light on, which we weren't supposed to do at all. I suddenly realized that and switched it off. We had to run out the front of the flats where we were living and through a café to get to the trenches, which were all open and full of sand. The American Negro soldiers were there, and our own soldiers, and all the people from the flats. The trenches were so quiet you could hear a pin drop. We could hear the drumming of the planes and people were looking up at the sky when a big cloud passed over the stars. 'Look! Duck down!' they said. 'They're coming in droves!' But it was just a cloud going over. Then, in no time after, they dropped three bombs – two went off, one didn't. They were aiming for the oil tanks along the coastline. They dropped one 300 yards from us, and there was dirt and flames everywhere in the air. Oh, I'd never seen anything like it in my life!"

Fortune would play out, and by virtue of a miscalculation the bombers missed their mark.

"Luckily, the tide was out," Nora explained. "Had the tide been in, it would've been a direct hit on the oil tanks and I wouldn't be sitting here today. None of my family would be here; everything would be gone."

Her sentiment toward US forces and their protection of Australia was equally strong. "There were thousands of Americans here for us, especially American Negroes, and I'm sure a lot of people forget that. I was in the thick of it, I know what the Americans did for the war. If we hadn't had them behind us, Australia would be a lot worse off."

When asked about present times, Nora lamented that many younger people are unaware that Australia was ever attacked. "A lot of people won't believe Townsville was bombed. A terrible lot don't even know Darwin was bombed," she said. "Young people can't be ignorant of these sorts of things. Instead of going to these riots and protests, they should be told what happened in Townsville and Darwin. These young ones today don't want America to go to war now, but they have no idea, they don't know what war is like. My children know what it's like. It's a dreadful thing."

---

* In all, the towns of Broome, Derby, Drysdale, the Port headland and Wyndham in WA and Mossman and Townsville in QLD were bombed, but the worst to have been bombed were Darwin, Katherine and Milingimbi in the NT.

It certainly was a strange tale to hear, especially given the contemporary context and youthful attitudes toward a history in which Australia had indeed been attacked as recently as 60 years previous. Had many people indeed already forgotten? Or, like me, did they sometimes act with good intention and end up thoroughly planted deep in sand with regretful afterthoughts?

32 – Conflicting Aussies

History is the version of past events that people have decided to agree upon.

– Napoleon Bonaparte

AT THIS STAGE I had read a few books on Australia's involvement in wars. For a small country, its always done more than could be reasonably asked for little official credit.

The earliest conflict was the 1886 war in Sudan, and since then Australia has put troops into the Boer War, both World Wars, the Korean conflict, the Malayan Emergency, Indonesia's confrontation with Singapore, the Vietnam War, Iraq War I – Desert Storm and East Timor, to name only a few.

In WWI – with a population of only five million people – over 415,000 (or about 10 times the current army) of all Australian men between the ages of 18 and 45 eagerly bounded up to enrol in WWI's only volunteer corps. Of that amount, four-fifths took to the field and a staggering 65 percent of them were killed, wounded or taken prisoner. Of the 60,000-plus fatalities, nearly half lost their lives in seven weeks, during the disastrous Somme campaign of 1916. For comparative purposes, Australia lost one man in five in that campaign, while the British lost one in 10.

The most firmly etched moment in the Australian psyche is the WWI Gallipoli campaign, when Australia had more casualties than any other nation. 75,000 allied troops (of which almost half were Australia and New Zealand Army Corps – or "Anzacs") were dispatched to seize Constantinople (presently Istanbul). Many of the Anzacs were being thrown into battle for the first time. The well-armed and well-entrenched Turks fought vehemently to defend their homeland and smote 10,100 Anzac lives and wounded a further 24,000.

And casualty statistics weren't all that were abysmal: so, too, were the conditions. In the height of the summer, 200 Anzacs a day were evacuated from grubby and cold trenches with all forms of sickness and disease and exhaustion. It was indeed one of Australia's saddest moments.

I did, however, manage to read one story that made me smile – that of the last important cavalry charge in history. In 1917, Australian cavalier soldiers and their brethren were in dire need of water, as well as being part of a larger campaign to capture the Turkish stronghold of Beersheba in Palestine (now Israel). Two light horse regiments – one from Victoria and the other from NSW – consisting of 800 mounted men, simply got on their horses and charged in staggered rows across three kilometres of flat terrain, directly toward the well-entrenched enemy.

The adversary opened fire with their arsenal of machine guns, rifles and other artillery, even an aircraft, at the on-rushers, who were wielding their bayonets like swords for maximum effect. The intrepid Aussies gained their objective and plunged into trenches to engage the very surprised Turks in hand-to-hand combat. The Turks lost 60 of their own that day and another 730 surrendered. For their part, the cavalier Aussies suffered 31 dead and 36 injured (no stats on the horses).

WWII would prove no more favourable for the young and overly ambitious nation. Australia sent over half a million troops to help her allies in Europe, of which over 23,000 came home wounded, and 39,000 never came home at all. As Hughes put it, many Australians felt that "having been shipped out of Britain as criminals, they were shipped back as cannon fodder; so that, when peace came, the survivors could return to their real mission as Australians – growing cheap wool and wheat for England."

What was more immediately domestically frightening was that Japan had captured much of Asia (including parts of then Australian territory Papua New Guinea) and Japanese bombers delivered payloads along the top lip of Australia, while submarines slid into Sydney Harbour to shell a Naval craft and lob shells into Bondi.

An American/Australian initiative turned the tide at the Battle of the Coral Sea and Prime Minister Curtin announced,

> ... I make it quite clear that Australia looks to America free of any pangs as to our traditional links on kinship with the United Kingdom ... we shall exert all our energies toward the shaping of a plan, with the United States as its keystone ...

The Vietnam War came about at the time when many Australians were becoming somewhat perplexed about their allegiances in the wider world. It was then that Prime Minister Whitlam pulled Australia out of Vietnam, quashed obligatory national service and set about making Australia a cross-breed communist/capitalist nation, just when the hand of the Queen of England dissolved his tenure by proxy in 1975.

Australians have since played mainly peace-keeping and clean-up crew roles, earning much distinction for their reconnaissance prowess.

* * *

As you might imagine, to read any material on war is to get lost in a conflicting myriad of political, economic, social and statistical smoke and mirrors. But for Jasmine, 71, another interviewee courtesy of CWA referral, war wasn't all bad news. In fact, it brought childhood joy.

Jasmine's mother, Margaret, one of 19 children, came to Australia from London on the advice of her physician. Her nerves were wracked by WWI, for she had lost a fiancé and had borne witness to the horrifying deaths of friends and family in the crowded English air raid shelters during German bombings. The doctor's remedy for her anxiety was clear cut: take up smoking and move away from England. Margaret took that advice, started puffing and moved to Perth, WA, where she had a cousin.

For employment purposes, she moved to the extremely remote town of Onslow, WA, population 30 plus her, located in the baking desert. So small was Onslow that when she arrived her first sights were of camels, because the town was being moved. She would eventually meet and marry John, a pioneer whose business with his father in Adelaide had made him and his brother broke; they had headed for the searing hot north to find work and clear debts. John and his brother changed occupation regularly until they took a lease on a sheep-sheering station 27 miles from Onslow. Two boys and two girls, the third youngest being Jasmine, came into the picture.

The station of her youth and the surrounding area were, according to Jasmine, "very hot, barren, dry and desolate." It covered 162,388 square acres and was regularly whipped by winds of 100°F. (Onslow's major claim to fame is that it was the location where the fastest and strongest wind in Australia was recorded: 246 kilometres per hour in 1975). The photos she showed us reinforced the words: parched red earth and arid scrub – true roasting Australian outback.

A one-way trip from their station to Onslow took three hours in their old truck. As a result, Jasmine rarely attended school, though she completed grades one to three in only one year. Her class was taught by a 14-year-old senior surrogate because the teacher had fallen prey to typhoid. She was then taught by correspondence, which involved the arduous process of having assignments mailed, administered by mother, mailed back for marking and then returned. The mailman came once a month. Supplies, such as butter, would come their way only once every three. You do the math.

"Growing up there was wonderful," remarked Jasmine, to the Mad Nomads' mild surprise. "We used to play desert games and chase snakes.

We found things to do." (Maybe it' just me, but my ideas of fun are far removed from chasing the most venomous slithering creatures on the planet; but, hey, I guess you have to do something). Work was a priority over school, so Jasmine and siblings learned the sheep-shearing trade.

From 1926 to 1944, as if this picture wasn't already one of toughness, a decade-long drought and two massive floods were of the order, forcing the family to live in the shearing quarters while they constructed their homestead on higher ground. All around them (and we're talking areas the size of countries), neighbouring stations were being foreclosed by banks and returned to the government as crown land. The sole income of Jasmine's family was sheep-shearing, and despite the hardships, Jasmine's father – who possessed a talent for building concrete tanks – was able to keep the station running by storing water in his tanks when it was made available.

During the war years, outback stations were required to identify and report any aircraft (friend or foe) that flew over their space. Consider that there was no two-way radio or telephone and the trek to town was three hours by vehicle. Consider also that the family got war news on the receiver radio, which they ran for two hours a day off the battery of the old truck. John, who had a chart of the world, would listen to the reports and plot the progress of the war in Europe with inserted pins. If they were lucky, the children were allowed to listen to the one-hour radio program *Blue Hills*.

There was a procedure put forth by the government of the day regarding air raids in the outback: evacuate stations by word of mouth. Papa John had converted one of his concrete water tanks into a makeshift bunker, complete with sandbags, back-up supplies and beds. However, Mama Margaret, who, you will recall, had a stark traumatic abhorrence for anything trench-like, refused to take her children there and would instead rush them into the surrounding sand dunes. The bunker became a play area.

John filed his station financial reports against the grim backdrop of his neighbours (who didn't have his skill with water tanks), and given the state of the land, bank agents didn't believe what they read and tried to foreclose on the station. A court battle ensued and the bank lost, then appealed to a higher court. While trying to get to the proceedings with his defensive evidence, another flood blocked John's route, and as a result, he lost the station and had to move the family to Onslow with their only remaining possessions: the old truck and 50 pounds. The year was 1942, and John had just turned 60 and had five mouths other than his own to feed.

Jasmine was 10 years old at the time, and she told us that the war years, despite the other factors, were quite enjoyable. Onslow had swollen to eight times its population with an infusion of American troops. Exmouth Gulf, a distance away, had been established as an American naval and air force centre and Onslow became a ship and submarine servicing point. The Americans commandeered the Great Hall and some homes for their operations, and also established a tent city.

Shearing quarters in the town became boys' and girls' quarters, and the children all played together as never before due to their previous isolation from one another. They would run off into the desert, play bush games, climb trees and persist in the ludicrous enterprise of chasing snakes while mums packed their lunches. The American soldiers played games with them on the beach and news of war never trickled to the seen-but-not-heard children.

In total, four air raids went over Onslow, though there were a great deal more alarms. Blaring sirens would often raise the call and every chink of light had to be extinguished. The only place that had electricity was the Great Hall: everyone else had lamps and torches. All forms of correspondence were censored, thus army boys and citizens alike read mail with gaping chunks cut out of them.

We interviewed Jasmine in her rural NSW home. She had left that lifestyle long ago to pursue various work around Australia. She did a stint for the Australian Tax Office in Melbourne, but in those days, once a woman married she was forced to quit work to remain at home. Only war widows got positions, though temporary ones.

At the time we were speaking to Jasmine, protests and calls to avert the war in Iraq were in high gear across Australia. People were wearing "No hoWARd" shirts, but things were seeming very inevitable. Thanking Jasmine for her tale, we moved on to Cessnock, where we did some community radio interviews with a CWA member and met Brian Andrews, the local historian.

We learned that the Hunter Valley was a region that had had its share of heavy recruitment and wartime losses, mostly in France. In the early years of WWI, there was such conviction of rapid victory that men departed from a northwest location of NSW and marched for 500 miles to nearby Maitland to collect conscripts, who were billeted along the way by town folk. It was kind of Mad Nomadic, come to think of it. The event was billed as The March of The Wallabies, and two battalions of men enlisted and headed to war by ship.

Casualties mounted beyond belief and the dire need for replacement troops surged. Between 1914 and 1916, the population of the Hunter Valley (including Newcastle, Maitland, Kurri Kurri and Cessnock) was 10,000, just over half of them women. 1,800 troops from the area never came home. The figure of losing half of your men, then, is grave indeed.

But Australians do have the capacity for humour in dismal situations. As the contemporary news offered that Australians were not receiving Prime Minister Howard's decision to back America in its Iraq II efforts, Brian told us a humorous regional tale to lighten the mood, an incident that I dubbed "The First Act of Australian Financial Terrorism."

During WWII, there were four old hotels in the nearby town of Kurri Kurri run by a gentleman named "Joe." As a measure to raise funds for WWII, the Australian government issued bonds and encouraged people to buy them from the local banks. Because Joe ran drinking saloons, he collected his revenues mostly in coin form and had to allow space in his cellar to stack his profits. One day, he walked up to the bank with bags full of coins and purchased a 100-pound bond in equivalent coppers. There were 240 coppers to a pound, thus bank tellers had to make sure that 24,000 coins were indeed present for the exchange. They were not happy, but had no recourse.

The next week, Joe returned to the bank (with help) to purchase a 300-pound government bond in the same manner. The bank was obviously less enthralled with the deposit of 72,000 coins, but were equally bound by tender law and ancient accounting systems. Needless to say, the amount of time spent counting and ledgering everything did very little for the war effort, and thus a man was able to protest war by supporting it.

With that, the Mad Nomads made for Newcastle at a time when some protestors in Sydney began the deplorable practice of throwing golf balls under the hooves of police horses during demonstrations in order to "help" the anti-war sentiment. I respect the right to protest – but to harm animals in the process? Such people, I think, deserve to be left in the baking desert with poisonous snakes and no lunches.

33 – Gutsy Art

NEWCASTLE (WITH A population, including the Hunter area, nearing 590,000) is still acridly seen as a dirty industrial town. In 1804, it was called Coal River and dubbed "Hell in New South Wales" by Sydney's most obdurate convicts, who had been deposited there so that the nice convicts could be left alone. In 1915, BHP Iron and Steel Works opened, and for many it was the sole source of remuneration and the only reason to live there. Then in 1997, the steel operation clammed up, and two years later (or 16 years short of a centenary celebration), BHP packed up and left altogether. Newcastle immediately went into a huge slump.

Aside from an earthquake it suffered in 1989 that damaged property and killed 12 people, Newcastle is today a thriving coastal university town with a trendy arts scene. There are said to be more artists there per capita than anywhere else in Australia, as well as lots of home-grown musical talent and splendorous beaches – and the wine region is just in their backyard. Nevertheless, it is hard not to notice, beyond the beautiful bikinied babes, a smokestack or two spewing smoulder in the distance.

Thanks to a phone call from Fay, we arranged a visit with Newcastle legend Anne Von Bertouche, a well-known local with a vast collection of art and paintings. At the time of our arrival, she had bequeathed her collection to the Newcastle Regional Art Gallery, a legacy that enthused the town, the gallery and the art community to no end. As we walked up the driveway to her homestead, she flung open the door and before we could say a word, ushered us to the back entrance. She pointed to a small, handwritten paper sign that contained the underlined words "No WAR." Having made her mute statement, she sat us down in the beautifully decorated home-studio in which she lived.

From the outset, she commanded the interview (possibly because she was very hard of hearing) and right away stated the following:

"To my mind, the present state of the world is appalling. Murder and mayhem and stand-over and greed, wanting the oil. No war. My feeling about art works is that they are really the most important things in the whole world – creative work, the work of one person's hand and one person's imagination, something that didn't exist before and is brought into being by one person. It is the only one in the whole world – whether a painting, a drawing, a poem, a piece of music. The creative work is the important thing in the world because it represents the person, the individual, of whatever race, of whatever age. The person has created something that did not exist before. And everything else, such as the thought of war, is so appalling and so abhorrent. My collection of artwork, which I have gradually acquired over the years, I am so happy to bequeath to the Newcastle Region Art Gallery, because there it will be public property and people can go to look at it: it will be theirs."

Anne and her late husband dropped out of administrative work in Tasmania to pursue hippy lifestyles of writing and painting. A decade later, they moved to Newcastle and opened an art gallery shortly before buying out a building set to be demolished and revamping it to become a bigger gallery and home.

And what a beautiful home! Diffused light streamed in from an A-frame roof, and the whole interior permeated a peaceful, secluded atmosphere – perfect for viewing or creating art. It looked in some ways like a little cobblestone alleyway in Europe, but with a roof over it.

Anne's lifetime collection was actually on exhibit at the Newcastle Art Gallery down the road, and so after our interview, we dropped in to have a look. It was impressive, but then I was informed that the exhibition space (about the size of my high school gymnasium) was hung with only 120 of her best, and that amounted to but one-third of her total collection! If there's one thing you could accuse Anne of, it was good taste. All the works were obviously the product of great talent, conveying substance and depth. Her inspiration for the grand donation to Newcastle Gallery had been born early on, when her father took her there as a child and told her: "[The art works] are ours, you can't take them home, but you can come here everyday and look at them because they *are* ours; you don't have to pay."

Later, when the Mad Nomads were far away in another portion of the country, we would learn that Anne Von Bertouche (who was in her 90s) had passed away. Her massive art collection was then handed over to the city of Newcastle, and we felt privileged to have met her while we could.

After our interview with her that day, we steered south again and headed back to Sydney, where we would become entangled with scandal and a strange hippy.

34 – Pulling Teeth

PRESIDENT BUSH GAVE Saddam Hussein 48 hours to turn himself in or "Face the consequences." The United Nations pulled their inspectors out of Iraq.

Coming back to Sydney was an overloading experience, as country gave way to concrete. After the string of adventures, home-cooked meals, fresh air, characters and wide-open spaces, the gridlock and noise was quite the culture shock, even if we had only been away a little over a week. Blend with that the deep and fascinating stories we had gathered thus far, and coming back to the fickle and mindless mayhem of Australia's biggest city was like suddenly being distracted from a really good book. Instantly, my thoughts were dashed as I contended with all the diversions. Louise was scheduled to have her wisdom teeth removed, an appointment made prior to the Mad Nomads project, and she joked that our search for wisdom and hindsight had to come back this way, anyhow.

During the 1960s and 1970s, when the Vietnam War was the focus of America's eye, there was invariably much public backlash, draft-dodging and protesting. An unforgettable quote comes from an unforgettable man – famed boxer Muhammad Ali. At the time, he was fighting an adamant and symbolic out-of-the-ring battle with the US government not to be drafted and sent overseas as a soldier. When asked by a reporter if he knew what and where Vietnam was, the spry-eyed boxing poet replied, "Sure I do, it's on TV." No truer words could be spoken, for thanks to advances in photography and film that could be shipped back in time for the evening news, Vietnam also came to be known as the first-ever "Lounge Chair War."

Since then, the trend and technology have continued. People all over the world tuned in for streaming updates on Iraq War I (which featured gritty aerial shots from bombers), and the hunt for Osama Bin Laden and his operatives in Afghanistan. And then it happened again, just as we washed up on Louise's father's doorstep in Sydney: Iraq War II, The Search For Something, was launched. It had been a long time since the others and I had stared at a TV, and there in the living room the coverage began on the tube. Perpetually on screen was this one image of Baghdad, overlooking a portion of the city that was apparently about to be subjected to "bunker busters." Were it not for the trickling and impish movement of vehicles along some of the roads in the frame, the image could otherwise have been a still photograph. Along the bottom and sides of the screen trailed an overload of information announcing that Australia had committed 2,000 troops, or about 0.06 percent of the total allied forces. Over this were the voices of a correspondent and the main news anchor, and they seemed to be running out of things to say.

"I believe that was the same car that just circled the block, Bob," said the correspondent.

"Maybe he was lost," commented the anchor. "I got lost once on a street and went around it twice," he added helpfully.

All the news channels carried this one camera angle with their own commentators over top. It was an O.J. Simpson trial rip-off: second-by-second analysis, expert opinions, predictions, statistics and reviews, but ultimately no action. It was worse than watching an Australian cricket match. Oddly enough, our immediate local sphere of reality was eerily mirroring the global goings-on.

Aaron and I dropped in on 258 Bondi to say hello, and things were in a right tizzy of tribal skirmishes. Aaron had long joked that he would make a great dictator, but humour is often based on truth: since our departure, leadership had broken down and anarchy reined among the newly instilled regime of residents. There were millions of stories coming from the mouths of our friends over deals and side deals and who was staying and who was paying what and what about getting bond money back?

Then there was the contentious issue of the latest phone bill, heavy with the balance of a three-digit integer, and no one was jumping up quickly to claim their portion. The real victim in all of this would have to have been Matt, who, much like the UN, was good enough to hold onto the lease and let people stay, despite his departure for a new life. An act of espionage led the landlord to discover the situation, resulting in a notice of eviction because too many people were living there. 258 Bondi, like Iraq, had a deadline on its occupants to get the hell out.

Of course, none of the in-fighting and gossip had anything to do with me, or Aaron. We had absolved ourselves of the place when we left it in the hands of the new clannish governments. Nevertheless, we couldn't help but be privy to a shelling of opinions and a bombardment of back-stabbing and phone calls.

But then, like in all war times, a hippy would come along to make the Mad Nomads laugh in these true moments of madness.

* * *

A few months previous, when he was seeking sponsorship for his branch of the project, Craig had placed an ad in *Metro Screen* (a Paddington circular) for a documentary cameraman. While Louise, Aaron and I were in the Hunter Valley, both Craig and I received numerous emails and calls from a respondent named Roger, who claimed that he "liked our ethos." Both in our written and spoken encounters with him, it soon became blazingly apparent to Craig and me that Roger was a few exposures short of a full roll of film.

"I have just had a natter with Craig," said Roger in a heavy and drumbling English accent when we established phone contact, "and I am very excited about your Mad Nomads. Perhaps we could, how shall I say, combine creative forces?"

Soon after, I found my email inbox riddled with his messages, which were composed in the most curious and scattered manner. He wrote in a fashion of real-time dialogue, as if we were having a live chat instead of a ping-pong email session. Ideas flowed from him, and it was out of sheer curiosity that we agreed to meet Roger upon our return to Sydney. It would turn out to be a much-needed moment of insanity in the terse air of the destabilizing forces playing out in Iraq and Bondi.

Louise, Aaron and I met him on the porch of the now-beleaguered 258, a safe and public place to meet any nut, in our opinion. We took stabs at guessing what he looked like based on the emails and jumpy conversations I had had with him. Turns out we weren't too far off the mark in thinking he was some kind of older hippy.

"I just drove up from Bundeena, where I live. Delightful to meet you all," he said upon introduction. Bundeena is part of the Royal National Park south of Sydney, and indeed this man looked as though he had just been ejected from the bush and the concrete level in Bondi might be a bit much for him. He was classically unkempt and raffish. He had aged and Hulk Hogan–like leathery brown skin that had never known sunscreen, brightly coloured garb and dirty feet as callous as elephant hide. He also had a wild and straying glint in his eye, an uncertain jump in his mannerisms (*Seinfeld* fans: think Kramer) and a capricious beard that made clear that his occupied mind had kept his hand at a wanton distance from a razor.

I can't in all honesty record here that we all actually "discussed" anything with Roger, for it was more like a one-way stream of consciousness that was uncertain of its direction.

Roger was in the business of "healing" (read: experimental medicine and alternative herbs and stretching and massage and such). In conversation, we learned that he had served in the British military and in the Middle East years ago, but obviously something had happened to derail him. He was also the self-professed innovator of "Reality A/V," an intricate method of filming documentaries. While simultaneously passing around loose papers of his credentials (printed in the most deplorable ink-jet colour schemes and with heavily pixelated photos), Roger spoke in tangents we couldn't follow. He wanted badly to be part of the Mad Nomads as a cameraman, and said that we should combine efforts and have "Mad Nomads, (plural) plus ONE Mad ... Nomad (singular)." One of his sheets even reflected his concepts.

"We need to stand up to the media lapdogs in chains," he cried passionately, fire in his eyes. "We need to create, to destroy the corporate mindset. We need Mad Nomads, plus ONE Mad ... Nomad, and it should all be done in Reality A/V."

"Roger," I interjected in a rare pause, "don't forget that we're sponsored by a number of corporations. Our project is one of seeking understanding and hindsight in troubled times, not what you're talking about. We have responsibilities to the people who gave us gear."

"Right! Exactly!" he said in a moment of clarity. "I follow you ... I could *follow* you! Yes. Around Australia. In my car. Meet up at certain points and get footage with my unique A/V Reality style," he replied, and presently his hands took to flaring about. "Even if the car breaks down, it could be part of it. Yes. True Nomads. We could show those media lapdogs, those pigs in power! Mad Nomads, plus ONE Mad ... Nomad! Brilliant! I absolutely love your ethos ... your aura, your vibe. I feel the energy."

No matter what we said, Roger somehow thought he was part of the plot. We would reiterate what we were all about, and somehow he would bring it back to the "hideous and overbearing system" that we were destined to expose and overthrow. Bless him, for he was a kindred spirit, but he just didn't get it.

Then we dared to ask the question, "What is Reality A/V, anyhow?" We weren't prepared for what happened next. Roger burst up as though lightning had struck and vaulted his sinewy frame into standing position on the wooden bench of the porch. His body and mind moved in a free and detached form, though sometimes there seemed to be agreement between the two to convey a united message. As he spoke, his limbs glided through the air like octopus tentacles.

"Most cameramen and media lapdogs film from a distance, you see," he pontificated friskily from his new elevated position. "Scripted, prompted, you see, far from the heart of the subject. They don't provoke, they can't reveal, they are scripted and directed. I get into it! *I* provoke! I run up and ask direct questions. I draw a person out of their shell. I make the camera part of me, brilliant, yes, part of my arm, part of my being!" he continued in a physical crescendo. He was defiantly building to something.

"Like this one time at a festival in Bundeena, there were these dancers performing as animals," he said as he took on beastie manifestations. "The press were in their allocated gallery, their chains, you see, but I went up on stage with my camera in one hand and my whole body doing the EMU DANCE!"

Then it happened: Roger was dancing somehow with one leg in the air, one hand pretending to hold a camcorder and the other hand in the shape of an emu head thrusting jerkily forward and backward as if grabbing air seeds. Louise, Aaron and I looked at each other, and it was obvious that we were all restraining nervous laughter at the sight of this leathery hippy prancing around like a high-minded Australian flightless bird with a camcorder, but Roger, bless his heart, just kept going, lost in the moment.

"Emu dance! Emu dance! No one knows that I am filming. I capture reality! Reality A/V! Yes, the true reality. Not like those programmed media!" he crowed.

How we managed to remain polite by not bursting out I will put down to strict astonishment and straight-up dumbfoundedness. To my mind – and later we would all agree – Roger was the type of guy who would be good to have a beer with, a long yarn, share some jokes, spend some time by Bundeena Beach with his "herbal medicine" in a non-committal sort of way. From a strict business point of view, we could certainly not assimilate him into the Mad Nomads trip: he would have been quite the liability.

I imagined what that might be like, even putting aside his ungainly appearance. All too easily did I conjure scenarios of sitting down with some dear elderly woman in the quiet comfort of her own home, willing to share a tale of hindsight with the Mad Nomads plus one, and Roger suddenly ploughing into her with some awkward question, or worse yet, having to bring the woman to hospital (in our Britz with evident logos) with injuries stemming from an unchecked and stray emu jab.

We promised to stay in touch and possibly drop by Bundeena, but after that Roger drifted slowly out of our lives ... sort of.

We instead took Jody into our fold, a travelling friend of mine from Whistler, who fused her petrol money to ours for the trip to Melbourne. Together, the four of us prepared to head away from Sydney and down the southern NSW coastline. (As it turned out, Louise had made a mistake. She didn't have to have her wisdom teeth pulled, her appointment was just a check-up, so we hadn't *really* had to come back to Sydney). The rest of the trip would be a lot different than our initial week. All the home-cooked meals and warm beds we enjoyed in the hospices of friends and family in Port Macquarie and the Hunter Valley would not continue; instead, our accommodation took on a more mobile form.

We returned to the Britz depot with our beloved Nissan Patrol and swapped it in for a four-berth, 3.4 metre-high Explorer Motor Home! The Britz people think of everything. In our new mobile home was a shower, toilet, four beds, full kitchen (including gas stove and microwave) and lounge area. But that wasn't all: sleeping bags, pillows, towels and a full range of pots, pans, cutlery and, yes, even a toaster were all part of their ethos. All we needed were our clothes and gear.

The Mad Nomads PLUS Jody left the hullabaloo of Sydney and the media lapdogs behind and headed for the open road. Indeed, when travelling at a safe distance from the redundant flicker of the CNN channel or the crumbling regimes of Iraq and the 258 Bondi tribes, the world did seem a better place. To boot, we were treated to a gorgeous sunset as we barrelled south past Bundeena, and we made absolutely sure that Roger was not a reality upon our tail.

35 – Smouldering Shrinkage

THE STATE OF NSW was known as "the shrinking state." Parallels between Australia's most populated region and that of the same in the US – California – no doubt exist. Aside from the immediate allusions one might make about a gold rush pioneer past, surfing culture, wine-making, long-lasting cars, the movie industry, litigation patterns and fact that you can ski and suntan in the same day, it is surmised that the NSW coastline is also eroding, and might even get chomped off all together.

I once read an article about a man in the US state of Arizona who was selling beach-front property on the premise that California would eventually fall into the ocean. If I remember correctly, he had some sucker ... uh ... *success* with his prophetic doomsday real estate endeavours.

Similarly, there are theories circulating that global warming might stir a titanic tidal wave – known as a "tsunami" – in the South Pacific. It could possibly head toward the Boomerang Coast and crash terminally 250 kilometres inland. If this holds true, then Canberra might one day also have beach-front property, so maybe the forefathers did exercise foresight, after all, in choosing the presently disdained location for a capital. You will be happy to know that I came across no parallel real estate scams while I was in Australia, but because things are five to 10 years backorward, consider yourselves warned if *you* one day become a gullible property prospector.

"So is why is NSW shrinking?" I wondered aloud to myself (as I often do when I write). One-third of the Australian population lives in NSW, and two-thirds of them are in Sydney – and both figures are on the rise. I then thought that perhaps it referred to the shrink in Christianity. The real reason, however, is that the designation used to be the name for almost all of Australia. When Cook named his discovery New South Wales, it covered the Gulf of Carpentaria to Tasmania and all the way inland to New Holland. When the First Fleet came, it grew to include as far west as the centre of the country. But over time, each colony established itself and took more and more away from it, the last severed appendage being the Australian Capital Territory. Thus, NSW presently stands as the appellative for the fourth largest state, covering only a tenth of the continent. Even at that, it is still roughly seven times the size of the UK and has an estimated 1,900 kilometres of pristine coastline.

By all accounts, NSW seems the most blessed of all the states in Australian federation. It is the most temperate and geographically diverse. There is baking-hot outback and ski hills, sundry forests, the Blue Mountains and endless beaches, as well as the lion's share of pasturelands along the fertile Boomerang Coast.

I was reading all about the state while relaxing on a beach where we had decided to stop a few days to recover from Sydney. We had taken in the picturesque Jervis Bay before barrelling south to Narooma, a not-too-touristy little seaside town where we chanced upon a quiet caravan park next to a beachy paradise. It was so nice, in fact, that we couldn't resist staying another day, so we did.

It wasn't the warmest time of year to be swimming in the ocean, but sure enough, people were. Before me, a man wearing Speedos presently emerged. Why any man would wear Speedos – which in Australia are aptly called "dick-stickers" or "grape cups" – in the first place is beyond me, and most sincerely in frigid water the advantageous puffiness of boardy shorts could surely not be ignored, but there you have it. Unfortunately there are actually quite a few Australian males who commit the faux pas, even in fashion-savvy Bondi, so maybe there was a whole other credible reason for naming NSW the shrinking state.

My moment of anatomical consideration was thankfully short-lived, for I was soon to up and explore the surroundings more thoroughly with the three others. The azure ocean and teeming vistas of Narooma were second to none, and aside from the Speedo man and few others, we had the beach to ourselves. This solitude lent itself well to exploration, and we ambled over incredible coastal terrain, rock formations containing numerous little jacuzzi-like pools and caves, passing one rock hole that was in the shape of Australia (or a dolphin, according to some locals). We stayed high and walked along a golf course at the edge of the world before coming into the town of Narooma. The bay area bragged a few bobbing boats, some oyster farmers and fishermen with their customary fan club of outsized pelicans. From a distance, we even spotted the fins of dolphins and some lazy seals lying on their flanks, enjoying the ocean currents.

Having refreshed ourselves, we climbed back into our Britz and drove for the "Mexican border," which is what the residents of shrinking NSW call the diminutive state of Victoria, because it's south, shares a telephone area code with Tasmania and hence is "second class." But I don't think so. I like to think of Victoria as the "No Bullshit" state. (Presently, Victorian license plates are inscribed with the words "The place to be," which is also the slogan for some municipal libraries. Other VIC plates have inscribed "On the move," which many joke is short for "On the move to NSW.")

Victoria is the smallest mainland state – covering 3 percent of Australia, roughly the size of Great Britain – and home to one-third of total Australian population; three-quarters of Victorians live in the centrally located Melbourne area.

Victoria began life as its own colony in 1851 and then joined the Commonwealth of Australia in 1901. I call it the No Bullshit State because though it's small, it doesn't have all the other useless things the other big Australian states have, such as endless desert and murderous outback. Almost all of its area is inhabitable or useable to some degree. Within a day, you can hit a wine region, canoe, ski or visit the beach, so it's kind of like a small Europe.

Our road went inland, drawing us away from the sparkling waters of the ocean and hurling us into farmlands. We rolled over hills that were dashed with lone trees and scattered boulders, past paddock after paddock of cows and horses and their tell-tale whiff. We had travelled back in time again, once more passing ancient farmhouses, old rusty yet sturdy trucks and men wearing overalls. Strange turn-offs offered roads to tantalizing locations such as Croajingolong, Noorinbee, Narrabarra or Murrungowar.

The towns we coasted through posted populations of 100 to 300 citizens, and had all the trimmings: old-fashioned general store, court house, post office and people who nodded to each other, not to mention petrol stations that pumped fuel through curved jukebox-like apparatus and rung up totals in Las Vegas–style spinning numbers. One town had a set of traffic lights, and let me tell you that we had contentedly forgotten those existed in all our country driving – what a feeling! Our path advertised koalas and kangaroos on the familiar yellow diamond signs and, sadly, the mangled, car-impacted bodies of these creatures strewn roadside attested that they were in fact abundant, but not streetwise.

There is no shortage of evidence that Victoria abounds in natural beauty, but the trade-off is that the weather is moody and colder. Sweaters were most often necessary and it seemed as if clouds thought Victoria was "*the* place to be." Soon, however, indicators that Victorian nature can be harsh availed themselves upon us, as well. Signs alerting people to the dangers of flooding became apparent and large vertical rulers with increments up to two metres above road level stood along the highway.

As we pressed further into the "Garden State," the scenery ahead of us appeared as though hidden behind a giant sheet of tracing paper, the sun filtering through in tell-tale eerie gold and orange hues. The smells of crisp air were replaced by the wafts of burning trees and we came into a place where bushfires and back-burning were still very much ongoing and real.

We scrutinized our Lonely Planet guidebook for a caravan park and made for a town with the creative name of Lakes Entrance in the south. Imagine a street near a river, lined with nothing save motels and caravan parks and tawdry mini-putts bearing some of the cheesiest and tackiest concentration of fronts I think I have ever seen in one location. It seemed the town's whole existence was geared toward the transient tourists, or possibly a place where unnecessarily vibrant paint was disposed of on all buildings. We rolled into a caravan park at dusk, cooked dinner and made for bed.

Don't let my initial description of the town detract from the actual area; it is quite pretty. The next day we meandered about the river front where lots of black swans were putting on shows in murky water that appeared too low. It was evident that drought had struck hard even this far south, in an area known for its lakes. We then crested a sand dune to stumble onto the beautiful 90-mile beach, which bends off over the horizon so you can't see either end.

Our business lay elsewhere, though, and we headed away from the lakes to effect an interview in Swift's Creek, a blink-and-miss town just south of Omeo (pop. 300). The area had been heavily affected by the bushfires and drought. The region had at one time been one of the roughest gold-mining towns during the 1851 rush, but now serves as an entrance for hikers to surrounding bush land and mountains. The one-lane highway snaked into the hills and we passed some pristine wilderness along some very tight curves, which someone had actually named Pig and Whistle and Jews Pinch.

Although we spied a small fire here and there, the massive amount of smoke we saw over the hills was apparently back-burning efforts ... but one never knows. A sign displayed what one would think impossible, "Road closure may occur due to snow," and only added to the sensation that this is a tough area where snow and fire can coexist and damage as one. We arrived in Swift's Creek under golden light and pulled up in front of the Uniting Church, where we were supposed to interview another CWA lead, but instead bantered with her husband.

Reverend Robert, a minister in rural Victoria and NSW, has been a fire marshal for over 40 years in a district that spans 500 by 200 kilometres. Weeks before the present interview, the area around Omeo and Swift's Creek had burned for three months straight.

"We didn't know what day of the week it was; we started in January and counted up to day 56. It wasn't until the end of the fire that we suddenly realized it was March and we'd been fighting fire for a quarter of the year already," Robert said.

For the most part, Robert didn't actually believe that the fires were deliberately set. In the strange world of Australian bush, lightning was more likely the culprit, striking a fuel-heavy area. In the seemingly endless tracts of land, Robert confirmed that it is indeed impossible to predict how big some fires get, not to mention how tangled any administration is in how to deal with them. Some people believe that it is an act of God.

"I believe in a higher power, of course," said the minister, "but I don't know if God intervenes in quite that way. This is a natural event. The problem is lack of back burning."

And mad things do result. "If you get close enough, it will cook you. People die fighting fires," he remarked grimly. "Visibility got down to less than 20 metres, and for two whole months the sun was just a red dot in the sky. We were sitting under smoke from horizon to horizon. It got so dark that even the chooks [chickens] went to bed!"

Despite being one of Victoria's worst fires, the brunt of the damage was done to crown land or forested areas, though freehold regions (pasture, outbuildings, fodder, haystacks and livestock) were not spared.

"It was a miracle no human life was lost," said the minister. He commented that some people lost homesteads and, worst yet, most if not all of their livestock.

In assuming the tandem role as a minister of God and a fireman, he further stated that many people "are furious and will never forgive you; others understand it fully." He said, "It's a bit hard to think rationally when your house has just been destroyed and the fire tanker isn't there."

Often it is simply a case of too few resources for too many fires. "If there are more houses burning than you have tankers," he said, "How do you weigh it? An injured fireman is no good to anyone. And a dead fireman is a total waste of resources."

And his buck doesn't stop there, for even after vanquishing a fire there is no rest for him. He puts down his hose and picks up his bible, and then the healing process of getting people over the shock of their charring ordeals begins. He provides personal visits to homes and community groups and observes many cases of stress, depression, forgetfulness and changes in sleeping and eating regimes.

"After the fire, you sit down and think about the rest of your life; where it goes from here?"

He went on to say that very few people have come to him to seek guidance from the church, but he is not surprised. To live in the region, you must be comfortable with isolation. Aid does come through in government and fundraising initiatives, from organisations such as the Lion's Club, Apex and other such groups.

Behind the minister was a set of maps with red markings to show current blazes. "It's under control now and everything is fairly well contained," he said, "but there's a lot of bush that hasn't been burnt and it's still dry. There's a lot of ground fuel so another lightning strike could start up another fire, even this late in the year."

Given the cloudy state of Victoria, that wasn't all too unlikely.

It certainly added a new slant to things as we thanked the minister and drove back south again. The *Book of Australian Facts* pegged the seventh and eighth placings in a top-10 list of disasters as bush fire catastrophes. On "Ash Wednesday," 1983, 72 people lost their lives in 64 blazes pressed by 100 kilometre-per-hour winds that ravaged parts of Victoria and South Australia. In 1939, 71 lives and 1,000 homes were lost to bushfires just east of Melbourne. Not mentioned (because no one died) was a fire in 1985 that burned out an area in Victoria equivalent in size to Yosemite National Park in the US.

Now, about 600 bush fires a year burn through Victoria's bush and national parks.

As we left, I thought much about reverend Robert's closing remarks. "I notice there's [a fire] down south that's a long way from the others ... so we're on edge again, listening out for the sirens. We're not out of danger yet."

36 – Melt Down

CHALK UP ANOTHER wonder in Australian business practices, one that even shocked Louise and Aaron. Consider for a moment our present lifestyle: we had our home on our back and would drive well into the dusk hours to cover empty kilometres. By the time we reached a destination, the darkness did little to help us know where the hell we were. In fact, popular Australian singer John Williamson wrote a song called *Old Farts in Caravan Parks* about the "grey nomads" – retirees in motor homes with all the time in the world to escape Victorian winters and kick up dust without worry. So we knew we weren't the only ones.

Trade case study: if you were running a caravan park, what would be your peak hours and how would you staff your business? Hardly a taxing business question, I know, but would you believe that most shut their doors at six in the evening? We were flabbergasted by this, and time after time along the journey, across all the states we touched, we would roll up to caravan parks at eight or nine o'clock, cash in hand, and find no one to let us in. Some offered you the opportunity to call ahead and they would wait, but when remoteness prompts no mobile phone reception, the problem becomes obvious. In most instances, once we hit a remote town under the pitch black of country nights, we had little choice but to find an inconspicuous and non-official location to park and sleep. We lacked options, you see.

We were rewarded sometimes for ignorant night plot-staking. Grace did favour us occasionally with a beach, a river with kayakers, sand dunes and, in one instance, some beautiful wetlands in Gippsland, South Victoria. Yet chance wasn't always on our side when we stumbled out in the mornings to realize things looked quite different in the daytime.

In one situation, we awoke to realize that we were blocking someone's home. Another morning showed us that we had parked next to a pub. Our crowning moment came in questing for a roadside toilet facility to accommodate our female companions. We couldn't find one and under cover of dark pulled into a place that looked full of other caravans. Poor Louise and Jody would have to bush it, finding a tree to crouch behind with the jumpy cone of a flashlight, but with the wonderful luminosity of a new day, we realized we had parked only metres from a children's playground, and a perfectly good toilet block lay just beyond that*!

---

* If you are wondering why we didn't use our motor home toilet, it was because whoever used it was obliged to clean the holding tray after.

To add salt to our wounds, there was an apple orchard yonder, and I had gone to bed hungry for want of a snack. To make matters worse, all other caravans had taken off, which left us with a lot of 'splaining to do if a police officer had decided to include our provisional parcel in his or her patrol.

You would think that such a staple in the Australia tourism industry would at least be a little more practical. Certainly by sight we were not the only ones who didn't wish to be tied down early when plenty of klicks could still be clocked. Then Louise pointed out that perhaps the idea was to encourage all caravans to hunker down before dark.

"Why would that be practical? Less kangaroos killed?" I asked her musingly.

"Yeah, maybe. Or maybe because children are tired of coming to their favourite playground and finding some camper's shit laid in dark ignorance in their sand box," she replied.

She did have a point, you know.

Well, the smell certainly became a reality in the next segment of the hindsight voyage. By invitation from a branch of the Lion's Club (affiliated with the CWA), we headed for the town of Toora in south-central Victoria. The region looked so much like Ireland or Scotland that I half expected to see a leprechaun or a roaming bagpiper filling the emerald dales with his wailing notes. It was so out of place in my mind, because I was expecting Australia to be mostly brown hues, but there we were in a hilly zone of verdant glens, upon which were farms and animals with their farmy whiff.

We slung our Britz into the hills and noticed huge spiralling white windmills. Indeed, the place was windy and cloudy, typical Victorian weather, but at least this region took advantage for the ends of creating energy.

Our hosts were Graham and Irmela, who at one time ran a caravan and camping operation on their property, the Warrarra Bushland Retreat. A sign at the entrance informed us that due to the out-of-reasonable-control cost of public insurance liability, they had been forced to close 18 months previous. We parked our home in a treed camp spot and plugged in to the functional but unkempt site. We then took off to explore the highlands by foot. All visuals pointed to sheer rural life: signs warning that stock crossing the road had priority and mailboxes were fashioned from buckets, cauldrons and even milk kegs. Old trucks and car chassis were being swallowed with time and neglect back into the earth. One rotting auto carcass was even rigged to be compost container.

Graham and Irmela's farm was a nice one, with goats and sheep running around and the clucks of chickens in the background. Graham's massive shed looked to contain more old cars, boats, tractors, bikes and tools (among them a pitch fork and some old farm apparatus) than a lifetime would allow to organize. In the centre of the property was a weeping willow tree hung over a small lake that was besieged by bulrushes, and a red canoe.

We hiked to nearby Agnes Falls, which is listed as being Victoria's highest cascade of water, but were molested en route. Along the way was a seemingly endless supply of blackberry bushes (one of the worst land-consuming weeds ever to be introduced to Australia) and wild apple trees. We gorged on the free food and promised ourselves we would return with Britz and bags the day following.

We were lucky there were no police around, for we were rather circumspect upon reaching Agnes Falls, owing to our orgy of fruit munching. Our hands looked to be fresh from the scene of a bloody murder and our limbs were scratched from thorny struggles to get the fat berries at the back. I allow that I am a man of few vices, but free blackberries and sour apples is one of them. It wasn't long before I ingested more apples than humanly possible and my stomach turned into a bubbling cauldron of volcanic activity.

Agnes Falls was nice, but nothing spectacular. It seemed very dry (due to drought of course) and was actually hard to see as it trickled into an angled chasm. We hiked back home, but I was soon waylaid and separated from the others and would arrive home much later ... The apples called to me!

Then I noticed that I was being watched. By cows. Yes, cows. Whenever I walked past a pasture, they would cease whatever it was they were doing (always one of two things: eating grass or shooting out what used to be grass) and give me that "cow stare." Their eyes were spaced far on either side of their heads and sometimes wisps of drool seemed to find wind to string onto in an alarmingly free fashion. When I realized that I would not be winning any staring competitions with them, I disengaged myself and went on my merry way.

The Toora Lion's Club threw a BBQ in honour of the Mad Nomads visiting their area and we gathered under the shelter of a large tin-roof shack housing a beer fridge, chairs and tables, gas barbecue and a crackling fireplace. It was there that we regaled and drank away with a grand turn-out of well-wishing locals and farmers. They all brought platters and we satiated ourselves to capacity on their healthy and naturally grown foodstuffs. One kind farmer even brought us a huge jug of fresh cow's milk, which found a good home on our morning cereal for days to come.

Pieter (a Dutch-Aussie farmer with a heck of a strange accent), armed with a silver goblet of grog, called Louise, Aaron and I over to pin Lion's Club badges on us and welcome us to the fold. When the munch was over, we all sat around the fire and heard Banjo Patterson* poems recited by local farmer Bruce. We met many ladies, as well, and made some connections for Mad Nomad interviews, which we followed up on in the days to come.

The evening continued in such a fashion as to cause the pile of empty beer cans to exponentially exceed those that were full. Eventually, however, even in my two-beer-induced state of wandering vision, I noticed the crowd thinning, as wives found husbands' ears to pull and whisper reminders into. I have no doubt that for some of the boys, it was probably the most action they had had in years. Sitting with the lads, beers in hand, telling old yarns to new ears, more beers, hearing someone with a different accent, giving him beers, making the world seem a simpler place, be*hic*ers – what more could you ask for? One farmer did require lifting from his seat, but the others dutifully found their feet, albeit swayingly, and looked back at our intimate semi-circle with wistful gazes as they were whisked off by the wives. (To be fair, people in their line of work do have to rise at five o'clock.)

The fresh milk and air helped clear our heads the following day and we headed into the little town of Toora, in the valley. When I say little, I mean only a few streets: one main one, and not much else. There were crooked facades and sinking pickets, and were it not for the presence of asphalt and cars, one could picture horses tethered outside the pub. The Bank of Victoria building on the main street looked as if Ned Kelly might come storming out of it any minute, and our Lonely Planet guide dubbed Toora "the town that time forgot."

We took the time to appreciate the area, and in driving around, we passed the irresistible Poop Fellow Me Creek. Despite the name, the country is unquestionably fresh and vigorous, and there is also quite an air of honesty. Out front of many a homestead were containers or little cleared areas holding pumpkins, apples, oranges, flowers, fertilizer, worms for fishing, knitted clothing and other curious affairs for sale.

---

* One of Australia's most celebrated poets, most notably for his piece "The Man From Snowy River."

Forever unguarded, these small posts of entrepreneurial endeavour operated on the honour system, which seemed never to be in question. Take something and just leave the money in an unlocked box, mate; no worries. Thankfully, none of them seemed to be going out of business due to crime – a comforting thought, these days.

Then, on one day in particular, while I was strolling at sunset in the hills with my camera and tripod, I dropped my cable shutter release along the way. That evening, I returned to Graham and Irmela's estate cussing the loss of this vital piece of gear in the vast expanse of knolls. To my absolute surprise, they produced my cable and said that someone had found it! I can't begin to point out what a literal needle in a haystack finding my small cable was, not to mention having someone know where to find me and, even then, to follow it up by returning it! Say what you may about how backward and stuck in time rural communities are: their redemptive benefits are beyond reproach.

By invitation, we visited Bruce's farm, where his wife, Catherine, had a project of raising a strange bunch. Louise thought it would make a great interview (despite the fact that the couple were far from elderly), and that it did.

Catherine was English in origin, but had married Bruce the Victorian farmer and set her heart on the delightful small-town ranch life. She showed us a strange sight: a pack of Alpacas – tall animals with long necks that looked very out of place in the green hills of Victoria. An Alpaca looks much like a llama, but is actually part of the camel family, its ancestry rooted in Chile.

Sick of cows, Catherine got what she called her Alpaca "starter package" – two pregnant females and an infant – and soon two more followed. They were an odd-looking bunch of creatures, to say the least. Alpacas have large bulging eyes, but the pupil is a mere slit. They do look odd when they are shorn, and one of them had such a tuft of hair on her head that I immediately thought of Buckwheat or Macy Gray. But like all animals, the babies always look so cute and puffy and cuddly.

The four of us quite enjoyed watching the farm kids play with these animals, and our ears perked when Catherine talked about the Alpaca mating ritual.

"The male comes making his chortling noise," she said, "and if she's receptive, she'll sit down and he'll mount her for about 15 minutes, chortling away the whole time ... that noise has something to do with making her ovulate. After a week or so, you bring the male back to her and if she's conceived, she'll spit at him!"

Strangely familiar, I thought to myself. But one can't blame the gal, for if he does his loud job correctly, she's up for an 11-month pregnancy.

"They give birth in the daylight hours," Catherine continued, "around about midday, very civilized. Only about 7 percent have a difficult birth. Half the time you don't even know it's happened. You go out and check them and half an hour later you come back and there it is, there's a baby."

The fleece of an Alpaca (softer than sheep's wool) is a prized commodity, for it can be made into carpets, jumpers, hats and even a wedding dress or veil derived from the felt.

The price of an Alpaca has dropped markedly of late. Louise grinned large when Catherine told us that males are worth a lot less than females, but, as reflected in the human world, the role of the male has changed significantly in recent years. Owing to the fact that they will stomp on any fox they see, their services as a flock protector have become very welcome, indeed. And don't assume that they are all brains and no brawn.

"There was a case where people had to leave their farm because the fires were coming and when they came back they couldn't find their sheep," said Catherine. "They thought they had all burned. It turned out their Alpacas had led the whole flock right over the back, down to the river, and they were all safe."

Tit for tat: it was my time to smile at Louise when it was revealed that Alpacas are the very antithesis of Sydney women: low maintenance. You clean them, you feed them, you mate them, you shear them and trim their feet. Point.

As we stood there, I really appreciated the rural life, for it truly is quite peaceful. Fresh air, honest folk and good, old-fashioned work. Sadly though, rural Australia is facing the world-wide trend of diminishing numbers and runners to the cities. And there is an alarming thought in all of that: the people who are being put out of business and whose communities are being whittled away are those who know how to grow food and rotate crops. Enter, as a small alternative, the Alpaca, who was the new-guard source of protection and bushfire patrol. Thanking Bruce and Catherine, we took our leave for the next interview.

"We need to get back to basics," was Eva's advice when we asked her what she had to say to the younger generation in these troubled times.

"I think I am lucky to have had the upbringing I did, because we had to be self-reliant."

Eva has been in the Welshpool area (down the road from Toora) all her life, watching through time as her town changed from being prosperous to being forgotten, as industry moved away, taking the youth with it. We interviewed her at a hall where she was cleaning dishes and helping the ladies out.

"The youth often leave for Melbourne looking for work, as there are no opportunities for them here," she said while drying her hands. "Everything has to be done by the older folk, which gets harder every year, of course. Once that person retires, the business shuts down and the town dies a little more."

Although only a child during WWII, Eva has some very unique memories, the likes of which none of us had ever heard. She recalled that the children of the town would collect scrap metal, such as the aluminium foil caps off bottles, tubes and toothpaste containers and take them to school every week. This raw material was then collected by the government and sent off to Melbourne to be melted down and made into ammunition! (Had I dropped my cable shutter release in 1942, it would no doubt have served the same purpose – as an implement of shooting – but in a way that took lives instead of pictures).

As abstract as that may be, it certainly is sobering to think that recycling can actually be deadly.

"[The war] was so far away we were not in danger of being bombed," Eva continued. "As a child, it was more exciting. Mine sweepers used to operate out of the harbour, clearing mines laid by Japanese submarines in Bass Strait [the water channel that separates Victoria and Tasmania]."

But she pointed out that the real danger to Welshpool and surroundings in 1942 wasn't the Japanese: at the time when they had the least men-folk, a tremendous bushfire swept through and smote the town heavily.

"We were lucky," said Eva; "the fire did not get us, but many families lost everything and would have to rebuild. I think kids should be educated more about death to get a greater appreciation for it, because we should not be scared of it. It is how life is."

Another sobering lesson she had learned as a child was that of tending the graves of the dead, which went a long way in teaching her about mortality. Later in life, Eva was awarded an Order of Australia Medal for her community work in the area (she even opened the town hall's new toilet block!) and she continues to outpour her spirit into community projects. For her, family, friends, community and taking the time to do things properly are very important. Eva, who is still watching her town diminish owing to a lack of jobs, conveyed that even in troubled times, she hopes that these very basics will not be forgotten, and be of equal importance to future generations, as well.

37 – Real McCoys

MAYBE YOU HAVE a grandparent who spins yarns about growing up with no electricity, telephone or hot water, taking a pony five miles to school through floods and fire, but these next two are the real McCoys.

"Those were good times ... hot water, wow! You start to live!" exclaimed Bill with a laugh. We were conversing with him and his wife, Lorna, at their home along the picturesque stretch of waterfront promontory of Port Welshpool, where they have been in retired residence for 32 years, after three decades of farm life.

When Bill was nine years old, in 1934, floods unleashed colossal landslides and washed away property, livestock and roads. His family's tally of lost stock stood at seven horses and some 90 cows, not to mention the trouble in getting to school on a pony. But elemental forces are a strange thing in Australia, and Bill would echo that the 1942 bushfires blazed the area "as far as the eye could see, burnt," he said. "All the blue gum trees were alight, wind and sparks flying off."

"The fires had been started separately by farmers to burn rubbish off land," interjected Lorna, "such as timber, blackberries and so on. Winds picked up and merged several different fires together and then it all got burned up."

Their descriptions of sovereign back burns colluding into a flaming landscape was powerful, and prompted us to ask them what people would do if they lost property due to someone else's rubbish-eliminating tactics.

"In those days, even if you knew who lit the fire initially, they had family so you just didn't say anything. If you lost property, you just rebuilt – that was life," she shrugged. Picture it with me for a moment: this carbon copy of lush and verdant Ireland all wrapped up in flames. And it was even worse before. When Lorna's father (one of 13 children) was young, he witnessed a bushfire turn his home to cinders.

"My father was lucky," she remarked, to our surprise. *Lucky?* We failed to see the point, until she put it comparatively. "Some people had been burned out and had to rebuild four or five times," she explained. "It was never talked about or brought up, you just got on with it and started over. I am learning things about the past now that no one ever talked about."

It seemed that their luck continued, in a manner of speaking, for in all their years of farming, neither Lorna nor Bill suffered any great loss due to bushfires, other than some blazed hedges, a few burned out creek bridges and other minor chars.

Sadly, though, children and adults alike lost their lives in such blazes. A fire in 1906 smote the lives of nine children in the area who were making their way home from school. They dove into the street gutters only to have the flames blaze over them and take all the oxygen out of the air. "There is a mass grave at the Toora Cemetery with their names on it," Lorna told us.

"So while the fires of 1942 were going on, how did WWII fit into your lives?" asked one of us.

"Well, there was some food rationing, but the effects of war in this area were negligible," said Bill. "Most of the men were shipped off to fight, but we were children then, and mainly just produced food for troops –"

"– and collected aluminium!" interposed Lorna. "It was used in the making of aircraft and bullets, I believe. But we never really knew back then."

And that wasn't all they didn't know at the time. Lorna and Bill, and many others in the area, never knew that Darwin was bombed as badly as it was until well after the war. It was an uncle stationed up there that informed Bill of the heavy damage done by Japanese bombs.

"The women had to get the work done," said Lorna. "Soldiers coming home were shocked to see female train conductors and women performing tasks that the men usually did."

WWII did, however, bring about some remarkable advancements for all farmers. When the Americans came over, they brought with them machinery like planes and ground vehicles on tracks (bulldozers, tractors, etc.), not to mention chemicals that were used to eradicate a rabbit problem.

But what was initially technological excitement was also part of the death knell for the region's industry.

"Where there used to be five families, there is now just one," both of them expressed. There also used to be some fisheries, but the government had to close them down. The discovery of oil in the Bass Strait area brought some work; now, though, people fly out to the rigs instead of raising their family in the town. It was sad for them to see, but in their fashion, they just got on with things.

Some books I dug up later reflected their feelings numerically. In 1960, Australia had 300,000 farms, and by 1999, this figure was down to 100,000. Farms were actually growing between WWII and the 1960s, but then it all reversed horribly. World markets crashed and income from wool and meat tumbled by 36 percent and 70 percent respectively. One stat held that the "exodus from the bush" had some 35 farmers a week quitting their land, and those who remained plunged into debt (as many as 80 percent of current farmers are said to be in arrears) as their farms got one-third bigger with one-third less people tending them. Currently, one in 11 Australians live rurally, down from one in three in 1947.

Some of it can be blamed on globalization: today, it is cheaper to import oranges from Brazil (which apparently keeps costs low by bulldozing the rainforests and using cheap labour) than to grow them on Australian farms and truck them into the cities. Small Australian towns reported that in some places, 40 percent of their young people couldn't find work. One economically minded author states, "The rural regions now have the next highest youth suicide rate in the world to New Zealand." He then claims some of it can be safely attributed to American business practices.

In the United States, most businesses had been small and family owned until the concept of shares and "big business" came in around 1860, largely due to the railroad companies. The American practice of businesses being owned by shareholders who had no real interest in the land other than turnover profit was an odd concept for farmers to grasp. Decades later, when Australia adopted some of the ideals of capitalism, farmers were soon introduced to bewildering words like "credit" and "debt," "liability" and "speculation" and "return on investment."

What is subtly ironic in all of this is that Iraq was actually the first open market system in the world. Around 8,000 BCE, during the New Stone Age, Iraqis had very highly developed systems of agriculture and advanced skills in the herding of animals. They traded surpluses with neighbours, and that freed up time for people to become artisans, entrepreneurs and so forth. At the time of our interview with Lorna and Bill, the American forces were in Iraq dropping bunker-busters in a search of Saddam Hussein. It is interesting to think that some 10,000 years previous, Iraqis had been the pioneers of mathematics and trade, and now an advanced superpower was dropping bombs on them. Time does weird things.

"Youngsters still don't know everything," said Lorna when we asked what she might have to say to the younger generation. "I can say something, but they won't listen. They have no idea of what happened before them and what we and our parents had to put in for it. When we

first got married, we had a push-bike each and we had to build the rest."
Both of them chuckled. "Nowadays, people don't seem to want to face
up. Handouts have come over the generations. In our day, if you didn't
work, you didn't get any money. Don't forget the basics, that is what I
have to say, such as how to grow food to supplement your food source,
because what if the supermarket goes under?"

We thanked them for their time and we headed to the Toora Cemetery,
where indeed we found an *l*-shaped mass grave with the names of the
children (some very young) who had been consumed by the bushfires
of 1906. We paid our respects, then headed to Toora's community market
where the whole town was out, and passed on our thanks to hosts and
all involved.

At their suggestion, we took in the marvellous Wilson's Promenade
National Park, a spectacular region covering the southernmost peninsula
in Victoria. After scrambling into the hills and taking in the stretching
and curved vistas of ocean and ambling green foliage, we then did exactly
what most young people from rural Victoria do: we headed for
Melbourne.

38 – Oh, the Webs We Weave

AS PACKED TOGETHER as we were on this trip, we were all respectful of one another – a situation that typically, in my travel experience, doesn't always result. We were even developing military-like algorithms such that two of us would set up the beds or the dining area or cook in staggered fashion, while the other two were out brushing teeth or walking. Our individual idiosyncrasies, however, were spilling out and beginning to be noticed.

Louise, for one, was blighted with the convention of always speaking softly or dropping off in already low decibels of dialogue. A few drinks and she would raise the volume, but otherwise one was hard pressed to hear most of what she mumbled. The quirk was rendered worse when she drove or rode as navigator, for the cockpit could be noisy. Sometimes I would miss a turn-off and hear,

"I told you to turn there."

"What?" I would blubber.

"I told you to turn back there," she would faintly reiterate.

"Sorry, I didn't hear ya, Lou," I would reply while looking for a u-turn.

"No worries."

"What?"

Aside from that, and a snore every now and then, I have only good things to write about Louise. But then again, neither of us Mad Nomad–men could ever say anything bad, quite simply because the strong and silent vixen had the dirt on us!

Of all the commonalities Aaron and I shared, the mutual curse of sleep-talking was probably the largest one. It wasn't a dirty secret, it simply couldn't be by its very nature, and both Aaron and I openly warned anyone misfortunate enough to try and steal winks in the same vicinity as us that they may get an earful of unwitting claptrap.

We swapped tales of our affliction in open discussion. Aaron told us that one time his family heard noises in his bedroom, and upon opening the door, they found him clinging to the wall like Spiderman. He was having a dream about getting across a river on a slick vertical surface, and still thought he was until they woke him up.

While we were sharing a room at Tim and Fay's Hunter Valley home, Aaron illuminated all the lights one night at a very wee hour of the morning.

"What are you DOING?" I sputtered, as one does when awoken at strange times.

"Spider ... did you see the spider?" he asked groggily, eyes barely open.

"What spider? No spider. Spider sleeping," I stammered sparingly, resolved to slip comfortably back into unconsciousness. "Shut the light!"

He did, then turned on the table lamp next to my head without explanation. I half-dreamed that I was a piece of paper stuck in a photocopier with a jammed light bar before I hit the kill switch and Aaron slinked back under his covers in a muffled decision to sleep horizontally again.

But hey, I've done worse – or so I am told. Once, in Whistler, while sleeping in a bed with two side lamps, I reportedly opened them both up and pointed the glaring beams onto my sleeping friends.

"What the &*#* are you doing, Allan?" came the inevitable cry from my roommates, and I wasn't quite sure myself. "Are you trying to land a plane? For God's sake! Shut up and sleep!"

There was also the time that my brother Simon won't let me forget. Our family was camping and my sibling and I were together in a domed tent. Apparently I felt that we were trapped in a bubble and tried to force my way out of it, which resulted in the whole campsite being stirred as well as me collapsing the tent; then I slipped back into my sleeping bag with everything fallen on top of us. I could go on forever (and probably do, unbeknownst to myself).

Well, the trend continued in the snug sleeping arrangements of our Britz on most nights. Louise and Jody would tell me (and the author would like to note that he never could verify these testimonies, though he generally accepts them as true by sheer witness turn-out) that I once apparently cried out in my sleep, "Its April! And I'm an April Fool!"

So frequent were such outbursts that I would soon have a daily verbal from Louise on the subject of the incoherencies Aaron and I blithered in the twilight zone. She even threatened to dedicate a web article or two to our insentient theatrics! Well, that never happened, thankfully, but it did enter my mind that Louise might be so quiet because she never got to sleep much and thought the wiser of wasting her limited energy.

Once we arrived in Melbourne, we were extended the generous hospitality of my friend Natalie, a Canadian pursuing her master's in criminology on exchange at the University of Melbourne.

Years ago, I had loaned Natalie my backpack and given her a kick in the ass to prompt her to go to her ancestral Ireland, and we had stayed friends ever since. Oddly in line with her scope of academia, Natalie had at one time been a victim of a heinous crime, perpetrated by me, though I will plead insanity if she ever takes the matter to a magistrate.

Some months previous, when she had just arrived in Australia, I invited Natalie to take a one-hour flight and visit me in Sydney. When she arrived, she complained of a skin irritation and unhappily showed me a spreading red rash along her stomach and face and on her lips. I, on the other hand, showed her the sights, which invariably included the eastern suburban beaches. By unspoken invitation, we both crashed in Aaron's room at the 258 hostel instead of returning to Darling Harbour and the concrete jungle where I lived at the time.

One evening, we watched the epically long *Lord of the Rings* on DVD, a tale full of hobbits and Dark Riders and ugly orcs with terrible dermatology problems of their own. Natalie and Aaron went for their respective beds at the conclusion, but because I was addicted to a video game called *Halo* and because Matt had the video game system, I took up a controller and unleashed pixelated fury.

The premise of *Halo* is fairly straightforward: basically, you're a cyborg soldier who's trying to save the human race from evil aliens. There are all kinds of guns and grenades, tactics and vehicles, and when the computer-generated ground lay awash with alien bodies and blood, I noticed the real world clock had chewed up about six hours and it was three in the morning! I still hadn't saved the human race yet, so I bookmarked my progress for a later battle. Conversely, all blood in my body save that in my nimble thumbs had long ago coagulated, and I peeled myself with pins and needles from the sofa, managing solely the task of eliminating the glow of the TV before covering the few metres to the bedroom to crash next to Natalie on the spare fold-out. I was soon sound asleep counting sheep.

Then the sheep turned on me.

Aaron would also turn witness against me and verify what happened next, though I have no idea how he could. Evidently, in the frame of mind of eliminating orcs and evil grunting ETs with plasma rifles, I pushed Natalie, who lay in her peaceful state, and cursed her alien ways. Because she was comfortably curled up in the foetal position with her back turned to me, I assume I thought that I would be able to successfully gun-butt her with my imaginary cyborg rifle.

I didn't physically harm her (there were no bruises), but a bit of unconscious manhandling supposedly went on while I said in strong and muffled tones that she *would not* eliminate my species. Aaron, even in his semi-conscious state, somehow managed to say, "Stop!" (possibly because he was in the role of traffic cop in his own never-never land), and I guess I must have.

Natalie was visibly incensed, but nonetheless found it funny and would joke about it in a way that I will never live down. But I have a comeback if she doesn't let it go: Natalie is arachnophobic and bug-o-phobic (which is a strange affliction to have if living in the land of giant insects). Whenever she brings up the subject of my drowsy misappropriations, I just ask her, "What's that crawling on your shoulder with hairy legs?" The case is then quickly dropped as she sprints off, tailed by a siren-like *eeeeiiiiee* and hands flailing.

I have no doubt she could pen an award-winning thesis on the destructive power of media and interactive gaming on the subconscious, but like Louise, she chose not to write about or publish the details of my affliction. I'm sure Roger would have delighted in filming it while doing the 'sleep-talkers foxtrot', and prove his lap-dog theories and many more, but we'll stop there.

To bring it all back in line with the Mad Nomads cause and the fact that we had a motor home in a large city, Natalie thankfully did not let past events prevent her from extending her good-humoured hand of mateship in allowing us to crash in at her apartment. I promise to thank her in my sleep forever more.

Melbourne, a grand Victorian city, known in the 1880s as "the Paris of the antipodes," got its reputation for all the profits that resulted from gold discoveries in nearby Ballarat and Bendigo (about nine-tenths of total Australian bullion, according to some sources). The population jumped from 77,345 to 539,000 in only 10 years, owing to some 1,800 new immigrants getting off in Port Melbourne per week.

Then as now, Sydney was always looking for a chance to snub Melbourne – who had stolen its thunder – and articles appeared in the *Sydney Morning Herald*, saying, "In a word, nowhere in the southern hemisphere does chaos reign so triumphant as in Melbourne." Not only were ships missing crews, but every other business lost staff to shanty towns that were swelling to over capacity. *Everyone* was digging.

A few rebellions and a generation gap settled Melbourne back to semi-normality. Those who had the money lived flamboyant lifestyles – until a bank crash spun Melbourne into a depression. It would again flourish into the early 20th century before the Great Depression hit and one-third of local bread-winners were out of work. Today Melbourne has rounded out to become a living quilt of cultures. Then many ran off to Sydney.

I had always made fun of Melbourne, not because I had ever been, but because it seemed the thing to do in Sydney. It was peer pressure. Having been a Sydney-sider for 16 months, just the act of physically arriving in Melbourne made me feel instinctively as if I had been dropped behind enemy lines.

The rivalry is of course very real. Has been since the beginning. Take this small example: in 1841, Sydney offered the independent-minded Melbourne their very own supreme court judge, one Justice John Walpole Willis. In their youthful jubilance, Melbourne-ites failed to smell a rat or check his background. He was one of the strangest justices in the Commonwealth, removed from British Guiana following a tearful petition, and fired from service in Canada for heated quarrel with the attorney general. When he returned to England, he was quickly offered to Sydney, who spun him down to Melbourne.

Willis' first act in Melbourne was to disbar a lawyer because he had a moustache. He then took to lambasting leading citizens, disbarring barristers for silly reasons, and holding litigants hostage to tell them how to plead. All of that in the first week. Sydney was laughing itself silly, though they finally had to step in and give the lunatic his pink slip after two years and a series of embarrassing judicial movements.

Twenty-some years on, in 1868, Alfred, Duke of Edinburgh, was sent on a round-the-world trip by his mother. Smug Sydney-siders were already bragging that they would entertain their guest so well that he would forget about the other colonies. However, everything went wrong. A very intricate naval manoeuvre in Sydney's Harbour failed to coordinate: it started raining heavily, fog completely blocked the view, the fireworks got soaked and 4,500 choir boys almost froze to death. People mumbled it was Melbourne weather, and possibly a curse.

Then, at a fundraiser, Duke Alfred was shot point blank in the back by a spectator as officials dove into ditches and another dignitary was shot in the foot. This was Sydney's worst nightmare. The Duke, nevertheless, survived the attempt. The police found evidence in the shooter's hotel room that he had been in Melbourne two months previous, and immediately tempers flared that it was "a Melbourne plot," some say their revenge for having been sent Judge Willis.

In truth, the shooter was a feisty Irish Fenian who wanted to kill all English society. The shooter claimed insanity as his defence, and his sister from Ballarat came up to testify that the nights in Victoria were cold, and her brother was preoccupied with mosquitoes, unfair mining license fees and attacks of craziness. In his spare time, his hobbies included collecting swords, daggers and pistols.

The next major conflict between the cities happened when Australia was federated, and the only way to make either duelling child happy was to put the new national capital city in the middle-of-butt-fiddle-nowhere and call it Canberra.

Nevertheless, Melbourne grew bigger than Sydney and every major Australian corporation put their headquarters there. When Melbourne got the nod to host the 1956 Olympics, Sydney-siders saw it as a call to arms, and since then the script has been flipped and everything shifted to Sydney: company head offices, population, fashion, film, most major industries, you name it. It seems Sydney looks down on Melbourne these days. For now.

As far as landmarks go, Melbourne is undoubtedly in the humped and cross-beamed shadow of Sydney. It doesn't have a Melbourne Opera House and the West Gate Bridge is an eyesore more than anything worth a trip over. The major downtown area, by early design, was actually built inland and away from Port Phillip Bay, so the waterfront will never really be on a postcard either: to get to a nice beach, you have to drive a couple of hours.

What makes Melbourne great is its people. Melbourne is a sister city to Montréal, and I instantly felt at home when I explored it. Everywhere were advertisements for international comedy and jazz festivals, art openings, car racing and horse betting. It had a major casino, musicians were gainfully employed, cafés were bustling, restaurants hopping, people dressed as they pleased and no one seemed to take grand airs.

Aside from a bizarre driving habit (exclusive to Melbourne) called a "hook turn" – in which traffic gets into the left lane to block perpendicular traffic, to turn right – I fell in love with Melbourne. It also made me realise that, unlike many Sydney siders, as an Australian, you don't have to be obsessed with real estate. In Sydney, at the time, there were endless property reality shows* and whole segments of the newspaper set aside for the same ends. But not in Melbourne.

We only spent a few days in Melbourne, mostly to catch up with friends, check emails and shop cheaply. Jody remained there while Louise, Aaron, Mr. Britz motor home and I headed for Port Melbourne,

---

* The Block, Location Location, Hot Auctions, Backyard Blitz, Auction Squad, Burke's Backyard, Renovation Rescue and Better Homes and Gardens.

where we drove into the gapping stomach of the *Spirit of Tasmania*. It would be a long, 10-hour ferry ride to Australia's only island state, and when we discovered $2 schooners (this time, beers) at the bar, Louise suddenly found her boisterous voice. I was tired, so I went back to the motor home and took a nap, hoping that I would not wake up sleep talking.

Least of all, in a nation of inbred aliens.

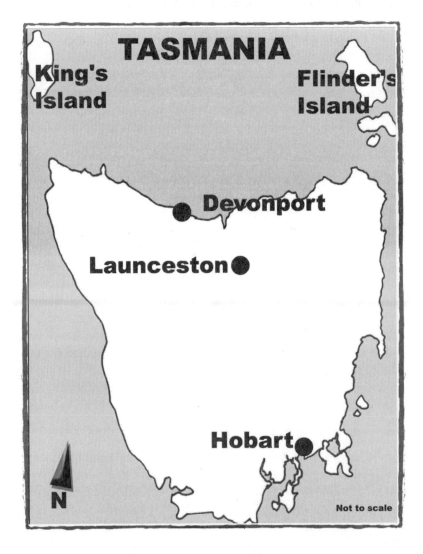

39 – Port-Soaked Reality

TRAVELLING BY ROAD forces one to appreciate the truly fragmented climates and mixed peoples. Australia is more continent than country. Nevertheless, there is one thing *all* mainland Australians see eye to eye on: making the isolated and bottom-most state of Tasmania the target of national jokes and inbreeding innuendo. It is the most singular, undeniable and consistent national trademark. I was even a victim once when I was dared by some blokes to ask an Australian girl named Sheila to see her map of Tazzie. It seemed a straightforward geographical question, but in hindsight I should have consulted a map and got the joke before innocently asking her to, in effect, hike her skirt.

As a visitor to Australia, I was always insulted if an Aussie asked me what part of the USA I was from. When the affront was made I would politely retort, "Actually I'm not American, but I know how you Kiwis can't tell the difference." It usually worked, unless of course the person was actually from New Zealand (and it took me a while to tell the accents apart), but then – with my growing knowledge of the pecking order – I would say, "Sorry, I know how you Tasmanians are," and that would defiantly drive the point home. (Unless, of course, they were Tasmanian, then I had no lower rung to go to for a comeback – though Queensland has been suggested as I write this).

Tasmania is to Australia what Australia is to the world: an island often ignored, with portions still unexplored, backward, but at the end of the day, a treasure trove of mystery to those who make the effort. So separate from Australia is Tasmania that some Australian friends of mine earnestly thought that it would be cheaper for me to fly in and out of Hobart than New Zealand in order to fulfil the requirement of being outside of national borders in procuring a new visa!

South Australian police once captured a man in Adelaide who was also wanted for crimes committed in Tasmania. The police detective told the reporter that the Tasmanian and South Australian magistrates were in discussion about "extradition" to Tasmania once the "crim" had done his time in SA!

Upon our arrival at the ferry station in Port Melbourne, a quarantine officer came onboard our Britz and ordered us to eat or throw out all our hard-picked Victorian apples on the spot. (Oddly enough, we came back to Victoria with Tasmanian apples and no one said a thing. The quarantine was one way).

Changing visas *outside* of Australia?! Extradition?! Quarantine?! Being sub-Kiwi by definition?! Tasmanians were to Australians what Welshmen were to English, or Belgians to Europeans: the bottom of the heap. And what of all this business about Tasmanians looking a little too forward to family reunions, hoping to meet that someone special? When I asked one New South Welshman what Tasmanians were like, he retorted with, "Well, they're just not symmetrical mate, if you know what I mean?*"

Maybe his statement was unduly influencing my thinking (a visual placebo), but presently some of the people on the ferry didn't look to me to have all their features line up. Then again, they could just as well have been from Melbourne or Germany or more likely Wales, come to think of it. My hairdresser in Whistler was Tasmanian, and she was a sunning specimen – had everything in the right place, if you know what I mean!

But the truth about Tasmania would soon out.

We docked in Devonport, on the northern tip of the island, at sunset, and the rays of dusk spreading over the green isle were intense. We rolled off the drop plank and I immediately started scanning for evidence to prove this well-held Australian theory of Tas-ackorwardness. I would accept no hearsay. We tuned in to the local radio station in time to catch the top stories of Tasmania.

"Flinders Island [a small island just north of where we landed] finally has mobile phone reception, after years of lobbying the Tasmanian government," the news reader announced with pride, "and over the next few years, residents have further assurances that $2 million will be invested to bring internet and video-conferencing to the region."

We passed petrol stations and convenience stores with signs proudly displaying, "NOW accepting EFTPOS [direct debit from bank cards]." Another roadside curio was that some signs displayed town names in (brackets). I didn't understand that one. Did it mean (*town down this road but don't tell others*)? Or maybe, (*town to be completed, but this will be its name*)? Perchance all towns with their names in brackets (*didn't have mobile reception or internet but were lobbying the government*). Whichever the case, the signage was good enough to lead

---

* The only reference I could find about early Australian settlers marrying their cousins was that of Lt. King of the First Fleet, who married his. He had taken some convicts to Norfolk Island on Governor Phillip's orders. He suffered, I suppose, island fever, which might have been mislaid onto Tasmania.

us to a caravan park, and right there along the street that weaved between camp plots was a sign that looked exactly like a speed limit posting: it was white, with bold black lettering that spelled: "SPEED LIMIT: Walking pace only."

The case to expunge rumour was looking bleak. However, Tasmania does have its compensatory charms. People don't know that Tasmania has given the world so many things, such as ... such as ... Errol Flynn! That's right! Haven't seen any of his movies, but the name is familiar. Then there's Bugs Bunny's spinning and slobbering nemesis, the Tasmanian Devil. Where would that wascally wabbit be without his anti-hero? And I love apples, and Tasmania is known as the "Apple Isle."

What was clear to me was that mainland Australians were surely hypocrites for making fun of their southern isle–dwelling brethren, at least the Australians who watched TV. Despite how they may sneer, all Aussies with a glowing boob-tube stood strongly united to award a Tasmanian woman $250,000 for doing sweet nothing! Yes, that's right! Regina was her name (if you don't know her, don't stress). She wasn't the sharpest knife in the drawer, a bit slow on the uptake, she overused the word "bugger" in a really annoying shrill aucker accent, but she had lots to say about her fish and chips business in Tasmania. The shop, her marriage and her dog had been her life up until she became a *Big Brother* housemate and did bump-kiss for several months while being eavesdropped upon by millions. Then the trans-national votes were polled, and she was the last one standing.

So proud were Tasmanians that Reggie was one of theirs that residents of the Apple Isle wrote her name with their bodies on a field as she flew over them en route home. Then they had a parade in her honour in Hobart, made Reggie's Fish and Chips a household name and started Reggie Mania (which lasted only a few frenzied seconds longer than the glowing minutes of previous winners when the reality show ended). The Lord Mayor of Hobart came out to award her something – the key to Hobart, or was it the promise to remove the brackets on signs designating her home town? Or was it an EFPTOS debit machine or his assurance of video-conferencing in two years for the shop? I can't quite remember.

These people have spirit, Tasmanian spirit, and they love their little battlers, even if some of them in the Flinders Island area couldn't be updated by mobile text message as to Reggie's *Big Brother* movements until recently.

* * *

Tasmania's compact terrestrial scale was such a welcome: I cannot underline how much of a relief it was to see signs with distances in denominations of less than three digits, and most often two. You can get anywhere in three hours or less, instead of a brain-numbing stretch of days or weeks on featureless highways.

Tasmania is the world's 24th largest island*(Australia being number one), and covers less than 1 percent of the Australian continent, holding less than 3 percent of the total population; almost half of Tasmanians live in the capital city. It is written that the island enjoys a population spread of about 6.7 people per square kilometre, which is put into sharp perspective if you consider that Bangladesh has exactly twice the area but 726 million people sharing it.

Dutch explorer Abel Tasman had named his 1642 discovery Van Diemen's Land to honour the governor general of Batavia, Anthony Van Diemen. Had Holland's sea exploratory agent been a bit quicker, had he had a bit more funding and gone a smidge more north, modern Australians would today be speaking Dutch instead of English, though either way I am positive they would have introduced a complex lexicon of slang. Instead, Abel went off into what is now the Tasman Sea before exploring New Zealand and some South Pacific Islands. According to records, while in Tasmania, Tasman never married any of his cousins.

Geographically speaking, Tasmania is a stretch mark. It is the last land-link between Antarctica and Australia, and as such it is a pretty cold and snowy isle. Central Tasmania is said to get 300 days of frost a year and Hobart is in the books as getting 160 days of rain a year. It's a place where you need to hold people closer ... just to survive.

In 1803, Van Diemen's Land became a dump for the brutish. One calculation has it that four out of every 10 convicts were forked out of Sydney. They were considered the lowest crust of England's lower crust and Tasmania was the lowest form of punishment: coarse, dangerous and isolated. On a smaller and slightly behind scale, Van Diemen's Land suffered exactly the same fate as Botany Bay: it was a settlement that moved about on the brink of starvation in an alien world. The only variation, it seemed, was that Englishmen developed nostalgia for England in looking at the chilly, rainy and green Tasmanian landscape. The settlers had to survive for the most part on kangaroos, as they received no supplies or visits from New South Wales for 18 long months.

---

² It is about the same size as half of Ireland.

Many tried to escape, only to wind up in Tasmania's foreboding and mountainous dense interior forests. There were tales of some convicts resorting to cannibalism to stay alive. One escapee apparently wandered back to the settlement babbling insanely with pieces of human flesh in his pockets; the others – those who couldn't catch kangaroos – died eating each other, while dreaming of sailing 14,000 miles back to England if they could but steal the right ship.

Though the first governor of "Tazzie," who came to be know as "Mad Tom" Davey – because he was a drunken lunatic – as well as those governors that followed, might help to explain a little about Tasmania's bizarre courses.

Davey had been a young Marine on the First Fleet. In his spare time at sea, he used to practice the art of wrinkling his scalp, moving his skin in all directions and making faces, reportedly some comical and others grotesque. But Davey had one huge fan; Lord Harrowby in England, and in life, it's who you know. In 1812 – for no reason that can possibly invite admiration for intelligent and sober reflection – Lord Harrowby asked Davey to tenure an application to be the first governor of Van Dieman's Land.

Davey didn't like his very dull wife. Keeping the appointment a secret, Davey tried (and almost managed) to set sail without her. Nevertheless, she showed up on the jetty determined to go with him, managing to pack only what she could grab quickly.

After breaking his ribs in a spectacularly miscalculated jump that was intended to impress his crew, Davey had to sit out the rest of the trip, under doctor's orders, watching his dull wife decorate her only bonnet. By the time they arrived in Hobart in 1814, he hated that bonnet. His first act upon docking was to order his steward to bring him a bottle of port, which he deliberately poured all over his wife's decorative headgear … while she was wearing it. Amazingly, she said not a word.

Davey then debarked, muttering inaudibly, with his jacket off and his sleeves rolled up, and began walking past soldiers who were in a rush to put together a last-minute military salute. When Davey asked the soldiers what they were doing, they replied, "Going to meet the new governor," to which Davey simply raised his hat and wrinkled his scalp. Davey immediately complained it was too hot and asked the soldiers the way to Government House. His pseudonym "Mad Tom" was coined by those very stunned soldiers when, moments later, a lone woman, wearing a damp bonnet, and carrying her own luggage, squelched up the path, reeking of port, and asked said soldiers which way her husband went.

On royal occasions, Davey would breach a keg outside Government House and ladle out rum to anyone who came by ... Until, of course, the contents of his ladle forced him no longer to remain erect against gravity. To boot, and to the further embarrassment of his wife, he openly cohabitated with convict women.

Meanwhile, Australia's first bushrangers emerged in Tasmania. Davey confronted the problem by enacting his own form of marshal law which – possibly unintentionally – gave carte blanche to all bushrangers to get away with all short of murder and then come in under amnesty. After an exchange of letters, the British government fired Davey in 1816. He immediately turned his hand to farming, and failed miserably.

The next governor of Tasmania was the very sober Sorell, who, although he was a good leader in many respects, had abandoned his wife and seven children for another woman (the sister of a brother officer) in Africa and – to the shock of many – his illegitimate fling bore him another seven children.

Regardless, Governor Sorell managed to break major crime rings. In Hobart, he hanged as many bushrangers as he could capture and put one bushranger's head on a spike at the border of settlement to set an example. One of the tools in his arsenal was a new prison called Port Macquarie. The Tasmanian Port Macquarie was the worst spot in the English-speaking world. It was on the forlorn and very wet coast of western Tasmania – a place where no one has ever, or will ever, live. Escape was impossible, for the harbour was a rare tidal bottleneck known as Hell's Gate that lead to lots of nothing, with a dense forest behind the prison and a tangled mess beyond that.

The position of Tasmanian governor was then snapped up by the controversial George Arthur. He was a very devout Christian military man who had fought against Napoleon and governed the convict colony of British Honduras before going *under* Down Under. Tired of running to Sydney for orders, Governor Arthur was largely responsible for severing Van Diemen's Land from NSW and naming it the separate colony of Tasmania in 1825.

Arthur then created the first Big Brother society. He turned Tasmania into a police state with a rigid bureaucracy. He created a registry of everyone on the island, with records of their birthdates and physical characteristics and any other notes he deemed necessary. He controlled everything through his new field police. All was reported to him and he even sized up all newly arrived convicts with his own eyes. It was said that he knew everyone: he was the ultimate cop.

He also went about erecting terse laws against intimacy between convicts and free settlers and, what's more, any marriages between relatives. If anyone fell in love with someone they shouldn't, Governor Arthur would hear about it, separate them and give them each a bible as a guide to repentance. So in reality, Tasmania became an early Australian colony with the heaviest legislation against marrying your cousin ...

However, it is conceivable that it may have caused an underground rebellion.

PRESENTLY, THE MAD Nomads found it bloody cold. We purchased thicker sweaters and we even donned tuques (or "beanies," if you will). We would awake our first few nights shivering in our Britz beds and subsequently got wise to the idea of slipping into our sleeping bags fully clothed as if we were in Artic snow tents.

Hobart (pop. 193,000), Australia's second-oldest city, is more of a small European fishing village than a metropolis. Its central area has cobblestone streets on slight angles squeezing between old fashioned stony buildings and leafy parks, and a gorgeous port with boats both old and new. Hobart is presently known for its well-heeled university and a thriving arts scene.

I got in touch with ABC Radio in Hobart and they did a phone interview with me about the Mad Nomads project. Not long after, my mobile rang (a bit of a foreign sound because I hadn't heard it in so long) and on it came a woman's gruff voice.

"How are you, you sexy North American BEAST!?" she rumbled.

"Fine ... and who is this?" I inquired politely. I thought maybe it was Kiwi Simon playing a joke on me, as he had left me messages when I was often out of range on the journey. He loved to pull my leg.

"My name is Joanne. I just heard you on the radio. Delightful project you have there, Mr. Nomad," she replied in a quieter timbre.

I still wasn't sure if it was a joke or not, so I measured and edged my replies accordingly, but it turned out to be a real person who had gotten my number off of our website following the ABC interview.

"I think what you're doing is WONDERFUL!" she said, her voice now fluctuating between happy and sad tones. "And I have ... some suggestions."

What followed in dialogue lead me to believe that I was engaged in yet another phone conversation where the caller might be at half an arm's length from a recently full – but currently empty – bottle of OTC uppers.

"I came to Tasmania to DIE!" Joanne bellowed, and I was taken aback. "I am sick. I have cancer," she continued in a lower tone, "and there isn't much time left." Then she flipped tones again, happier. "I was once a star in Melbourne," she reminisced. "I acted, I sang, I have so many connections. I want to read you a poem, do you mind?"

"Uh, no ... uh, yes! By all means, please read," I stammered in reply.

She recited to me a poem penned by a friend of hers, one full of melancholy and twisted fate, and she began to cry, her deep voice quivering. I can't remember the words, but it was about war and losing loved ones, and corrupt governments. At the conclusion she seemed to be wiping up tears.

"How *saaaddd* is that?" she finally said after a sniffling pause. "How awful." Then suddenly, as if she had never read it, she said, "So how long are you in Tasmania?" with all the sing of joy.

"Only a week," I bumbled, unsure if I should match my tone to hers, from Jekyll to Hyde. "Um ... did you have a story for us?" I pressed.

"FUCK NO!" she cried, and erupted into a deep and grinding laugh/ cough that induced my reflexes to launch my mobile handset to arm's length from my eardrum. "No, you don't want to see me," she furthered, then in a whisper that brought me to fit my ear tightly back to the handset she said, "Take down these numbers, I want you to interview these women. *They* have stories." I jotted down the three names and numbers, but ultimately one number didn't work, one lady was out of the country and the other was in north Queensland (and we never made it that far).

"The world is so sad. But so happy. Good luck on your journey. Mine is just about over," and with that I never heard from Joanne again.

There was something about this Tasmania.

When I told Aaron and Louise about Joanne's phone call, they raised their eyebrows. Nonetheless, the Mad Nomads had lined up a local interview through a Lion's Club contact, but she was only available to speak in a few days so we wound our Britz northwest of Hobart into the hills.

Green and lush, flowing with waterfalls and teeming with animals is the best way to describe the postcard images I had seen of Tasmania before arriving. With that layout, I could swear the shadow of Gandalf or his wandering hobbits, or maybe Zena The Warrior Princess, would not be too out of place. The landscape we passed was indeed similar, but it lacked that striking emerald glow that would complete the frame.

Many of the vast tracts of glens, hills, woods and land were in hues of brown, dotted sparingly at times with parched and dead grey trees. Perhaps the Evil Wizard had come instead. But it wasn't black magic: it was the driest summer on Tasmanian record in 125 years that had done the deed. One source had it that interior Tasmania receives rain on average seven days out of 10 (comparable to the British Isles), but the Apple Isle had been affected by the Australian drought.

While we were driving inland, I was plying through some books on Tasmanian nature and her first peoples, and I feel obliged to spend the remainder of this chapter telling you a little bit about them.

But I warn you: what follows is very graphic.

The most internationally known local is the Tasmanian devil, always shown in photographs with the large pink and red interior of their agape mouths and sharp teeth ready for action. Contrary to belief, they don't travel in self-generated tornados and break through things while slobbering inanely.

The devil is said to be the size of a bull terrier. It has short black hair, stumpy legs and paws like a dog, but ears like a bat and whiskers like a cat, and it qualifies as the world's largest meat-eating marsupial. It has earned a very ugly reputation, for it disembowels prey and engages in bloody squabbles over carrion with shrill and piercing screams. Apparently – if it gets half the chance – it will even eat its own young.

The devil's favourite dish, however, is its own cousin, the marsupial wombat, a stocky little bear-like creature half a metre tall that munches grass. The devils will invariably settle for wallabies, possums and birds, but also things that smell vaguely digestible, such as tea towels, rubber slippers and leather boots. They can reportedly eat one-third of their own weight in an hour, which is like an average human eating 50 large steaks in a sitting.

As I write this, there are hardly any of them left. Any devils alive today are either living in the remote areas of Tasmania or in 20 Australian and two overseas zoos. The devils have never gone on record for killing humans, though there are unofficial accounts of sleeping campers being attacked. Scientists who try to gather data on them have one major obstacle: the devil is apparently really putrid-smelling.

Further offsetting are their mating rituals. The male of the species will fight off rivals before dragging away a screaming female by the scruff of her neck. He then starves his captive (sometimes up to 10 days) and keeps performing his motions until he is sure she is pregnant. Then he leaves and the poor woman is left to birth up to 20 babies that stick around for 10 months. Increasingly distressing in all of this is the fact that she only has four nipples, so most devil babies die if they aren't able to muscle in for milk. It is not uncommon, I read with disgust, for babies to attack the mother and tear into her if they are not fed. On top of that, she has to worry about a male coming back to have them for dinner. And if her little tykes make it past all of the above, half of them are killed in the wild, anyhow.

But the Tasmanian devil is blessed with a strange ability: it has a high tolerance for pain and the prowess to resist infection from open soars. It can walk around with wounds that would incapacitate most other animals, and it is still not known how they can do this. One scientist thinks that the devil can mentally stop bleeding, while another just boldly suggests that they are too stupid to know pain.

A lesser-known but no less spectacular creature was the Tasmanian tiger (Latin lovers: *Thylacines*), who was one freaky-looking dude. Some describe it as a "pouched dog with a wolf's head," but to me it appears as if someone sewed together a lot of different animals and set it loose to breed with others. It was marsupial, but sadly there are none left to look at. In the early 1900s – even though it was the last of its kind and only existed in Tasmania – farmers sought to eliminate the *Thylacines* because it attacked their livestock. The Tasmanian government placed a bounty on its ugly head and by 1930, the tiger was thought to be completely eradicated. However, even today many locals (and an assortment of tourists) claim to have seen some in the wild. Some fisherman tell tales of strange animals having a go at their bait, and their descriptions do match the characteristics of the tiger, or perhaps a relative that has developed unnoted. Regardless, many in the empirical community just dismiss testimonies as fishermen's yarns with roots in boredom and alcohol. In 1972, a French expedition briefly searched for the tiger, but nothing was found.

In 2003, there was a local news story about 200 cattle being mutilated and killed by what farmers think was a Tasmanian tiger or something like it, but no one seems positive what exactly the predator was. Once again, calls to extinguish the bovine killer were raised, but because the *Thylacines* is listed as extinct on government books, there was some confusion as to how to legislate funds. So essentially, for all we know and until documented proof can be procured, it could also be either a yeti or a land version of the Loch Ness Monster.

But I do have my own plausible theory. I read somewhere that though the coming of man to Australia lessened numbers of some creatures, it increased others. The bush fly plagues many parts of the continent today. This annoying insect multiplied exponentially as white settlers imported some 30 million cattle to graze and drop an estimated 300 million piles of shit around Australia, and the fly thrives in that. Conceivably, the stink of it all revived the dead tiger to eliminate the problem. Call me crazy, but wait till you hear about the next Tasmanian enigma.

The Aboriginal Tasmanian is thought to be altogether unrelated to the mainland natives. When Abel Tasman arrived, he never logged seeing any, though he did spot smoke from campfires. The first official European sighting of an Aboriginal Tasmanian was scrawled in 1772 in the diary of Frenchman Marion du Fresne, who had landed on the island on his way to Tahiti. His crew was attacked and in avoiding the flying spears, they managed to kill one native and bring his body back to the ship for examination. It was proclaimed, "We could see that their natural colour was reddish and that it was only by habit of keeping close to a smoky black fire that blackened them thus."

Tasmanian Aboriginals looked like no one else. Their noses were flat and they possessed a completely different head of hair, as well as "reddish and ill-tempered eyes" (or so said du Fresne's log). A broad conjecture was reached that the original Tasmanians must have come from some other point of origin, but as you might imagine, why and how they came to such a cold and remote place is even harder to fathom than how the first mainland Aboriginals touched down on the northern brim of Australia. The theory that all Aboriginal Australians came over the Indonesian archipelago was placed seriously into question. Some religious theorists went as far as believing that they were people from the Book of Genesis, who may have been scattered by the hand of God during biblical flooding, or possibly by Noah's Ark. Those of the science cloth furthered empirical studies. It was conceivable that the native Tasmanians had braved a long route to get to the bottom and, once there, had witnessed land falling into ocean. Like their mainland counterparts, they seemingly never bothered making anything to sail away with.

One very confused branch of inquiry arose owing to linguistics. On his Antarctic voyage, James Cook stayed in Tasmania for a week and attempted to speak with the Tasmanians using words from the three main languages of the South Sea and other Pacific islands, and met with no success. Eleven years later, William Bligh called in to a beach near where Cook had been and came upon a crew of naked Tasmanians. He gave them gifts and tried to speak with them, though they spoke quickly and sounded, as Bligh's diary said, "like the cackling of geese." It seemed that Tasmanian natives boasted five distinct languages, such that even when recorded and played to other Tasmanians, none could understand the other.

To name a few other theories – all with the common thread of their arriving by raft – Tas-Aboriginals have been thought to be descendants of New Caledonians, exiles from Hindustan (southern India), ancient Europeans, African castaways, half-breeds from Dutch voyages and (given their small stature) far-removed Asians. Naturally, each theory has been disproved.

All kinds of data was collected and compared: hair and skin samples, the shape of the skull, cast of the nose and profile of the eyes – you name it. So sought-after were Tasmanian remains (especially by scientists who were trying to link humans to evolving monkeys) that at one time, there was a burgeoning trade in excavated Australian Aboriginal skulls and scientists would mark some as "Tasmanian" to increase their value, even if they weren't. We can only begin to imagine how many false conclusions might have been drawn as the result of greed over pure scientific reward.

And, I am sad to report, despite all you have read here (which is only the tip of the iceberg), to this day no one theory has proven predominantly plausible over the others, and scientists are still simultaneously scratching the surface of the issue and no doubt their heads. Perhaps the physical differences mutated over 9,000 years of isolation and random processes from the mainland tribes, or maybe they just married their cousins.

Some islands off the coast of Queensland held the remains of Aboriginals who had markedly different traits than those of the mainland. What seems certain (that is to say, what most scientists agree upon) is that Tasmania has been separated from mainland Australia for at least 12,000 years as a direct result of the sea rising some 6,000 years before that. The swell was the very same that sheared Kangaroo Island from South Australia and Flinders Island from Wilson's Promontory in Victoria.

So all things considered, Australia and little cousin Tasmania could have been the staging grounds for the rise and fall of several varied societies, possibly related, perhaps not, and quite conceivably none of them knew of each other. Stranger still are the habits of one of Australia's most famous wild dogs, the dingo. Early white explorers were quick to notice that dingoes followed men and their convoys, even while knowing that they would be scalped if captured; but whether they followed for companionship or scraps of food, no one can be certain.

So yet another mystery enters the Australian annals. Did the Aboriginals and dingoes have a relationship? Did dingoes and

Aboriginals team up on the Tasmanian tiger and wipe it out on the mainland before white cattle farmers did so in Tasmania? But where did the *dingoes* come from? We'll stop there, before all our brains explode.

I must end this chapter on a very disgusting and sad, but necessary, note. The Tasmanian Aboriginals are the only Australian Aboriginals to have been completely eradicated. None survive today.

The stories, starting from about 1804 and going for a brief time, are grim and brutal. Tas-Aboriginals were often slaughtered at point blank with guns for no reason. Although some survivalists might legitimately argue in favour of saving a starving colony by killing off competition for food sources, by 1806 many bushrangers were reportedly hunting natives for sport alone. One of the most sickening cases was that of James Carroott of Oyster Bay. He captured a Tas-Aboriginal couple, killed and decapitated the man and then made the traumatized wife wear the severed head in a bag around her neck as a "plaything."

And children were not spared horrible indignities. I read of a time when whites cut the cheek off a native boy and forced him to chew and swallow his own flesh, and then made women do the same. Some Tas-Aboriginals were reportedly killed to make dog food. A campaign was next proposed that offered 150 armed convicts a ticket of leave if they managed to kill a quota of Tas-Aboriginals, and that was how many convicts got their first guns and graduated into bushranger-hood.

Then some settlers came up with the notion of "Black Line," a sort of flushing campaign. Hundreds of troops and convicts boasting 1,000 muskets, 30,000 rounds of ammo and 300 pairs of handcuffs spread out into the woods in 1830. Over seven weeks, they closed a human fishnet along the Tasman Peninsula – but all they managed to capture were two tribesmen and a boy, and the rest were somehow missed.

An early version of apartheid was tried next by Governor Arthur. But the plan didn't work and historian Hughes summed up the plight thus: "Die they did – shot like kangaroos and poisoned like dogs, ravaged by European diseases and addictions, hunted by laymen and pestered by missionaries, 'brought in' from their ancestral territories to languish in camps."

Some estimate the early Tasmanian indigenous population as having been between 3,000 and 7,000. However, by 1835 there were only 150 and by 1855, there were 16; in 1869, only one true blood was left. She apparently lived in fear that when she died she would not be buried traditionally, and she was right. A funeral procession was held for her in 1873 and her body was buried, against her wishes, in a Protestant cemetery. Later, it was dug up and de-fleshed, her bones put in an apple crate unceremoniously and forgotten for several years before ending up strung together in a museum. In 1947, people protested and her skeleton was removed. In 1976, over 100 years after her death, her bones were cremated and her ashes spread over the waters of the D'Entrecasteaux Channel, as she had wished.

All told, it took whites about 75 years to wipe out the indigenous Tasmanians, who had been there for 30,000-plus years. Some historians go on record as to call it the only true genocide in English history.

THE MAD NOMADS crept into Mount Field National Park in time to take up residence at a caravan park. Before the sun sank, my Nikon cameras, some Fuji film and I managed a quick 10-minute huff down a path of green to Russell Falls, shown in pamphlet photographs as a waterfall of flowing proportions. What I arrived to was a beautiful cascade trickling down from several levels, but let's just say it wasn't as full-figured as I'd expected, for drought had slimmed its scale.

When the daylight was all but gone, the bushes around me came alive with bounce. The path back, not to mention our caravan site, was soon besieged by gangs of bennette wallabies (like kangaroos, but smaller). The next day, I emerged into dull sunshine to find Aaron and Louise staring down at what appeared to be a small and mobile pin cushion. It was, in fact, a bumbling echidna. And we never saw, heard nor smelled any devils, despite plentiful photo postings.

That day, we hiked into the forests. The ground and surroundings were covered in moss and massive ferns that forced green at the top but that were based in brown, drought-ridden bottoms. We were in "tall trees" country, passing stumps and fallen trunks that stretched off to infinity. It was the kind of scene wherein at any moment, a three-foot imp with pointy ears wearing a green tunic, with exaggerated buttons and a orb sized belt buckle, curved wooden shoes and a stove-pipe hat might pop out of a community sized stump smoking a pipe, squinting with curiosity at your passing and say something like,

The dwarf of Tasmanian big trees I be,
Mistress of the waterfall seek thee,
But first you must answer these questions three.

Then you blink, he's gone and you hear laughter echoing through the woods. OK, maybe that was just my impression.

One tree we crossed was labelled as towering 79 metres above us. The tallest one in Tasmania measures 98 meters, just shy of the world's loftiest tree in California, which rings in at 111. But I'm easy when it comes to competitions of height: to me, any tree that shoots out of sight in vertical or fallen horizontal direction classifies as "big."

We pressed on along the path, which was coloured by mixed green and russet light filtered through the high tree canopies, and stopped at various waterfalls for breaks. Let me tell you that no water tastes better then when it taken from the source in the Tasmanian wilderness.

Thank thee, mistress of the waterfall!

"Allan, you're not sleep-talking standing up are you?" Louise would ask with her pen poised and her eyebrows cocked.

"Nay, lady of the Mad Nomads fellowship. Be us cousins?"

She would then gently ease my Tasmanian water from my hands with a reassuring gaze that it would all be OK.

We then drove back in the direction of Kingston, a suburb of Hobart, to effect the interview we had arranged. As we drove back, we noticed that the clouds looked a little different. In fact, they weren't related to rain at all; rather, they were palls of thick bushfire smoulder pouring off of some of the mountain tops. It was said, once again, to be controlled back burning, but I have learned that "fire" and "control" in the same sentence is never a guarantee of incendiary restraint in this country.

Along the way, we spotted something very unusual, aside from the "walking pace" speed limit signs. It was so unusual that it caused Louise to post a web article entitled, "Mad Mailbox Masterpieces," for which as I supplied supporting photos. You see, rural Tasmanians take their mail boxes VERY seriously. When you don't have mobile reception or the internet, I suppose there is no choice, really. We drove passed estate after estate, and wrote Louise,

> The first [mailbox] we noticed was a miniature house – cute, but nothing crazy. A few doors down was an old milk bucket and barrel painted like a cow, complete with attached head, legs and tail. Getting better. And then came the full-sized trail-bike, the tractor, the lawnmower, the butcher, the life-sized man and his dog, a Tasmanian devil and several more masterpieces, until we hit the ultimate – a full set of swings with dressed-up teddy bears in the seats.

Wondering whether or not to be happy for the art or concerned for the mental condition of those with too much time, we sped up to way past "walking pace."

We arrived outside of Kingston under darkness, and guess what? The caravan parks were all shut up for the night. Surprise, surprise. We began circling dark back streets – rather unsuccessfully – looking for incognito. We eventually came upon a grassy shoulder near an obscure intersection, promptly parked, ate dinner, took cold showers (which consisted of us splashing water on ourselves in our shower chamber) and then settled into bed all rugged up for the cold night.

A knock fell upon our door. "Great," we thought. "Cops or angry locals." Plans of knocking the knocker out ran through our heads and we opened the door, preparing to be told to move on. We didn't expect the sweet face of 18-year-old Rachel, who was on her way home from dance class. She greeted us and offered our band the chance to park in her driveway just down the road. We didn't know what to say, other than to gratefully accept the invitation.

We then met Rachel's parents and their three other children in their stately hillside house. They munificently offered that we use their showers, their phone, their internet connection, have some food and just to make ourselves part of the family. As you might imagine, we were gob-smacked by the quick trust these people of round ears and normal stature bestowed upon strangers parked along a roadside. After a warm shower and some chats with the whole clan, the Mad Nomads bedded down in our parked Britz for the night. The following morning, the father knocked on our door at about eight o'clock and told us that though the whole family would soon be going to school and work, they would leave the house open for us and would we lock it before we went? So after doing our laundry and taking real showers, we left a colossal thank you note for this family of unrivalled generosity. I finally had my proof: Tasmania is a great place, behind in some ways perhaps, but very far forward in its acts of random human kindness.

As we made moves to leave, we noticed suddenly that although the mountains had been on fire at the close of the previous day, the passing of 12 hours had made the weather British again. It was raining, windy and bone-cold. Even the horses in the fields wore jackets. This was a perfect day to interview!

We pulled into a comely retirement village in Kingston to meet an incredible woman who had lost her first husband under a veil of secrecy. Edith would tell us the story of her three marriages – all of them to air force pilots! Her third husband Robert was also present as we chatted with them in their cosy living room.

Edith, who grew up an only child after her mother died when she was six, was drawn to the Royal Australian Air Force (acronym also sounding like a plane, RAAF) and a "life of adventure, no responsibilities and a chance to go anywhere," she said. "I guess you don't think about too much when you're only 19."

Despite a dispute with her father (who had to sign her up given her age), she got her way. For three years she was an Air Force driver, steering everything from ambulances to airstrip vehicles to parachute packers. This was a life she wanted, and "certainly there were a lot more men, let's be honest," she candidly allowed with a smirk.

Her first husband was Geoff Tuck, a RAAF pilot of quite some merit. Geoff was a training commander for a long spell, eventually being posted to Papua New Guinea, where he flew low-level spying missions over enemy troops, before being shot down and eluding capture by "crawling from the plane wreckage and steamy jungle with a broken back." But the most dangerous mission was yet to come. When the war ended, he returned to Australia as a high-ranking test pilot, flying very secret missions that he couldn't even tell Edith about.

Edith knew very little about Geoff having to go to England to pick up a Canberra bomber and bring it to Australia, though she did know that it was equipped with a self-destruct button should he land anywhere else but Australia.

The couple had two children, a boy and a girl, and were posted – with no notion of the tragedy about to befall them – to Woomera, in the windy, dusty South Australian outback, which was then a town of 3,000 built for military personnel and their families.

In 1954, the Tuck family received orders to move to England. Edith gathered their two children and took them back to Tasmania to say goodbye to her father before they returned to Melbourne to set sail across the globe. Geoff, she states, was not well upon their return.

"He said he was very sick and he had a lump in his neck, which was analyzed as a cyst. A doctor removed it on a Tuesday and that Friday I received a call from the chief medical officer. He told me that it was incurable and terminal." Geoff deteriorated quickly, going from "a physically fit man to dead in no time, full of cancerous things." He died in 1955, five months after his mysterious mission. He was 34.

There was no explanation for why he passed away so abruptly. Edith received no compensation, and she had no job and no place to go. The youngest child was aged three months and the elder four years. Her father remained in Hobart but bought her a small place in Melbourne while she drew a war widow's pension from the government. She did manage part-time work sometimes, but, "With children that young, who get measles and mumps at school, I could hardly work while caring for them. We never had day care in those days. We got by."

What she found out over time was that Geoff had been on a mission for the British government. Setting off British atomic bombs in the South Australian desert (the largest of which had a yield of 25 kilotons) in the 1950s was all the rage. Geoff had been sent to Maralinga (an Aboriginal word meaning "thunder") that sits on the edge of the Victoria desert and apparently once housed hundreds of secretive scientists and service personnel.

"The planes were seemingly kitted out with instruments to test what effects atomic dust would have on an engine, or so I was told much later," said Edith. "To this day, we still don't know much about the Maralinga atomic testing. The British government is, apparently, still looking into it and the Australian government had nothing to do with it."

Geoff only flew around a mushroom cloud, but one year after his passing, Edith discovered that the whole team of related personnel had also died quite suddenly after the test day. She drew out a paperback book with a disturbing atomic mushroom cloud on the cover and the title *Maralinga, British A-Bomb, Australian Legacy* written in white block letters. In the back of the book were columns and rows of names, including Geoff's. All the names listed had cause of death as either "cancer" or "lymphoma." While squinting at the inside front page, she said, "How many in total, we may never know."

Among the many affected, but not the listed, were the local Aboriginals, who are likewise seeking compensation from the government. Today, the area around Maralinga has been deemed "unsafe" and cordoned off for hundreds (and some say it may take thousands) of years, until the radiation returns to normal levels.

(In some later research, I discovered that the Maralinga explosion was at least recorded. In 1995, the Japanese cult Aum Shinrikyo (who objectified ending the world) released nerve gas into the Tokyo subway system, killing a dozen people and frightening the hell out of everyone else. It was later revealed that the cult owned a 500,000-acre property in the Great Victoria desert of WA. The group had covertly tested a nuclear blast on Australian soil and it took the Australian government four years to figure out that it was more than a seismic disturbance. It was apparently 170 times more powerful than the most powerful explosion recorded in WA. What's more, the French government was caught testing nukes in the South Pacific Ocean, not far from the Great Barrier Reef. I could go on, but it only leaves me wondering what else has gone on in this thinly populated region without being recorded).

Seven years after Geoff's passing, Edith married widower Ian, also an Air Force pilot, who brought his four children into the equation. "I could write the book on blended families," Edith allowed. "I thought I could make it all work, but it was hard." The marriage lasted for over 20 years, before Ian passed on.

So, how does one get through a tough childhood, losing a husband under such vague circumstances, being a widow with children during war time, raising a merged family and leading an RAAF life? "You just get up and keep going," was Edith's straightforward reply. And she had, for at age 80 she had married childhood friend Robert – also ex-RAAF and son of a Gallipoli survivor. At the time we chatted with them they were about to celebrate their three-year anniversary.

As for current world conflicts, Edith is amazed by the images that come across her television. "It is unbelievable what you see on TV. Children and women in battle – it's horrendous. But there is so much we don't understand. Today's conflicts are so different from anything we have ever heard of or seen. We are hearing of women leaving messages to their children at home as they go off to war, and that to me seems wrong, how mothers can go away and leave their kids. I guess I don't wholeheartedly agree with this equal-opportunity business."

We thanked Edith for her story and made way to the door absorbing the massive lessons she had taught us about life and resiliency. "There is always someone fighting with someone," she said at the close of the interview, "dreadful as it is. I don't like it, but the bible says there will always be war."

And with that, we headed out into the cold of Kingston.

OUR TIME IN Tasmania was running out, and we still wanted to take in some of the sights, starting with Freycinet National Park. We hiked an exhausting five-hour circuit, mostly uphill – very good exercise, indeed, for our growing "car asses."

We crested a vantage point that offered us the vista of the thin sliver of land known as Wineglass Bay. The view shown in postcards is that of a shimmering inlet of inviting aqua-hued water that turns lighter as it hits a golden white beach, which itself becomes lush forest. It certainly was the right view, but with the thick cover of grey clouds it wasn't quite the postcard. However, when we walked to beach level, we were stricken by the array of colours – especially some very red moss that clung to the rocks.

The following day, we drove to Cradle Mountain National Park. The long drive inland through winding hills and switch-back roads brought us into opaque views of the emerald mountains. The vegetation looked a lot less brown here, and more animals popped out now and then. Cradle Mountain is spectacular. The name is derived from its profile, and indeed many people were holding up babies and being coordinated by snap-happy camera-toters trying to make the photo look like the babber was lying in the curvature of the mountain naturally. (I didn't have the heart to tell those with their point-and-shoot cameras that the viewer doesn't truly represent how the photo will look).

The area is one of grey rocks battling green foliage on inclines, with the rocks of Cradle Mountain appearing to be holding a race to the sky in their spiralling fashion. The lakes at the bottom lend only too well to the scenery. We walked around Dove Lake and breathed in the bush lands before arriving back at our vehicle and motoring off to seek a campground. We found a caravan park and managed at length to locate our assigned spot along dirt paths winding labyrinth-like through dense forest. We should have noticed that there was no street-lighting, but we didn't, and we all headed to the showering facilities without flashlights as the sun was sinking. Upon emerging from the facilities, all of us got separated in the dark. We couldn't see a metre in front of us through the pitch and wandered around the maze-like campgrounds, sometimes getting off trail. Aaron later testified he had discovered a pole in the middle of the path "at testicle level."

Once we did manage to find each other (and our Britz motor home), Aaron sat incensed with his most unenviable of wounds and we passed the rest of the evening away at the local hut, which was equipped with a fireplace to combat the cold. The most horrible thing about slumbering in a sleeping bag in cold temperatures is that you automatically curl up into foetal position in an attempt to keep warm, but when you finally stretch out, you discover regions of your sleeping bag that are still possessed by arctic demons. You recoil in frigid fear, sometimes venturing gradually back into the offending zones in an attempt at spreading the heat, but ultimately you sleep in a paranoid dread of the cold and the unknown areas of your sock-like cover.

Our final day, however, proved to be the worst, weather-wise. We did a final hike along Dove Canyon Circuit: over terrain seemingly designed for mountain goat balance tests. It was slippery rocks and roots territory, thrown on angles not too far from, say, 60 degrees. Painted posts marked the trail and, without them, bashing through the woods on slopes angled to favour gravity would be hopeless. The track wasn't even really that, I realize as I think about it now. The hike was beautiful despite the cold weather, which gave way to a chilly drizzle, but the kicker was a sign *at the end* of the hike marked, "Caution: Trail Not Maintained." Right …

We passed some dense primordial woods with trees and ground covered in grassy moss. I could almost swear those trees were watching me, or might try to grab me, but maybe my brain had frozen. We passed several serene babbling brooks and waterfalls, winding through the lush backdrop, the best one being oddly enough at the end of the hike near the parking lot. I forcibly wondered if Tasmania's rough landscape made them do things backward and not tell others.

And thus, with our time up, we retired to Devonport to catch the ferry. It would be another 10-hour ride back to Port Melbourne, so we sought the solace of the $2 beer. Louise got her voice back and when she began bending the ear of some American cowboy at the bar as we were approaching the mainland, I took my Nikon, tripod and a large lens to the deck in an attempt to photograph Melbourne's skyline silhouette behind the fog.

As I clicked away, I felt as if I was being watched and turned to see a middle-aged gentleman standing near my flank stealing glances at my camera and the view. He wasn't appropriately rugged-up for the outside weather, and didn't seem to have a reason for being there, either. He wasn't smoking, enjoying the fresh air or taking pictures, so why wasn't he inside?

Once he saw that I had noticed him, he approached me in the way that a spy approaches a possible contact, or "asset," constantly looking over his shoulder. Any minute I expected him to speak a line of subterfuge code like, "The weather is better when the wet duck walks backward on the moonlit beach," to which I might reply, "But the monkey scratches when the tree tilts," and we would exchange microfilm.

"Sorry to bother you," he said instead, "but I'm a bit of a photo enthusiast myself. I couldn't help but notice your camera."

We then launched into a friendly conversation about photography. I proudly showed him my sponsored Nikon as the wind and cold continued to pound us on the deck. As we spoke, he stole nervous glances at the window of the ferry.

"Keeping an eye on your bag?" I probed jovially. His behaviour became jumpy to the extent that I half expected a trench coated figure to emerge and gun him down. But his was a fate worse than death.

"My wife hates it when I do this. She just likes those point-and-click cameras, doesn't understand or appreciate why it takes so long to set up photos and cameras," he said, once again looking back. "I used to be part of a camera club, but had to quit," he added quietly, as if she might be listening through the glass pane.

"Don't look now!" he snapped with his mouth covered. I quickly made it seem as though I was turning my head to crack my neck, and thus by a quick glance caught the disapproving gaze of a woman through the porthole. It might have been the glass, but her facial features didn't appear to line up.

And then our conversation ended and, as if being signalled by a noiseless whistle, he briskly offered a goodbye and thanks before bilking off back into the warm world of indoors.

My lens and I turned back toward the approaching Melbourne skyline to rattle off some more shots. I stole glances indoors every now and then and caught the long face of that chap, seated obediently with the expression of a child recently deprived of candy, next to his overbearing wife with her dour disposition.

Albeit a brief one, it had been a phenomenal time in Tasmania. I got to thinking that for all the sacrifices previous generations had made to guarantee an open way of life for their children, it was certainly sad to think that it didn't always translate into direct freedom for all. The photographically inclined gentleman I had just bantered with was sure proof that that indeed spirit-crushing dictatorships could still go on latently in free places like Australia. Poor fellow.

Alas! The moment of clarity! The misunderstood and bent truth about the magic of the smallest Australian state was upon me! The "Apple Isle" had the power to make people realize that no matter how mysterious the world may be, in some inexplicable way, so many things in life can be somehow ... related!

Try as I might, I couldn't get a clear photo of mainland Melbourne, for it was simply too foggy.

How do you like them apples?

43 – Snakes, Ladders and Other Devious Roads

IN KEEPING WITH the theme of clarity, the truth about Melbourne must now out.

In the mid-1800s, it seemed that snakes were biting reasonable citizens all around the settlements and those who didn't die from the venom died from terror. The thought occurred to John Underwood, who was serving a sentence in Tasmania, to create a snake bite cure that he could mass market. Underwood had been working in the woods often and thus had ample time to observe serpents. He realized that, if treated immediately, snake bites were rarely fatal, and in certain seasons the venom was not as potent as in others.

When he got his ticket of leave, he went about creating a concoction and then undertook a very personal promotional campaign. Underwood would draw a crowd, pull snakes out of his pockets and let them bite him, feign that he was dying before horrified citizens, and then swig Underwood's Majic Antidote and suddenly be good to go again. He was soon making a mint and thinking about expanding outside of Tasmania – namely to Melbourne, where there would be a larger market and, of course, less Tasmanians.

But Joseph Shires had his eyes on Underwood. Shires came from a similar background and decided to muscle in on the trickery. Pretty soon, there were two snake cure kings, both denouncing the other as fake and selling their own elixirs at their orchestrated live promotions. The rivalry came to a head in 1860 when they both rucked up in Launceston, in northern Tasmania. One-upmanship, bravado and a shouting match led the two to agree that a no-poisonous-snakes-barred competition should be held before a large crowd to prove who was the real McCoy. The event gathered a large audience and the two tried to outdo each other by pulling snakes out of hats and pockets; before long, a plethora of diamond, tiger, taipan, whip and carpet snakes were swarming all around them. It was then agreed that instead they should each produce one snake and let it have a nibble on the other, but before that could happen, Underwood and Shires came to blows and the snakes never got their chance. Shire's entourage managed to kick Underwood's gang out of the tent; thus, in Tasmanian eyes, Shires *had* to have the better product.

Underwood remembered his original plan to go to big-time Melbourne. Sadly, once he got there, he somehow lost his spark and failed to sell anything. Then one night, a snake that was sleeping in his shirt decided to put its fangs into Underwood's diaphragm and the man was out of business ... because he was dead.

Meanwhile, Shires had cornered the Tasmanian market, had then steamed to Melbourne; by 1868, he was a success and a star. A Victorian police magistrate named Drummond began to openly doubt Shires' demonstrations, saying that the fangs had either been removed or milked, but many just told him to shut up. So to prove himself, Drummond concocted the half-baked idea to rush Shires and demand his snakes bite him instead. "All they do is talk," Drummond had said of the elite class he hung out with; "I'll actually do something!"

Shires was reluctant about the private test, but after enough badgering (and after being offering a hefty fee) he gave in and the two rented a private hotel room and invited several eyewitnesses. Shires tried to talk Drummond out of it, but the magistrate presented his arm and said, "Let your snake bite that!"

Shires then let one of his tiger snakes bury its fangs in the flesh six inches above Drummond's wrist. Meanwhile, downstairs, the landlord of the hotel was very suspicious of the noises and – after his knocks went unanswered – put his shoulder to the door to gain entry. The proprietor crashed in on the befuddling scene of pale witnesses, a man holding a tiger snake and a police magistrate stumbling around the room screaming deliriously for a doctor. The landlord then went for a cab to rush away Drummond and came back to throw Shires into the street.

Drummond's doctor was not in, and so time was wasted in rushing him to another, who was quite perplexed (as you might imagine) at hearing that a tiger snake had been *invited* to bite his patient in a private hotel room. The doctor couldn't do much, and ordered Drummond to come back the next day.

Shires rushed his antidote to Drummond's home. Sadly, no one would let him in and Drummond died. Shires was arrested on charges of manslaughter. At his trial, which by all descriptions was flamboyant, Shires was found not guilty. Nevertheless, the vindicating verdict did little to help slumped sales of his antidote and he went from riches back to rags.

It might shock many Melbourne-ites (also known as "Yarra Yabbies"), who poke fun at Tasmanians, to know that their "Marvellous Melbourne" was founded three decades before the above narrative by some snaky

Tasmanians in what some historians call the greatest land grab in British imperial history.

David Collins, one of the men who helped establish Hobart, had sailed around the coastline of Victoria in the early 1800s to look for new pasturelands, while at the same time deterring any French from doing likewise. He found a spot and trawled 310 convicts out, but after only six months, the "barbarous country," as he called it, was abandoned. Some convicts ran over the sand dunes to die in their search for China, but most just hopped back on the boat to Derwent River to help build Hobart. Collins died in 1810 and it was rumoured that he had been struck down by the hand of God for the sin of consorting with the women of Hobart – usually with his good friend "Mad Tom" Davey.

By the 1830s, John Batman (the son of convicts sent to Van Diemen's Land) had helped found the 14-member, Tasmanian-owned Port Phillip Bay Association. He went up the Yarra River where he spotted some Aboriginals sitting around the area that Collins had been looking at a few decades earlier, and exclaimed that it would be a great place to raise sheep. Batman then duped the traditional landowners out of a 243,000 hectare parcel of land. The indigenous people had no idea what trading was, of course, and as compensation for being shuffled off of their ancestral home they received 20 blankets, 30 knives, 12 tomahawks, 10 looking glasses, a dozen pairs of scissors, 50 handkerchiefs, 12 red shirts, four flannel jackets, four suits of clothes and a 50-pound bag of flour.

The governor of NSW was not impressed by the zigzag methods through which Batman had acquired his stake and swiftly took it away from him, then offered it for sale at a low price. Batman, despite no longer being its owner, still managed to settle with his wife in what is today Melbourne, but he suffered terribly. Some believe it was Aboriginal voodoo, but Batman was actually afflicted with syphilis; he had to be wheeled around the settlement in his decaying condition and would die horribly four years after making the dodgy land grab.

Over time, the settlement – despite earning a reputation as being a place where escaped convicts would most likely flee – grew in spurts and jumps and was named after British Prime Minister Melbourne in 1837. Three years later, it had a growing population of 10,000 people, thanks in large part to the energetic John Fawkner, a driving force behind the new settlement and the individual who would become known as "the grand old man of Victoria." Fawkner was once a publisher, then a publican, then a self-taught bush lawyer before lending his zeal to the fledging Melbourne. When he died, 15,000 people filled the streets to pay final respects.

This was of course the very opposite of the sinful Collins and the swindler Batman who died in obscurity and no one remembers them or other Tasmanians who pushed snake cures not long after.

Once we docked back in Melbourne, we sought refuge at Natalie's place for a night and then stayed another with my friend Ingrid. Many months previous, Craig and I had met Ingrid (on vacation from her native Melbourne) on Sydney's Manly Beach while Natalie was visiting, and we had kept in touch with her since. I told you Melbourne-ites are cool! She was by trade a teacher (and a person who had never been assaulted in a sleepy delirium).

Kim and her parents were also generous in their hospitality. You may recall that Kim was one of the original 258 Bondi cast members and a good friend of my former roommate Jen. But our time in the café city built on swindled circumstances was short-lived.

Jody, our companion since Sydney who had stayed in Melbourne while we were in Tasmania, headed off by plane to Cairns with a view to travel down the east coast. Another friend of ours would be joining the Mad Nomads in Adelaide, and thus with great big thank yous to Nat and Ing and Kim, we headed to the Britz depot to trade in our four-berth Explorer for two other vehicles. We were issued a Hi-Top and an Elite model, both of them two-berth jobbies. The Hi-Top is a small modified Toyota van, but don't judge it from the outside, for the interior is fanciful; it was designed for two people plus a child, and has all the Britz trimmings: little kitchen, fridge, beds, storage space and all the bedding and kitchen ware. The Elite is a Mercedes with a long wheel base, more of a luxury, and it, too, is equipped accordingly.

With great excitement, we drove west out of the sprawl of Melbourne, destined for one of Australia's most famous stretches of thoroughfare running along the southern lip of the continent: Victoria's Great Ocean Road. Picture a place where the divergent forces of liquid and solid nature converge on a battlefield of patience and time. With eroding power, the ocean pounds away in wave after wave of relentless onslaught against the stalwart, stubborn and russet landscape. Now arbitrarily fling a thin but long sliver of concrete, much like you would a string over rocky shoals, between the two battling elements, and you have the Great Ocean Road. It is out of this world.

With green and undulant hills on one side, and sheer and startling drops to the ocean on the other, the one-lane highway slithers between the two but offers pull-offs for the seemingly endless beaches along the way. Surfers clad in wetsuits barrel into the white blitz, families have picnics and lovers snuggle up. Every now and then, we crested a hill to be offered a vista reminding us that this really is the bottom of mainland Australia.

Before 1918, all the coastal Victorian towns were linked and accessed either by boat or very rough inland trails. Then after WWI, the project of building such a scenically blessed motorway was born in the spirit of paying homage to fallen troops. It employed 3,000 ex-servicemen and when the Great Depression hit, the project took on "susso workers" before being completed in 1932. The stretch runs 300 kilometres and is dotted with famous little seaside towns and farms and stretches of rain forest and hills and all the other things that make it spectacular.

Along the way, we saw lots of unmarked police cars. Apparently some drugs had washed up on shore and a bust was effected by the Victoria Drug Squad, netting what the news folk tagged "the largest drug bust in Victoria's history." They also bagged some illegal immigrants, who wound up in the Woomera Detention Centre.

By nightfall, we managed to reach the parking lot of an Australian landmark almost as over-featured, photographed and hyped as the Big Red Rock on the international stage: the Twelve Apostles. Although the moon was full and attempting to be forceful, a heavy conglomeration of clouds blocked it and rendered the night freezing. We parked our Hi-Top and Elite and wandered down to the cliff's edge, where the world drops away into the ocean. We didn't see much, but we could sense the presence of the grand rocks and vaguely trace the freestanding silhouettes of the closer ones.

Now here is one of Australians' undeniable attributes: they aren't capitalists when it comes to national treasures. Years ago, when my brother and I were taking a road trip across the United States, we found it annoying that most locations of note had fees attached. I could understand some fees, but we had to pay to look at the Grand Canyon, we had to pay to drive our car through a hollowed-out redwood (which lasted mere seconds), we had to pay for parking – we had to pay for *everything* in the USA.

But in Australia access to most things, even something as huge and renowned as the Twelve Apostles, is free! One outdoorsy Englishman in particular was over the moon about the fact that in Australia he could veer off the Great Ocean Road and fish or go for a swim and not have to pay someone to be on their land. An American echoed the sentiment, only he also appreciated the fact that you wouldn't find yourself at the business end of a shotgun or a lawsuit if you mistakenly trespassed on someone's land. More likely an Australian would buy you a beer and ask how you're going.

For all the other crazy fees Australians paid, they at least had the sheer delight in enjoying their own vast land thriftily. If Europe or America had the Twelve Apostles in their jurisdictions, you can be sure there would be a theme park and $80 tickets, big mascots and turnstiles, not to mention overpriced cheeseburgers. But not here. Not yet, anyway.

Because we couldn't see anything, we curled up in our Britz campervans and awaited the next day, hoping that someone would scare those clouds away.

I hopped out of bed early and ran down to the viewing area with my tripod and cameras. Indeed, someone had scared away the clouds and the full moon was now highlighting the eerie shapes of the Apostles. It was cold, and though I was dressed in several layers and wearing a tuque, I was shivering. I manipulated the controls of my camera gear with frigid hands.

In the distance I heard what sounded like children fighting or being forcefully handled. When you are standing in a silent night with a full moon, noises will play with your imagination. It wasn't children, I later found out, but rather penguins on the beach below retreating into hidey holes before the sun rose. And that it finally did!

The sky turned a multitude of pastel colours and the moon retreated over the horizon, rather sheepishly leaving a silver trail on the water. The shapes of the Apostles became more apparent and down the coast we could perceive an ocean mist that shrouded the land. It was, all told, an amazing sight. There they stood, the stubborn stone masses that used to belong to the land, being bashed by white frothy waves in a ceaseless procession. One day they, too, will become part of the ocean floor.

But I'll back up a few minutes here. As I stood there in the pre-dawn hours, a middle-aged gentleman ambled up with the telltale waddle of a photographer. He went about setting up tripod and camera body with dangling cable shutter release. We gave each other a professional nod as we both struggled to keep warm while executing our art. As we snapped away, we chatted about photography and life. Then, once the sun was up, he started packing up his gear in a mad rush.

"What's the matter? Are you on a tour bus that's about to leave?" I asked.

"No, I'm in the parking lot like you. Wife wants me back for breakfast," he said as he unscrewed his cable shutter release hurriedly.

"Right now?! But you'll miss some prime shooting time," I said, photographically alarmed.

"Well, my wife doesn't like all this photography biz, she says it takes too long, prefers the quick snaps," he said as he collapsed his tripod. In response to the look on my face, he added, "We have a compromise. She gives me sunrise and sunset, and I give her the rest of the day."

"Hardly equal amounts of time," I retorted.

"Whaddya gonna do?" he said hopelessly. (Head for China, I thought to myself). He packed up his kit and said, "Nice to have met you," and then made for the parking lot in magnetic fashion.

"Hey!" I yelled and he turned around. "Do you by any chance have a relative in Tasmania, or one who travels there by ferry with his wife? He used to be in a camera club?" I ventured.

"No, not at all. Why?" he replied.

"Oh, nothing," and with that he went off to the parking lot, where I have no doubt a foot was impatiently tapping.

Aaron and Louise joined me and we watched what Louise would note as, "A v-e-r-y slow-motion changing of the guard: the day shift worker taking over from the night shift."

To be honest, there aren't actually 12 of the Apostles to really see. From the lookout, one can easily spy seven – five on one side and two more over the opposite cliff – and so it is thought that either five have joined forces with the ocean floor or (and this is officially written) the discoverers might have taken great poetic license while using mind-expanding chemicals. Wrote Louise for our website, "The obvious comparison is of the Seven Dwarfs. In fact, they used to be called the Sow and Piglets, as there is one large rock and a trail of smaller ones."

It was kind of alarming to note that the coastline, made up of clay and limestone, is eroded by wind, waves and rainfall to the tune of two centimetres a year. The cliffs simply crumble and get massaged out of existence.

The Twelve Apostles are the most famous pull-off on the Great Ocean Road because they just happen to have been stranded close to each other and line up conveniently. The rest of the formations along the Road are much larger, but they are laid along a larger spread. They, too, have names: Ard Gorge, London Bridge, Arch and Grotto, Bay of Islands and Bay of Martyrs.

Ard Gorge has a sad tale associated with it. In 1878, after a long journey from England, the *Lord Ard* clipper ran aground at a very early hour and killed every one of its 55 passengers and crew, save two. One 18-year-old woman (a non-swimmer) managed to grab a piece of wreckage and float into the gorge where she was heroically rescued by a local apprentice officer, also 18, who had also raised the initial alarm, but not in time to save anyone else. Rumours soon flew of a romance between hero and damsel in distress, but in reality, the woman returned to Ireland and the two never stayed in touch.

For its part, London Bridge used to actually connect to the mainland, until a catalytic moment in 1990 sheered the annex and left two tourists stranded. They were rescued by helicopter, and it isn't written if they stayed in touch, either.

After we drank our visual fill, we got back on the famous highway and eventually it turned inland, away from the elemental battlefield, into the dry zones. We were now headed for Adelaide, the capital city of South Australia, where a friend and some twisted destinies awaited us.

IN THE EARLY 1990s, the Victorian government offered $250,000 to anyone who could discover the wreckage of a fabled ship. The reward has since expired without being demanded, but if ever someone did find it, Australian and world history would have to be rewritten.

Legend has it that the *Deliens World Map* was published in 1567. It was speculated to have been traced in 1522 by Portuguese mariner Cristovao de Menoca, who reputedly hugged a significant portion of the southern Australian coastline, calling it Java La Grande. The diagram apparently ended abruptly at what is today Warrnambool, at the western edge of the Great Ocean Road, which the Mad Nomads were presently driving on. Historians hypothesize that one of his three ships must have sunk near Warrnambool and thus caused him to abandon the project and never return.

In 1836, two shipwrecked sailors claimed they saw the remains of a large mahogany ship near Armstrong Bay, not too distant from Warrnambool. Up until 1870, there were other sightings and suppositions that the wreckage was covered over by shifting sands. Then again, it could also have been the product of imagination. If such a ship were to be found, it would mean that Menoca's expedition did reach Australia in the 16th century and thus the factors of early settlement, mixing with Aboriginals and the title of being the first Europeans to find Australia would have to be rewritten.

One of the reasons it might have been so hush-hush was because, at the time, there were treaties between Portugal and Spain, which divided the world in two rough exploratory halves and Australia was in the Spanish bit. If the Portuguese had discovered anything Down Under, then it would have been considered illegitimate.

Historians got excited when two Portuguese cannons were found on the northwest coast of Australia. The exhilaration floundered when it was realized that there was no additional wreckage – the big guns had washed up with no human companions. Furthermore, it turned out that they were copies made in Asia. And it looks like the early Portuguese ships in Oz will always be a mystery, for an earthquake in Lisbon in 1755 destroyed several early sea charts, such as *Deliens*, that were reputed that have had Australia on them.

I kept an eye out, and read that 1,188 shipwrecks (more shipwrecks than anywhere else in the world) lie just off of Victoria's pernicious and foggy coastline, but I never saw the fabled ship or any others as the Mad Nomads pulled away from the Great Ocean Road.

The greenery of farmlands and the canopies of cloud gave way to the heat and golden flatlands of South Australia. We crossed the border into the "Festival State" under the hospices of a heavily orange sunset reflecting on wispy clouds. A series of tunnels and ear-popping inclines brought us into Adelaide. By all outward appearances, it was the reverse of Sydney: roads were straightforwardly laid out and all was visibly named.

Well, I wasn't wrong in my assumptions, as I read that Adelaide was one of the three best-planned and most charming cities in the world, alongside Washington, DC, and Edinburgh, Scotland. Three-quarters of SA's population live in Adelaide, but the whole empty state sums only one-tenth of Australia's population and equally covers just over one-tenth of the entire continent. It has 37,000 kilometres of coast and inland SA earns the distinction of being the driest state in Australia. Consider that harder for a moment. This is the driest state on the flattest and driest continent in the world. Perplexingly, though SA is almost entirely desert, one-fifth of its area has been set aside for conservation. I wondered how one might go about protecting desert, and realized that I was entirely the wrong person to be mulling over such things.

What seems to be an immense source of pride to all South Australians is that their state was the *only* Australian colony that wasn't created as a place to send convicts. It was apparently settled by equal ratios of men and women (unlike the other testosterone-heavy colonies) who came of their own free will. But in hitting the books, the assumption is somewhat ambiguous, and SA looks to have been founded by a paedophile.

The founder in question was actually a political theorist who had been convicted of abducting a 15-year-old heiress. While in the brig, he and another inmate read avidly and heard stories of Kangaroo Island (just off the coast from Adelaide) from a cellmate who happened to be a ship captain. Having never been there themselves, the two industrious prisoners hatched a plan to settle the southern part of Australia with free men and labourers and put their proposal to the English government in 1829. The business strategy hung on the principle that investors would get rewarded with land development and labour dividends.

In 1831, the South Australian Land Company was formed at exactly the same time as the entrepreneurs gained their freedom. Ultimately, their brief was rejected and the two men abandoned the idea altogether, only to have it revived in London in a slightly different way by explorer Charles Sturt. By 1834, the colony of South Australia was formed and free settlers headed off two years later to make SA the only colony to have begun without convicts.

Nevertheless, it seemed that there wasn't much foresight exercised, and upon arrival the settlers didn't even have a base or a loose concept for a settlement. They set up provisionally as surveyors bumbled about the desert looking for a sound alternative to erect a capital. In the process, debates raged over two prime locations, and the present location won out more or less by default and Adelaide – despite early warnings about a huge lack of water supply – was founded.

A few markedly noticeable things happened in Adelaide's history, though these events are separated by long spells of inactivity. A spike in 1967 occurred when – after the near four-decade tenure of a dry-as-a-SA-fart governor – a young and charismatic governor took over and intellectuals, artists and thinkers began flooding in and tearing down old mentalities, importing banned books and organizing festivals. Things were rolling toward the 1980s, however the catalytic governor left and so did most of the action. Next, the Bank of South Australia collapsed, ships saw no use in docking so far away from Melbourne or Sydney and in 1994, Adelaide lost the Grand Prix to Melbourne, which it has since tried to win back. Then, of course, the geographic location isn't ideal – worse than Canberra, if such a thing is possible. Murderous desert and ocean are its entourage, nothing is really close to it and – despite the early warnings – Adelaide is still plagued with fresh water problems.

Nevertheless, looking at the residents one may conclude they don't really give two cents worth anyhow. They have some of the world's greatest wine, they are far enough away not to hear the whine of Sydney or Melbourne and they have lots of taboo reading material and still a fair few festivals and major concerts. So maybe it ain't that bad being obscure.

Our first stop would be to pick up Sybille (Bille for short), 25 years old and one of the many Germans who had lived in 258 Bondi. She is the quintessential German: built tough, aquiline face and crazy blond Einstein hair that looks lionish when she rolls out of bed. She had studied English in Sydney, travelled around a bit and would join us as a fourth token on our Mad Nomads journey on the leg from Adelaide to Darwin in the Northern Territory. She was clean, reliable, courteous and always on time, without fail. Plus she had petrol money, was a dedicated driver and wanted to practice photography and ein English, which immensely spruced up the long road trip.

We next coasted into the local Britz branch, where we effected a trade to reduce us from two vehicles back to one. We drove off in another of their four-berth creations known as the Adventurer, an aptly named set of wheels dubbed by Australian Travel Show *Getaway* as a "motorized Swiss Army knife." Its design is unique and rooted in South Africa, where it was first constructed by a military who had spent nights in lion country. At heart it is an off-road four-wheel-drive Toyota Hilux, riding high on suspension that makes driving on rough feel like sitting on a slinky. The Adventurer may be small-looking on the outside, but out of the roof unfold two platforms with pre-opened tents and drop-ladders, and from the side you can launch a sun-blocking awning. A folded table slides out the back, and from within you can draw out chairs, a stove, a cooler-like refrigerator (an "eskie"), cutlery, towels and sleeping bags. It even has a tap under the rear bumper! I had played with Transformers as a child, and the Adventurer was like one of those robots that turned from car into small city. I was in heaven.

We tarried long enough in Adelaide to check emails and grab a snack, then took our new robust Britz from asphalt into the land it craved – destination: Flinders Ranges, 500 kilometres northeast of Adelaide. It wasn't long before urban gave way to what some people termed "the *real* Australia" – the baking and dusty expanse of bona-fide Aussie outback stretching in flat tracts in all directions.

The people who sparsely populate the area have a sense of humour about their harsh reality. Along the way, we spotted such roadside creations as giant cockroaches with pitchforks, a guard tower and a huge farmer, among other strange shapes that dotted an otherwise homogenous horizon.

Amusingly, even the government of South Australia tries to make their barren, ruthlessly ruler-level and otherwise featureless portion of the outback more appealing by putting in "scenic lookout" points along the highway. The logic of these pull-off spots struck as us non-existent by virtue of the sheer indifference in elevation. The choice boiled down to seeing the static outlook from the comfort of a moving and air-conditioned vehicle or from a sweltering and stationary position by the road, where swarms of flies will descend if you dare become a component of the exterior. In fact, if we had stopped and stepped out of our Adventurer, slighted elevated as it was on its suspension, we would actually be *stepping down* onto the lookout.

The desert is mystical. You can literally see other vehicles and towns many kilometres before you cross them. The land is barren and itchy-looking, with hues of arid red and sand mixed with the ever-present grey-green clumps of dried-out scrub known as spinifex, which crackles under your feet if you walk on it. The sky seems so much larger and competes with the disc of land to occupy the majority of your field of vision.

This openness can be scary yet strangely magical. Driving along sealed roads in a vehicle with litres of water is one thing, but whatever possessed the early explorers of Australia to make inroads into regions that exist seemingly only for the purposes of deadly demise makes my head spin. Furthermore, how they managed to convince their horses and camels to continue into the baking heat and endless flies that can bring you to the point of screaming dementia, I will never fathom. Indeed, many never returned or went mad and drank their own urine.

45 – The "Real" Australia

THE BACKORWARD THING about a nation that loves winners is that it celebrates in its early inland explorers the biggest losers. You hardly ever find flashy mention of the plodding and orthodox types like Sir Thomas Mitchell, who was described as being "a worthy surveyor and government man who did lots of good work in New South Wales and Victoria" (yawn). No, you won't hear of him or his ilk. You'll hear about all sorts of failed explorers whose only credits were that they were willing to barrel unprepared and impetuously into the Australian centre and die horrible deaths. These stories are much sexier than some British guy with his socks up around his knees and a methodical and logical approach to mapping such a strange country.

Interior Australia is not a place for the sane. One explorer, Englishman Charles Sturt, was ordered to explore the inland river systems in 1829. He went and named the first large river he found the Darling (after the then-governor of NSW) and then found another river that had already been named by Australian explorer Hume, and called it the Murray (Hume was a proud Australian and his name had been taken away by a proud Englishman, but don't worry folks, Hume did get a highway named for him later on). When Sturt got further inland, he didn't find much to write about.

However, the most famous Australian explorers were the unlikely team of Burke and Wills (no relation to me, as far as I know).

Robert O'Hare Burke, an eccentric policeman from Ireland (described as "impulsive, charming, short-tempered, reckless and brave; a contrary and fatal mix") was known to muddle his bearings not only on the small Isle of Ireland, but on his own slender patrol-beat. His knowledge of exploring was on par with a fish's knowledge of snow capped mountain peaks.

How such an unlikely candidate managed to tie his own shoes, let alone be chosen expedition leader *and* solicit 60,000 pounds of sponsorship (the most expensive expedition in Australian history) is a tantalising story. There was a need, at the time, to build an umbilical-like telegraph relay from isolated Melbourne up the belly of the country to the East Indies and onward to Europe. Someone had to go and make the first crossing of the continent from south to north.

For his part, William John Wills – a young doctor with a decent British background – got the title of "surveyor."

Burke and Wills and his crew then packed way too much stuff and lost their lives. In reading what they packed (which included stationary office furniture, four dozen fishing lines and scores of fish hooks (for rivers they never found) and 1,500 pounds of sugar), I had flashbacks to high school wilderness camping trips when city girls would pack hairdryers, dozens of shoes, pagers, truckloads of make-up and plug-in mini-TVs in their rolling suitcases and arrive at the bus depot in SUVs. As instructed, the rest us had brought one slender backpack and one set of clothes, and stood gob-smacked by such inexperience.

Despite a huge send-off party in the streets of Melbourne, I have no doubt that parallel gob-smacked expressions were worn in 1860 when Burke and Wills and co. set out and managed to slowly cover a small sum of murderous interior kilometres (in the height of summer, no less) before they reached a location called Cooper's Creek in Queensland.

Thinking that smaller groups might progress faster, Burke, Wills and two others – King and Gray – asked a team to wait for them while they attempted to reach the Gulf or Carpentraia in two months. The trip took double that, their rations lasted a quarter of that, and Gray fell dead on the return voyage.

The parched trio then headed back to Cooper's Creek and their waiting friends, but arrived only hours after the latter had quit the camp to head home. Burke would find a note in a bottle under a spot marked "Dig" and discover that they had just missed the others. For unknown reasons, instead of following their original track down the Darling River, the three delusional explorers decided to make a 240-kilometre attempt to a police outpost near what was ironically called Mount Hopeless. They scribbled a note and buried it, but failed to put any markers indicating that the note was there.

Almost immediately after they blundered off, the other team came back to make one last check, but because Burke had left mail in the box but failed to raise the flag, the other team assumed they had not come back and gave up looking for them. It read something like those sitcom scenarios that take place in a long hallway with lots of doors and people who just keep comically missing each other. Even more ludicrous, Burke returned again (moments after) only to discover his note was still unearthed, so he went back to the other two and died with Wills. King managed to survive and was rescued.

What saved King was a larger underestimation among white explorers: the interior-dwelling Aboriginals. As white explorer after white explorer threw himself at the merciless interior, many died babbling mad and dehydrated short distances from underground water sources or went hungry as they passed perfectly edible plants. They also, for the most part, couldn't hunt or capture native Australian game and would contract infections and irritations that could have been easily remedied with local shrubbery.

All the while, the Aboriginal Australian found plentiful sources of life. They had a mastery of bush "tucker" and some experts go as far as saying that they enjoyed a richer diet than any European ever did.

(However, almost every food eaten in Australia today belongs to species introduced to the continent in the last 200 years. But it's all enjoying a comeback these days. To name but a few of the Aboriginal dishes currently enjoying popularity in high-end restaurants: eel, emu, sautéed kangaroo, stewed crocodile, plump insects or grubs, lizards, roasted frog as well as bush plums and lilli pilli ice cream, and an array of bush berry jams and sauces*.)

Owing to their deep belief that the land owned them, each generation of Aborigine knew when to move about as choice blossomed or faded. To cite one small example, there are today about 120 edible plants between the car park and the beach at Wilson's Promontory in southern Victoria, and like most hikers, I wouldn't have had a clue until I cracked a few books open. Even then, I wouldn't be able to guess which plants could be eaten and how.

However, their most incredible ability was that of mimicry. A white explorer in Tasmania was speared in the calf and screamed, "Oh, my leg," to which the Aboriginals responded by chanting, "Omyleg." In southern Victoria, in 1836, boring explorer Thomas Mitchell kept hearing what he thought to be a Scottish woman in his camp, though none was actually there. He found out that the speaker was instead an Aboriginal called Tommy Came-last, who was imitating a Scottish lilt he had heard at Portland Bay, on the distant coast.

The Aboriginals' decibel dexterity would send bandicoots running from bushes, coax eels to swim into their hands and cause crabs to pop out of crevices. To the astonishment of many, some Aboriginals could stamp their feet on the ground and cause a certain frog that retains water to jump out from the comfort of its hole thinking there was thunder, only to be grabbed and squeezed like a lemon for its juice.

And so, as the ancient European empires were rising and falling a

---

* Kangaroo, crocodile and emu meat are some of the best forms of meat in the world, low in fat and high in protein. However, because the Europeans brought cattle to Australia, the beef industry strong-hands any competition, and thus a natural and possibly profitable Australian abundance goes untapped.

long distance away, Aboriginal Australians were discovering ways to elicit precious water from sources as dry as Mars and passing this knowledge on to each newborn who would, generations on, watch stupid white men perish unmercifully in the desert, started – as you might imagine – as they noticed piles of fish remains next to Aboriginal camp fires.

With time, some explorers got smart and rounded out their company with Aboriginals who could seek water or summon dinner (but because the whites used thirsty horses and camels, sometimes their skills were considered irrelevant). Indeed, an Aboriginal seemed to know how to find just enough for what was needed, and treated anything over and above that a waste. I suppose you could say that they were true environmentalists.

We would be doing some of our own inept exploring shortly.

46 – Pounding Away

IT PROBABLY WASN'T the wisest move, and despite the native expression that only madmen and Englishmen walk in the daytime between 10 in the morning and two in the afternoon, our foursome hiked, drenched in sweat, up the steep ridges of the Wilpena Pound crater, Flinders Ranges, as the sun was approaching its searing midday position. We, in a small way, did exactly what silly white explorers Burke and Wills had done, only we had lots of water, sunscreen, hats in manageable backpacks and – best of all – no office stationary fixtures.

The rocks and earth were golden, the trees and scrub dry and threatening, and it may well have been the heat, but I started to imagine faces and figures in the craggy cliff facades we passed. We did make it to the top, which rewardingly offered us a vista of a big bowl. It was a concave microclimate flaunting green trees and grass – something like what you see on a Jehovah's Witness pamphlet, the Promise Land – and outside the rims were expanses of parched horizon leading off to the raised crests of the Flinders Ranges. It was hard to imagine that these two areas could coexist, but South Australia is a region blessed with micro-climates.

The "pound" is a cratered impact spot from some meteor that struck the Earth a very long time ago (it is still being guessed precisely when). Apparently, the bowl is 17 kilometres long and eight kilometres wide, containing 8,960 hectares. When I couldn't fit the whole view into my wide-angle camera lens, I generally accepted this as true.

The word "wilpena" is Aboriginal for "place of bent fingers," and the spot is generally considered to be the emotional centre of the Flinders Ranges. By the 1850s, the region was deemed beyond hope for cultivation, but the crater was used to rear horses who roamed freely because they couldn't escape the natural enclosure (makes sense if you want to save cents on building fence). Some 50 years later, a family leased the whole pound and cleared it out for wheat farming. Despite some initial success, they abandoned their plot in 1914 and left a trail of rusting pieces of 19th-century farm equipment as they retreated. By 1945, someone failed once again when they put up a resort; however, only a year after that an amazing, unrelated and uncelebrated event occurred.

A geologist was digging not far away when he found, to the disbelief of the scientific community, fossils of the earliest traces of multicellular life anywhere on Earth. "Ediacaran" (plant and animal) fossils have been found elsewhere in the world, but in the Flinders Ranges sleep their ancestors from the beginning of time, perfectly preserved. As to whether grand archaeological digs have been arranged, I am not quite certain, but it only underscores that no one really knows what went on here in prehistory.

About 30 years after the resort failed, the government decided to turn the Flinders Ranges into a national park, and things seemed to have improved for the area. The name Flinders might ring a bell: yes, it was Matthew Flinders who first sighted the low-lying region in 1802, before going on to champion Australia as the name for the new continent and record doomed Trim the cat's biography in a Mauritian prison.

That evening, as we were walking lost around the massive camp area, we happened upon a congregation of children and adults singing along to the Aboriginal tunes of Arthur, one of the Flinders Ranges National Park's Aboriginal rangers. A fire roared to combat the cold evening.

Some of the children suddenly spotted two kangaroos bouncing around in the periphery. For those of you who think kangaroos are cute little animals, let me advise you that they are also the most vicious of street fighters, and more entertaining to watch than any boxing match. In fact, these two particular kangaroos reminded me all too much of the two Glaswegians with whom I had celebrated Christmas the year previous.

The roos would be peacefully eating or browsing side-by-side and then without warning start fighting. They lock up much like wrestlers do, then circle for a bit, unleashing combinations on each other. A few slaps, jabs or punches to the head from the top arms is the most common offensive, but they also slip in low kicks, high kicks and tripping moves with their powerful hind legs. Then, if possible, one might unleash the mother of all kangaroo finishing moves by leaning back on its tail and firing off a mighty double drop kick to the opponent's mid-section. Then, as quickly as it all began, they separate calmly, scratch, let bygones be bygones, eat a bit more grass, take a casual hop around and then just randomly fling themselves at each other.

We managed to speak to Arthur and tell him about the Mad Nomads project, and he provided us with a lead for a stellar and insightful interview. The next day, we headed back in the direction of Adelaide, stopping off in a small town, and it dawned on me that not only were we in the real outback Australia, but I was seeing many more Aboriginal

Australian people than I had previously collectively seen in populated NSW, rural Victoria, Tasmania or the major cities.

They were everywhere: sitting in circles under trees, drifting by the side of the road, resting in the shadows of stairwells, roaming here and there. Some were even sleeping in public spots (and in one case, sprawled out across a sidewalk) and no one seemed to pay them any mind. It was as if they were just part of the scenery, another tree to walk past. All non-Aboriginal people, tourists included, treated them as less than as even remotely peripheral.

As I write this I will not for a second pretend to have any solutions or suggestions; in fact, like even the most revered historians, anthropologists and politicians, I am more puzzled the more I read and hear. There is so much that we don't know about the Australian Aboriginals' culture or their mores, spiritual minds and deep relationship with the land – or even how they got there in the first place. It's an unravelling process, but it isn't all hopeless, for slowly progress is being made on both sides.

We next entered Hawker (population less than 500) to speak with Arthur's cousin Pauline, who is a member of the local tribe. She had her own tale of rebuilding to tell.

Four years previous to our meeting, in a rapid six-month period, Pauline traumatically lost three close members of her family. Her cousin, aged 32, was diagnosed with a rare form of liver cancer and left behind a 12-year-old daughter. Four short months later, Pauline's brother, 37, whom she described as "a brilliant guitarist with some mental issues," died of a massive heart attack due to his involvement with drugs. On the heels of these events, her aunt passed on from liver cancer. It was a massive blow to the family, but Pauline has managed to be a mother and a mentor to her immediate family and the community at large.

"I worry about my health often: cancer has been a real killer in my family," she offered through some coughs. Pauline was presently fighting the flu, had recently had an operation and was still recovering from a back injury after falling off a horse. She spoke to us in a building that used to be a garage but now was carpeted, furnished and decorated with Aboriginal posters and ornaments.

"I was lucky, in a way, because I grew up in two worlds. I am very proud of my Aboriginality. It's a culture that is still a living culture, the stories are still alive. But I also got some education from the white man," she said.

The first decade of her life was spent on a cow and sheep station of some 600 square kilometres. "I loved being a child in the bush," she reminisced. At an early age, she learned how to drive cars and bikes, ride horses and raise animals, as well as spot, spear and prepare kangaroo and other creatures. She was educated for three years by School of the Air before coming to Hawker and working in nursing, falling in love with a cowboy and having her first child at age 18.

She has raised three children on her own and keeps herself busy with varying work, such as fencing the cemetery: "There is a lot of history there and I want to make it beautiful for when I go, whether I have to work in 45°C or not!" But her major plans for herself, her children and her grandchildren are to promote Aboriginal tours in the area.

"The Aboriginal ceremonies were ended in 1948 by the elders. Alcohol had filtered into the community and many began living the white man's way. The elders, who were very traditional in their laws, were concerned that under the influence of alcohol, members might leak out information that could result in the punishment of the whole tribe, so they stopped teaching," Pauline explained.

Recently, a market has been growing in Aboriginal tourism and traditions. "My mother grew up traditionally. Although Aboriginal people didn't get rights until the 1960s, my parents taught me not to sit and dwell on the past but to think to the future, because we have to make it a better place for all of us and our future generations."

To that end, Pauline worked for the Education Department, instructing new teachers in cultural awareness and in how to speak to people in communities. She also assisted with school outings, taking children into the bush to demonstrate the old way of life. "I like to take groups out while telling stories on site. You get more of a feel of the place, instead of reading from a book. Its good for the kids; they don't get bored."

Pauline found it equally rewarding to work in the unique Operation Flinders program run by the SA police and some councils. Young offenders are taken out of prisons for a week and put in the bush. They are obliged to walk eight to 10 kilometres a day laden with backpack, food and gear from point to point, where a bushman or traditional miner tells them stories and teaches them about bush food and the old ways of the land. They are also taught how to prepare indigenous meals as their hosts sing Dreaming Time songs. Pauline's role was one of running a cultural stand where she taught kids how to make damper bread, eat kangaroo and learn Dreaming Time stories.

Not all young offenders take so easily. "Some people can't handle the bush. One girl threw herself down a mine shaft in an attempt to get flown back to Adelaide. But she only ended up with some bruises and had to continue the trip. Didn't work too well," she chuckled.

One bush character "used to sit up in the hills with a laser pointer and flick it on the group every now and then to freak the kids out and remind them that they weren't alone and couldn't get away," she said.

Another time, she was sent a rich American girl who was on a "punishment trip" to learn how to fend for herself. "When she arrived, she had on make-up galore, changed clothes three times a day and was used to maids and servants doing everything for her. We stayed in shearer's quarters with a bunk bed and a dining room with a few old chairs. To take a warm bath, you needed to gather water and stoke a fire. We had to hand wash our clothes and she would hang her wet jeans out with 10 pegs on each leg," laughed Pauline. "In the end, she'd had a good shock."

Regarding her own culture, she feels that it does indeed take a village to raise a child. "That is one of my aims, hopefully in the future, to get more young people out there on these trips, give them an identity. Everyone needs a helping hand once in awhile."

Pauline's grandchildren are taking a deep interest in what she does, as are others, though the biggest challenge is getting people together and getting on with things. Despite the finish of the SA government grant, Pauline keeps her dream alive day by day and with some of her meagre personal funds.

"Beware of the kangaroos on the road," she advised us as we were getting up to leave. It was dark outside. As we headed out of town, we noticed that as predicted, the roadways were littered with packs of the bounding Australian icon. We followed Pauline's advice and took it slow, because in the end we all wanted to reach our destinations safely.

THE AUSTRALIAN OUTBACK station is an amazing thing to see – even though you can't really see it. Whereas the word "paddock" in England means an enclosed meadow, in Australia it means a field that extends for hundreds of square kilometres. Pauline's childhood station had measured 600 kilometres square, and she considered it small. Save for a fence, a rusty old windmill and a flock of sheep here and there, you wouldn't really know these terrains are used to raise animals as you drive past them on the highway. But having 1,000 square kilometres per farmer does make sense: in lush and wet England, a farmer can allow more sheep to graze per square kilometre, but in outback Australia, you need a lot more kilometres for the same quota. The vast stations apparently pretty much run themselves.

There were other hints of what once could have been: a repetitive presence of abandoned ploughs, wagons, tractors, cars and trucks, brown and red with rust and neglect, becoming part of the ground again. Every now and then the land would be dotted with the old crumbling bricks and basic structure of what was once a homestead, sometimes with a fireplace hearth still intact. Apparently, until the 1970s, it took weeks and months for stockmen on highly trained horses to gather large herds and hold them in yards until market. Nowadays, helicopters do most of the work with ground teams, so farmers rushed to the cities for work.

The towns we trickled past boasted populations of between 50 and 1,500 people. Identical signs advertising the historic birthplaces of obscure poets and outlaws, as well as old railways and mines, were ubiquitous and beckoning. The main streets are all lined with old-fashioned western cowboy–looking facades and bubble-shaped petrol pumps. Gruff-looking men tipped wide-brimmed hats to everyone and walked around with gusto and rolled sleeves, some to their old and curved and cherry red 1950s trucks. Here was a place where time had no meaning and hardship was a dish served hot and endless.

Of all the 19th-century outback tales, none matches the rags to riches narrative of the "Cattle King," who turned the interior to his advantage. Sidney Kidman, born in Adelaide, ran away from home at age 13 with a one-eyed horse and five shillings in his pocket. He ended up at Mount Gipps (now called Broken Hill, a desolate, middle-of-nowhere outback town 1,200 kilometres west of Sydney), where over the next decade he plunged himself into all kinds of varied affairs. His real ambition, however, was to own property, and he managed to purchase a half-share of his first property near Alice Springs.

With time and unrivalled aspiration, this once-poor rag of a kid owned or partially owned over 100 stations from the Gulf of Carpentaria and the Kimberly's in WA, to NSW and SA. By moving his animals from one of his stations to the next, he managed to deliver all his cattle in prime condition for market and avoid the effects of drought and tyrannous distance between points. Estimates of his ownership are of some 170,000 square kilometres, an area twice the size of Tasmania. He died in 1935 in Adelaide with many a shilling, and no doubt many horses of perfect vision.

"I took the kids out of school, the wife and I quit work and we drove around Australia in a motor home for three years, doing odd jobs and living in different communities across the land," said Bob with pride.

The Mad Nomads plus Bille were relaxing with Bob and Gail, whom we had sourced through my old roommate Shanni. They were kind enough to let us deploy our Adventurer in their driveway for a few nights and show us their town of Burra. We presently sat in their quaint living room having a chat and a drink.

"Yep, it was a grand time," Bob continued. "We met so many fascinating people, had some escapades and lived in so many different climates," he said with zest. "But there is much we did not get to see," he added ruefully. Bob has a brazen white beard and a glint of adventure in his eye. He looks like Santa Claus with a flask of whiskey. His talk of his three-year travelling sabbatical made the Mad Nomads realize that with only piddly three months (one gone already) to attempt getting around as much of the continent as possible, we stood to miss quite a significant portion. It put much about Australia into perspective: stuff the big stations, this whole country is outlandishly oversized.

We had been thrown a visual curveball upon arriving at the threshold of Burra, northeast of Adelaide, for no sooner had the outback dust settled behind our vehicle then we were into a green area. We passed a generous river banked with weeping willows, ducks mulling about and lush plants everywhere – an oasis in an ocean of sand. Bob explained that the difference between the Burra Valley and a few kilometres over the hill was the difference between two and 18 inches of rainfall a year!

In only two years, Burra grew from nothing into Australia's seventh largest town by virtue of the discovery of copper. Burra also earned the unofficial title as the eighth wonder of the world for its role in ending a small economic depression. It had a population of 5,000 people by 1845 and produced a staggering 5 percent of the world's copper supply. Then the industry and people floated out, but the town still has a look of its not-too-distant vestige. There are plenty of historic lookouts and inoperative mines to gaze at, and the town centre, though sleepy, has the feel that at one time real men swaggered about with ropes, buckets and picks and a penchant for an evening beer and a kangaroo brawl.

The following day, Bob was good enough to show us around the place and take us to the latest thriving "*c*" industry in Burra: not copper but cider, as well as wine-making. It was a bit out of place to see apple trees, especially since I associate apples with Tasmania and dreary cold, but there they were, in the heat. With South Australia's pockets of variable climates, wine production was a big enough business to give the European wine-producing nations a run for their money.

Bob was also good enough to introduce us to Edith, a Burra local, who had a very chilling tale to tell. In what is every woman's nightmare, she had lost three children between 1957 and 1964.

"It was so horrible," she told us in a low soft voice in her living room. "There is no real way to describe how one feels when you lose a child."

Edith brought 12 children into the world. "Never my idea," she joked, "but my husband wanted a large family." Her children were all born one after another, thus 11 and a half years separated the oldest from the youngest. Sadly, though, she would lose a quarter of her offspring in tragically different circumstances.

The first misfortune occurred when the child was aged a mere 12 months. He drank kerosene by accident and died of poisoning. Years later, Andrew, aged eight and a half years, had a freak heart attack while sleeping and doctors could not explain why. The last incident occurred when one of her sons, aged 19, was in a car accident, dying instantly as the vehicle went off the road through a guard rail and his torso was sliced nearly in half.

Each member of the family had to cope and seek solace in their own way. "My husband was a farmer and used to drink," said Edith. "When our son perished in the car accident, he never touched a drop again." The siblings, being close in both age and kinship, had some psychological scars, but managed to console each other.

The community of Burra came to their aid and Edith involved herself with Compassionate Friends, a non-denominational group of people who have lost close family and who gather for emotional support. Edith took each day as it came, and still does. "Some days you dwell on things and get really sad. Other days are better, and you keep busy and active and happy."

Edith was raised in Burra from the age of seven and, in a common echo of all our rural interviews, she, too, has seen her little town change. "Most people you don't know anymore," she offered. "Everyone used to know everyone, and now the population is dropping and mostly strangers come and go. The town used to be 2,000 people and now it's 1,500." Our Lonely Planet book put the figure at 1,200.

Edith keeps active despite her losses, the latest being her husband, who passed on from cancer in 2000. She leads a quiet life alone in a home that is often tranquil but swelling with activity when any or all of her eight grandchildren come up to visit from Adelaide or other areas. Edith is also an active member of Meals on Wheels, which aims to help elderly people who cannot easily gather their own groceries, and helps out as a volunteer at the leisure centre. "I love old people," she smiled.

As we left her home, she grabbed each of us in turn for a big motherly embrace. "Good luck," she said softly. "Drive safe." And that we did, happy to see that despite massive losses none of us could ever comprehend, she still found joy in her life and reason to smile.

"Ja, I vood like to keep her. She is *soooo* cute," said our German Bille, who had sat in on the interview.

"You can't just keep people in Australia," we had retorted jokingly.

"Ja, I know zis," she said sternly. Then I heard what sounded like a penny rolling through her head and when it landed she added, "It vas a joke, ja?"

"Yes, it was a joke, Bille."

"Das ist cool."

We thanked Bob and Gail for their yarns and hospitality and drove back into the desert for a more famous South Australian setting: the Barossa Valley, where odd things were about to unfold.

"There's more to the Barossa than booze!" called out a strange woman in a supermarket parking lot. In her online chronicles, Louise wrote,

> Spotting us as tourists, stocking up on bread and cheese to accompany our wine, she felt obliged to give us a local's tip. I couldn't imagine what more these famous vineyards could offer. "Such as?" I asked, with hope (or perhaps just a glaze) in my eyes. "Well, I've just come back from a quilt exhibition – simply wonderful it was," she shared, then gave us directions. "When you get out of the car park, turn right and take the first street." When we got out of the car park, we turned left and took the first winery. There was drinking to be done.

Barossa is an hour outside of Adelaide, and though the valley is only 32 kilometres long (a mere dash of oasis in an otherwise brown and sandy state), it pumps out an unbelievable one-third of Australia's vintage. In Australian exploratory tradition, the region had been named for the friend of an explorer but ended up being misunderstood and misspelled by cartographers as Barossa ("hill of roses").

The early settlers were devout German and Silesian Lutherans who were persecuted in Prussia. A wealthy South Australian businessman heard of their plight and financed their escape in 1838 to Port Adelaide and then to Barossa, where he thought they would make fine colonial pastoralists. The Germans immediately set up quaint bakeries with *streuselkuchen* and *bienenstich*, and delis with *bierwurst*, while others held oompahpah lederhosen recitals outside.

The current population is about 18,000 and half are of German descent. Interestingly enough, they single-handedly turned around one of Australia's largest drinking habits. Up until 1960, Australians mostly drank beer and sherry (some estimates stand at 96 litres of beer a year per Aussie), but when wine was offered up, a new statistic tipped the alcoholic scales: 201 litres of wine per person per year goes down the Australian gullet. Nevertheless, with averages of 901 litres per person per year being consumed in France and Italy separately, there is still some catching up to do.

When WWI broke out, propaganda was trumped up in rigidly British Australia and Germans became the concentrated target of enflamed paranoia. One rumour circulated that teachers in South Australia took down Union Jacks, stomped and spat on them and raised the German flag in their place. Whether or not it was true (and I am assured it was not by one book) mattered seemingly little, for in 1917, all teaching of German was prohibited in South Australian primary schools and 49 Lutheran schools were closed down.

Towns such as Klemzig, Hahndorf, Blumberg and Lobethal were all renamed Gaza, Ambleside, Birdwood and Tweedvale. German names and titles all over the state were altered, except for the most important one: it seems that in their furore, South Australians missed the fact that their capital city was named for Queen Adelaide, the German wife of William IV of Britain and daughter of the Duke of Saxe-Meiningen, and left it as is (way to go guys).

However, one of Australia's most unlikely wartime stories came from Holtsworthy Internment Camp outside of Sydney, where 4,200 Germans (most from SA) were rounded up and imprisoned in 1915 for the war effort. Over a period of eight months, the inmates were frequently streaming into the sick bay with broken arms and cracked skulls. The warden, one Lt. Col. Sands, was very concerned with all of this – especially since the wounded seemed to be the more intellectual types instead of the brawlers. Sands couldn't get answers, so he decided to resort to unorthodox measures.

He set up a miniature secret service and found out that 30 rough Germans, known as the Black Hand Society, were at work in the compound extorting protection money from the wealthier inmates. Even with profiling, Sands could not identify the 0.7 percent of the camp who were the Black Hand. The head of the gang was one Hans Portman, who used pipes and bars and henchmen to exact his suppression. One large man in the camp, Hilderbrandt, was never touched by the Black Hand because of his size, but when he tried to protect some people he, too, ended up in hospital, not saying a word to the frustrated Sands.

However, when Hilderbrandt went back to the camp he gave a speech that inspired the others to stand up for themselves. Before long, hundreds of Germans were running about and grabbing whatever they could. Sands heard the ruckus and assumed that a break-out attempt was being made, though when he saw that no one was approaching the boundary or gate, he had to reconsider, and thus decided against sending his 50 troops to quell the 4,200 fired-up Germans.

Before long, the bodies of Hans Portman and two Black Hand goons – thumped well into unconsciousness – were thrown over an eight-foot fence; amazingly, only Portman died. The interned Germans then settled down and started singing and laughing and dancing. At a coroner's inquest, the doctor congratulated Sands on his handling of the affair, despite the fact that no one was ever arrested for the crime.

With the passage of time and the ending of the war, hysteria and scapegoating died down and many of the original German appellatives in SA were reinstated, and the blessed and wined Barossa retained its cultural heritage. Surprisingly, Bille wasn't too pleased about the German lilt of the area.

"Oh no! Zere are too many Germans! Everyvhere! I leave Germany to trawel and I see Germans. No, no, no! Das ist nein gut. I vant to speak English!" she said.

We took a big break in the Barossa Valley, and went from winery to winery with dignity until we found ourselves at Tanunda's Main Street gazebo for a performance, whereupon we lost that dignity. Being the

"Festival State," South Australians do excel in drinking, eating and music. Playing that evening was a five-piece band of high school boys. We had taken up position on the grass and laid out all our "herby, spicy cheese and goat cheese, red cheese and brie, crusty bread and rye bread and pumpkin bread, and we dipped it in the olive oil and balsamic vinegar and the artichoke antipasto stuff" (Louise's diary), plus our assorted wines. I dashed off to take photos of the sunset from a higher vantage and would return to a very glazed and loud Louise.

"That guitar player is *sooooo* hot," she slurred, looking gamely toward the gazebo.

"Ja, sure, he ist OK, und he ist also young," Bille replied looking at the adolescent in question. "Fourteen or 15, maybe."

"Hot. So hot. I want to talk to him," and with that she was off.

She did chat with him, scruffy youth that he was, and he blushed. Content that she had made the effort, we peeled Louise away from an act similar to what had landed the founder of South Australia in prison and went to camp off the night.

The next day, Louise wasn't very talkative and didn't even attempt to report what I might have blithered in my sleep. But then again, the whole group was fairly mute with bloodshot eyes, so I took the necessary steps to swap in our Adventurer for yet another Explorer motor home in Britz Adelaide. We would need a good shell, because our next reality would be a very long and sober one: we started driving up the forbidding and isolated centre of Australia.

48 – Mirage

COULD THE SCORCHED Australian continent have held teeming and green spreads full of Jurassic creatures? Had there once been a big lake in its middle? Why does Australia line up with South America and not share its properties of climate or have its own Amazon? Its life appears to cling to the slimmest of margins.

There is evidence to suggest that dinosaurs enjoyed a plentiful life. A 1991 discovery in a marine portion of Victoria revealed fossils and rock pools that used to link Australia to Antarctica 115 million years ago. Although dinosaurs looked to have arrived in Australia about the same time as other species, their breed would have remained un-evolved and isolated, with ancient regional characteristics.

Present-day Australian pelicans have beaks that average 47 centimetres long, which is the longest of all the world's other 10,000-odd present-day bird species. But consider this: Australia was also home to the largest bird that ever lived – the *454 kilogram* dromornis, a long-extinct relative of the emu. That is one big-ass bird!

I couldn't help but imaginatively impose such sights over the landscape that we were presently barrelling through. Theories have it that giant breeds of wombat, marsupial*, emu and bat existed long ago, thus copious amounts of water and plants would have had to be around to justify such outreached growth.

In 1837, scientist Ludwig Leichhardt was examining a collection of massive ancient marsupial bones. He surmised (like many others) that such creatures were still grazing near a verdant river. He wrote to a friend, "I should not be surprised if I find them in the tropical interior." But this from a man who dropped flour in the desert and scraped it up with dry leaves to make porridge for his starving exploration team.

A quick background: Leichhardt was a Prussian/German explorer who bumped around the regions of northern Queensland and the NT, taking along, of all things, 550 kilograms of flour, 90 of sugar, 40 of tea and 10 of gelatine, slung on the backs of 16 bullocks and 17 horses. He did quite well, considering, but a second attempt to cross from Moreton Bay (Brisbane) to Perth was his last. Neither he nor any of his party have been seen since. Some remains thought to be his and a coin were found, and theories of his fate have abounded, but without any concrete

---

* Including giant "red kangaroos," who apparently reached a couple of metres in height. Today, kangaroos ring in between 74 to 140 centimetres tall.

evidence to back them up.

At all events, it is my belief that he died yelling "Das ist scheize!" about not having found any of those giant marsupials. But beforehand, hundreds of millions of years ago, giants most probably did roam around undisturbed for a very long, lush time.

As we drove through the type of featureless land that covered about nine-tenths of the continent, I could only imagine through literature what might have been. I wondered how many giant footprints were out there, as of yet undiscovered. Then I noticed something that all state governments seemed to be more currently concerned about. There were many signs discouraging people from sleep-driving, and (if you were lucky enough to catch a signal) public service announcements geared toward the same end filled radio air time. Holidays, especially Easter, are when road accidents mount exponentially as Australians barrel around their empty country to see each other. It is a real problem.

There are several contributing factors to sleep-driving, including long and monotonous distances, lack of sleep, alcohol, speeding and animals. Along the way, we passed sombre little crosses or stakes that marked accident sites (if the stake is black, that means death; if it's white, that means bad injuries). And there are very creative reminder signs everywhere: "Don't sleep and drive"; "Survive the drive"; "Drifting off? A 15-minute powernap could save your life"; "Grow old: drive safe"; "Wake up or stop the car" (which might as well read "If you are reading this, good work"); and my personal favourite, the very straightforward "Drowsy Drivers Die." And there are supporting actors in this effort: a plenitude of places to pull off, some with little water towers in the desert or picnic tables in the shade of a rare tree. Senior citizens sometimes sat by the road with fly nets and coffee and offered to give anyone who stopped a hot cuppa and a chance to stretch the leggies and hear a yarn.

However, sheer boredom wasn't all that was stacked against the outback driver. Dusk and dawn marked significant periods of animal activity, most notably that of kangaroos. Evolution may have shrunk them, but it hasn't instilled in them the fatal effects of man's vehicles or the hypnotic powers of gleaming headlamps, as there were always broken bodies along the bitumen.

Rarer was the possibility of hitting camels, who had been left to roam the deserts of Australia after helping build the nation (there are said to be 100,000 of them meandering about). We did see some of them along the way, missing their bridles. We spotted, too, lots of roaming emus (an estimated million of them dwell all over Australia, from the deserts to the snowy mountains), and they are one of nature's strangest mutants. Despite being flightless birds, they can rocket along at 50 kilometres per hour for short bursts and then cruise at 35 to 40 kilometres per hour for 10-minute intervals; they can also bound four metres in a single stride. If cornered, they deliver a sledgehammer kick with a talon boasting a 15-centimetre-long claw.

If, for example, you were inbred and stupid enough to taunt one (and I read several accounts of stupid tourists doing so), even at 24 metres an emu could close the distance between you and it in six fast seconds and slice you open from neck to torso quicker than you can say 'what the fu...' and watch your guts ooze out and hit the ground as you slump into a dead heap.

However, to paraphrase Forrest Gump, stupid is as stupid does. Emus are pretty stupid themselves and will attack anything shiny, like a button or a coin, thinking it is an edible seed. People wearing buttoned shirts have been pecked to death or put into hospital. Yet while most other animals are ducking into shade at midday, emus can comfortably exist in temperatures exceeding 40°C, thanks to some creative breathing and blood reallocation systems. To boot, they can eat almost anything and are the last survivors of their kind. Their relatives – the moa in New Zealand and the ostrich in Africa – are both now extinct in the wild. But the strange twist is that Australians did deliberately try to get rid of emus.

There was a national call-up in 1932 to use 500-round-a-minute Lewis guns from the Royal Australian Artillery to shoot the crop-wrecking buggers out of existence. The attempt failed miserably because the emu was just too quick to be shot. Recently, however, things have turned around and emus are now big business. Many are raised in captivity for their low-fat, high-protein, beef-flavoured meat and France has become the largest market for Australian emus. Hardly any of the bird is wasted: the skin is used as stippled leather, feathers are sold as cushion stuffers, claws turned into jewellery and eggs into ornaments. Emu oil, which the bird stores in its thick layers of fat, has long been an Aboriginal skin balm used to combat arthritis, and is now making its way into pharmacies. Any dead emu bodies along the road are quickly recovered. Today, emu theft has become a major crime.

Australians, however, do instinctively find humour in all things, including road death, and at one remote truck stop bathroom I chatted with a trucker who told me that once a driver fell asleep at the wheel of his four-by-four and drove headlong into the desert. When he woke, he was hopelessly disoriented and lost, evidently out of petrol; he couldn't find the highway and died a thirsty and sunburnt death. But not before the flies drove him mad as well, apparently.

"To this day his remains and ute lie in the sand somewhere, and no one dares look for them. That's true, mate," he concluded. I found the whole story a bit hard to swallow and put it down to rural legend, but after jostling his member to make sure their was no further leakage, the hefty bearded driver walked away from our communal urinal assuring me it was God's truth. (I noticed that he didn't wash his hands and that on the wall in front of me above the urinal someone had written, "The future is in your hands.")

I have no doubt that true facts didn't get in the way of this trucker's story, but one thread of it was assuredly true: there is a lot of space without road that can easily swallow someone up without a trace. To travel the region by main road and car nowadays is not very perilous, for people are constantly driving along it. But then again who was I, or anyone, to know how many people went charging unconsciously into uncharted areas never to return; and the only possible person to see them last was a sleepy truck driver who told tales at the piss-trough and had little regard for hygiene?

Have I mentioned yet how truly mysterious this country is?

The outback is a tantalizing place. It is eerie to think that if not for the highway and a pub every day or so, you could be in a place yet untouched by man. "Next petrol/pub: 500kms."

We had also set in motion our radio's seek button, to hear music or news, and then forgot about it as its digits dialled fruitlessly. After hours of silence, a faint radio wave that the tuner triumphantly caught made us all jump. If it was a cricket match, we preferred static. Drowsy Drivers Die. Drowsy Drivers Die. Drowsy Drivers Die.

The first European to stand in the centre of Australia was John Stuart, on April 22, 1860. The next day, he climbed the only hill, raised the Union Jack and named the mound for his friend Charles Sturt (no "*a*"). No one knows why the name was changed on subsequent maps to Stuart, but I suspect that it is the only time in Australian history that a letter has been added to a word instead of taken away.

I was brought out of my own dreamy world by Bille who suddenly cried, "Is das eine snow!"

"Snow? Must be a mirage. Where?" one of us replied.

Sure enough, there in the distance our troop collectively spied huge basins of glistening snow in the inhospitable scales of land. It had to be the most visually odd juxtaposition, and was possibly something related to road vapour, but as we drove on the snow glittered blindingly larger in swaths of baking earth and turned out to be not frozen water, but its antithesis: salt lakes! We *had* to stop for this, and we crept to the edges, testing first with feet, and then walked out. I don't quite know how to describe the feeling of standing on a lake of salt, but it was strange. Someone had comically stuck an inverted surfboard fin in the saline mass, and it really did look like an unmoving shark.

Our enjoyment of this remote scene was cut short by the desert bugs. We were descended upon by flies with military tactics that targeted every orifice in the head. We quickly scraped up some salt with a Tupperware container to use it for cooking and beelined it for the safety of our Britz. Nevertheless, some flies did manage to breach our interior.

49 – Getting Nicely Baked

WHILE THE US-led coalition was bombing away in the desert-ridden country of Iraq, the Mad Nomads pretty much lost all contact with time and the outer word. We spent some weeks driving through the desert, never really knowing anything more than sunrise and sunset. Our desert was very peaceful.

It wouldn't be until another long spell that the monotony was broken again, and conversely we weren't given the opportunity see it from a distance. Literally, one minute we were seeing nothing but highway, then we rounded some man-made mounds and BAM: Dust-ville, so-called civilization in the middle of nowhere. Signs are ubiquitously posted warning that a step in the wrong direction will introduce you, at the speed of gravity, to the dark recesses of any one of 250,000 very deep and still-open shafts.

We had just hit the famous mining town of Coober Pedy, an Aboriginal term for "white fellow's hole in the ground." It is 534 kilometres from the nearest big town (Alice Springs), 948 kilometres north of Adelaide, and it has a population of 4,000 people. It is, you understand, isolated. It wasn't like any "settlement" I had ever seen. It looks like the end of the Earth, and that's probably why films like *Mad Max III*, *Stark* and *Ground Zero* were filmed there. There is an old spaceship mock-up dumped in the middle of town among the other Hollywood set leftovers strewn about the place.

You could easily place Luke Skywalker here, feverously negotiating with a dodgy extra-terrestrial for a turbo-trans-coil-60-parsec-blast-converter while two droids – one gold and jumpy and the other silver, domed and chirpy – waited outside arguing over their short term future. Coober Pedy's residents and visitors live (and all businesses operate) in dugouts and underground facilities excavated out of the man-made hills. It's a perfect prototype Bedrock – no droids allowed.

The climate is extreme in Coober Pedy: temperatures range from 50°C in the day to freezing at night. As we rolled into the area, the alien factor was increased by the amount of people wearing funny-looking fly nets over their heads. We didn't laugh long, though, for when we stepped from our vehicle, flies descended on us in a frenzy that gave the sufferer the appearance of a karate champion on amphetamines battling invisible enemies.

Along the way, our motor home had been subjected to what sounded like an intense hailstorm. The exterior was awash in bug guts and impact points. Masses of horribly disfigured and mangled insects were riddled into the front grill, Mercedes symbol, bumper and outcropped edges of the vehicle, and Aaron proclaimed it "an insect holocaust."

"Zose poor animals," said Bille sadly when she saw the mess and flicked the leg of an oversized grasshopper that was protruding from a wedged position.

"They're not animals, Bille, they are *insects*," one of us corrected.

"Nein. Zey are little animals, no?" she asked expectantly.

She did have a point, her German logic was sharp. Anywhere else in the world but Australia, creatures of their bulk would certainly qualify to be described as such. They could leap motor homes in a single bound, and many died trying. We just opted for simplicity and nodded back at her.

So what brings people to a place like this, hell on earth as it was? I loved Coober Pedy, myself, and so did the rest. We wandered around the mine shafts, piles of burrowed-out earth and dumped and rotting equipment, junked cars and shelled-out buses, before resting from the heat and flies in an underground church. The two mainstays of Coober Pedy are opal mining (Australia actually produces 90 percent of the world's opal supply) and tourism (and, I am guessing, filming, as well).

The townsfolk are quite diverse, both in their backgrounds and reasons for being here. There are lots of Greeks (running the restaurants), Serbs, Croats and Italians, as well as people from Hong Kong and groups of itinerant Aboriginals. Louise sourced that 60 percent of the population had migrated from south and eastern Europe after WWII, evidenced by the Italo-Australian Miners Club and the Greek and Serbian Orthodox churches.

We met Terry in our meandering, a Hong Kong man struggling to speak English, who claimed to have been in Coober Pedy for 25 years. He lives in a bizarre home atop a hill surrounded by strange leftovers from Hollywood: bits of computers, simulated alien equipment, pieces of spacecraft with blast marks, not to mention stalagmites with human heads and aliens in them and pipes coming out their sides. He is an opal trader and, after showing us his wares and seeing that we weren't buying, he switched to plan B.

He gathered us around and opened a tattered and ripped Chinese-English textbook that contained words and phrases. Apparently, the book was meant to have been accompanied by a series of cassette tapes, but Terry had lost those or possibly traded them for a turbo-trans-coil-60-parsec-blast-converter. He asked us to sound out words and syllables as his pencil glided underneath, scrawling their pronunciations in neatly drawn Chinese characters. We admired his resolve to learn the language and, taking our leave, headed on to see the other sights of this strange place.

"Oh no! Do you sink it vill take me 25 years to learn zee English?" asked Bille with a pout.

"Only if you live in the desert, Bille," I replied.

Again I heard the sound of a penny dropping inside her skull. She spurted, "Cool! I have good chances zen! Oh Ja! Das ist cool!"

From the Coober Pedy Returned Serviceman's League (RSL) clubhouse, we heard the sounds of people and drums. We arrived in time to see a smattering of folk in a loose parade, heading off into town to commemorate the Australian soldiers who fell in WWI, WWII, Vietnam and other conflicts. It was Anzac Day, when Australia stops to remember the sacrifices of her soldiers. Australians have a really strange way of paying homage: they celebrate by doing drunken and illegal things.

That evening, our team could not refuse the Anzac Day tradition of hanging around the RSL bar to catch a few yarns from the old boys. The bar was real outback basic, and patrons ranged in age from a few months old to really old. Yes, there were even children in the bar scurrying around and playing in dirt as the elders drank merrily.

"I like the remoteness because when people get together, it has more meaning," said one man. "People in the cities just ignore each other. It ain't friendly, mate. You won't die from a speedy life out here, either; there's no rush." Then he turned away from us to yell, "Twenty dollars on heads, mate!"

The tradition in the pubs on this day of remembrance is one that is unique. The game they play is called "two-up," a fairly straightforward gamble involving a paddle, two coins and a simple double heads or tails outcome, thus putting the odds at one-half. Now get this: two-up is illegal in Australia, *except* on Anzac Day! That's right, only on this special day when the nation pays tribute to fallen soldiers can people gather at drinking holes and play the game that the soldiers once played with their meagre wages in stinky war trenches. Well, certainly the people in the Coober Pedy RSL weren't holding back as the crowd yelled, jeered and flashed money around a dirt square. Every now and then, two coins would quickly gain and lose altitude, then they were hailed or booed depending on who had won and who had lost.

At one point, all the lights went out, the gambling ruckus quelled and people stood in solemn silence while a poem was read out to commemorate fallen Anzac soldiers. It concluded with the words "Lest we forget," words repeated in chorus from the dark crowd. The lights then came back on and the feverish gambling began all over again, as if there had never been a moment of silence. Gotta get it in while the cops allow it, I guess.

We headed on into town to seek more action. En route, we passed the youth hostel (underground, naturally) to find a bunch of American kids on tour who revelled at the novelty of being 19 years old, in the desert and legally consuming alcoholic beverages. We made quick pace to the local boom-boom club, where Louise had a beer with a priest whom she had seen drinking at the Anzac dawn parade.

It is hard to describe, but this town so obviously ugly on the outside compensated by having so much inner beauty. Louise met Susie, a guide at the Umoona Museum, who stated, "In Coober Pedy, it's what inside that counts. Here, nobody cares how things look. Nice things just get destroyed by the heat and the sand, anyway. You might have a nice car as your highway car, but around town you just drive the cheapest one you can find. Most of the buildings are old because it's not worth building anything new. It's so far to go to get materials, it's not worth the drive to the city. If you take a look inside many of the houses, you'll be surprised how beautiful they are. That's where people have their nice things. In the city, people are more concerned about how things appear on the outside, but we don't care about that, we care about what's on the inside."

While poking about on our final day, I went to a bank machine to pull a few dollars out and metres away, some little Aboriginal children were playing in the sand next to a man who was sprawled across the walking path. I punched in my PIN, took the money and walked off, but stopped when I noticed the children running to the ATM. They couldn't have been more than five or seven years old.

"How do you think he did that?" asked one to the other.

They stood there wide-eyed for a few minutes and punched buttons and touched the screen, hoping money would magically sprout out. For all the things in the modern world that most of us take for granted, there are still children in first-world countries who don't understand what purpose they served. Consider that for a second. By all appearances, here before me were direct descendents of the oldest continuous civilization in the world.

I know I come back to this point a lot, and I don't mean to sound infatuated, but I am very taken by such thoughts. In just over 200 years, their cultural world had changed so abruptly, that these children didn't know that one needs a bank account, bank card and a PIN to operate an ATM.

Then again, they also didn't know about latent bank fees and scandalous CEO retirement packages.

When their button-mashing proved fruitless, the children dashed back to the side of the man and reinitiated their dirt games. The man managed a grunt, a bit of movement, then went inert again with his mouth gaping wide, and the children giggled as they stared into its black void. He had obviously been drinking hard.

Whether dereliction among Aboriginals is a result of genetic indisposition to alcohol, chronic addiction or losing their heritage and never becoming full members of the new society is still in refute. However, one study undertaken in the 1960s revealed that Aboriginals of the past 1,000 years knew more about self-medication than most pharmaceutical companies today.

Getting stoned was nothing new. In 1831, an explorer in Tasmania came upon a group of Aboriginals tapping a cider eucalypt in full bloom and – after they giddily stumbled off giggling – he took a sip himself and wrote that it tasted "like sweet cider."

Explorers Burke and Wills scored the first-ever printed record of taking the Aboriginal sedative known as pituri, which they found to be "quite intoxicating." The natives also had know-how regarding the leaves of duboisia (among the leaves, bark and sap of other plants), which they could use to poison drinking waters where animals fed. They could equally use the plants to induce eels or fish to swim drunkenly into their hands.

Admittedly, they came upon this knowledge quite by trail and error. There can be no doubt that with the sheer toxicity of Australian nature experimentation led to considerable death and serious baked brains on both animal and human sides.

What the Europeans did was introduce Aboriginals to the notion of inhaling – instead of chewing – many of their known leafy substances. It struck some as strange that for a culture so bent on using fire and burning all that was around them, Aboriginals never actually thought to roll one up and toke away. I can't imagine what the scene of the first

Aboriginals and the first white men sitting around and smoking the first intercontinental fatty looked like, but it was probably similar to many white people's first years in college: lots of coughing, laughing, red eyes, a few placebo jokes, and curiosity about the availability of sweet, calorie loaded foods.

Nevertheless, even drinking and smoking habits that lead to abandonment aren't always clearly explainable in one presumption. So again, I arrive at no solutions, nor can I substantiate or deny what I read or hear in any of my own research. I am a stranger here myself. Like anything that comes to an outback place like Coober Pedy, theories too can get lost in voids or fall into deep holes, and end up as bent tales told by strange outback drivers pissing in remote troughs.

IT WOULD BE another mindless tumble until we crossed over the border into the Northern Territory. For comparative purposes, the massive and vacant states of Queensland and Western Australia are roughly equivalent in population spread; respectively 1.7 people per square kilometre and 1.5. For its part, the NT, which covers 16 percent of the continent, has a population spread of 0.1 people per square kilometre! The entity also only has 0.1 percent of Australia's total population, and half of them live in the capital city. I say entity because in many ways the NT is part of Australia in geography only.

For the longest time, the region was just another empty appendage of NSW, before essentially being given away to the colony of South Australia in 1863. It was only made a territory of the Commonwealth in 1911, and wasn't even allowed to administer itself until 1978. In 1998, the NT held a referendum to become a state and I imagine they took one look at New Zealand, which enjoyed full benefits without having to be a part of it all, and decided to stay a territory. The citizens of the NT (also known as "top-enders") don't hold parliamentary seats in sleepy Canberra, just representatives, who apparently do even less than politicians. The odd twist is that if top-enders don't show up to vote in federal elections, they get fined anyhow.

It seemed to me vaguely familiar; something of mutated KFM 'Kelvinator' – things being put on paper with purpose and nods and smiles before speedily lining garbage cans. Top-enders are equally obliged to vote during national referendums, even though their votes don't actually count. I'm not sure about this, but when I read that 20 percent of the region's population is Aboriginal, I got an inkling that perhaps the top-enders were cast as an entity of extras even on the political scene.

Much like any similarly rugged and pioneered region of the world, the NT grew up having a population of more testosterone than estrogens. Men were men and sheep were scared. In 1828 it was calculated that there were 3.34 men to every woman, and it appears that that hasn't altered much. I could be completely wrong, but I thought I saw Louise smile when she read that figure.

So spare in population is the NT that the School of the Air was started in 1951 in the continental dead-centre town of Alice Springs. It was the brainchild of Adelaide Miethke of the Royal Flying Doctors Service, who used his own radio transceivers to supplement correspondence courses while he was in the bush. A class can have up to 15 students, all of whom live on stations hundreds of kilometres from each other. In the 1990s, there were still a dozen "classrooms" running over a four million square kilometre area. Teachers apparently still attempt the valiant benchmark of visiting each outpost once or twice a year. Nowadays, assignments that used to be mailed and were subject to rain-season floods are done by fax and internet and satellite. I am sure it's less forgivable for kids these days to tell teacher on live link-up that a dingo ate their homework, or that they can't "attend school" because a monsoon took their house away.

I came to think about living in isolation in a monotonous desert, as well as the concept that blind people are compensated by having heightened levels in their other senses, such as acute smell, taste, hearing or touch. They in fact sense things that many of us who have vision overlook. I found it easy to think in the outback, you see, and was often day-dreaming. And then I thought about those early peoples who never even had real homes in the desert or even courses by correspondence, but rather only the hand-me-down wisdom.

And it seemed then that the bigger blindness regarded our understanding of one of the world's most ancient religions.

The concept of Aboriginal Dreaming Time is easily summed up, but rarely comprehended in its entirety. Most works I read left writers exhausted for words.

"Dreaming Time" is a very rough translation of "Altjira Rama," meaning "to see and dream eternal things." It is Aboriginal religion, though it doesn't have a version of the bible or a Koran or Torah or Dead Sea Scrolls.

The belief is that the world was put together by spirits – or "djangs" – who took on different forms (plant, animal, human, other) to create, teach or maintain, well, pretty much the natural order of things. "Dreaming Time" stories, as well as dances, ceremonies and wall art, all served to keep the information flowing. It was almost like a human internet – an ancient system of woven erudition that could be accessed only by people who were "dialled" in. And so, when "balanda" (white folk) arrived just over two centuries ago, they were not "connected."

For the Aborigines themselves, Australia was born in the sacred Creation Time. Even today many Aboriginals disregard scientific discoveries such as those of Mungo and Kow Swamp and other archaeological sites because they claim that their ancestors have always been here and cannot be back-dated. And maybe they're right. One expert wrote, "One cannot 'fix' the Dreaming Time; it was, and is, everywhen." There are no words in Aborigine, apparently, for "yesterday" or "tomorrow."

It seemed to early Europeans that many Dreaming Time traditions fell deep into the realm of the sheerly ludicrous. In one case, a starving tribe perceived that greasy-looking eggs resembled a man's testicles and thus they refused to eat them, despite the fact that it was the only food that was around at the time. There are several other cases of certain Aboriginals denying themselves perfectly good food because a djang banned chewing it until the following season.

What most early balanda failed to realize was that many other religions also practice fasting and abstention from certain meats or foods. I ask you, then, had Aborigines created the first kosher?

When Christianity was taught to the Aboriginals, they found the idea of eating a wafer (meant to represent the flesh of Christ) and drinking wine (his blood) to be very primitive and repugnant practices. So isn't that a case of the teapot calling the kettle black? And it gets better.

In 1978, Frank Gurrmanamana, an Arnhem land tribal elder, visited Canberra, his first visit to a major Australian city. Much like his ancestors, he seemed to regard white people as substandard. He was unimpressed with escalators, jet planes and all the other gadgetry of modern life. He was more interested in the patterns of street layout, the maps of the city and the relationship each house on each street had with each person. He asked his surprised white hosts who carried out the rituals to tie people to their lands. He found it inconceivable that land could be sold off arbitrarily with no attention paid to religious ties. He was further disgusted by the lack of rules to govern marriages, and concluded openly that white people mated as indiscriminately as dogs.

However, there have been some agreements. The Aboriginal Dream Time had no theories for how the sky, sea and land came to be formed. When the white man bunged them into schools taught by missionaries and offered the explanation of a ubiquitous Christian God, many Aborigines agreed that it was possible a God put it all together even before their mother djang emerged to hatch the first offspring and scatter them to procreate.

But when it came to believing in Christianity's Adam and Eve as the first human couple, the Aboriginals had a good snicker. Given the span of time they had been around, who was dreaming now?

As the Mad Nomads grinded north on the Stuart Highway through the deadpan mass of no distractions, it was all too easy to start zoning out. The drive felt more like running on a conveyer belt than progressing on bitumen, and reaching a petrol station or a pub was heralded as a triumphant occasion. Any water we garnered from "public" fountains or hoses tasted like a bad and piss-warm concoction of chlorine and plastic tubing, so we spent heaps on marked-up bottled water.

The land we passed resembled African savannah and I could certainly say that the sight of loping giraffes, sleepy lions and spry zebras would not have been too out of the ordinary. Of course, there were none. As we killed kilometres, the scene altered to saturated crimson earth. I guess "Mars-like" would be the best description – and was one supplied in most books – especially when the sun rode low in the sky and the ground appeared almost alive and breathing. Indeed, when you are in the mystical centre of Australia, all you have left to do is dream, therefore anything seen in the red sea of nothing is always something more.

I started seeing things: faces, shapes of animals, shimmying movements and other figments I would have paid scant mind to in more crowded circumstances. I could only begin to imagine how heightened this natural mental drifting would be if I actually wandered into the desert with the sun, heat and flies, and suffering from hunger and thirst as others had done and only some had lived to speak about.

We arrived at Erldunda, which I am guessing might be Aboriginal for "lonely white fellow's petrol pump and pub," a few hours south of Alice Springs and 244 kilometres east of where the famous Big Red Australian Rock lies. We noticed that the solo female pump attendant had an English accent and asked her what she was doing in the middle of nowhere.

"I was travelling when me car broke down in the desert," she replied jovially as the litres and dollars spiralled upward, "and I had only enough money to have it brought here to Erldunda. The part I need is expensive, and there was a job as attendant here so I thought, Why not stick around for a bit? I love it out here. There may not be much to look at, but you meet the most fascinating people ... and the sunsets and stars are wonderful. Won't see that in England. OK, your total is a gazillion billion dollars. Thanks."

Well, she didn't say a gazillion billion dollars, but outback fuel is marked up about 80 percent because of remoteness, so she might as well have said that. Because we had arrived after dusk, we rolled into the adjacent open-plan dirt lot – a free camping area – and slept the night away.

The next morning, we would set off to see Australia's most famous landmark!

51 – Throbbing Red Centre

IT PROBABLY IS the distance at the end of the day. Has to be. It sits 450 road kilometres southwest of Alice Springs, the closest major town, and the closest major city to Alice is either Darwin, at 1,494 kilometres north, or Adelaide, at 1,512 kilometres south. Even if you fly to Yulara, the tacky desert resort 15 kilometres from the Big Red Rock, you still have to see a lot of nothing to see the something.

After days of featureless driving, paying desert diesel rates and quaffing nauseating water, we were very ready indeed for that promised reward. We even got over the disappointment of having to pay $15 each just to get into the place (watering – or should I say *sanding* – down my previous revelation that most natural things in Australia are free), and we were in the frame of mind that Ayers Rock had better be a very special something to see for all we had been through to put in an appearance.

It's not like we haven't seen it before. You would have to be living as a hermit in a cave on Pluto not to have seen it at least once in a photo or in a book, or on a calendar or youth hostel wall, with its glowing scarlet mystique. Most people in the world can't even think of Australia without immediately conjuring Ayers Rock, yet most Australians haven't even seen it themselves.

The colour scheme of the region might have been stolen from the tubes of an old television that has had its swatches all muddled up. Infused in the striking red earth are charred black trees that look like toilet brushes, grass of gold, a deep blue sky and jade and grey scrub, and circling above the bizarre scenery are birds with massive wing spans curled at the edges where at any second a *Star Trek* away team might beam in unnoticed with phasers set on stun.

And "bizarre" seems also to describe the story of one of Australia's most enigmatic figures. Roughly 100 kilometres west of Ayers Rock, Harold Bell Lasseter collapsed and died searching for a rich reward. In 1897, when he was but a strapping 17-year-old prospecting in the desert, Lasseter claimed that he had found an abundant gold reef, but subject to faulty instruments and bent imagination, he lost the location.

After a determined 33 years, Lasseter raised enough interest and capital to mount a sponsored expedition (including an aircraft) from Alice Springs. After numerous misfortunes, the expedition fell into disarray, his sponsorship dried up and everyone doubted Lasseter's credibility, so he set out alone with two camels who eventually bolted and left him stranded without supplies. He amazingly managed to arrive at Irving Creek, near the original place he found in 1897, before he died a desert death. A tree with his name and the inscribed date of "2.12.30," along with his diaries, were recovered; a year later, so was his body. It seemed that he sincerely believed he was on the right track, though to this day the reef has never been found.

Lasseter's Last Ride, published some years after his death, told the tale, subject to some major alterations. Apparently, the author took grand poetic license and transformed Lasseter's original claim of a quartz yielding three ounces of gold to that of a ton. The writer claimed that the reef's "yellow stuff was ... thick as plums in a pudding."

And then in the middle of all that, along the present-day Lasseter Highway, lies Ayers Rock. Well, gold or not, it's worth the visit!

Draining distances, nasty water and siphoning monetary considerations are suddenly forgotten, and no matter how many images you may have seen, nothing, and I mean *nothing*, prepares you for the presence or the scale of real thing. From Yulara, it doesn't actually look that big, but when you move closer it grows and casts a magnetic force on your sight. It is arresting.

Ayers Rock rises 348 metres above the ground and truly does not look real; indeed, you keep thinking it might not be. Once I was closer up, I could swear it looked like a Hollywood prop and I expected to round a corner to see it supported by a mass of beams. It has strange markings and curves on it, and depending on the angle of the sun and cast of shadow, it is easy to make out faces and shapes and animals and bodies in its shell. I was glad that I don't abuse drugs, and I recommend that anyone who hallucinates or is paranoid avoid the landmark, because it will convince you that things are watching you as you take your three-hour, medium-paced walk around its 9.4-kilometre circumference. A thunderstorm will apparently push the alchemy of light into the surreal.

Ayers Rock was supposedly first spotted by explorer William Gosse in around 1873; Gosse named it Ayers Rock for the governor of SA. He was otherwise on a mission to find a road from central SA to Perth, though that mission was unsuccessful. Gosse had unknowingly beaten a disheartened Ernest Giles to the punch by only days. Poor Ernie was still a bit depressed for having lost his friend Gibson in the harsh desert (the name Gibson was then given to the desert that ate him), and probably could have used the discovery to lift him.

Ayers Rock remained inaccessible to most non-Aboriginal people until the mid-1950s, after which it became a very over-trodden tourist destination. Geologists date it back about a hundred million years and assume that it is the remains of a larger geological feature that has been washed away. Ayers Rock was listed as a World Heritage Site, and in 1985, it was ceremoniously handed back to the Yankunytjatjara and Pitjantjatjara peoples (collectively, the Anangu – pronounced *arn-ang-oo*) by the governor general. The more traditional and respectful name of "Uluru" was reinstated over Ayers Rock and the Aboriginal stewards in effect leased the region back to the National Parks, and will do so for another 99 years. The Anangu have put up a painting to reflect white and Aboriginal people sitting around Uluru in a joint council to protect it.

Most people don't realize that they are staring at something some scientists tie back to the tearing of the super continent Gondwana. The region is reportedly a scar from early continental tectonic movements. But to the Aboriginals, Uluru was brought about in the Dreaming Time creation stories by their wandering ancestors. The Anangu people request in writing on several multilingual notices that, out of respect for their culture and ancestors, no one climb up the revered monolith. Upon arrival at Uluru their ancestors – the Mala – took the traditional route to the top, which had great spiritual significance. They have a name for non-Malans, "minga," which may sound like an Italian swear word but is actually Aboriginal for "ants that crawl on mounds." They further state that death or injury on Uluru deeply saddens their people and spirits.

But as we found out, it is not absolutely forbidden to climb upon it and we arrived at a full parking lot to see a whole lot of mingas scrambling up along a chain-linked path. We were torn, because while we did heavily respect the Aboriginal traditions, we so wanted to see the view – and who knew whether any of us would ever come here again. So we opted to climb – with all due respect.

It was a hellish ordeal. The possibility of falling off, even with the secure hand rail, is very real and if winds or heat act up, park wardens completely close down the dangerous path without second thought. The geography of Uluru is one of many steep angles, the marked and chain-aided lane stealing up along the least abrupt portion. Even then, everyone has to adopt a clambering dog position in going up, and a slide-on-butt posture with feet-as-brakes when coming down. Many people were also in the popular doubled-over-trying-to-catch-my-breath stance.

Apparently, there have been over 35 deaths on Uluru, most related to heart attacks or breathing difficulties. One man madly chased his wind-blown hat over an edge in the delusional belief that gravity had taken a coffee break. It's not hard to fathom that any member of an emergency medical response team would have to drive a long way to reach the parking lot, then risk their own necks climbing, so your health is pretty well understood to be in your hands if you undertake the slog to the top.

Shortness of breath and throat-burning thirst certainly caused our foursome to halt every few seconds, yet we crossed many people who couldn't make it up even a quarter of the conduit and who were returning shakily to the bottom with defeat written on their exasperated faces. Staggered as we were, we all managed to crest the summit as the sun was lowering, and couldn't believe how much sheer nothing and scrub stretched as far as the eye could see. On the very linear horizon due west of us was the silhouette of bumps that looked like the kind cartoon characters get when hit with oversized mallets or anvils. We found out that they are known as Kata Tjuta or the Olgas, another monolith site 30 kilometres away.

The sky then got angry with brilliant colours, mauves and oranges and deep reds, and the distant clouds contorted, giving the appearance that the heavens were being licked by raging flames. It is difficult to fully capture how intense things can be in the red centre of Australia. We scrambled back to the base under darkness and camped the night, returning at sunrise to see Uluru glow that absolute blood hue it is famous for. To see the real thing is magic.

In 1939, onlookers at the Coogee Aquarium near Bondi were shocked when a shark vomited up a tattooed human arm. The arm used to be part of one James Smith and police traced his last-known whereabouts to a forger and get-rich quick schemer named Brady. Brady was arrested for the crime, though owing to the untimely murder of the only possible witness, the jury had to acquit Brady, for there was no body, witness or confession. Even when Brady was on his deathbed and told that he could never again be retried for the same crime even if he confessed, he maintained that he never killed Smith.

I bring this little tale up for two reasons: first, because I found it in the same book on unsolved Australian mysteries (of which there are a plethora). Second, because the tale had huge parallels with the 1980 Uluru tale known as the "Dingo And The Baby" (often parodied as "The Dingo Ate My Baby" from the Merrill Streep film "A Cry in the Dark.")

Nine-week-old Azaria Chamberlain vanished from her family's tent in a busy campsite near Uluru. Lindy Chamberlain, the mother, frantically raised the alarm that led to a search. Lindy had claimed that she had possibly seen a dingo take her baby from the tent. Azaria's body was never found, though some of her clothes were. The media swooned for two years over the case, and public speculation led to Lindy's and her husband's arrests – respectively for murder and being an accessory – despite a complete lack of a body, any eyewitnesses, a plausible motive or even a confession, just like the Coogee case.

Nevertheless, a jury found them guilty and the court meted out life imprisonment to the mother and 18 months to the father, who was released immediately on a good behaviour bond. Lindy and several supporters put in an appeal, she was released after three years, and then went through two more lengthy appeals and a public inquiry to quash her conviction. A decade following the "trial by media," she wrote her autobiography, telling her side of the tale. Regardless, the mystery remains unsolved.

And I have brought the latter tale up because it has similarities to what was about to happen to the Mad Nomads: we almost went missing in the desert.

THE FOLLOWING DAY, we headed over to the other bumps, about which a debate remains ongoing: are Kata Tjuta (the Olgas) a better set of rocks than Uluru? They have a smaller circumference but higher domes (500 metres), are less touristy and are constantly visible along the flat horizon from Uluru. The Olgas are also too steep to climb and one can't really walk around them with any ease. There is a quick-dash level path between the domes that places you in the shade with a chunk of greenery before terminating at a wooden platform that looks over an impassable pile of boulders. As far as taking side in the favouritism debate, I think it is apples and oranges, and the most impressive thing I found was a sign that said if you head further west there is nothing for thousands of kilometres before Karagoolie or Perth in Western Australia. I'm a simple man at times.

The next day, we headed to a place dubbed "photographer's paradise": King's Canyon.

"Zey are like pancakes," Bille observed of the surroundings that we were presently hiking.

"Yea, and kind of like the place where Coyote chases that elusive emu the Roadrunner and tricks him into some bizarre anti-gravity demise along the ridges," I offered.

"Ja, sure … Vat? I did not understand vat you say. Please, again," she retorted, digging out a pocket translator.

"Yummy pancakes, Bille, nice pancakes," I said.

"Ja … Pancakes. Cool," she agreed, content with her accurately expressed observation.

Aaron and Louise were way ahead of us by virtue of the fact that Bille and I were shutter-bugging at every turn. The landscape was impressive as promised. Rock walls shoot up at a steep angles and all around are spires of layered rock, like piles of mom's flapjacks. The local flora contrasts with the rich gold-red colouration of earth: eucalypts of pale white bark and intense green leaves stand next to brambly and scorched trees that look like petrified black lightning bolts in reverse. There are no guardrails along the top rim of the gaping gorge, so a missed step can land you 200 metres below lifeless.

"What are you doing, Bille?!" I cried, alarmed that she was standing right on the lip of the fierce drop while the wind was blowing.

"Its *sooooo* cool up here. I vant to take photos," she answered, seeming blissfully unaware of what the combination of gravity, velocity and hard surfaces can do to a human body and the soul animating it. She dangled her legs over the edge with a huge grin as I dropped a log into my pants

Below, Aaron and Louise had found the Garden of Eden – a hidden and hollowed-out microcosm in one of many lush gullies, with a billabong and surrounded by birds and a blossoming miniature jungle. They went for a welcome dip with other hikers but I never managed to get there because I was otherwise occupied trying to pry Bille and her camera away from bungee jumping *sin* cord.

We returned to the motor home drenched in sweat, but in time to catch the surrounding rocks and area stoked flaming red by another flawless outback sunset. Aaron took the wheel as night fell and would ingeniously do something the other three of us had dreamingly failed to do in our rotation as chauffeur: he had a gander at the fuel gage.

"Um, when is the next petrol station?" he asked, trying not to sound alarmed.

"Curtin Springs," one of us replied from the back of the motor home. "87 klicks. Why?"

We made it about half that distance at a snail's pace when headlights appeared in our rear-view mirror and we opted to flag down whatever help we could get. A large SUV stopped and turned out to be a travelling family, who said that they had just passed an Uluru park ranger and he would be along shortly.

True enough, we waved down the next vehicle and it was an officially marked pick-up truck driven by an affable man named Graham. We asked if he had extra diesel, which he didn't, so Louise and I jumped in with him, leaving Aaron and Bille in the Britz to wait for our return.

We almost didn't return.

"I just came back from an international Aboriginal meeting, aye," Graham offered as he drove, and we noticed that, indeed, he did have the features of Australia's first peoples. In conversation, we learned that he wore many hats: tribal leader, community liaison officer, park warden, desert patrolman and currently hero to stranded people without diesel. His territory extended thousands of kilometres from Western Australia all the way to Queensland, yet he still hadn't seen most of it. He also travelled the world on committees and councils dealing with international land rights and cultural think-tanks for shared issues.

"We now have Uluru for 99 years, aye," he said "and the government is returning many more sacred lands back to the Aboriginal peoples over time. Land rights are important because –" But we would never hear the end of that sentence.

To our alarm, he veered sharply off the highway and jumped the truck into the scrub and desert, pressing down on the accelerator. He gritted his teeth and gunned harder and suddenly we noticed the profile of a scared kangaroo in his headlight cone, who just managed to skim clear of the massive bumper bar mounted on the front of Graham's ute. The frightened Skippy bounded off into the desert and instantly Graham tore back onto the asphalt and continued as if nothing had ever happened – like those movies where people imagine things in cutaway scenes that don't really occur.

"Missed him," he said calmly. "I'll nail the next one and throw him in the tray. Good dinner."

"Is ... uh ... kangaroo meat ... um ... good?" I asked, trying to seem cool with his impulsive and unexpected off-road vault.

"Traditionally, the men eat the meat and the women make a delicacy out of the guts. We use every part of the animal; nothing goes to waste," he said.

We arrived at Curtin Springs with no further fresh dinner vehicular homicide attempts, and luckily someone was at the station to give us a jerry can and some diesel. We rejoined Aaron and Bille, thanked Graham and drove our motor home to Curtin Springs, where we found another dirt lot full of caravans and cars and people camping for free.

We took up position around a burning campfire with a pack of travellers and one chatty 40ish-looking Aussie bloke from Adelaide commanded the conversation. A couple of Dutch travellers had asked him about Aboriginals, and he spent his evening ranting about the government spending too much money on people who just go walkabout.

"Have youz all seen the burned-out cars along the highway?" he asked the group openly as he stared into the fire. Most of us nodded, for certainly we had seen a fair few charred and forlorn chassis strewn by the wayside.

"That's the abos, mates ... That's government money lying there, burnt. They have no concept of ownership or maintenance. They're a bloody nuisance," he said while lifting his tanned marshmallow from the heat of the coals.

However, "walkabout" is misunderstood. I personally think that Aboriginals foresaw something that many modern people still don't. Wrote Blainey, "We are so accustomed to stressing the material merits of the sedentary life that we can easily overlook the fact that the Aboriginals often suffered when they were anchored to the one spot."

Is it laziness as many believe? Or an inner spirit calling to them? Did they suddenly drift along old paths laid by their ancestors to fulfil ancient yearnings? It seems beyond the scope of what I can write here, in fact beyond the scope of the millions of pages and research documents written to date.

However, maybe they looked at white men chained to buildings and desks and computers that they themselves had no strong bonds with and thought, "Sod this." That I could understand. Maybe they have the courage most people don't to just walk away from such a terrible and unfulfilling nine-to-five, Monday to Friday, two weeks of vacation a year existence. Despite government programs to hire Aboriginals, I don't remember seeing any in the offices of that telesales Many Excuses hell I first worked for in Sydney and – lest we forget – I, too, got caught up in the undelivered ME lie and then went on a naked walkabout into the plaza.

"During the 2000 Olympics in Sydney," continued the marshmallow-cooking man, "the government just swept them under the rug again like stunned mullets [people completely bewildered]. Bloody oath!"

He then immediately resumed a good-natured exterior and offered the bag around to all the circled travellers. I knew that despite what he and others might say, the issues were layered and complex and required much more than a squishy approach. But I took the marshmallow from him, speared it on the end of my stick and thrust it in the fire until it turned brown. I couldn't retort or add to the conversation, because I had no solid knowledge or experience to give him in return for his views.

After breakfast the next day, we made for Alice Springs, where the most engorged penis lay in wait for us.

53 – Bulging Penis Spiders

"OH MY GOD! It hurts so much!" cried Mark in heavy aucker. We all looked down to see him nursing the space betwixt his legs where a massive bulge beneath his jeans was readily discernible and menacing.

"I need a medic! Spoon, get me a medic, mate. It hurts!" he screamed.

Just minutes previous, Mark had vowed that he could drink a schooner of beer through his penis, and disappeared into the bathroom to emerge with a swollen member in his pants and lots of concerned onlookers.

"It's gonna burst, mate! Spoon, you have to drain it out with yer mouth, mate! Please help me!" he tried again, and Spoon burst out laughing and told him, "Bugger off, or I'll just cut her open."

Moments before, we had moseyed into the swinging doors of an Alice Springs bar that was decorated with dubious yellow posters of outback desperados playing cards and pointing pistols, cowboy boots on the ceiling, saddles and horse reins and bull horns along the cross beams and a wooden floor upon which people chucked dispensed shells from the peanuts garnered from bar-side buckets. While sitting quietly tending to our drinks, we couldn't help but notice the loud antics of Mark, Spoon and Spoon's wife, Emma. They were about our age and garbed in cowboy hats and leather boots, jeans and chequered shirts with sleeves rolled up.

Presently, Mark turned his distended nether region on Bille and screamed, "Help me out, fair lady! Don't let a cowboy die this way, mate!"

"Oh no!" laughed Bille. "Vat vill happen to you? I don't know!"

Mark then turned to Louise, who was doubled over with laughter, and produced an empty beer mug from the zone in question, which reduced things back to normal and put a big smile on his face.

The gang of them were rodeo members touring the country on a circuit. They had started out in Melbourne and were heading for Darwin for a big event, stopping only in the Alice owing to a brief mechanical problem.

One beer led to another (except for me, the always designated driver, of course) and at their slurred invitation we found ourselves and our Britz parked in a field on the outskirts of the city next to their motor home, which also doubled as a mobile stable for two steeds. After setting up some chairs, we lost Spoon for a moment and then found him face down and unmoving in a bale of hay near the tethered horses.

"He can usually take a lot more," slurred Mark, barely standing over his pal, "but I reckon he's tired. Aye, Spoon? Tired, mate? Get up, mate!" and he gave him a little kick that didn't appear to rectify anything.

There isn't much else in my journals about that night, except waking up to see Louise outside our motor home in Mark's swag and Mark sleeping in a pile of hay without. He looked like he had landed there instead of placing (or pacing) himself. Once everyone had stirred, they invited us to come and see them in action at a rodeo near Darwin a few days on. So with lots of promises to see each other again, we went our separate ways.

There isn't really much to say about continental dead centre town of Alice Springs. Nowadays, it's just a stop-off point with a big shopping complex, lots of internet cafés and hostels. There is nothing really magical about the place: you don't actually feel like you are anywhere remote once you get there. It is just anytown, anywhere, really.

The town was originally called "Stuart" after the explorer, but it for some reason adopted the name Alice Springs for Lady Alice Todd, wife of Sir Charles Todd, in 1933, when the location was one of a dozen repeater stations in the telegraph line that went up the belly of the country. As far as any water springs went, I'm not exactly sure if there were any; nonetheless, lack of water isn't a reason to give up hope of having a boat race!

The annual Henley-on-Todd Regatta is held in Alice Springs each year in August. Complete boats with sails are raced along the dry, sandy bed of the Todd River, propelled by the legs of the crews, who remove the bottoms of the boats and hold them up as they would a barrel if they were naked. Apparently, the first one was held in 1962 and since then international attention and crowds have come to see people peel around in vessels deprived of base hulls – something like driving a car with Fred Flintstone.

As we pressed north, we started to perceive what we thought were unmoving kangaroos along the roadside. They appeared small and scattered at first, but then we noticed that they were actually little mounds of rounded earth, some red and some brown or gold. As our course furthered, the size and variety of shapes grew – some round and others like chiselled citadels or fanned-out sandcastles. We found that these numerous marvels of engineering were termite mounds. Amazingly, these little insects mixed saliva with a grain of dirt (and no doubt immeasurable patience) and built these massive castles to keep them comfortable from the exterior temperature. They were, in essence, building millions of little Coober Pedys all over the Northern Territory. Their handiwork was presently becoming a ubiquitous feature of the roadside, giving competition to the burned-out car bodies.

We made for a NT mystery known as Devil's Marbles. The sun plopped down over the horizon as we reached the pull-off and a trucker informed us that we had just missed an authentic Aboriginal sitting on a rock. We had missed the perfect photo opportunity by minutes!

I glanced over the bearded and tattooed trucker to his set of wheels – and there were a lot of them. On the front bumper of his rig were two huge and bold-lettered signs reading "ROAD TRAIN," and behind trailed a lot of linked-up cabooses. Road Trains are pretty scary things, the leviathans of Australian highways, and we would see and pass many of them.

The vans can sometimes be about five metres high; Australian Road Trains are the biggest general freight-carrying vehicles in the world, roaming over millions of empty square kilometres. The only vehicles that come close (and even then, not really) to rivalling them are the 35-metre-long double-trailer trucks in some US states. In Australia, the Road Train can sometimes stretch more than half the length of a football field and the maximum allowed – from bull bar to tail lights – is 53.5 metres.

They carry food and cattle (sometimes 150 in a shot, with 115 tonne loads) and some have 62 tires (and 12 spares), each of which drivers must inspect for punctures. Along the way, the verification is done with sticks instead of by foot – lest an angry snake be coiled around the axle and looking to take out his aggression. To drive one, you apparently have to know how to shift through 18 gears; what's more, you can't reverse, so you better be able to proactively size up potential u-turns by eye. The max speed is about 85 kilometres per hour, and the trucker I spoke with advised me never to stop abruptly on the highway if I saw a Road Train in my rear-view mirror because, well, the drivers are trained to plough through obstacles rather than braking.

Well, we couldn't make much out of Devil's Marbles in the dark, so we parked and admired the unhindered constellations. It is only when surrounded by such imposing sights that one starts to think about the meaning of life and one's place in it all. I am sad to report that I have no ground-breaking revelations, but I did think about my late grandmother and my recently deceased godfather, and my family and friends. I also realized that I had no clue about what was going on in the world, how Iraq War II was progressing, if it was at all, and I wasn't all too bothered about that. I think more people in power should sit under the stars in the desert once in awhile to get perspective, but that's just me. It might be more politically correct to pass gas in the desert anyhow.

The next morning, we strolled around the site just as it was being saturated in red and gold by the magnificent sunrise. I can understand why Devil's Marbles is considered a mystery: massive round boulders (many significantly larger than our Britz motor home) were perched in strange and mind-bending positions. Some were almost perfectly balanced and stacked on areas no larger in diameter than a car tire, while others were scrunched together as if they were huge and less symmetrical Lego pieces. In some ways it does look as though some giant may have spilled his bag of marbles onto the flat ground and just left them as they were. The area covers about 1,800 hectares and is related in a small way to Uluru.

How, I hear you asking? Aboriginals hold that their djang ancestors set the place up for ceremony; to scientists, however, it is another link to an even further past. They are considered part of Australia's underlying skeleton – the proverbial bones, stripped of what used to cover them. They are thought to be remnants of mountain ranges forged when tectonic plates crashed together and then tore apart.

As we headed toward Darwin, the landscape finally changed and became increasingly muggy and tropical and less desert-like. Signs everywhere warned us not to swim in rivers, as crocodiles "can cause serious injury or death." Other roadside markers advised that the area was prone to flooding levels of 1.4 metres or higher. The termite mounds were also reaching incredible heights: one we stopped at rang in at four and a half metres!

We decided to pull into Elsey National Park to enjoy the Mataranka Hot Springs for the evening. As we rolled in, who should we spot but our cowboy friends with their dogs and horses! I knew instinctively that we would be in for another night of comedy.

Once parked, we walked the few hundred metres into the jungle, toads springing from our path, to the thermal pools of crystal clear water (fed by underground sources), surrounded by panadunus palms. Thankfully, this was all free! As we relaxed in the hot springs, Bille grimaced and pointed up. About three metres above our heads were whole webbed communities of hand-sized spiders with long legs strung between the overhanging tree branches.

"Zose are dangerous animals!" Bille managed with concern.

"Don't worry about those insec– ... animals. You leave them alone and they'll leave you alone," I retorted, content to relax without hindrance in the bath's warm water.

"Vat about zee crocodiles?" she asked.

"Not here," I replied.

"I vant to see von," she said, and then swam off with her eyes just above water level and her body slithering.

Thankfully, we didn't.

Later that evening, we strolled into the bar where men with crocodile teeth in their hats drained cans of golden ale. The walls proudly displayed photos of a time when a massive flood had washed out the premises. Lines on the wall way above our heads denoted where the water level had crested, and one of the pictures was shot from a helicopter showing the submerged building with the owner flailing his arms for rescue on the rooftop. I don't know who would want to remember that kind of trauma, but I found out that top-enders celebrate the strangest things, such as simply living another day.

Because the Mad Nomads plus Bille plus three rodeo riders plus some of their friends didn't find much action in the saloon, we all decided to have a night dip in the thermal pools. Moments later, we were all splashing about when one of the cowboys conceived of a competition to separate the men from the boys. Who, it was demanded, could dredge the heaviest rock from the depths of the pools and lay it on deck?

Competitors drew breath, sunk below the surface to troll for increasingly larger slabs of sunken rock. If you have ever taken the distinct privilege of farting in a full bathtub, you can easily picture the ensuing scenario. Tumultuous bubbles burst on the surface and the muffled sounds of submerged, yet forceful, activity could be discerned. Then a head would break back into the air, screams would find less to dampen their volume, and the competitor would either complete or fail the final swing.

In the end, Spoon rang in champion, as he shot up with slab after slab of impossibly burdensome rock with the devoted screams of a weightlifter under an Olympic barbell.

The next morning, we had another dip and found puzzled people wondering how so many unmanageable rocks had been laid in procession along the deck.

"Spoon's Marbles!" I reflected.

We drove onward and stopped at a showground next to a prison in Katherine, a couple of hours drive south of Darwin. Mark, Emma and Spoon were in their preparatory stages and we wandered about the rootin' tootin' rodeo grounds. We were a tad bit out of place, as we weren't wearing any cowboy hats, big belt buckles, jeans or boots amongst the caged-up bulls, bucks and horses. We muscled a good seat near a character who could have been half of ZZ-Top and had a vantage over the arena.

CLANG! It wasn't long before the show began, the crowd cheering as heat after heat of bulls bucked out of cages with men bobbing on their backs, trying to last eight seconds without tasting dirt. Mark came out to manage the task one-handedly on some behemoth that tried viciously to show him the ground. Spoon was in two events, first jumping from his horse to wrestle an escaped steer and then bull riding. He managed eight seconds, as well! Emma was in a horse course, sashaying around barrels in the dirt against the clock, and she placed well.

They were walking a little funny after the event, especially Mark and Spoon, but they invited us to pull our Britz into the showground and camp next to them. Nearby people were square dancing and drinking their merry way into oblivion. The next morning, we thanked the trio for all their kindness and wished them well upon their circuit. To Bille's excitement, and our consternation, our next destination would be the location where *Crocodile Dundee* was filmed.

54 – Losing Germans

"BILLE!" AARON BESEECHED. "We are not going that way! It's dusk, it's a swamp and there might be crocodiles!"

"Ja! Und I vant to see von! Das ist cool," she answered from down the path. It seemed that the penny in her head was jammed.

Presently, we were standing near a swamp where another recently posted pictographic panel announced that crocodiles might well be murking about. Bille, the brave German charger with no fear, had forged ahead and Aaron was voicing the very real concern that the signs hadn't been put there for fun.

"Come back!" Aaron said. "It's too bloody dangerous."

"No vorries, mate!" Bille answered as she mounted a rather long zoom lens on her camera. "I vant to see zee crocodiles."

This is a transcript of an article published a few days later in the *NT News*:

> Swimmer Tells How Crocodile Dragged Tourist to Her Death: A tourist swimming in a billabong felt a 4.5 metre crocodile brush his leg just moments before it dragged a 25-year-old German woman under the water to her death. She was one of several tourists who ignored warning signs when they slipped into a park billabong for a moonlit dip ... A ranger announced, "We are flabbergasted, absolutely amazed that people ignored the park's warning signs." After a seven-hour hunt, they harpooned the crocodile and recovered the victim's body ... The tragedy was the first fatal crocodile attack in the park for 15 years.

In research I would conduct posthumously, I ran a search through major periodicals of the past decade on "crocodile" and "Northern Territory" and the computer almost crashed. Tourists and locals alike had been flashed out of existence, but some had survived to tell trembling stories to journalists. Some articles claimed that if any one of the 50,000 known crocs in the NT get a hold of you, it could be days before your remains are found – if at all.

One of the saddest stories was that of a man whose last vision of his daughter on Christmas Eve was her hand fading into the watery ruckus of two seven-metre crocodiles who had decided not to share. He had been boating with her along a river. He lived to mourn her, albeit badly mauled. Soon after, retaliatory hunts on crocs were undertaken while the NT government pleaded for calm.

Presently, there was another story afoot about a crocodile that scared the shorts off of a tourist who walked leisurely out of a beach pub not far from Darwin to find a limousine of scales and teeth sunbathing near the entrance. This croc, captured and relocated, was apparently the 86th caught in the Darwin Harbour that year.

Amongst all the adaptations and introductions of foreign species that have gone on in Australia, crocodiles are one of the few creatures that have not evolved one iota. They are the world's largest living reptiles, unchanged for nearly 200 million years. They are such refined and perfect killing machines, so fast and efficient in the execution of their prey, that nature has neglected to streamline or update them.

Although they are a year-round concern in the NT, the wet season (when river banks overflow and dams burst) can see many crocodiles slither into territory they normally wouldn't. Given the size of the region, it isn't easy to get signs up in time or track their locations.

We managed to coax Bille back onto a trail consisting of more land than mysterious murk, and that transcript you just read happened to another 25-year-old German female. Immediately, however, we were besieged by insects of all shapes and sizes. The heat was thick and muggy, even after sundown, so even if one could minimize one's movements to the sole act of slow breathing, 10 kilograms of sweat would still be shed.

Later, at the motor home, we prepared dinner with dingo howls in the backdrop, which seemed to come closer with each burst. Then, when I took the flashlight and toilet paper and headed for the dunny some metres off, I continually heard a peculiar shuffling noise in the bush. If I stopped or shone my light into the dark thickets, the sound would cease, and then reinitiate. Thankfully, I survived to defecate and write the words you are currently reading.

In trying to sleep, we dispensed with covers and sheets and all lay in bed trying to pretend that we were not melting into the mattresses. *Bzzzzzzzzzzzzzzzzzz*ings whizzed by our ears, and it was obvious that despite our efforts to close the door quickly, whole gangs of bugs had invaded our Britz and would not stop until they sucked the blood from our salty skins. If the dentist drill sound stopped, it was a signal to venture a guess as to which part of your body the critter had landed on so you could swat it. Then your whole body tingled with itch, and any movement would cause you to sweat even more profusely. It was not a comfortable situation.

"I HATE ZEEZ ANIMALS!" screamed Bille, who shot up from her bed in heated frustration. "I vill kill them ... kill all eine little animals so I kun sleep," and she flicked on the lights. To our absolute horror, there were squadrons of grasshoppers, spiders, moths, mosquitoes and other twitching things lining our ceiling like planes on an aircraft carrier. It was bug fest, and we grabbed magazines and rolled up newspapers to eliminate swath after swath of them. When our ceiling lay speckled with blood spots and squashed bug bodies, we lay down again and turned out the lights. *Bzzzzzzzzzzzzzzzzzzz.*

Lights on! There was a fresh batch of troops and we had no idea where they had come from. No matter how many we killed, they replenished, like the mythical hydra dragon: slice off one head and three grow back. So went our first night in Kakadu National Park, where it seemed Paul Hogan (a.k.a. Mick Dundee) hadn't been as plagued in his movie.

Kakadu is a World Heritage listing and the major draw for tourism in the top end. It spans roughly 20,000 square kilometres and houses 1,600 plant species, 275 bird species, over 75 reptile families, 25 different types of frog, and, surprise, some 10,000 species of insect (I am sure we killed at least one of each kind that first night). Topographically, Kakadu is a place of sandstone escarpment plateaus, river systems and flood plains with numerous billabongs, savannah woodlands, fringing woodlands and monsoon forests. It's also home to 50,000-year-old wall art from the Bininj (pronounced *bin-ing*) and Mungguy (*mung-goy*) Aboriginal peoples.

(In reading the park pamphlets, you can't help but ask for help when confronted with words like Anbangbang [*un-bung-bung*] or bawardedjobgeng [*bad-bon*]. The main languages spoken by Kakadu natives are Kunwinjku, Gun-djeihmi and Jawoyn, which replaced the ancient tongues of Gagudju and Limilngan and I'll leave you to it to figure out how to say those.)

Other notes of interest regarding Kakadu were warnings not to go near or swim in any rivers or swamps, no matter how inviting they may seem. Hmm, what else? Stay on roads, use fire in designated areas, don't take photos of sacred Aboriginal sites. But of all this, considering that most of the world has been discovered, reading the following in the Kakadu handbook made me do a double take: "Traditionally, Bininj/Mungguy do not greet each other every time they meet. However, most Bininj/Mungguy are used to non-Aboriginal people doing so and may expect a 'hello'. However, some Bininj/Mungguy find constant eye contact uncomfortable."

During our séjour, some areas were unfortunately closed due to flooding, though we did manage to hike and enjoy what area was available. We combated the heat with dips in shady billabongs and lagoons, some of them blessed with waterfalls, and all of which were posted as waters not infested by crocs. The signs did not, however, announce the other troublesome plague: tourists.

Areas slicked by sun cream occupied large parts of the water surface as tour after tour of dawdling, plump and camera-toting tourists came along. In uprooting ourselves for sheer want of less people, we toddled off into deeper jungle, where a ranger had told us another less-visited billabong lay. True to his word, it was there, but en route I was speaking with Louise with my head turned and almost wandered straight into a titanic web with a spider the size of a splayed adult foot sitting in the centre. To boot, while I was taking some snaps, swamp bugs bit my legs into a state of itchy irritation that lasted for an eternity. The sheer heat of the NT seems to make all things heal slow, and I would have scabs on my feet and legs for weeks.

We also managed to squeeze in a nice sunset over the wetlands and some cliff climbing on layered spires of rock, and Louise and Aaron got up at sunrise to cruise the Yellow River and see crocodiles and bird life. But of course you can't go far in any part of Australia without a bushfire, and one evening we drove down a road flanked by blazing grass and, beyond, a charred and smouldering landscape.

We then headed west of Kakadu to a region rumoured to be civilized. Some more toothy adventures would await, and we would lose our German companion in the kafuffle.

"PEOPLE WHO DON'T want to be found won't be," said the owner of a local internet café in Darwin. "I get guys in here who show up in their four-wheel-drives from off 'the track,' beer between the legs, smoke in the mouth, shotguns in the back and dead pigs in the tray. They come to burn CDs, send emails and download DVDs." He then handed me a receipt for my web-time; where it said "name," he had written "passer-by."

I don't blame them. Darwin is the only spot to do just that, for it is the only place around with this many buildings and streets for thousands of treacherous kilometres. I found out that "the track" meant the Stuart Highway, the only road in or out of Darwin. To the north is the pernicious ocean, to the east, Kakadu National Park, and then the tangled and forbidding Arnhem lands beyond that; to the west is more steaming jungle, and then endless searing desert. Darwin is closer to Asia than it is to any other city in Australia; Perth is 4,298 kilometres off, Sydney 3,917, Brisbane 3,774, but Bali is only a two-hour flight away. The closest foreign capital is Port Moresby, Papua New Guinea, some 1,815 kilometres directly east and gently north. It's a rough place.

The first NT settlers (half of them convicts) were dispatched to the region in 1824, mainly to discourage French and Dutch interests and partially to establish relations with trepanning fishermen from Indonesia. Fort Dundas, on Melville Island, was the first settlement along the shores of the Apsley Straight, but it was abandoned four years later owing to remoteness, bad health, conflicts with the Larrakia Aboriginals (who killed the party's draughtsman, J.W. Bennett) and destructive storms. Another attempt was made at Raffles Bay, a deep inlet 200 kilometres northeast of modern-day Darwin, but a year later it, too, was deserted.

And so the story was repeated, as location after location was abandoned. Only the township of Victoria lasted 12 years before being forsaken. When the NT was forked over as part of South Australia, the idea for a northern capital for shipping and trade enjoyed a renaissance, resulting in expeditions mounted by explorer John McDouall Stuart. He reported favourably of his overland discoveries and in 1862 claimed that the top-end region had great agricultural potential, as well. Several sites were considered, and one area 50 kilometres northwest of modern-day Darwin (called Palmerston) was about to become the capital when arguments broke out about why other alternatives had not been considered. Two years later, Port Darwin* was recommended and ignored as another expedition was thrown together. In the end, over two decades, the telegraph line and the gold rush made the provisional camp a capital by default and the name Darwin was written in 1911 when the NT separated.

There had been several stories in the papers about backpackers having gone missing or been hijacked under sinister circumstances. An English couple had broken down on the "track" and assumed help was at hand when someone approached them. Instead, the male was murdered and the terrified woman taken captive. She managed to escape, bleeding, and get help and flee back to England. But it wasn't all in the NT. In a related story from 1995, the bodies of seven backpackers were found mutilated in the forests of NSW, and the deranged criminal was sentenced two years later to life. In 2000, 15 backpackers died when a Queensland youth hostel was set ablaze. The arsonist was convicted for the crime two years afterward. What's shocking, though, is that the NT seems to have more violent stories in ratio to its slender population. And I could see why ...

Darwin has a gaping chip on its shoulder: a loose-knit community where fresh faces come and go and are never cause for comment. In our time here, I would meet all kinds, including several pearl divers on break. Diving for pearls is one of the NT's biggest businesses – and you can earn good money as a diver – however, it is isolation work: out to sea on boats and camping on islands. Divers usually work six days a week for a month and a half and then piss away their earnings in their fortnight of debauchery.

I befriended a few glazed-eyed divers who said they could get me work if I wanted, though after they slowly explained how much time they spent underwater, I thought the wiser of inhaling nitrate at long stretches, only to get lonely, and further intoxicate myself silly in Darwin.

Rumour also has it that Mafiosi like the region: getting rid of bodies undetected is easy, especially when banks break in the wet season. Just over 91,000 residents and itinerants, as well as untold species of animal and insect that kill horribly, call Darwin home.

---

* Named so in 1839 by John Lort Stokes, Commander of the *Beagle*, to honour his old friend the scientist and naturalist Charles Darwin, with whom he had shared a previous voyage in South America. Little did he realize that Darwin's popular theories of "evolution" and "survival of the fittest" would actually be a way of life in the area for human settlers, as well.

And it has been rebuilt a few times. Darwin was bombed to smithereens by Japanese forces in 1942 and then flattened by a cyclone 32 years later. To add to that, there isn't much one can do in the wet season of November to April, when monsoons wash out roads and the exterior humidity level swivels its dial to "bake quickly." On the other hand, the dry season, from May to October, is said to be cooler and more bearable, and somewhat less dangerous. The Mad Nomads arrived between seasons.

Nevertheless, we had been drinking urine-warm water all through the desert and it hadn't been since Adelaide that we had seen so many urban features. We realized that the last time we had spent any time in a real city for more than hours was Melbourne, almost a distant memory. That was part of Darwin's limited appeal, like the ski fields in NSW and Victoria, or a lemonade stand in the desert: there was no competition for yonks.

We easily found parking for our motor home along a major downtown street on the first evening. When I say downtown Darwin, I mean a couple of streets by a couple of streets. Although it may be a city in title, to my eyes it barely qualified as much more than an outback town. As I stepped from the interior of our Britz, it felt as if someone had opened the door of a pizza oven. A big wall of muggy heat smacked me. The others were getting ready so I waited outside while doing my able best to move as little as possible in a concerted effort to make my deodorant last longer. Something rustled in the tree above me and a little nut or piece of fruit with teeth marks bonked off my noggin.

"No! You won't get me!" screamed a bearded man in the distance, standing bolt upright on spindly legs and pointing into the air as if someone was trying to arrest him.

"Sits 'own, mate," grumbled one of two other men of mange seated on the bench from which the bearded bloke had just launched himself against his invisible foe. The three of them were obviously vagabonds, one of them an Aboriginal wearing two hats (one on top of another) and the other two looking as if they had just emerged from a day in the mines, circa 1850. They were filthy and sinewy, their whiskers hung low and skimmed their chests and the telltale bottle-shaped brown paper bags lay close at hand amongst a collection of trash in a shopping cart.

"I'll kill ya!" he cried in a tone like the rumble of an old four-wheel-drive as he swung at the air, twirling himself around before crashing headlong like tumbling timber into a bush, where he remained twitching for a moment. The other two snickered, their eyes bleary and their movements sluggish, but the darker man with two sunhats seemed in his own world.

Louise, Aaron and Bille emerged from the motor home as another chewed-up piece of alimentation fell on my head from the tree. Whatever it was up there munching in the branches, it didn't think much about who might be below. We made for town as the bearded drunkard in the distance started chasing something or someone while emitting a gruff string of curses and sometimes a throaty and terrified bawl. Another bush came to interrupt his dissemination of demons.

We wandered down Mitchell Street, also known as the backpacker zone. There were a couple of hostels, some five-dollar meals and a healthy helping of bars and pubs, and nearby was a place where people sat around hoping to sell their used caravans and cars. Once we found a free table at a pub, we sat down, moving as little as possible while awaiting some cold schooners.

At the bar, Louise had nodded g'day to three cowboys while getting our drinks and presently one of them strode up, cocksure of conversing with her. He summed up his life in a matter of seconds.

"Originally from Zimbabwe," he said with a slightly tinted Australian accent. "I can speak English and three blick fella languages. I work with an Aboriginal blick fella, but I can't speak his talk or any surrounding abo blick fella talk. Those over there are me brothers," he indicated the two other cowboys, "and we live on a station 1,000 kilometres west of here in Western Australia. I can brand about 250 sheep and cattle in an hour, up at four o'clock, to bed at 11 ... Couple days off, came to Darwin for some drinks. Perth is too far, but sometimes we go there."

We could see that he had had a few, and when the conversation lulled he added, "I can't read or write, but I can run a station. Yep. Run a station real good." It was obvious he was out of things to say about his place on Earth, so he turned to Louise and mumbled something the rest of us didn't hear. Louise shook her head side to side dryly, then he got up, pulled on his belt buckle, tipped his hat and sashayed assertively back into the bar.

"What did he say, Louise?" we asked.

"He 'fancied a shag' and I told him to bugger off," she replied matter-of-factly. I took it that she had dealt with hard-line Australian men before. "He's probably in there telling his brothers that I dig chicks." We glanced over and the gesticulations between them certainly looked that way as he joined his two siblings in a consolation beer.

It was that night that three monsters would take our Bille from us: she had reached the bottom of her bone-dry savings account, not to mention the end of her visa, and she also had a prepaid plane booking back to Europe. While Aaron and Louise remained at the bar, I would take her to the airport for the red-eye back to Melbourne, and then she would go onto Europe for a life of earning more money to travel again.

It is very hard to get lost in Darwin, even at night, it's that small of a place. If you look at a map, the first noticeable attribute is that the centre appears hollow where the airport is, and that there are little boroughs around it. Nevertheless, Bille and I were rerouted by a police roadblock, at which the cops informed us that they were looking for someone wandering about with a shotgun. Great. Wonderful. My first night in Darwin, Bille's last.

We made it in time for her flight without being served a buckshot and I bid Bille a great trip home. In many ways, I could understand her situation, for I, too, was running out of money fast and my ETA visa was close to expiring. I drove back to town to rejoin the others at the pub, but ultimately I would be a wet blanket and head to bed early while they stayed out.

"Hey, guys," said Louise, reading the local newspaper the next day. "Do you remember that guy who got kicked out of the bar several times? Aaron, you would; Allan was at the airport with Bille."

"What about him?" Aaron said between mouthfuls of cereal.

He stopped chewing as Louise flashed the *NT News* our way.

Charges Over Theft: A 25-year-old man arrested after he was allegedly found with explosives in the centre of Darwin has been granted bail. Police said that he was arrested last night after he tried to force his way into a Mitchell Street bar. Police said they searched his vehicle parked nearby and seized a quantity of explosives. They said a stash of explosives were also found in his hotel room. He was charged with criminal damage, trespassing, stealing and offences under the Dangerous Goods Act. Conditions of bail include reporting and residential conditions.

Darwin does have its advantages. A traffic jam is considered to be three cars backed up at eight o'clock on a Monday morning, and parking in the ever-available spots is only 60 cents an hour or $1.80 for the day. The thick air guarantees that the sunsets are dramatic each and every evening. And as far as its denizens, Darwin is home to starchy military personnel and hippies living in trees along the foreshore, as well as Aboriginals, backpackers, loopy scientists, eccentric artists and potty poets.

The town is chock full of four-wheel-drive vehicles geared to the gills with engine snorkels and caked in red earth as if rigged for missions to distant planets. Many vehicles also sport large and bloodied mounted roo-bars (like the front of a snow plough but with an empty frame of a shovel), in case animals don't get out of their way. Darwin is the adventurer's paradise.

Blessed and cursed, too, is Darwin for its harbour and endless beaches. A little-known fact is that Darwin's harbour is 22 times larger than Sydney's, but you can't swim in the beautiful waters unless you're a pain freak or suicidal. Very evident signs are posted along the shoreline: between October and May, box jellyfish breed in the area and "Cause severe and painful injury or death" (mind you, they could really be around any month).

A box jellyfish can range in size from golf ball to volleyball. They look as if they're the result of some experiment gone awry – as if someone hurriedly flushed a condom down the toilet with limp two-minute noodles trailing behind. A mature jelly fish is called a "medusa," and it can have up to 40 tentacles, each capable of stretching two metres. These tentacles contain minute stingers called nematocysts, which are so tiny that 1,000 of them would fit on the head of a pin. These nematocysts contain a hollow thread that can spring out, pierce the skin of their prey and inject venom that can "kill a person in two to three minutes" (this from a pamphlet circulated to tourists with the title, *Living with Box Jellyfish*, which may as well read, *So, You Decided to Come to Darwin*). Although the venom is intended for infusion into small fish and prawns, box jellyfish are the only creatures that can venomously kill a human in less time than it takes to cook those two-minute noodles.

Locally, and in the past 100 years, the box jellyfish (scientific name, *Chironex Fleckeri*, "the most venomous animal known to science") has taken more than 60 lives and caused untold cases of blistering and hellish pain. It was advised that people carry lots of vinegar, for despite being a great addition to French fries with salt, it could also be used to sooth the fires of hell upon your skin. You can be sure I searched for the creature in the databases of recent periodicals.

When the Mad Nomads arrived in Darwin, the latest story was of a 21-year-old who was stung by an irukandji jellyfish, five kilometres out of Darwin's harbour, when he was scuba diving. Despite wearing a wetsuit, he was lashed across his face, then pulled screaming from the water and doused liberally with vinegar. He was treated at the hospital for "horrendous pain." My real point in telling you this *NT News* snippet, however, is that it was on the same page as a story titled "Australia's Only Singing, Piano-Playing Dingo is a Howling Success With Tourists" and another article about a bird that can whistle mobile ring tones.

A quick visit to the Darwin Museum put a few things into context. One section is dedicated wholly to the creatures of the region: stuffed sharks and pickled snakes, deadly fish and prickly jellyfish, bitey insects and huge, hairy spiders. The captions were filled with the words "venomous," "bite," "aggressive," "sting" and "death."

And if that isn't enough to make you consider re-reading the fine print of your health insurance policy, beyond is a section devoted to Christmas Eve 1974, when something no one expected levelled Darwin. Today, most people don't even know about it, or more likely try to forget. By all accounts, it was just another quiet evening in Darwin during hurricane season, which in previous years had been windy and rainy but had never translated into too much more. But this particular Christmas would come to be classified as Australia's largest natural disaster, though it isn't really unless you were an insurance company.

While families gathered for the holiday, a funnel of fury flattened Darwin, erasing three-quarters of its then 12,000 homes and prompting an evacuation of over 25,000 people by air and over 9,000 by road. To this day, there is no fixed death toll, as "the disaster was of such magnitude – with people missing at sea and the number of itinerants in Darwin at the time, an accurate count of victims was not possible," says the *Cyclone Tracy Information Sheet* (one source, though, did put the casualties at 66 dead and 112 injured). Darwin lay a twisted mess, and no one had been prepared for it. Apparently, Darwin had been hit viciously three times over in the previous 77 years by other cyclones, but none as bad as Tracy, which pressed in at over 250 kilometres per hour.

Ninety percent of all property was damaged beyond repair, and as I gazed over aerial photos in the museum, I couldn't believe that it was the same place in which I now stood. The only thing linear about the photos were the roads: everything else was just a chaotic and corrugated destruction. In one ground-level photo, a building and a car lay in ruins and the owner had released some anger by spray-painting "Tracy, you bitch" across the brickwork. In another image, a sheet of twisted aluminium metal was spray-painted with "Keep out – we still live here" and mounted on what used to be a building.

I then went to listen to a looping audio bit of a recording someone had managed to make of the sound of the hurricane. I tell you in all honestly that when I heard the monstrous roar and the sound of pieces of things scraping on the ground and cutting things to ribbons, "fright" doesn't begin to describe my feeling, though I could swear I felt my rectum do a dry rehearsal of the advances stages of terror. The voice-over said, "That sound is the most horrible sound in the world."

No shit.

56 – Adventures in Smuggled Forensics

WE HAD THREE weeks of sponsorship remaining on our tour and the plan had originally been to wind up in Perth, another 4,000-plus kilometres of barren nothingness and extreme fuel prices and rancid public drinking water along the northern and western coasts of the eccentrically large continent of Australia. As crazy as Darwin is, we decided to make it home until sponsorship expiry, and just as well we did, for it did have a relevant history for our cause.

We decided to get with the program and traded in our Explorer motor home at the Darwin Britz office for our final vehicle: the Bushcamper, or "Bushy," a hearty and modified four-wheel-drive Toyota Landcruiser equipped with basic facilities and a hi-top roof that becomes a bed. This thing is made for the outback, tough as guts and raw as meat. It wants to eat rocks for breakfast, bush for brunch, bumps for lunch, drink rivers for tea and diesel for dinner. It sits high on a sturdy suspension, has a snorkel and massive tires marked Desert Duellers. Now we blended in with all the other Dundees of Darwin, and decided to take her out in Litchfield National Park, about an hour and a half's drive southwest. The park spans some 1,500 square kilometres of largely untouched landscape, including monsoon rainforests, tabletop ranges, sandstone escarpments, large groves of cycads and spring-fed creeks.

The road in was bumpy and harsh. En route, we passed ever-growing termite mounds. Because we were driving a Bushy, we were presently members of a large NT subculture – we could embark on any and all jungle paths marked "4WD only." We did get lost at one point in the jungle, but were rewarded by emerging onto fields dotted with miniature cities of termite communities, some two and a half metres high! In some ways it looked like a diminutive Martin Place: huge grey and flat constructions clumped together. Although they may look like sandcastles, the termite mounds are as solid and stable as any boulder, and no less forgiving. I read some accounts of people crashing into them, which resulted in serious injuries to them and their cars becoming write-offs.

There were tell-tale signs that the hand of fire had come through the area. The earth was scorched and as we walked, ash sprayed out from under our every step. On the horizon, smoke was moving closer to our position and when we saw flocks of birds fleeing the area, we wisely decided to high-tail it out of there, lest we found ourselves surrounded by a wall of flames. When I returned to the same spot a week or so later for photo opportunities, I was glad to see a fresh green re-growth gilding the once-seared ground. In a national park pamphlet, I read the following poem, written by Bill Neidjie of the Bunitj clan:

This earth, I never damage
I look after. Fire is nothing, just clean up.
When you burn, new grass coming up.
That means good animal soon,
Might be goanna, possum, wallaby
Burn him off, new grass coming up, new life all over.

A note beneath explained that only since 1980 has the park management and the Bininj/Mungguy worked together to reduce the number of fires at the end of the dry season. "Using fire wisely, for the right purposes at the right time, will ensure Australia's unique environment is maintained for present and future generations," it concludes.

Our first stop was the popular Wangi Falls, which were a very welcome respite from the oppressive NT's exterior intensity. Louise and Aaron took the time to get a massage from one gushing waterfall while I relaxed in a plunge pool and then looked for things to climb that I probably shouldn't. Because the Wangis are just off a sealed road, they are quite full of tourists, so Bushy and the Mad Nomads and their Lonely Planet guidebook said, "Nah-uh."

We put dirt and bumps beneath our tread and bashed in a *Tomb Raider*–like fashion down jungle track, forging through two rivers, to get to Sandy Creek Falls. Was it ever worth it! We had the place to ourselves for awhile and fully enjoyed the massive waterfall and pool. I found cliffs to climb and high places to jump off of, but before long, some tourists arrived and their guide pointed to me as an example of what not to do.

After camping out the night, we continued our quest for crocodile-free areas. We couldn't resist another off-road jaunt in Bushy, so we made way for the Lost City, a large collection of sandstone formations that could look like Mayan ruins, but only if you'd had enough to drink, or smoked the right substance, first. We weren't too impressed, but we enjoyed swapping driving duties and feeling rather Indiana Jones-ish.

After another night of camping, we assailed Buley Rockhole at sunrise, which was an amazing way to wake up. No one around, a river with really deep plunge pools and cascading water – who could ask for more? We took the liberty of filling our water bottles at source. An hour's bush walk alongside a babbling river on a path slung with endless webs and massive but idle spiders put us at Florence Falls. There, I happily discovered more surfaces to scale and cliff tops to jump off of than I could handle. I received worried (but I prefer the word "jealous") looks from tourists when they saw a human form in such high and dangerous locations. I did bash my shins and slice my big toe in one foray – when I was in a Spiderman-like position on a high-up precipice – but I made it to the top and jumped a hell of a long way down into the pool.

We headed back to Darwin, wiping dirt from our teeth and grit from our eyes, with a better appreciation of the four-wheel-drive culture, and I bandaged up the flaps of skin on my toe.

"Hey, Allan! Meet Twitch," Louise yelled loudly from the bar, the beer flowing in her veins. Seconds before, I was minding my own business absorbed by the TV above the pool table; it was playing a hockey match, of all things. I know diddly-squat about hockey, as I never follow sports; however, I am sure you will agree that anyone would be captivated by the circumstance of watching an NHL game in Darwin when, in the middle of winter, the thermometer reads 35°C at night. Nonetheless, I turned around to where a jittering person was waiting to make my acquaintance.

"I'm Twitch," said the woman, who looked a bit undernourished in her red dress. She had a head of shoulder-length flaxen hair and a burning cigarette in her hand.

"Why do they call you –" But I didn't have to finish my question. She was moving oddly, akin to those suction-cupped dancing Elvis dolls that people put on their dashboards. Then suddenly she shuddered and her eyes rolled back in her head while the lids danced randomly like the doors of a cuckoo clock. I was taken aback. She stopped for a few seconds and then starting shaking in the fashion of someone who has been handed a live toaster and pushed into a full bathtub.

While I stared in amazement, some local on my other flank suddenly leaned over and said, "Stay away from Twitch, mate. Don't bother."

"I wasn't ... um ... bothering. I'm watching hockey," and I made a SWAT team signal with two fingers from my eyes to the screen. "But say, isn't it cruel to call this woman Twitch?" I ventured.

"That's what she calls herself, mate. Stay away," he warned. I looked back at the woman and she was nervously smoking her cigarette. I didn't know what to say so I just nodded and she twittered back some form of acknowledgement ... I think. I turned to the local.

"Does she need vinegar?" I asked earnestly, but the stranger was distracted and didn't reply.

At that moment, Tony leaned over both the bar and my shoulder and said, "You don't want any of Twitch, mate; keep clear. She's a man-eater." Tony was our new best friend and Darwin saviour. More on him in a moment.

"Man, I'm just trying to watch hockey," I said, and then a band came on stage and Twitch flinched off somewhere else and Louise shot me a smile.

Aaron, Louise and I were in a bar formally known as "The Cage," along the Casurina foreshore of Darwin. We had been invited there by Tony, and presently the well-known local band Dr. Elephant graced a compact stage that was wedged in the corner. The lead singer, also named Dr. Elephant, was a hefty individual with Pavarotti pipes of gold. Although they belted out covers, they did so exceedingly well. After the show, I went up to congratulate the band and the singer on a job well done, but he looked nervously at me as I approached.

"Thanks," he replied in a terse tone. "Yea, thanks, mate." I didn't understand then why he was so edgy, but I would eventually find out (and so will you) in the small world of Darwin.

I turn now to Tony. We back up for a sec to an evening on a patio.

"So there I am in bloody New Orleans, 19 years old," Tony said in a heavily aucker accent while blowing smoke straight into the air. "And I was surrounded by black fellas – American negroes. They were going to mug me, for sure: two white blokes had been killed there recently, and I found out later it's one of the hottest crack spots in the US. But then I said something and by pure coincidence one of them had seen *Crocodile Dundee* and fancied me accent, so they didn't rob me, no worries, and they took me out drinkin'! I can't remember much after that, except that I was on some stage surrounded by wide-eyed negroes and I was talking pure shit, mate, tellin' yarns, spinnin' sagas. They didn't understand what I was sayin' but they liked the sound of it. They let me out the back when I said I was tired and I got a job at the local youth hostel, where I slit the throats of some sheep and hung them to drain the blood in the shower. Happy days, mate. Put a sign up, no one went in there, no worries ..."

Tony took the last drag off his cigarette and continued. "Was working with some Irish and a South African bloke who was drunk and fell down the stairs and knocked out all his teeth. He was buggered."

Then he lit another cigarette and said, "I grew up in rural Queensland. Crazy place, mate. When I was a kid I had a GATT-ling gun and fitted it to me jeep. Went off into the bush and fired it at some galahs [pink parrots] sittin' quietly in a tree. All you saw was feathers and smoke and while the feathers were still falling the coppas came up saying, 'Give it 'ere, mate,' and then took off. Happy days ... Then one day, me old man got his gun to shoot a pig and the bloody bullet rebounded and went into his mate's knee. All dad could say was, 'Get up, mate, we got a pig to kill!' Yea, he was a tough bastard, me ol' man. He had been run over accidentally with his own jeep previous to that. He was in the hood tinkering with the carburettor when his foot slipped off and the jeep lurched forward and over him, putting tire tracks across his chest. Got up cursing and kicked the thing!"

All I could think was that Quentin Tarentino had to call this guy. We had met Tony while asking about places where we could sleep in our vehicles in the Darwin area.

"Come stay with me, guys, no worries," he had said casually. He gave us his mobile number and after our Litchfield adventure, the Mad Nomads thought, "Why not?" So we called him, a brave thing to do if you consider how people disappear in Darwin. He invited us to the bar in Casurina where he was a bartender. The bar was known as The Cage because that's where fist and face and bone used to meet every Tuesday and Thursday, and mostly when people got dole cheques. Recently, the place had been cleaned up with a dress code and some biker types to keep the peace.

Tony was tall and had a lean, spare figure with a keen, eager face and a glint in his eye that told adventure never lay far away. When we were walking into The Cage to find him, I put my hand up to open a swinging door with sectioned glass panes. My arm went through nothing: one glass pane was missing and I crashed into the door frame with my arm fully extended out the other side.

"That was where a bloke's head went through the other week," said Tony as he poured us all drinks. "An abo came to the bar with a spear before that, and his mother was behind him toting wood. A week later, somebody came looking for him with a shotgun and unloaded three shots into the bar while driving by [I realised that it was the same night I had taken Bille to the airport]," he said dryly, sliding me a cold one. "But no one was hit and the bouncer just pissed him and his gun off. Nice to see youz, how ya going?"

"Good. Just wondering if that offer to stay with you is still good?" one of us asked.

"No worries." And he went off to get his keys and then give us directions. "Just tell me flatmate its oo-right. He's a bit of a nervous bloke, works as a forensic scientist and he hangs with the coppas, who get in his ear about robbery, so he gets all pumped up. But make yourselves at home. I finish late, two or three o'clock, and have another job at six in the morning, but just bring me the keys when you wake up. Happy days!"

His shared apartment was beautiful, right along the Casurina foreshore, overlooking the ocean. It didn't have a lot of furniture, but it was spacious and clean. In the living room was a pile of thick books with titles like *Psychology, Biology, Infectious Diseases, Dentistry, Arson, Blood Patterns, Organic Chemistry, Anthropology, Fingerprinting, Bite Marks* and more. I never did meet Tony's roommate, the forensic scientist; the other two did, but apparently they were polar opposites – Tony the easy-going bloke who slept very little, and this other guy who was uptight about strangers coming into his home at odd hours with Tony's set of keys. Because it was so hot out, Aaron and I slept in our boxers on the balcony and Louise stayed inside.

"Are you sure your flatmate doesn't mind?" we asked Tony one night.

"Probably does, but stuff him. Loosen him up. I'm not worried about youz guys stealin'. Me flatmate's so good at what he does, he'll know where you are before you do!"

WE ALSO TOOK in the Mindle Beach market, a weekly outdoor bazaar with rows and stands flogging commodities such as didgeridoos, crocodile-teeth hats and local Aboriginal artwork. In the background somewhere, a guy wearing an Akubra* cracked tunes with two whips to market his wares while a white fella gave a concert on four didgeridoos simultaneously. Then as evening fell, fire-twirlers, bands and dancers came out on a stage area.

I noticed that quite a few police were on hand and had parked their patrol trucks nearby. On the back of these trucks were fitted cages. The constables stood around the fringes of the show and as the night progressed grabbed unruly and drunken Aboriginals and tossed them into the paddy wagons. I saw it happen over weeks, like clockwork, and it prompted me to wonder just what legal system Aboriginals actually belonged to. The answer is: To Be Announced.

In 1996, an argument between Aboriginal Stephen Jungarrayi and his nephew broke out and the nephew was killed accidentally in the struggle. Jungarrayi was arrested in Darwin, imprisoned for 20 months (the length of his trial), convicted of manslaughter and sentenced to four years in prison, but was immediately released because the judge recognized that Jungarrayi should not face two punishments for the same crime. Jungarrayi, you see, was willing to be tried by the Aboriginal courts in his own community.

Jungarrayi was a fully initiated member of the Warlpiri clan, and when the magistrate released him, he travelled 700 kilometres to his "dry" community of Lajamanu. Lajamanu has population of 1,000, is 200 kilometres from Tennent Creek (which, if you're counting, is 504 km north of Alice Springs) and is a place of continuous isolation in wet seasons. He would face what his people called the Yarrawa, the Warlpiri word for "blood."

The Yarrawa tradition, in older times, would have resulted in Jungarrayi's death, though present-day tribal elders were aware that times had changed. They instead pronounced a word that means "two laws" – a mixture of Aboriginal and white law, though their traditions override the latter. In the place of full-blown Yarrawa, the elders simply re-enact a ceremony that would otherwise be deadly.

---

* National Australian wide-brimmed hat. Akubra is an adopted Pitjantjatjara word (circa 1872) for a head covering made with the soft under-fur of rabbits.

The whole community, including the children, gathered to watch. Jungarrayi was held up by his kinsmen. He was speared eight times in the legs until his muscles were torn to the point he could no longer stand, and then his sisters and mother beat him over the head until blood ran, and then he blacked out. Apparently, at one point he woke up, only to receive a hit from his own mother's nulla-nulla, which delivered him back into unconsciousness. Nearby, an ambulance stood in wait and Jungarrayi was airlifted to Katherine Hospital. Jungarrayi – against the orders of doctors – checked out after five days barely walking and with his head and legs heavily bandaged and speckled with bloodspots.

Jungarrayi's story was one of many instances in which a blend of new and old legal systems has been sought. It was one of the more extreme cases, but it nonetheless opened a Pandora's box of opinions. Should there be the due process of trail, or rather the ancient custom of dealing with punishment as quickly as possible? And who should dole it out? Amnesty International claims that cases like Jungarrayi's are "cruel and unusual," and thus a human rights violation. On the other hand, the governments face pressure under "reconciliation" to restore lands and traditions to the "stolen generation" and to leave them be. The sword is double-edged.

While we were in Burra, South Australia, we met two missionaries who had spent years in Hermannsburg* – a desert settlement 130 kilometres west of Alice Springs. They told stories of Aboriginal criminals being brought back to their communities for tribal punishment. In some cases, certain individuals were never seen again and were presumed dead and mutilated. Others would often be seen hobbling around in a beaten state.

Yet it appears that some Aboriginal reprisals have been quite toned down in recent years. In the past, they practiced not only spearing and beating, but also genital mutilation, such as the ritual of sub-incision, whereby a man's penis is split open from tip to tail. When I read that, I crossed my legs.

But then you have to ask yourself this: *who* is considered an "Aboriginal person" nowadays? The last known nomadic Aboriginal couple gave up their existence in 1979 in Western Australia's Gibson Desert to move to a township. When tribal elders are asked, some say that over 40 percent (and possibly a lot more) of the full-blooded Australian indigenous population is uninitiated and mostly living non-traditionally in white cities. On top of that, many more are of mixed

---

[2] Hermannsburg is famous for the Aboriginal painter Benjamin Landara. When people saw the vivid colours he used to employ in painting the Australian outback, they thought he was prone to exaggerating. That was, until they saw it for themselves.

blood and don't belong in either category. In a 1996 census, 352,970 people claimed to be indigenous Australians, an increase of 30 percent from five years previous.

It is a curious place, this Darwin, this NT, this Australia. I was sitting one day with my laptop in the Britz when an Aboriginal approached me and asked for money. When I said no, he told me to give him my laptop. When I refused, he shuffled off to get friends. I decided to drive off to the library, where I noticed something odd: a week-old *NT Times* was spread on a table with a huge photo of Dr. Elephant, the singer I had congratulated for his great voice at The Cage only days earlier.

I read that he had been attacked recently while leaving a gig. His group was approached by "a man with an afro hairstyle." The individual told Dr. Elephant that he had enjoyed his singing and then suddenly pulled out a knife and stabbed another musician in the eye before punching Dr. Elephant in the stomach, asking if he wanted "to fire it up." The stabbed musician suffered a shattered socket, partial loss of vision in one eye and nerve damage to his face. Dr. Elephant was not seriously injured in the early-morning assault, but he was shaken up. I guess that explains why the good Dr. Elephant had been so frigid when I had approached him: I hadn't cut my hair in almost three months, and he must have had an unnerving sense of déjà vu.

One day, my mobile rang and the director of the Australian Centre for Photography put me in contact with some Darwinian friends of his, through whom I would garner some interesting locals to interview. First, though, I was going to meet Aaron and Louise when I crossed two familiar British girls I regularly bumped into around central Darwin. They were both travelling and working their way around Australia and seemed very dialled into everything that was going on in backpacker's circles. They had the peculiar habit of finishing each others' thoughts, as if sharing a brain.

"Hi, Allan. Did you hear about Jake?" one of them asked.

"Who's Jake?" I queried, having met more faces in Darwin than I could name.

"He's that bloke from Nottingham –"

"Oh, maybe you don't know him, but did you hear what happened?" interjected the other.

"Just got the news from Jessica, remember her, from Brighton?" reiterated the first, and before I could answer, the other butted in again.

"Get this. We just saw Jess and Jake wasn't there, so we asked where he was –"

"They were on a tour in Kakadu with a group and they stopped somewhere –"

"Yes, and Jess said he went mad!"

"Completely *mad*!"

"Apparently started yelling obscenities –"

"And chasing cars –"

"And jumping on bonnets. Even tried to take a tire off of a moving Britz –"

"And he was saying really strange stuff –"

"Loopy, crazy stuff –"

"Then the cops came –"

"To calm him down –"

"Then he fought with them and grabbed one of their guns and shot at them!"

"But the bullet went between the cop's legs and hit the road –"

"They arrested him and it looks like –"

"He's going to get done for attempted murder of a policeman!"

"He went troppo!"

Finally I had a chance to speak, so I asked what "going troppo" meant, and the verbal tennis match began again.

"Going tropical –"

"Going absolutely off your nutta."

"Senselessly daft –"

"Crazy ... What time is it?"

"We gotta go to work –"

"See ya."

The town criers were on the money, though. The story appeared officially in the paper the next day: "Tourist Tries To Shoot Cop." The official police details exactly matched what the girls had said, and the suspect was being treated for brain swelling.

Later, I would also speak to someone else who confirmed this well-held "troppo" theory.

"Everyone knows about it. It's what happens up here in the NT. Your brain swells with the heat and if you drink it gets worse. You just lose control." Apparently, troppo was an American word absorbed after WWII, along with the word "spine-busting."

I met Louise and Aaron, who had found a hotel that didn't monitor who was using the pool; we took advantage of it on the really hot days. I told them I had an interview lined up, and they said they would be happy for me to go alone.

I set off and was about to bin my parking voucher when I noticed the municipal logo written at the bottom:

"Darwin – different every day."

NEAV WAS FIVE months old, or so she thinks, when the Australian government took her from her mother.

Between 1900 and 1970, Australia was going through the torrid motions of what is today called the "Stolen Generation." The government passed laws that all half-cast Aboriginal children were to be seized by the state and put into institutions so they could learn the advanced living standards of the white man. In written legislation, Aboriginals weren't deemed mentally capable to raise their own children. Native babies were taken, some say torn, tears streaming, from their mothers and families by government hands and tossed into church run schools. It is today still a hot topic in that the practice only really ceased just over thirty years ago.

However, some think it was a good thing.

Neav was sent to an institution to be educated by religious teachers, though her life remained quite the walkabout.

Her mother was a full-blooded Aboriginal and her father a white Australian. She was placed in the Cullen Compound on Croker Island, located northeast of Darwin. The compound was run by the United Church and was comprised of a reverend and his wife, a teacher, a medical woman and 95 female "stolen generation" children. Her brothers and half brothers had been sent to far-off Alice Springs.

"I had such a happy childhood," she said. "We had such fun and learned so much." When Neav was eight years old, WWII broke out. "It was frightening. You think to yourself, 'Oh my God, what is going on?' You haven't got mum or dad; you're unsure of what's happening." During the Darwin bomb raids of 1942, the children were evacuated to a beach further east of the city. They could not get to Darwin by boat because the harbour had been obliterated and shipwrecks obstructed entry. There were also continuous air raids.

Because all hands were on deck for the war, the children, some as young as two years old, were asked to walk to Pine Creek several hundred kilometres south through Kakadu National Park. "We walked for days and days, weeks; the road wasn't paved, there was no one to pick us up. The army was busy setting up defences."

Once the group of displaced children arrived in Pine Creek, they were transported to Alice Springs by army caravans, then placed on a train bound for Sydney, a further 3,109-kilometre journey. There, Neav attended primary and secondary school south of Sydney. When she was a teenager and the war had been quelled, she took a long ship ride back to Darwin and the Croker Island Mission. She heard that her mother was desperately looking for her and so she went to see her.

"To see mummy again was shocking and happy and sad. On one hand, this was my biological mother, and she had adopted so many little black kids and raised them. But when I saw her and my brother sitting under the trees, uneducated, I felt so thankful for my education, thankful that I could speak and read and write. I thought, 'That could be me sitting there with them.'"

"That's me there, the old gin!" laughed Neav as she displayed photo albums full of images of her as a young lady. She would go on to have nine children in nine years! "The doctor would say, 'Oh, *you're* not back again, are you?'"

In 1974, for the first time in her life, Neav took a vacation to Adelaide with her partner to visit one of her grown children. While she was away, Cyclone Tracy struck and she returned to find her home as flat as a pancake. "I felt sick but lucky that none of my children were injured or killed," she said. Her house was subsidized by the Government Housing Commission, so unlike many Darwin residents, she didn't have to chase insurance companies. Instead, she lived in alternative arrangements until the government repaired her old home.

These days, Neav takes it easy "with a couple of beers." She collects stunning shells and looks forward to visits from her 18 grandchildren and 11 great-grandchildren. And so she should, after having an odyssey such as hers!

Wondering and wandering around the area, one can't help but notice the constant reminders of WWII. Air strips remain proudly marked along the Stuart Highway up from Katherine and veterans drive around with WWII license plates. Along the western esplanade of Darwin is a lookout with a panelled and pictorial history of what the harbour looked like after being bombed. Not far from that is a large "Lest We Forget" memorial, and around town, numerous dedicated plaques are plonked.

Ask most people from anywhere in the world about Pearl Harbour and the majority are at least aware that a port in Hawaii was demolished by a Japanese air raid some go further to offer that Ben Affleck was there. But ask most Australians outside of the NT about Darwin and some "think" it may have been bombarded, even though it is clearly stated all over Darwin that the aerial assault on February 19th 1942 was drastically worse than that of Pearl Harbour – and most assuredly bombed worse than the Hollywood-ized version with the pretty boy*. On that fateful day, 188 Japanese aircraft sank eight ships, destroyed 20 aircraft, killed 243 people and injured another 400, leaving Darwin in a smouldering heap. Over the next 21 months, 57 more bombing runs were effected, though none as destructive as the first.

The mood that permeated immediately after was one of confusion. The then prime minister of Australia had this to say: "In this first battle on Australian soil, it will be a source of great pride to the public to know that the armed forces and the civilians composed themselves with the gallantry that is traditional in the people of our stock." Flip to another source, and you read the following: "[It was] a national day of shame," writes Sir Paul Hasluck. These polar opinions needed looking into.

In northern Darwin, along another pleasant stretch of palm tree–lined foreshore, lies the War Museum. I couldn't resist a visit, and upon entering, I quickly shuffled into a dark room where a looping historical movie was about to begin again. It was a very old-fashioned, grainy black-and-white affair, showing acrid black clouds of smoke and Darwin Harbour in absolute ruins.

A wing of the museum housed wall-mounted photographs detailing the mass destruction, the sunken ships and the loss of lives, plus pictures of men in trenches, piles of sandbags, jeeps, nets and tanks along another wall. The laminated monochromes concluded near an aerial map marking hundreds of bomb hits in red dots; the diagram was just riddled in red. One photo, however, lightened the otherwise sombre mood: it was a shot of a reduced building – apparently what used to be a pub – and the owner had spray-painted "No beer after four bombs" on the crumbling wall.

Another room was chock full of display cases framing handguns, machines guns, knives, ammunition and swords. One very curious item on display had been found on a dead enemy pilot: a bible in Japanese. Outside in the yard were tanks, drums, bombs, propellers and turrets. Nearby was the 9.2" gun, a massive cannon that was bought for action and never actually used.

When I left the museum, I clambered back into the Britz, arm out the window, feeling like a G.I. on leave, and cruised slowly back down the foreshore. Along the way, I passed the man-made Lake Albert, the only

---

* I don't know why they say this, because the Pearl Harbour bombings sank 18 warships and felled 188 aircraft, and killed 2,403 servicemen, which is much worse than Darwin. I surmise that they mean as a percentage of population.

safe place to swim. Families were out and about, barbecuing and smiling and enjoying the sun. People were having beers, and not far off, a large children's birthday party was going on; some little girl was spiralling around because a balloon had entangled her. On the opposite side was the beautiful blue ocean and a couple of guys fishing, while joggers pounded pavement under a line of palm trees. It was hard to imagine that just a smidge over 60 years ago, planes had appeared on the horizon and hell was unleashed – nor that 30 years later, a cyclone decided to make Darwin part of its corridor of obliteration.

I headed to the library next, which is not far from the memorial or the old town hall, for I wanted to ply through a few books and, quite frankly, enjoy an air-conditioned building.

As I entered the main room of the library, I noticed that amongst the several paintings, there were two very notable ones. The first was of a cocksure and steely-eyed soldier with the granite gaze of victory in his eyes. The other was a wall-sized mural of Japanese planes coming in for a bombing run with muzzles blazing, while Australian gunmen sprayed return fire at them, expended shells singing out from their chambers. It looked like a scene from the back of a G.I. Joe box. By these accounts, you would think that they had defended themselves honourably, but I would find out differently.

Darwin was so unprepared, despite a message that bombers were coming, that they didn't sound the warning sirens until the bombs were dropping. The citizens and defenders were seized with panic and took to their heels on bicycles and in pushcarts, trucks, a road grader, an ice cream vendor's bicycle and even a sanitary cart. These "valiant defenders" began showing up in Sydney, Adelaide, Brisbane and Melbourne. Meanwhile, other reports revealed that many of the military personnel were pushing women and children and elderly out of the way to board a hastily organized train out of town. But it was not to be, because when some more sirens went off, the train conductor and crew panicked and bolted with an empty train, stopping to look back only once they hit the end of the line some 500 kilometres south.

A report released in 1972 backed all of this up. It outlined, among other things, that there had been no courage or leadership, a lack of training, a breakdown in civil administration, a panic-stricken stampede for the bush and a rampage of drunkenness and looting led by military police. Apparently, some troops were ready to shoot the police, who were taking advantage of the chaos and anarchy. When calm finally reigned in the streets, it did so only because nothing of value was left to steal.

But then I realized by reading another few sources that perhaps the top-ender folk had had good reason to run. The Australian government of the day had a war-time contingency; if ever Australia was attacked, all resources would immediately be sent to the Boomerang Coast, where men were to take up positions, all the while burning everything in their path of retreat so the enemy would have nothing. It was called the "Brisbane Line Scorch Plan," and it was basically a loose insurance that already thin Australian resources wouldn't be needlessly defending empty lands. If nothing else, the plan represented in black and white how the NT is pretty much its own place.

I watched a few Darwin-WWII stock videos and they, too, were just as divided as to whether or not Darwinians were heroes or zeroes. Some videos were obviously propaganda, but others were more scathing.

Meanwhile, I realized that I had no idea what was going on in Iraq War II, which had been raging for a few months by the time I was in Darwin looking into WWII. There were still many ongoing protests against the John Howard administration and much criticism of his hasty rush to sign Australians up for active duty under the Americans and the Brits, as well as against the warnings of most other nations.

I thought long and hard about the relationship Australia and the US had forged since WWII and it looked like another case of big, massive brother controlling teensy-weesy little brother. I could only conclude that the true stories of The Search for Something would not see light for another few decades. In my WWII research, I noticed that many books on the subject were only recently published, and they made the provision in their introductions that much more information was coming out now than during and immediately after the conclusion of the conflict.

While I was poring over Darwin's and Australia's conundrums, I couldn't help but ponder my own short-term future, which looked very bleak indeed. The Mad Nomads project would soon wind down and Louise and Aaron certainly weren't keen on returning to Sydney. They instead wished to travel onward to Western Australia, and I would have loved to, as well ... under any other circumstances.

My savings account was like a river bed in dry season with fees dressed as skiffs running across it and I had various obligations to return all sponsored gear, and pick up all developed Fuji film, back in Sydney. My Australian visa was days from running out, my credit card had melted and I was in no position to afford a plane ticket home – not to mention the fact that I still had lots of my stuff stored in Sydney with Aaron's brother. So in essence, I wouldn't have been able to go home yet even if I wanted to.

Just then came a ray of hope. My mobile rang, so I ran out of the library to answer it and it was Belle from Newks Promotions, asking how I was going. I had previously emailed her and presently she was asking me for a return to Sydney date as there was lots of work on the horizon, if I was interested.

But then another dilemma: where was I going to live? 258 Bondi was no longer, Shanni had moved in with someone else and the majority of everyone else I had come to know intimately were gone. New Zullund to the rescue! I received another call shortly after, this time from my friend Kiwi Simon the Prankster, and after I told him of my problem, he graciously offered that I take up a "choice spare room, aye, bru" at his place until I could get back on my feet.

Now consider this: Kiwi Simon had given me the advertisement that led me to KFM and Louise, he had given me free internet to research all sponsors for the Mad Nomads project and now he was offering me a thrifty place to live. I don't know what I would have done had I not met Kiwi Simon while handing out train station oat bars at dawn for DeVogue.

Now my only problem was the visa, and this would mark the third occasion of my quitting the continent of Australia just to remain another three months legally in it. This time, it would be slightly different: I would actually see more than just an airport full of people who bungled their vowels. I would fly to a location not far from Darwin, a destination most Australians know and have all recently been horrified by because, like Darwin, something very unexpected had occurred there that resulted in acts of cowardice and heroism.

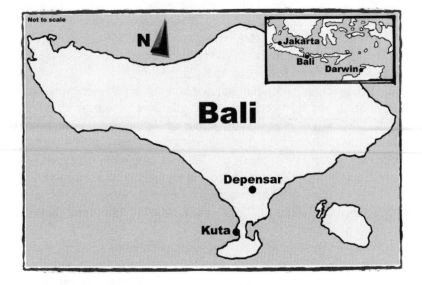

59 – Pecking Away

A LARGE-SCALE poster graced with the image of a fetching and colourfully dressed Balinese woman – her hands curved to form a flower and her head lowered as if nodding hello – was hanging just behind the customs officer who stamped my passport. In flowing letters above her were written the words, "Welcome to Bali." Next to her was a smaller sign, written in red on a white background in English and Balinese: "Drug traffickers will be executed."

"No seat belts," said Frankie as I reached for my shoulder harness. "Not in Bali." My unconscious habit, long drilled into me by ads and high fines, had no application here. The weekend return flight from Darwin to Bali, including hotel, transport with Frankie and meals, came bundled at a cost hundreds of dollars less than any no-frills overnight run I had taken from Sydney to Auckland.

As we drove, I noticed that motorized humans in Bali seemed oblivious to any notion of a safety culture. Most scampered about on scooters or mopeds, children or even whole families straddling the guiding column or rear bench without helmets. The streets were thin, potholed and very populated; nevertheless, traffic and human flow were harmonious by virtue of a language of horn beeps. The vernacular of the streets had a seemingly vast and profound vocabulary whereby toots could mean all of "Move over," "Hello," "Do you need a taxi?" or "See you tonight for that game of chess."

After checking in to my hotel, I awayed to an internet café and garnered my third online ETA visa, then strolled toward the beach, wondering what to do with myself for two days. I couldn't advance more than a few metres without someone offering me sunglasses or a shirt, a scooter rental, a massage or a drink, or even a bow and arrow. It fast became obvious that saying "No thanks" roughly is translated by Balinese vendors to mean, "Try harder and really hassle me and maybe – just maybe – I will change my mind and buy whatever knock-offs you want me to buy."

"Good price for you!," "For you, cheap, cheap!," "Aussie, Aussie, Aussie!" and my all-time favourite, "Free! Free!" were hurled at me as I walked faster with eyes to the pavement. If even slight eye contact is established, swarming results instantly and everyone refers to your physical manifestation as "My friend" as if for those few seconds before you say "No thanks" *again*, you really are the centre of their universe.

Kuta's narrow lanes are ramshackle and appear almost as if they had a hangover. When I reached Kuta Beach, I thought respite was at hand, but I was wrong. It was like a tennis match. "No surfboard, thank you ... No juice, thanks ... It's OK, I have lotion, thanks ... No, I'm fine, thanks ... NO, I DON'T NEED A SURFBOARD!!"

Rounding out the top five on the Balinese nationality guessing list were Australia, the UK, Ireland, Germany and Holland. I tried a little experiment, informing each new hawker that I was from a different country, and always they would reply with praise. "Niger! Good country." "France? Good country." "Iceland? Welcome. Good. Lithuania? Kazakhstan? Good. Bali welcome."

I concluded that to their eyes, I was part of a homogonous one-nation that existed just beyond Bali: Touristica. I then wondered why no one has put into operation the one single business idea that would sell the most: producing t-shirts, hats or sandwich boards that say "No taxi, no tours, no trinkets, no thank you," in Balinese.

With the passing of time, I could hardly blame them. Indeed, the beach and laneways were devoid of non-Balinese and a game of spot the tourist helped burn minutes. Those who didn't belong in either category were either women wearing hijabs playing in the ocean or smiling students dancing blissfully in the sand. Time after time, Balinese and Javanese students, Hindus and Muslims, would accost me in my sitting position with cameras in hand, practicing a bit of English by asking permission to take a picture with me. They were genuinely friendly and warm souls, quick to laugh and filled with questions.

I began to feel bad about my preliminary frustration, and then felt worse for being so broke that I couldn't help their little economy. There was a weight in the air, a realization that a tragedy had occurred just up the road and had come to affect this most peaceful of people, who really had had nothing to do with it. Much of their lifeblood's business had evaporated, though the real needs of their families had not.

I gathered that Australians had been their biggest customers until October 12, 2002. The Australian dollar never fetches a favourable exchange rate in the wider world, so Bali was an obvious preference for students, budgeteers and sports teams. Two English girls I met said that they were a novelty around Bali. "You can't buy a ticket to Bali in England," one said. "We got ours in Thailand."

"Usually this place is packed with Aussies and English, we come every year," said the other. "But not now, with all the travel advisories ... But we still come." In one article, a writer commented that 1.6 million visitors once came to Indonesia's most alluring tropical paradise every year, though shortly after the explosion, the statistic stood in the thousands.

While pondering all of this, yet more smiling Indonesian women accosted me and asked if they could take a picture of me with my beautiful wife.

Wife?

I glanced left and there was a blindingly blond and tall Dutch girl, minding her own beeswax. She agreed to a photo, and we looked at each other for the first time. For the next hour, we chatted as wave after wave of locals posed with the happily married couple from Touristica. "This happens to me all day," she said, and so we agreed in unspoken terms not to expel the fantasy to each new smile and lens.

I can't recall her name (basically because I couldn't pronounce it), but she soon rose to head off to pick up a new tailored suit, made for a really rock-bottom price, so I tagged along. We strolled through the homogeneous alleyways of Kuta as scooters beeped and sputtered past. Later that day, after I had eaten like a king at a restaurant and outlaid an amount of money that would have fetched me half a wormy apple in Sydney, I parted company with the Dutch girl, who pointed me in the direction of the Sari Nightclub and Paddy's.

I sloshed through the ankle-deep and murky water of an alleyway and ambled up to the location. It felt very strange to walk into an area that had been the focus of a well-covered global tragedy and now was deathly still. Presently, I stood in the place where so many lives had been taken in a violent manner, and so many horrid injuries had sent people to hospital. It was only seven months previous that images of the location were of fire and death, screams and ambulances, chaos and fear. Of the 202 deaths, 88 were Australian and 34 were Balinese. Standing in such a locale brings a feeling that is altogether eerie, painful and reflective.

The area around the blast site was still being reconstructed, although a Billabong surf shop and some other locals were open for what scarce business trickled by them in that haunted space. Hollow structures skirted with scaffolding surrounded the site of the former Sari Nightclub, itself enclosed in aluminium sheeting. A small corner was laid with wreaths, candles, photos, Australian flags and notes to loved ones.

It was with a heavy heart that I meandered about the streets. A few clothing shops sold t-shirts with "Bali Cry, 12/10/02," "Bali Bleed" and "Bali bombing, Bali cries. Please help Bali and come back" printed on their fronts.

I grabbed an international newspaper and glanced at the current stories. There had been a bombing in Casablanca. Algiers had been rocked by an earthquake and there was a war on a northern Indonesian island. Iraq War II was ongoing, and Amrozi's trial for the Bali bombing was underway, though it was continually interrupted by his extremist chants and boyish smile. Many Australians had flown to Depensar to follow the tribunal.

Not long after, I strolled to an open-plan structure overflowing with people. I glanced inside to spot hoards holding money in the air, yelling. When I penetrated further into the assembly, I peered into a pit wherein two men were priming cocks to have a go at each other. They fired them up, tied a blade to their talons and then blood and feathers flew as the crowd ejaculated responses to the pecking match. It might well have been a case of overload for me that day, but the world seemed such a violent place at that moment. I came away from the strange and gory spectacle of cock-fighting as night fell. It became apparent that the range of products in the streets of Kuta had expanded with the darkness.

"Smoke, smoke, weed, weed, man? Bang-bang women? Sniff, sniff coca?" offered a voice from an alleyway where I had previously been offered a scooter. "Women? Boys? What you want, my friend?" presented another down the way, from a location that used to have colourful Hindu items for sale. Some Balinese men shuffling about didn't even say anything at all, they just gesticulated. They tapped their nose, or their crotch. If drug trafficking was punishable by death, there certainly was a lot of living going on, but I suppose the theory of economics overrides: where there is demand there is supply, and I looked, to them, like someone from Touristica who typically demanded.

At one point, I got lost on my way back to my hotel, even forgetting the name of it, and stopped to ask directions by showing my room key with its hotel symbol on it. A kindly middle-aged gentlemen put his arm on my shoulder, affably pointed the way, and as soon as I thanked him said, "What room I send girls to? Or boys?"

"No thanks, the directions will do. Bye," came my curt reply. I ambled past pounding thatch-roofed bars and discos and some backpackers weaving with beer bottles from bar to bar.

The next day, I sat once again on Kuta Beach. The impact of Bali's street-level economic loss would be shown to me by Wayan, a burly Balinese grandmother who sat next to me and repeatedly offered me massages –

"Cheap." I had fended off many others before her, but she continued to sit by me.

"I am so sorry, but I will be honest: I have no money," I said frankly.

"Please. You pay later. I give you nice massage. Good massage. Where you from? Australia? England?" she said as she took my hand and rubbed it.

"I'm sorry, I am sure you give good massages, but I have no money," I repeated with even more emphasized candour, but it seemed hard for her to conceive that a Touristican could not spare some pittance.

"I trust you. You come back later," she showed me a name badge with her photo and an identification number. "My name is Wayan, number 27. Come find me. Cheap. Good massage. Germany? France? I give you massage now, you come back later."

No matter what I said, Wayan would not leave my side, and then suddenly her face contorted and in a melancholic voice she said, "Bali cry. Bali cry for Australia. Bali cry for tourists," and true to her words, tears did come from her eyes. Her emotions were real, not part of a pitch. She had nowhere else to go, and she told me how she was so poor because of the lack of business that her whole family, down to her grandchildren, were suffering. "I cry for bombing, business very bad."

I felt so sad for her. I felt bad for all of them, out there day in and day out, trying to scramble for the residue of what was once a relatively well-heeled touristy spot.

In the end it wasn't Frankie who drove me back to the airport, but another Balinese driver who was friendly and apologetic for his broken English, which he wanted to practice nonetheless. "I speak English because of tourists," he managed. He then conveyed the sense of loss to both of his linguistic and occupational practices.

I got on the plane back to Darwin thinking that though I was broke, I could have been a lot worse off.

"HOW WAS BALI?" asked Louise and Aaron when we were out one night at a soirée for writers. Sydney novelist Emma Tom, one of the undercover journalists I met while speed dating way back when, happened to be in Darwin on some conference and invited our crew out to where she performed (she's also in a band).

"Strange. Weird. Weird to see the site of the Bali bombing and how everyone is suffering," I replied. But things would get stranger still.

Later on, Louise and Aaron came steaming up to me, wide-eyed and with a woman in tow. She was gaunt and timid, looking somewhat like Popeye's main squeeze Olive Oyl. She wore a pair of thick glasses and peeped awkwardly about as introverts do. I think Louise spoke first.

"You'll never guess where this woman is from!" she said.

"Where?" I replied, confused.

"Bundeena! She knows Roger!" cried Aaron. "Can you believe it?"

Finally, Olive Oyl spoke for herself. "He's a hero in Bundeena. Brilliant man," she said with reverence.

"Yes ... he is rather creative ... He does Reality A/V rather well," I offered in a hopeless blather.

"He did a docco on me. Provoked some things out of me. Brilliant." She then smirked, nodded and drifted off to find a bowl of chips.

In Darwin, of all places.

Once the shock had washed over, the three of us talked about present business. Despite how much we had achieved on the Mad Nomads project, there was still much ground we never got to cover. I had to go back to Sydney – I was obliged, financially and contractually. Louise and Aaron wanted to stay on in Darwin and fan out nomadically on their own journeys.

"Man, you look so shaggy," one of them said. I hadn't cut my hair in months, so they had a point. The next day, I headed for the barber shop and met a friendly hairdresser who put me on the tail of a fascinating woman.

And so I interviewed the last Mad Nomads contact, a woman named Beth who, in 1974, almost lost it all.

"I love Darwin," Beth offered, along with some cookies, as we sat down to chat on her veranda. Originally from New Zealand, Beth became engaged to a man named Dan who, during WWII, occupied the unenviable position of rear gunner in Lancaster aircraft flown over the Pacific to dogfight Japanese forces. He fell in love with Darwin on his R&R visits and his proposition of marriage to Beth included a clause to relocate to the outpost.

Breaking with the notion of the times that women don't leave their home town, Beth agreed to Dan's proposal – having never even seen Darwin – and in 1950 boarded a ship destined for marriage and life in the far-flung tropics.

"I arrived during the most intense sunset I had ever seen in my life. I felt as if I was going into storyland," she said. "The harbour was still littered with wrecks from the WWII Japanese bombings even then, and the northern suburbs were bush land."

After her wedding, Beth became the first-ever civilian female in the NT to obtain the position of secretary to the staff officer of intelligence on the HMAS *Melville* while husband Dan worked in an electrical power plant. Half a decade later, she resigned with a bulging stomach and a new life on the way in the form of Ian, born in 1955.

Rather briskly in 1962, Dan took ill and was advised by a doctor in Perth that he had less than two years to live. He had developed cancer, since attributed to the war, and had to have one lung removed. Sadly, only three weeks later, Dan passed on, widowing Beth and leaving seven-year-old Ian wondering why dad wasn't around to take him fishing anymore.

Though the loss was sudden, Beth still managed to purchase their home and acquire a station as housekeeper for a doctor a few hundred metres up the road from her doorstep. "We had to eat, we had to live and I know Dan would have been proud of me, even if it was only housekeeping." Later, she would pull an 18-year stint with Qantas as a secretary to the catering manager.

The phone rang when Beth was setting the dinner table on Christmas Eve, 1974.

"Have you filled your bathtub with water?" a concerned girlfriend enquired.

"No, why?" replied Beth.

"There's a cyclone warning."

Like everyone at the time, Beth considered cyclone warnings in December a dime a dozen. She illuminated her radio only to hear the end of an early midnight mass broadcast from the Catholic church. "The noise you have just heard is the breaking of the stained glass windows," announced the reverend on the air. "The choir has just finished singing in darkness. And may God bless everyone of you tonight."

Son Ian, aged 19 at the time, was beckoned by his mother to help her collect all her plants when the sound of corrugated iron being torn filled the deafening air rush. Their neighbours had just lost their roof. Pinning their own door open in a move that could have broken an arm, Ian and Beth invited them to come and seek shelter in their residence. As the winds picked up and turned into a roar, her crying neighbour wondered out loud, "Will we ever get out alive?"

Then the roof began to lift.

"It's a horrible feeling to hear the roof just folding up like paper. The front wall of the house fell in, and my Christmas tree in all its glory flew across the room. In the end, three quarters of my roof was torn near clean away. The house bent over so far to the ground that I thought it would never right itself. We sat in the bathroom and waited, and I am sure every one of us prayed. Morning came with a deathly calm. We went outside and couldn't believe what we saw: devastation everywhere, but we were alive and none of us were injured, and we thanked God for that. Water from the sea was lapping the side of the road nearest my home and live electricity lines were everywhere."

Somehow they managed to find the BBQ, get it working and cooked up a turkey stew. "We had Christmas," said Beth.

Shelters were established and swelling to over-capacity, thus Beth, Ian and neighbours couldn't get in and had to remain at Beth's half-standing home. All shared one mattress and were subjected to rain once in awhile.

"There were no birds around," she described. "There was a complete stillness you can't explain. And the northern suburbs looked like a dropped deck of cards."

The town's water supply had been cut off. A pipe was set up and residents had to transport water in whatever containers they could muster or fashion.

"I ran into all kinds of problems with the insurance company. They wouldn't renew my policy and pay me. I eventually got it. Life goes on and you rebuild," she said. "Thirteen truckloads of debris were taken from my lot alone. Then the military came back to clear it."

Beth has been a member of the women's organisation Quota for 25 years, and presently she helps provide starter kits to battered women's clinics, as well as hand-knitting teddy bears for hospitals and aero-medical teams. She told me how during the rebuilding of Darwin, food depots were set up, and she was delighted by the feeling of using shampoo again.

"There was a wonderful spirit of friendship and sharing. I think we all realized that material things didn't really matter – the fact that we were all alive mattered most. Cyclone Tracy was a great tragedy for the people or Darwin. Many never came back, marriages broke up and lives were lost. I'm glad I stayed here, for now many years later I see the rebirth of our city and I often think, 'I love you, Darwin.' Life has been at times very harsh, but on the other hand, it has also been very beautiful."

I looked back at the comely home as I left and tried to imagine what Beth had described. I pictured the roof removed, the wall fallen in and the trees decorated with bits of the house. But I didn't have the benefit of memory, only imagination, and certainly I wouldn't have known what to do if I had been in her shoes.

With that, I bid a fond adieu to my partners in crime, Louise and Aaron, and the Mad Nomads fellowship disbanded as I boarded the red-eye from Darwin to Sydney.

Funny that the final interview topics had been cyclones and Qantas, because a metaphorical mix of the two came to swirl around me, and everything in my life came unhinged.

PART III
THE IMPLOSION

He is truly wise who has travelled far and knows the ways of the world. He who has travelled can tell what spirit governs the men he meets.

– On the topic of experience, from Hávamál, *The Sayings of The Vikings*

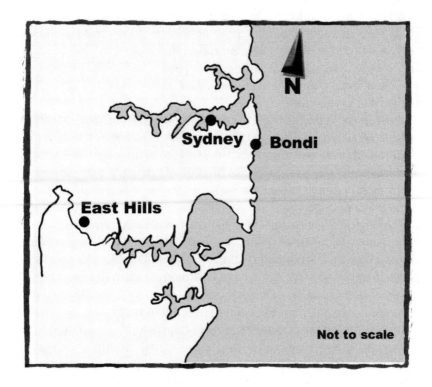

61 – Full Circle Twister

THE TAKEOFF WAS delayed owing to a medical emergency. The nocturnal flight is aptly named, for I arrived with red eyes at the quiet carousel of Sydney Domestic Airport. A wall-mounted TV ran the early-morning news. At the very time my flight had been in the air, another Qantas flight between Melbourne and Tasmania had been the subject of an attempted hijacking!

A rather well-built and tall male purser had constrained a deranged man. He had suddenly noticed the attacker running at him and the cockpit with, of all things, wooden stakes that looked to be door stops. In a scuffle, a female flight attendant was punched in the eye and the male bear hugged and pinned the assailant and was stabbed in the back of the head several times.

Later, I would find out that the purser emerged from hospital with 16 stitches on his marred scalp and the female with a large shiner. For his part, the attacker was thumb-nailed as a lonely, 40-year-old computer analyst from Melbourne, recently fired, Caucasian, with no connection to terrorism nor any known motives. Former co-workers said he was as a quiet, but likeable, guy.

The story shot adrenaline through the score of us awaiting our baggage with bleary dispositions. Then, just before the carousel produced my bag, another story followed that at the Woomera Detention Centre, more protests were underway against the treatment of Australia's refugees. A documentary promised to air that evening with inside footage of illegal immigrants sewing their eyes and lips shut and mutilating themselves to protest their treatment at the hands of the federal government.

Outside, it was bleak and wintry. I descended into the train station where I set off to my new home in a suburb called East Hills, 26 kilometres southwest of central Sydney. Watching the news that evening, I further learned that moments after I had left the airport, some bewildered elderly ladies had walked past dopey security into a "sterile area" and the whole terminal was clamped down.

I had been in the serene eye of quite a cyclone of events.

As you might imagine, I had to acclimatize myself to my new surroundings. I had just come from living a quarter of a year in mobile homes relocating from rural countryside to desert to Darwin. Back in Sydney, my senses were besieged.

Everything frightened me.

Things moved in a blurred motion that only true city dwellers don't notice. A Transpo bus roared past me with enough din to raise eyebrows at a Harley-Davidson-without-mufflers convention. Then a wailing ambulance blew by. Then a fire engine. Then cops. Then someone blared a horn and under that a speaker was spookaning, "You'll never pay full price again!"

I saw no parking, no engine snorkels protruding from vehicles and no Aboriginals lying around under trees. I felt as if I were right back to day one in Sydney – as if the Mad Nomads had been a dream.

The only difference between the feeling of that day of arrival and my first day in Sydney (some 20 months previous) was that I thankfully had a place to live. Kiwi Simon shared his East Hills abode with two other guys, though for a bunch of boys with piles of nudie magazines and an affinity for a bit of gambling and a few Jim Beans after work, they were the cleanest, most respectable and hard-working blokes I ever had the pleasure of living with.

My room was small and without furniture, but lucky was I for having such a friend as Kiwi Simon. The other upshot was that we lived adjacent to a major train station, so it took me only 30 minutes to get into the city.

All that aside, personally and globally, my mood was very cheerless. Once again, my lifestyle was minimalist. Two-minute noodles became my dietary staple and the low rent of my new hospice a godsend.

After dropping off all the sponsored equipment, I picked up my mail from Aaron's brother, who told me that a goods and services tax had been put on road tolls – which struck me as really odd, because how can you tax a tax? In my pile of gathered correspondence, I had letters from my banks advising that many fees were doubling and some other ones had been introduced; notably if you dared use a credit card or EFTPOS. I sighed and surmised that some executive banker was turning 40 soon and would need another golden parachute.

Another letter was from the Australian Tax Office, who still maintained that I owed them a chunk of change. I had been waiting eight months as their bureaucratic wheels sputtered and once again appealed their decision, shelled them with supporting documents and lost. I then took them to small claims court.

Then, by virtue of ample reception, I received a text message from my mobile phone provider to say that phone and text messaging rates were going up and a new charge for flag fall was in effect as of the week following.

The only moment of joy occurred when I strolled into Platinum Imaging's photo lab and picked up the 65 rolls of sponsored Fujifilm transparencies I had been mailing in from populated points with post offices along the way. I hauled them up the road to the Australian Centre for Photography and spread them on the light board with energetic anticipation and a shaking hand holding the magnifying viewer. I lost track of time as I dreamily relived the colours, frozen moments and splendorous scenery of the Mad Nomads journey. At least memories don't cost money ... yet.

My cumulative dire straits translated inevitably into staying home, as I could ne'er afford to do more than gather dust. Aside from constantly reviewing my slides with the sort of nostalgic sighs that only come with realising a vacation is over, I ended up watching quite a bit of TV and news and reading lots of newspapers.

At the time, the scandalous governor general had been ousted, but not without taking a massive pension for life that could possibly rid some third-world nations of debt. Many Australians were not happy about that one bit, and to boot, their medical social net and bulk billing were under threat.

Then Pauline Hanson was arrested for fraudulently registering One Nation in Queensland and obtaining almost $500,000 in electoral reimbursements. Both her and co-partner were found guilty, shackled and sentenced to three years in prison without parole! The irony was that Hanson was going to be put in a prison with many Aboriginals and Asians. She was strip-searched and tossed in a cell with no privacy. Her days begun at six in the morning with cereal, toast and fruit, then she was given a sandwich for lunch and a hot meal in the late afternoon, before lock down. Given my situation, I thought that a generous variety of food.

However, Hanson had a nervous breakdown and was medicated for depression. Many, including the prime minister, were screaming that this was all a bit too outrageous, even for Australian courts looking to go hardcore American.

Meanwhile, a murder went unnoticed. I received an email from a friend in the promotional world inviting me and others to a vigil to be held for Kane Mason, a 24-year-old Aboriginal. In scouring the major newspapers, I couldn't find any mention of the incident and asked her what had happened*. Allegedly, Mason – a member of a north-shore rugby team – was having a night out with his mates in Macksville, a central-coast NSW town, when he was shot by a group of three youths aged 15, 17 and 19. It appeared that his Aboriginality was the only motive, and his team-mates were all in shock. But it didn't make headlines.

Iraq War II officially ended and the hunt for proof of their cause began, though many Australians were still leery about having been an accomplice with the British and Americans. They weren't sure when any of their 2,000 military men and women were coming home.

Meanwhile, in Depensar, Bali, the trial of Amrozi the smiling bomber and his co-conspirators wrapped up and the judges were contemplating his fate. "Islam never teaches violence, murder or any other crime," one judge said. Amrozi was found guilty and sentenced to death, but that only made the killer smile wider.

The judge's decision seemed a toss-up between extreme Islamic martyrdom and letting the culprits rot in cells for life. While in the United States, most opinions supported swift capital punishment, many British (including parents of victims) held a quiet lunch to press for a commute to life in prison. As always, opinions from Australians were somewhere in-between.

Another bomb went off in a hotel in Jakarta. Around the same time, in Maroubra, a beach southeast of Sydney near the airport, a man walking with his five-week-old baby harnessed on his chest was jumped and beaten by a gang of five teenagers. The baby suffered a fractured skull, but thankfully the injuries were neither life-threatening nor too severe. She was released from Children's Hospital a week later to her bruised father. The public was in shock as to why anyone would attack a defenceless baby without motive. The assailants were captured and while exiting the courtroom, one of their friends pushed a cameraman and threatened to sue him for getting in the way, then spat on him.

All things considered, the world seemed a bit dark to me at those moments in time.

I went for a walk to clear my head and explore my new surroundings. This was the first time I had lived in Sydney and had not been near a beach.

Then I realised that everyone I really cared about – save a few – were

---

* As it turns out, there was some coverage of the event in the *Manly Daily*, a paper that enjoys a small circulation along the north shore of Sydney. There were also a few back-page articles in the *Sydney Morning Herald* and *Illawarra Mercury*.

gone. I hadn't seen my family in 22 months. I hadn't been sponsored to stay in Australia, nor had I married, nor was I willing to outlay money to leave the country every three months just to maintain this existence and have to deal with the Australian Tax Office. I wondered if I would end up in Woomera detention centre sewing my lips together in protest if I couldn't get a plane ticket to leave.

I love Australia. And I love Sydney – bar none, it is a beautiful city. Nevertheless, when you don't live near the coast or have money or won't be legal in a few weeks – or, for that matter, have many friends or any nearby relatives or a position as the head of a bank – the slant of light changes.

At that moment in time, Sydney suddenly seemed to have a heavy cost attached to it.

I WAS SAVED. By a few people. Well, sort of.

All of my amazing former casual employers – Newks promotions, Extras agency, Pinnacle waitering and Julia Ross temping – found it in their hearts to give me work and gradually, by sheer frugality, I began amassing some funds. It was now time to make my decision about my immediate Australian future.

The omens were not long in coming.

"Hi, I'm Pam," said a sparkly woman a Newks Group promotional meeting, "and our team will be working with you guys on this new promotion." She handed out meticulous manuals covering every conceivable contingency and launched into an airy and needlessly long speech on simple and straightforward affairs. After listing more guidelines than we thought humanly possible, she concluded with a bubbly, "We just want you to have fun," and I realized with horror that it was Krappy Field Marketing!

Our professional Newks team would have to work with *them* on a campaign. My heart went out to Belle, our wonderful Newks manager, scrambling to deal with KFM's trademark shifting schedules, their staff being double-booked or not showing up at all, venues being moved or cancelled, permits for the wrong day and so forth.

Alas, aside from that, I wasn't pleased about being a waiter again at sports events, least of all cricket matches. Extra work on film sets was just as drab, though I did see Craig – the former Mad Nomad docco maker – on a few gigs. This being said, it was the strangest thing to see him again and not be excitedly planning something.

Then one day I went to the supermarket where a butcher (sitting at a fold-out table between a section of grapes and cheese) tried to convince me to open an "Ezy" account. Outside, in walking past a car, I saw a bumper sticker that totted: "Australia! Love it or leave it!"

I got home and turned on the TV. Drawling idiots were yelling at each other in southern US accents over censorship beeps. They bashed each other over threesomes, altered sexual orientation and illegitimate children as crowds chanted, "Jerry, Jerry." I flipped channels to see more Americans, who really should have retained lawyers, being belittled by a shrewd woman in robes with a thick New York accent. *Ricki Lake* was next. During a commercial break, the only Australian accents I heard announced that *Australian Big Brother* got the nod for another season.

Then another ad encouraged me to tune into a slimmer selection of candidates on *Australian Idol*. The next promotion told me to stay tuned for a new episode of *Home and Away* (though now, I realize that it might have been an ad for *Neighbours*).

I flicked off the tube to a silent apartment and felt really far away from home. I looked at the door of my small bedroom and wondered if it was sturdy enough to sail 17,000 kilometres to somewhere with a variable climate. I was starting to believe – deep down inside – that I could probably at least make China.

All of these little omens culminated into one big epiphany when I opened my email. A friend had forwarded me a joke. It opened with a photo of a sensual blond woman with massive fake breasts in a bikini and beneath her was written,

"No matter how good she looks to you, somewhere, someone is tired of putting up with her shit."

That was it! I needed out of Sydney.

Then the world healed a little.

Bali was taken off the Australian travel advisory list. The Sari Nightclub and Paddy's Pub reopened and people returned. The two Qantas flight attendants from the fraught Melbourne to Launceston flight heroically returned to work. The three killers of Kane Mason were arrested, charged and held without possibility of bail. Although the drought had been bad, globalization allowed Australians to get their food from elsewhere. The Australian continent drifted another two centimetres north. I won my case against the tax office, though they made me wait another 60 days for payment (then the bank held my funds for 25 business days).

Nonetheless, I spent my every last cent on a ticket home, realising a heavy truth.

I had not swam with dolphins, dove the Great Barrier Reef or seen a platypus (one of Earth's strangest animals, stuck in time between a reptile and a mammal). I hadn't really learned how to surf, play a didgeridoo or throw a boomerang. I never got see if the rumours about Queenslanders' mental proficiency are true. I never got to visit Perth, the world's most isolated city, and see if the women truly are more beautiful out there*.

I hadn't done what you are *supposed* to do in Australia.

When I did get back to my home continent, it wasn't without an

---

* The distance from Sydney to Perth is equal to that between London and Moscow, and Perth's closest foreign capital is Jakarta, 3,000 kilometres away.

emergency landing owing to two blown engines. I had shipped off two crates of stuff with lead time, and they arrived significantly behind schedule.

Now coming from Australia, my old world seemed all very backorwards: there were no beaches, the weather was inclement, people drove on the wrong side of the road and toilet water spiralled concentrically the wrong direction when flushed. No one was spreading tar on their toast. Paper money seemed fragile. One-cent coins were still in circulation. I had to adapt to being able to talk on phones without worrying about time as a cost variable and listening to people speak using full words, which seemed wasteful.

And get this: the latest news was that large areas in western Canada and the US were threatened by smoking forest fires and experts were using the "new" ideas of selective forestry and back burning.

In flicking on the TV, I saw that a slew of cheesy new reality shows was pervading the airwaves. A news story announced that insurance rates for almost everything were about to go through the roof, if they hadn't already. Some of my friends were atavistic: they had evolved backward in my time away.

I began to miss Sydney and Australia, and recalled my final weekend.

I had taken the dawn bus to Bondi with my photographer friend Melissa, to watch and photograph my final Bondi sunrise.

Later that morning, my old roommate Shanni took me up the coast to Bonny Hills, near Port Macquarie, for one last visit with her family. Her brother-in-laws took me out at sunrise to watch and photograph them surfing. I sat contentedly looking over the splendorous beach, the blue ocean with its creamy waves and the golden sunrise. At that moment, a beaming elderly woman who was out for a dawn stroll accosted me. We got to chatting and I told her what I had been up to and she noticed my accent.

"How long have you been in Australia?" she inquired politely.

"Two months shy of two years," I replied.

"Oh lovely. Are you going to stay?"

"I am afraid I can't: my visa runs out and –" but I was cut short, and she changed her tone.

"I *can't* believe that they won't let a good bloke like you stay in this country," she said with inflected anger. "What is wrong with this place? There are all these illegal immigrants and boat people and people sneaking in and over-staying their permits and they won't let a motivated person remain. I tell you, something is wrong with our government."

"Um ... I actually want to go," I said, somewhat flattered by her indirect compliment and her gracious acceptance of my character without even knowing me. Her demeanour changed back to gentleness.

"Oh ... I see. Such a lovely country you're from. I hear it's just like Australia, but bigger and colder. I have a grandson teaching snowboarding over there." Then she turned to walk away, but not without asking that all-Australian question: "Did you enjoy yourself here?"

I suppose I had a flashback moment that many do in their later birthdays. I remembered that evil telephone booth from my first day, and realized it was only doing what it was programmed to do. I thought about the Russians, Bondi, DIY, my string of employment agencies, the dramas, the cast of characters and the amazing companies that came to support our Mad Nomads initiative. I thought about the women whom we spoke to. I wondered if I had read too much or too little, or just read too much into things. I briefly pondered the interconnectivity of the universe and pondered without conclusion whether the world had conspired for or against me. I thought about Australia, and why I ever went there. I wondered if mateship would ever become a part of the Constitution

"So?" she pressed, and I blinked and snapped out of my reverie.

I looked out to the surfing boys who were coming in to land on the beach. What a place to start a prison. I looked back at the expectant woman.

"I certainly did. Wouldn't have changed it for the world. Coming to Australia was the best thing I didn't plan very well. I would love to come back sometime."

With that, she nodded and grinned and walked off, humming a tune with the sun of a new day in the lucky country warming her back.

Acknowledgements

There were so many people who came forward to help in the making of this project. This list is by no means comprehensive, but if you helped us out, even in the smallest way, my thanks are a given.

Thanks, in no particular order, are due to:

In Australia:
Will Horner from Ted's Cameras in Sydney, Nick Boshier for DV cassettes and energy, Toora Lions Club in Victoria, ABC Radio, the Australian Centre for Photography, the Country Women's Association, Savannah Bekin and her boyfriend, Simon (in Sydney), for critical feedback and document design, Simon Cuthbertson (East Hills, NSW) for use of his internet and home (choice bru!), Maria Christou and Alasdair Foster from the ACP, Matt Tague for the DIY Tours, Melissa Clarke for photographic assistance and image contributions, Sybille Neher for photographic assistance and muesli, as well as all zee other 258 Bondi Germans.

In Canada:
Dad for the proofreading and constant feedback and Mum for support and love, Angela Bernier (Ottawa, Canada) for ideas and proofing. Thanks for encouragement goes to Juidth Isherwood of Shoreline Press Publishing.

Elsewhere:
Syreeta Clarke (London, England) for sponsorship feedback and Nina Waldau (Cologne, Germany) for help with my online forms.

Thanks for accommodation along the Mad Nomadic path:

Tony Crane (Darwin, NT), Bob and Gail Edwards (Burra, SA), Ingrid Labb and Natalie Crowe (Melbourne, VIC), the Hutchens family (Kingston, TAS), the Hudd family (Frankston, VIC), Graham and Irmela McIntyre (Toora, VIC), Edward Goldsbury (Hillsdale, NSW), Janet Henderson (Bob's Farm, NSW), Tim and Fay Woolley (Bolwarra, NSW) and Elaine Elsey (Port Macquarie, NSW).

Thanks for monetary donations via our website go to:

Alan Clayton (UK), Bruce Beatson (Toora, VIC), Taylor Sommers (Victoria, Canada), Sean Brehon (Limerick, Ireland) and Marie Bembrick (Cambridge, UK).

SOURCES

Internet

I consulted untold sources through web-searches.

Newsprint and Periodicals

I have derived much information from articles in:

Australian Geographic
BRW
Central Coast Herald
CFO Magazine
Financial Review
Illawarra Mercury
MIS
National Geographic
Newcastle Herald
Northern Territory Times
Sydney Morning Herald
Sunday Age
Sun Herald
The Age
The Australian Financial Review
The Economist
Time Magazine

Bibliography

Alcorta, Frank, *Australia's Frontline, the Northern Territory's War, 50th Anniversary*.

Atkinson, Ann, *The Dictionary of Famous Australians*, Allen and Unwin, 1992.

Australian Phrasebook – Understanding Aussies and Their Culture, Lonely Planet Publications, 1998.

Birmingham, John, *Leviathan*, Random House, 1999.

Blaikie, George, *Scandals of Australia's Strange Past*, Seal Books, 1976.

Blainey, Geoffrey, *Triumph of the Nomads*, Pan Macmillan, 1994.

Book of Australian Facts, Reader's Digest, 2000.

Bryson, Bill, *Down Under* (a.k.a. *In a Sunburnt Country*), Doubleday, 2000.

Bryson, Bill, *Mother Tongue*, Penguin, 1991.

Connaughton, Richard, *Shrouded Secrets: Japan's War on Mainland Australia, 1942-44,* Brassey's, 1994.

Clark, Manning, *A Short History of Australia*, Penguin Books, 1988.

Conway, Dan, *The Trenches in the Sky,* Hesperian Press, 1995.

FitzGerald, Stephen, *Is Australia an Asian Nation?,* 1997.

Flannery, Tim, *The Future Eaters: An Ecological History of the Australasian Lands and People*, Reed New Holland, 1997.

Hall, Timothy, *Darwin 1942, Australia's Darkest Hour*, Methuen, 2000.

Horne, Donald, *The Lucky Country*, Penguin, 1988.

Hughes, Robert, *The Fatal Shore*, Collins-Harvill, 1987.

Kingston, Margo, *Off the Rails: The Pauline Hanson Trip*, Allen & Unwin ,1999.

Lockwood, Douglas, *Australia's Pearl Harbour, Darwin 1942,* Cassell, 1966.

Melbourne Guidebook, Lonely Planet Publications, 2002.

Morrison, Reg, *Australia: Land Beyond Time, The 4-Billion-Year Journey of a Continent*, New Holland, 2002.

New South Wales Guidebook, Lonely Planet Publications, 2002.

Nicholson, Margaret, *The Pocket Aussie Fact Book*, Penguin, 2002.

Sheehan, Paul, *Among the Barbarians*, Random House, 1998.

Strachan, Graham L., *Globalisation: Demise of the Australian Nation*, Applause Press Pty Ltd., Logan Village, 1998.

Sydney Guidebook, Lonely Planet Publications, 2002.

Tales From a Sunburnt Country II, Reader's Digest, 1999.

Victoria Guidebook, Lonely Planet Publications, 2002.

Von Bertouche, Anne, *February Dark*, Hunningford's Lane Press, 1983.

Von Bertouche, Anne, *What Was It? Before It Was A Gallery*, Hunningford's Lane Press, 1989.

Walton, Nancy Bird, *My God! It's a Woman*, Harper Collins Publishers, 2002.

White, Charles, *History of Australian Bushranging* (Vol. 1 and 2), Golden Press, 1970.

Special Thanks

Anzac Memorial Museum, Hyde Park, Sydney
Australian Centre for Photography
City of Bankstown Library, Panania
Museum & National Gallery of the Northern Territory, Darwin
New South Wales State Library, Sydney
Northern Territory State Library, Darwin
War Museum, Darwin
Waverly Library, Bondi Junction